The Pacific War
and Its Political Legacies

The Pacific War
and Its Political Legacies

Denny Roy

Westport, Connecticut
London

Library of Congress Cataloging-in-Publication Data

Roy, Denny, 1960–
   The Pacific war and its political legacies / Denny Roy.
      p. cm.
   Includes bibliographical references and index.
   ISBN 978–0–313–37566–8 (alk. paper)
   1. World War, 1939–1945—Political aspects—East Asia.   2. World War,
1939–1945—Political aspects—United States.   3. World War, 1939–1945—Influence.
4. World War, 1939–1945—East Asia—Historiography—Political aspects.
5. World War, 1939–1945—United States—Historiography—Political aspects.
6. East Asia—Politics and government—20th century.   7. United States—Politics
and government—20th century.   8. East Asia—Foreign relations—20th century.
9. United States—Foreign relations—1945–1989.   I. Title.
   D767.R69 2009
   940.53'14—dc22   2008051407

British Library Cataloguing in Publication Data is available.

Library of Congress Catalog Card Number: 2008051407
ISBN: 978–0–313–37566–8

First published in 2009

Praeger Publishers, 88 Post Road West, Westport, CT 06881
An imprint of Greenwood Publishing Group, Inc.
www.praeger.com

Printed in the United States of America

The paper used in this book complies with the
Permanent Paper Standard issued by the National
Information Standards Organization (Z39.48–1984).

10   9   8   7   6   5   4   3   2   1

Contents

A Note on Names

For Chinese personal and place names, the text generally uses the modern version with Pinyin romanization, except in the case of very well-known people or places such as Chiang Kai-shek, in which I use the popularized spelling. In many cases I provide both (example: Mukden / Shenyang). I follow a similar practice with Korean names, where I prefer the Republic of Korea's Ministry of Culture and Tourism system for romanization and hyphenated given names, but I use the well-known spellings for famous figures such as Kim Il Sung. For Japanese names, I generally follow the Japanese convention of surname first followed by given name, with exceptions for Japanese who choose to follow the Western custom (such as Akira Iriye).

CHAPTER 1

Introduction

Honolulu, Hawaii, 2009

In a country that fought World War II almost entirely beyond its own shores, Honolulu is as steeped in wartime history as any city in America outside Washington, D.C. It is the only American city in which a battle was fought—the Japanese raid on Pearl Harbor on December 7, 1941. A Honolulu cable television program on "The 10 Worst Dates in Hawaii's History" broadcast in June 2006 had the Japanese attack on Pearl Harbor listed at number one. Pearl Harbor is now home to what are commonly called "the Alpha and Omega" of America's participation in World War II: the U.S.S. *Arizona* Memorial, which stands over the rusting, oil leaking remains of the sunken battleship and honors the 1,177 of its crew killed during the Japanese attack; and, moored nearby, the battleship *Missouri*, on the deck of which Japanese officials signed the surrender documents in Tokyo Bay on September 2, 1945. The museum at the *Arizona* Memorial, Hawaii's most-visited tourist attraction, shows a well-balanced short documentary film about the attack and its causes. A few thousand people per year take the "Home of the Brave" tour of military sites around Oahu, with the guide pointing out details of the Pearl Harbor attack that the Hollywood version omitted or misrepresented. On the street where I live is the 100th Infantry Battalion Memorial Building, a gathering place for veterans of the famed U.S. Army unit—nicknamed the "Purple Heart Battalion" for its valor in bloody combat in Italy—which was composed mostly of Japanese Americans from Hawaii. One of my family's favorite beaches is a few yards from the end of the runway of Bellows Air Force station on the windward side of Oahu, attacked by the Japanese as part of the Pearl Harbor raid and now disused. In 2006 the remains of a U.S. Navy pilot who crashed in Oahu's Koolau Mountain range during a 1944 training flight were found and identified.[1]

Despite this abundant historical scaffolding, understanding of World War II in Honolulu is in many ways poor. In her commentary on the Pearl Harbor attack for "The 10 Worst Dates in Hawaii's History" program, host Olena Rubin stated, "The Emperor of Japan said 'We have awakened a sleeping giant.'" This is a double error. Rubin's scriptwriter undoubtedly confused Hirohito with Japanese Admiral Yamamoto Isoroku, to whom Americans popularly attribute the "sleeping giant" statement. But the statement itself is evidently a myth, as there is no evidence Yamamoto actually made it.[2] More seriously, high-ranking U.S. Navy admirals standing on the deck of the *Missouri* or at the *Arizona* Memorial have recently given speeches repeating misleading notions such as these: that Americans who fought in World War II "defeated imperialistic tyranny and fascist hegemony," and that the Pearl Harbor attack created in Americans a "staunch national resolve . . . to confront tyranny whenever and wherever it lurks."[3] At my local public library, in the history books written for youths and young adults, I find discussions of World War II that barely mention the Soviet role in defeating Nazi Germany[4] or the U.S. policies in East Asia that influenced the Japanese decision to attack Pearl Harbor.[5]

While writing this book, I received a piece of direct-mail advertising from a company called Axis Lending offering to help me obtain a home mortgage loan. I found it curious that the term *Axis*, which Americans associated with Hitler, Mussolini, and fascist Japan for decades after World War II, could have now become an appealing name for a business operating in Honolulu. I contacted the owner and learned, as I expected, that she started her business with that name relatively recently, in 2003. She mentioned that she planned to move to a new company called Allied. I responded, "So you're moving from the Axis to the Allies? Good for you." But there was no indication that she understood the historical allusions that made for a striking and ironic coincidence.

My adopted hometown's knowledge and understanding of the Pacific War did not improve with the 2001 premier of the big-budget Hollywood movie *Pearl Harbor*, which was shown to 2,000 guests on the deck of an aircraft carrier in Pearl Harbor. Film critic Roger Ebert wrote of the movie, "If you have the slightest knowledge of the events in the film, you will know more than it can tell you. There is no sense of history, strategy or context."[6] Another reviewer called it "a cheerfully offensive rape of history that cheapens the lives of World War II veterans by making a dumb popcorn movie out of their suffering."[7] Light though it was on history, the film was still riddled with inaccuracies and fabrications. Although it disappointed U.S. audiences, the film's owner, the Walt Disney company, hoped to make $100 million from audiences in Japan. In addition to spending $10 million on a marketing campaign in Japan that hyped the movie as the "Pearl Harbor love story," Disney created a revised version of the film aimed at increasing its appeal to Japanese audiences. Among the changes Disney made was toning down the disparaging remarks about Japanese uttered by the film's American characters. Thus, to increase potential profits, Disney bent its presentation to make it less reflective of the deep animosity toward Japan that prevailed during the period the film purports to portray. Despite Disney's efforts, a spokesman for Japanese Prime Minister Koizumi Junichiro still dismissed the film as "quite fictitious and one-sided. Japan is portrayed as the enemy, and wrong. The United States is portrayed as right."[8] So this vacuous movie managed to illustrate several important points. The most highly viewed (and therefore potentially the most influential) historical medium is perhaps the least reliable. Accuracy and balance are not necessarily the main goals of the makers of a historical presentation (certainly not in this case). And most Japanese have a different interpretation of the Pacific War than most Americans.

What is true of Honolulu is indicative of not only a nationwide but a worldwide trend. Wars other than the Second World War have been called "the forgotten war" and "the unknown war,"[9] but over six decades since it ended, World War II and its Asia-Pacific component the Pacific War are becoming forgotten and unknown. America as a society knows little about the Second World War, and less with the passing of each generation. There is ignorance, confusion, and imbalance on the events of the war and their significance. The *Washington Post*'s Jay Matthews reported in 2004 that among 76 high school students interviewed in the Washington, D.C., area, "only one-third could name even one World War II general, and about half could name a World War II battle."[10] A history professor at Shepherd College relates that in a quiz he administers to new freshmen, "a majority consistently fails to place the Second World War in the right decade" or to correctly identify Winston Churchill.[11] Churchill does not fare well in his homeland, either. In a recent survey among British children aged 10 to 14, less than half could name their country's famous World War II prime minister, with many guessing Margaret Thatcher or Tony Blair. Only 17 percent could correctly name America's wartime president, with others giving the names of more recent presidents and even the actor Denzel Washington.[12]

Much of what Americans do know, or think they know, is distorted. Innumerable statements by American opinion leaders claim that it was America that won the war in Europe, and that the "D-Day" landing of Allied forces on the coast of France was the climactic battle of the war, when in fact the Soviets did most of the difficult work of destroying the German forces. Surprisingly, this view can even be found in today's Russia—a testament to the soft power of American cultural and media influence. Russian researcher Natalya Loseva reports that many Russian youths have become "victims of Hollywood." Gaining their understanding of the war largely through "movies and comic books," they "seriously believe that the United States and Great Britain won the war, with only symbolic help from the Soviet Union."[13]

Americans also like to think of World War II as a struggle in which the forces of goodness and liberty defeated the forces of evil and tyranny. Although Nazi Germany and fascist Japan were certainly odious regimes, the simple dichotomy glosses over the fact that the Allied side included imperialist Britain, the despotic Chinese Nationalist government, and Stalin's Soviet Union. The war "liberated" Western Europe, but doomed Eastern Europe to the grim fate of Soviet domination and sent parts of Asia (temporarily) back to European colonial status. Americans would also like to believe that they came out victorious because of their political and moral uprightness rather than their industrial and technological might. In a 2005 speech commemorating V-J Day, President George W. Bush mentioned a member of the Japanese surrender delegation in 1945 who later wrote favorably of American democracy. Bush quoted him as writing that the Japanese "weren't beaten on the battlefield by the dint of superior arms; we were defeated in the spiritual conquest by virtue of a nobler idea."[14] America has elevated its World War II veterans to heroic, almost mythic status—the *Greatest Generation*, as news-anchor-turned-author Tom Brokaw described them in his best-selling book.[15] Popular historian Stephen E. Ambrose asserts, "We did not have to fight Germany and Japan for our own survival—we did it because it was the right and decent thing to do" and because Americans "didn't want to live in a world in which wrong prevailed."[16] Without undermining due respect, we can recognize that being killed on a ship docked in port during a surprise air raid is not in itself an act of heroism. But during a visit to the USS *Arizona* Memorial in Pearl Harbor, President George Bush Sr. described the dead men below him as "great heroes, the greatest that any nation has ever known."[17]

PATTERN OF DISTORTION

From the phenomenon at work in the United States we can discern a pattern that is present in other countries as well, of which a glimpse was visible in the official Japanese response to the movie *Pearl Harbor.* Several processes are involved in the complex phenomenon of constructing the "conventional wisdom," which can include the community's generally held understanding of an important historical event. People filter what they see and hear through a framework of expectations: assumptions and preconceptions based on their experience. Another filter is interests. Some parts of a story or some ways of telling a story appeal to a listener more than others, appearing more supportive of the listener's objectives. These will likely be privileged over details that countervail the listener's wishes. *Gatekeeping* is inherent in communication: the storyteller, unable to relay every detail to the listener, decides which details to pass on and which to omit. Both the communicator's agenda and the presumed agenda of the audience factor into these decisions. Even where so-called historical facts are not in dispute, interpretation attaches causation, meaning, and significance to the selected events. Memories are shared throughout the community and passed on from one generation to the next. There is an interaction between memories of the past and the needs of the present. The past determines the present in the sense of shaping the ways we understand the present. But the present determines the past to the extent that today's interests motivate attempts to appropriate and repackage the past in ways that appear to support modern goals.[18] The collective memory is constructed along the way as certain parts of the story are kept and others discarded, and as a consensus forms around certain interpretations.

Distortions or imbalances are easily introduced into a community's historical conventional wisdom. The most influential sources of historical knowledge do not necessarily have an interest in presenting history accurately. Indeed, often the presenter has strong reasons to do the opposite, for political or financial reasons. Ideally we should be learning our history from acclaimed historians. The reality, however, is that the number of people who read the best history books in the field is far outweighed by the numbers who see Hollywood movies or hear speeches by prominent, agenda-driven officials or other popular commentators.

What does this mean for international relations in postwar Northeast Asia? Nations or other self-distinguishing subgroups will tend to favor historical interpretations that are consistent with their own values and that reinforce their own sense of importance and rectitude. Some of this occurs unconsciously. At the same time, present-day circumstances and interests may dictate that a group adopts a particular position on a historical issue because that position offers the highest short-term utility. Thus different communities within the region harbor differing interpretations of the Pacific War. Each community's view is typically self-centric and self-interested. These differences pose challenges in postwar interstate relations. International disputes rooted in history are good illustrations of the aphorism that in politics, perception is reality.

WE NEED TO UNDERSTAND THE WAR

Understanding the Pacific War, along with the larger global conflict of which it was a part, is an essential prerequisite to comprehending the composition and nature of today's political world. World War II accounts for the birth of the United Nations and the World Trade Organization, the membership of the United Nations Security Council, why Korea is divided, why the Third World was decolonized, how America became "the world's policeman," the drive for European integration, the fear of many Asians over Japan becoming a major political and military power, and many other important aspects of the political architecture within which we live.

International relations are largely based on judgments that peoples and countries make about themselves and about each other—who is a traditional friend or a traditional enemy, which people are victims deserving a break and which are inherently aggressive or warlike, what kind of policies will make one's state secure or invite aggression or retaliation, and so on. These judgments are mainly based on historical experience, of which the Pacific War was a gigantic dose. Our view of the past affects the choices we make today. History is a learning opportunity, providing lessons about human political behavior. In the case of an event as large as the Pacific War, the influence on people's conceptions of how the world works is incalculable. The war not only shaped the structure of today's political world, it also made profound impressions on humanity of what is possible, both positive and negative, when a major war occurs—on the battlefields, in prison camps, in national economies, within societies, and in high-level meeting rooms. It went a long way in setting the conceptual parameters within which we discuss many issues of international politics today.

The Pacific War (and even more so World War II generally) matters because our political and opinion leaders continually refer to it for guidance. Our discourse is rife with allusions to the war, both explicit and implicit. Stories of past events are subject to reinterpretation to underscore points the storytellers want to make about present-day political issues. When politicians and commentators draw from the Pacific War for ammunition in their debates about current issues, we are not equipped to judge the validity of these allusions unless we know the history ourselves.

The Pacific War is a potential source of wisdom that could inform today's policy debates. It illustrates, for example, the potential of competition for resources among major powers to lead to armed conflict. The desire to gain control of sources of key resources was the main impetus for Japanese expansion in the first half of the twentieth century, leading to its war in China and later to a conflict with the United States triggered by an oil embargo. This is relevant to today's discussions of the need for a mechanism that would allow for multilateral coordination rather than outright competition for energy supplies among the strong U.S. and Japanese economies and the voracious appetite of a rising China. To give another example, many Chinese military commentaries since the 1990s have argued that the United States would shrink from intervening to help fight off a Chinese attempt to conquer Taiwan if Chinese forces could threaten or carry out a punishing strike on a major U.S. warship such as an aircraft carrier. The Pacific War featured an analogous situation: Japanese planners, influenced by their belief that America was an epicurean and casualty-averse society, planned the Pearl Harbor attack in the hope that a stunning military blow would convince Americans to accede to Japanese control over the Asia-Pacific region. Although the raid succeeding in sinking or badly damaging several capital ships, the U.S. reaction was the opposite of what Tokyo hoped for. It is a precedent that should be of interest to the Chinese.

Conversely, lack of memory is tantamount to ignorance and naïveté, which hardly serve a people well. Indeed, they lay the foundation for bad behavior and poor policies. If inaccurate or incomplete interpretations prevail, the mistakes displayed during the war are more likely to be repeated, the successes overlooked, and distorted "lessons" employed to support unwise courses of action in the present and future. If there is value in knowing and understanding history, we squander this value if we get the history wrong. I am inclined to endorse the view of humanities professor Wilfred M. McClay that for

Americans, "Historical memory is as much a necessity to the preservation of liberty and American security as is our armed forces."[19] A similar point could be made for the other Asia-Pacific countries. For any nation, a sound understanding of its own history is essential to knowing how valuable aspects of its culture and society came about, what benefits they impart, what might happen if they were lost, and how best to retain them.

ABOUT THIS BOOK

Even if it is widely accepted that World War II, including the Pacific War, reorganized the political world and laid the foundation for the international relations that prevail today, a study that draws the direct connections between the war and contemporary political issues is useful and necessary. What happened in the Pacific War, and what are its consequences for today's international politics? The answer to either of these questions is insufficient and incomplete without the other. Therefore this book undertakes to answer both questions.

This book focuses on Northeast Asia—the area traditionally known as "East Asia" (China, Japan, the Koreas, and Taiwan) plus the United States, which is a regional power by virtue of its military presence and its great political and economic influence in the western rim of the Pacific. A study of the legacies of the Pacific War for Southeast Asia would certainly be worthwhile. I limit the present project to Northeast Asia to keep it from growing unfeasibly large, and because in my view Northeast Asia demands first consideration. This is an exceptionally important subregion because of its concentration of economic, military, and political power. It is also an area where debates related to the Pacific War continue to strongly affect interstate relationships.

This book undertakes to explain (1) the origins of contending interpretations of the war and (2) how those interpretations have led to the positions and policies of postwar governments and societal groups on issues directly related to the war. Tackling these issues will lead us to three recurring themes:

1. The linkages between the events of the war and the subsequent interpretations espoused by various groups.
2. The relationship between a country's dominant interpretation of the war and the county's postwar domestic and international political circumstances.
3. The interaction between elites and their own domestic constituents on the question of how to remember the war.

Each country has one or more unique interpretations of what the war means—not only what happened or did not happen, but also what aspects were more important, what lessons should be drawn, what issues remain unresolved, and how those issues should be addressed. These interpretations tend to be self-serving in that each of the countries in the region has a nationalistic view of the war that supports the postwar national political agenda.

Society and government are distinct actors in the process of reaching a community consensus on which interpretation is accepted as the mainstream version. Self-serving interpretations of important past national and foreign policies or the national role in an important historical event become part of the canon of national myths. Once this occurs, the national polity forms an emotional bond with a self-serving interpretation of history, the refutation of which implies national humiliation and loss of face. As Ernest Renan trenchantly observes, "Forgetting, and I would even say historical error, are an essential factor in the creation of a nation" and in maintaining nationalistic fervor.[20] Where a popular historical interpretation implies a certain course of action in the country's foreign relations, the members of a society who hold strongly to this interpretation will pressure their leaders to behave accordingly. Political elites have their own political and strategic agenda. They also have the challenge of maintaining legitimacy with their domestic polities. Where the opportunity exists, elites have incentives to invent history: spinning or jerry-rigging interpretations of history to gain domestic support for their preferred agenda. As products of their own society, however, elites are also subject to having accepted some of the same historical interpretations held dear by their countrymen, interpretations that imply certain nonnegotiable positions in their foreign relations. Thus elites can be both inventors of history and prisoners of history—constrained by the rhetoric of their predecessors and similarly constraining to their successors.

This collection of self-justifying viewpoints creates a proneness to strife, one of the ways in which Pacific War legacy issues become drivers of today's international relations. Nevertheless, the effect of Pacific War legacies on each Northeast Asian dyad is unique, reflecting the complexity of variables involved.

This book is partly history and partly political analysis. The first part of the book will briefly recount some of the major political aspects of the Pacific War. Obviously, any summary of the Pacific War this brief can tell only a fraction of the whole story. My summary will focus mostly on political events and themes rather than an analysis of military battles and tactics. This book is not intended as a complete military, diplomatic, or social history of the war years. Rather, my objective is to highlight facets of the war that are most relevant to a discussion of postwar international relations in the region. Knowing what happened during the war helps to explain the positions that various countries take on today's political issues related to the war. The aspects of the Pacific War I cover are: (1) the tremendous suffering of China under the twin burdens of Japanese invasion and the desperate response of the callous Nationalist government; (2) the growth of U.S.-Japan tensions that led to the Pearl Harbor attack and American entry into the war; (3) the remarkably savage character of the fighting in the Pacific War; (4) the American strategic bombing campaign against Japan; and (5) Japan's decision to surrender, with particular attention paid to the role of the atomic bombings. I include a chapter on the establishment of new regimes in Japan, Korea, and Taiwan as a result of Tokyo's surrender, events which mark a transitional period from war to postwar.

The history of World War II involves many issues that historians continue to debate. In undertaking to answer the question of what happened in the war, I have in some instances taken positions on controversial issues, positions that I recognize some readers may disagree with. Nevertheless, this project required me to make some bold decisions, which I have attempted to do with open-mindedness and serious reflection.

The second part of the book assesses the impact of those highlighted wartime events or themes on today's Northeast Asian international politics. I discuss in depth several political legacies of the war. First is the *Rashomon* phenomenon of Japan, the United States, and China holding to distinct interpretations of the Pacific War and what it implies for today's regional politics. Second, I discuss the "comfort women" issue as the most prominent example of wartime victims seeking compensation from a reluctant Japanese government. Third, I analyze how the history issue has affected China's postwar relations with Japan. Fourth, I examine the resilient postwar U.S.-Japan partnership as an outgrowth of Japan's defeat in the Pacific War. I devote a separate chapter to the postwar controversy over the use of the atomic bombs, which is one of the areas where a deep-seated divergence between Japanese and American views is visible despite the framework of cooperation between the two governments. A final chapter offers some concluding observations.

Some wartime events have become the basis of highly salient, acrimonious disputes in contemporary international relations. Others have been suppressed or marginalized, or are no longer commonly recognized as determinants of today's political world. The perception of relevancy of different legacies of the war varies greatly by community. Different countries have drawn different lessons from the war, based on both their unique wartime experiences and on the usefulness of (interpreted) Pacific War history in current political debates. The approach of the book is ideally suited to identifying inconsistencies in the impact of various legacies: which of those wartime events are salient today, which are not, and why.

We begin, then, with the war.

CHAPTER 2

China's Ordeal

Despite already having suffered through imperialist exploitation, a failed attempt at republican government after the 1911 revolution, and continued economic and political stagnation and injustice under a collage of regional warlord governments, the Chinese people still faced the culminating event of their so-called century of humiliation: the devastating Japanese invasion. The fighting in China was brutal; murder and other abuses of prisoners and noncombatants were the norm. The scale was huge. Historians outside China generally accept estimates of between 15 and 20 million Chinese civilian deaths resulting from the war, plus more than 3 million Chinese military personnel killed. The war displaced as many as 95 million Chinese refugees.[1] This cataclysm had correspondingly great political ramifications for postwar China.

The Nationalist government had its hands full with the project of building a unified and modernized Chinese state when Japanese expansionism presented Chiang Kai-shek's regime with an escalating crisis that impinged on Chinese domestic politics. Chiang did not intend to allow the Japanese to occupy Chinese soil indefinitely, but he hoped to increase the proportion of Chinese forces with high-quality training, armaments, and leadership before sending them into a war to drive out the invaders. He recognized the weaknesses of his forces compared to the relatively modern, well-trained, and well-equipped formations of the Japanese. Prior to 1937, Chiang's approach to Japanese encroachment was to trade space for time. This steady loss of Chinese territory to Japanese control, first in Manchuria and then in north China, was extremely unpopular among the Chinese people and increasingly undermined the legitimacy of Chiang's government. Chiang realized this and eventually changed his strategy. China would give up no more territory, but rather would meet future Japanese challenges with stiff resistance, forcing the Japanese leaders to realize that they could not conquer China and that they must seek an accommodation with Chiang.

With the beginning of full-scale war in July 1937, Chiang lost his breathing space and Japan waded into what turned out to be an impassable swamp. Both sides explored the possibility of a negotiated settlement. Proposals that Nationalist government officials made to Japan in 1937–1940 included the continued Japanese control of Manchuria, autonomy for Inner Mongolia, and Japanese economic and political privileges elsewhere in China. Whether Chiang would have actually agreed to and honored such concessions is uncertain. These negotiations might have been part of Chiang's strategy of using the threat of capitulating to Japan as a means of squeezing more aid out of the United States, Britain, and the Soviet Union.

THE NATIONALIST GOVERNMENT AT WAR

Generalissimo Chiang was head of both the Chinese government and armed forces during the Second Sino-Japan War and the Pacific War. Although by far the most powerful figure in the Chinese political structure, he operated within extremely precarious circumstances. Born in 1887, Chiang was the son of a merchant family whose father died when he was a boy. As a young man, he studied at a military academy in Japan before joining Sun Yat-sen's nationalist movement. Later he developed ties with Shanghai's Green Gang, which practiced extortion along with its involvement in prostitution, gambling, and opium sales. Chiang was the first commandant of the Whampoa Military Academy near Canton. Highly disciplined, courageous in the face of physical danger, and apparently uninterested in using his power to indulge in a sumptuous lifestyle, Chiang was also prone to rages and did not hesitate to order the executions of those who displeased him.

Even after the overthrow of the Qing Dynasty monarchy and the establishment of the Republic of China in 1911, China remained a mostly feudal country under the control of various regional warlords. Rising to the leadership of the Nationalist Party (Kuomintang [KMT] in Chinese) after the death of Sun, Chiang confronted the enormous task of modernizing a huge and diverse country while at the same time trying to achieve and maintain central government authority against challengers from both within and without. Chiang led the 1927–28 Northern Expedition to unify China under a KMT government. Although Chiang's forces succeeded in getting the KMT flag hoisted over most of China, it was a largely nominal unification, achieved in many instances by persuading the warlords to declare allegiance to the KMT. The necessity of compromising with many powerful groups rather than bringing them to heel was a major source of the KMT's ultimate failure in China. KMT-appointed administrators ruled only five provinces in southern China. This left Chiang to play a multilayered game that involved not only countering the Japanese invasion, but also managing his relationships with other domestic political and military groups that held varying degrees of loyalty to Chiang ranging from trusted allies to long-term enemies. He also had to fulfill the usual Chinese expectations of a national leader who claims to hold "the mandate of Heaven." The more of his trusted and well-equipped troops he lost fighting against the Japanese, the more Chiang risked leaving himself vulnerable to defeat not only by the communists, but also by regional armies that were still more loyal to their warlord leaders than to the central government.

Originally, the fledgling Chinese Communist Party (CCP) was a coalition partner with the KMT in the task of unifying the country under an effective central government. Both the KMT and the CCP received substantial Soviet assistance. During the Northern Expedition, however, Chiang split with the communists after his forces reached Shanghai. There he secured an alternative funding source in the form of loans from the city's bankers and industrialists, largely through extortion carried out with the assistance of Green Gang members. Thereafter Chiang launched several military campaigns to attempt to wipe out the communists, even as Japanese encroachment was increasing. Many of Chiang's countrymen were dismayed that Chiang preferred to fight his fellow Chinese rather than the Japanese. Zhang Xueliang (Chang Hsueh-liang), a warlord leader turned Nationalist general, went so far as to kidnap Chiang when he visited the city of Xian in 1936 in an effort to force the generalissimo to agree to join with the communists in a "United Front" against the Japanese. A shaky truce followed, but Chiang placed Zhang under house arrest for the next four decades. (The KMT eventually allowed Zhang to emigrate to Honolulu, where he died in 2001 at age 101.)

Although officially espousing Sun's doctrine of "Three Principles of the People" with its promise of eventual democracy (*minquan*, or "government by the people"), Chiang's regime was highly authoritarian. Reflecting the work of his Comintern advisers, Chiang's government was Leninist, with the ruling party dominating both government and the military. By the 1930s the KMT had established a police state in the areas under its control. It built a vast public security apparatus including the Military Bureau of Investigation and Statistics, led by Tai Li, labeled "China's Himmler."[2] The authorities harshly punished citizens who complained about the regime's manifest shortcomings. The regime maintained heavy-handed censorship of the press and intimidation of intellectuals and college students. The government gave license to a conservative group called the Blueshirts, whose members took it upon themselves to enforce traditional morality by harassing patrons of dance halls and cinemas and even by pouring acid on Chinese wearing Western clothes. Chiang appeared more accepting of fascist than democratic ideology. He made favorable reference to fascism in 1935, calling it "a stimulant for a declining society. . . . Can fascism save China? We answer: 'Yes.'"[3] Chiang's New Life Movement, begun in 1934, was an attempt to restore Confucian principles throughout China and, in Chiang's words, "thoroughly to militarize the life of the people of the entire nation."[4] In his speech launching the New Life Movement, Chiang spoke admiringly of Nazi Germany as a country that had broken the oppressive chains of war reparation payments imposed by the victors of World War I (the liberal democracies). Before the war, Chiang sent two officers to study Nazi political practices. His second son, Chiang Wei-guo, studied in a German military academy and twice met with Hitler. German generals Georg Wetzell and Hans von Seeckt served as military advisors to Chiang. They planned one of Chiang's so-called extermination campaigns against the CCP forces.

With Chiang focused on consolidating the authority of the central government, containing the communists, holding off the Japanese, lobbying the Allies, and keeping the Chinese economy from collapsing, the Chinese had abundant reason to conclude that the KMT government was no more concerned about the lot of the common people than the old monarchy. The KMT regime made little serious effort to better the lives of Chinese peasants, who made up most of the population and toiled in poverty, backwardness, poor standards of health and education, and frequent exploitation by corrupt local officials.

The pressures of the conflict with Japan worsened Nationalist policies that further alienated Chiang's regime from the Chinese people. In spite of its numerous and highly visible flaws, the Nationalist government was not completely ineffective or rapacious. It was making steady progress toward consolidating its control over China and maintaining a national economic growth rate of about 2 percent annually until interrupted by the Japanese invasion. The level of government appropriation of national wealth was below 10 percent, relatively low compared to other developing states.[5] The war, however, derailed the KMT's plans for political and economic development. Chiang pushed through a provisional constitution in 1931, and his party showed a strong interest in rapid industrialization from the time it ascended to power. But the Japanese takeover of Manchuria forced Chiang's government to begin diverting resources toward war preparation, which seriously curtailed progress in industrialization.[6]

To meet the endless need for more soldiers, Chinese officials virtually kidnapped young men from their villages, often marching them out with rope tied around their necks and wrists. Tens of thousands of these recruits died of starvation or disease en route to the battlefield. Wealthy families, on the other hand, could gain exemption from military service for their sons by paying off corrupt officials. Brutalized, given extremely low pay and meager rations, and poorly disciplined, Chiang's soldiers were notorious for pillage and rape in the Chinese towns through which they passed, often with the assent of their officers. Thus the ROC army was both victim and victimizer.

Widespread corruption and mismanagement, partly a consequence of the cronyism upon which KMT leaders relied to maintain the support of important domestic allies, contributed to rampant inflation, shortages, and other serious economic problems. In Henan Province, government confiscation of most of the 1942 rice crop caused a famine that may have killed between 2 and 3 million. Chiang's government punished *Ta Kung Pao*, the newspaper that reported the famine in February 1943, with a temporary suspension.[7] In 1938 Chiang ordered the demolition of Yellow River levees to create floods that would hamper the Japanese advance. The floodwaters killed many Japanese and destroyed much enemy equipment, but also killed hundreds of thousands of Chinese and made 2 million homeless. To deflect criticism, the KMT government claimed the Japanese caused the flood.[8] Still worse were the mass killings in the countryside. The KMT sought to liquidate all communities suspected of cooperating with the Chinese Communists. The result was indiscriminate slaughter of the residents of areas where large groups of communists had lived. The KMT also empowered local officials to get rid of townspeople or villagers (and, often, their family members along with them) against whom they held a grudge by reporting them as communists or Japanese collaborators. All told, political scientist R. J. Rummel estimates, during its period of rule on mainland China (i.e., discounting additional political killings after the government relocated to Taiwan), the KMT was responsible for about 10 million deaths among the Chinese people.[9] The Chinese civilian population suffered massive hardship and cruelty at the hands of their own war-stressed government as well as the invading Japanese.

The KMT's failure to inspire its own soldiers and its outrages against the Chinese population go far in explaining why Chiang eventually lost China to the CCP. The Nationalist troops who reasserted Chiang's authority in previously Japanese-controlled areas of China quickly alienated the local population, essentially stepping into the role of the defeated Japanese. In some cases Japanese troops and commanders actually changed uniforms and joined Nationalist units. The newly arrived Nationalists often looked down on their liberated countrymen as Japanese collaborators, worsening the usual looting problem. The Nationalist regime also reintroduced its currency at an exchange rate of 200 to 1, erasing the savings of countless families. At the end of World War II Nationalist forces outnumbered the communists 10 to 1 in troops (3.7 million to 320,000) and artillery (6,000 to 600). Three years later, largely due to surrenders and desertions, the Nationalists were down to about 2 million troops, while the communist forces had grown to 1.5 million, and the two sides had equal numbers of artillery.[10]

OVERMATCHED CHINESE NATIONALIST FORCES

China fought alone against the Japanese from July 1937 to December 1941, a period that exceeded the length of the U.S.-Japan conflict. Although the USSR supplied a thousand aircraft plus pilots and military advisors, Soviet aid dried up after the war in Europe began. Assistance from the Western countries was minimal. Chinese soldiers fought under numerous disadvantages. In general, the nationalist armies had organization, training, tactics, and equipment that could prevail in battles with warlord or CCP forces, but they were outclassed by the comparatively modern Japanese formations. Chinese industry and infrastructure were not sufficiently developed to properly supply Chiang's armies throughout the country. Much of the precious supplies delivered to China by truck from the west over the so-called Burma Road ended up for sale on the black market. Troops as well as recruits en route to join their assigned units were poorly cared for, and large numbers of them died of disease and starvation. The top American commander in China during the latter part of the war, Gen. Albert Wedemeyer, found that Chinese units were "unable to make even a short hike without men falling out wholesale and many dying of starvation."[11] This largely explains why Nationalist troops so frequently pilfered food and other goods from nearby Chinese communities. Much of the soldiers' equipment was inferior. An estimated 80 percent of Chinese-made hand grenades, for example, failed to explode when used in combat.[12] The greatest shortcoming of the Chinese armies was their leadership. Chiang had little trust in or control over the nominally Nationalist armies under the command of regional strongmen. The KMT-affiliated warlords usually employed their armies to strengthen their own local political standing rather than to fight the Japanese. The armies with close ties to Chiang were better trained and equipped but still often poorly led because many commanders were selected for political or personal loyalty rather than professional competence. Chinese generals demonstrated they could not successfully maneuver large units to avoid defeat or exploit opportunities. Some Chinese field commanders exhibited great bravery, but many proved incompetent or abandoned their troops when the battle grew hot. Chinese soldiers sometimes fought to the death, but on other occasions pushed aside civilian refugees in their haste to run away from the advancing Japanese. In contrast, the Chinese Boy Scouts (most aged in their twenties) developed a reputation for courage and reliability in their volunteer support roles. U.S. military adviser Gen. Joseph Stilwell said of them, "If all organizations connected with the Chinese Army were half as good as the Boy Scouts, the story of the war would have been very different."[13]

With the virtues exhibited by the Boy Scouts in relatively short supply, Japanese forces dominated the fighting throughout the war, winning most of their battles despite the Chinese frequently enjoying a numerical advantage. Chiang committed some of his best-trained forces to defend Shanghai in 1937. With the expatriate communities looking on, the Chinese fought well in defeat, bolstering Chiang's positions that China would be no pushover and was worthy of foreign assistance. Chiang's forces became dependent on outside suppliers for armaments to continue the fight as the Japanese gained control of China's major cities in the northeast and on the east coast. Japan would conquer territory containing most of China's industry and about half its population and agricultural land. The Japanese simply lacked the manpower and resources to seize and hold the entire country. Since the Japanese drove out the Nationalist government but maintained little presence in the rural areas of "occupied" China, various types of armed bands took advantage of the anarchy. They tormented Chinese communities with looting, raping, and kidnapping.

There was relatively little fighting in China after Pearl Harbor. The Japanese had already taken most of the areas they wanted, and, as historian Edward L. Dreyer observes, "Both the KMT and CCP essentially sat out the 1941–45 period, letting the USA beat Japan for them."[14] Japan formed a collaborationist Chinese government in occupied China in March 1940. As its titular head they recruited Wang Jingwei, formerly a highly ranked KMT official and a factional rival of Chiang. Wang had come to favor reaching a peace deal with Japan not only to save China from further devastation through war, but also to avoid either a communist takeover or excessive and debilitating influence from Western culture. Wang's masters were unwilling to grant him the autonomy that would dispel the suspicion that he was no more than a Japanese puppet ruler and therefore unappealing to the people of China. On a smaller scale, some local Chinese military commanders arranged unofficial truces with their Japanese counterparts, allowing trade to take place between Japanese-occupied and Chinese-controlled areas.

U.S.-CHINA RELATIONS

Americans sympathetic to China, often from missionary families or the business community, used their influence to urge the U.S. public toward greater support for Chinese resistance against Japan. Favorable images of the Chinese emerged in Pearl S. Buck's novel *The Good Earth* and in Henry Luce's *Time* and *Life* magazines. Both Buck and Luce had been raised in China, where their parents were missionaries. Another prominent aspect of the prewar history of American relations with China, however, was the anti-Asian racism that also colored U.S.-Japan relations. As the U.S. government promoted a positive image of wartime ally China, the contradiction with the anti-Chinese sentiment embedded in American laws became more glaring. In 1942 the United States finally abrogated extraterritoriality, a vestige of the "unequal treaties" imposed on China in the nineteenth century. Extraterritoriality meant Chinese authorities could not prosecute Americans who committed crimes in China, but rather had to turn them over to the U.S. court system. This arrangement had long been an affront to modern China, since it originated in a Western perception that China's legal system was corrupt and backward. The set of laws that limited Chinese immigration to the United States, similarly offensive to China, proved more difficult to rectify. At least 15 federal immigration laws passed between 1882 and 1913 specifically mentioned the Chinese. The combination of a narrow slice of the quota system and ineligibility for naturalization effectively blocked Chinese from immigration. Chinese seeking temporary entry into the United States as well as American citizens of Chinese ancestry routinely faced harassment by immigration officials. Furthermore, discrimination against Chinese residents had forced many of them into the virtual ghettos of Chinatowns and restricted them to low-status jobs. Congress discussed the issue for over a year in 1942–43. In December 1943, Congress finally revised the immigration program to allow a maximum of 105 Chinese annually to emigrate to the United States. An important factor in this modest outcome, which was opposed by groups such as the American Legion and the American Federation of Labor, was the argument that a China alienated by the United States might join the Japanese camp. As several commentators said, a Japan-China alliance not only threatened U.S. economic opportunities in the fabled China market after the war, but also portended a possible future "race war" in which white Christian civilization would be hopelessly outnumbered by non-Christian, non-Western Asia.[15]

After the Pearl Harbor attack, China was a full-fledged ally and U.S. aid greatly increased. American Lend-Lease assistance to China eventually reached more than $1.5 billion, although this was only 3 percent of the total Lend-Lease help the United States distributed to all recipient countries.[16] The Americans had several strategic interests in China. First, China was a potential base for offensive operations against Japan, particularly a bombing campaign from Chinese airfields. Second, the Allies worried that Japanese troops in China might choose to continue fighting after Tokyo agreed to surrender. Finally, Roosevelt feared that a collapse of Chinese resistance would free up Japanese troops to invade India or Australia.[17] For these reasons Washington wanted to strengthen Chinese forces to the point where they could do the job of destroying the Japanese army in China, a job that in the early years of the war seemed necessary. The U.S. government therefore wanted and expected Chiang to commit his forces to battle against the Japanese armies in China. To facilitate this, the United States increased aid to China, provided (often unwanted) military advice, and granted Chiang considerable prestige. Over British objections, Roosevelt held up China as one of the "Big Four" Allied powers and included Chiang's government in some of the major Allied conferences and declarations. Churchill thought granting China such status was "strangely out of proportion" and "wholly unreal."[18]

To its great frustration, the American leadership discovered that Chiang, who was officially the commander of Allied forces in the China theater, had a separate agenda. A contest soon developed in which Chiang's government and the U.S. leadership each tried to persuade the other to shoulder more of the burden of fighting the Japanese in China. Chiang unsuccessfully lobbied for up to a million U.S. soldiers to fight in China.[19] On the other hand, Chiang tried to employ his own forces sparingly—especially those led by his most trusted comrades, the graduates of his Whampoa Military Academy. In Chiang's famous formulation, "The Japanese are a disease of the skin; the communists are a disease of the heart."[20] American entry into the war almost guaranteed Japan's eventual defeat, which meant the Pacific War for Chiang was a period of preparation for the final extermination campaign against the communists. Chiang sought to win the maximum amount of American help, to channel foreign-supplied materiel toward his loyal troops and away from the communists, and to minimize U.S. interference with the pursuit of his objectives.

Chiang saw his American and British allies as untrustworthy, arrogant, ignorant, and self-interested. The Anglo-American "Europe First" strategy understandably dismayed Chiang. Chiang and the other Allies frequently disagreed over the conduct of the war. One example involved Burma. In a campaign to defend Burma in 1942, Chiang committed some of his best forces, under the overall command of Stilwell, to assist British troops. The Allied campaign failed. In Chiang's view, the British did not fight hard enough and Stilwell allowed the Japanese to surround and defeat the Chinese troops. Yet Stilwell blamed the defeat on poor Chinese leadership. In 1943 Chiang persuaded the Allied leaders to attempt an amphibious invasion of Burma. They soon cancelled the operation, however, after obtaining Stalin's pledge to enter the war against Japan once Germany was defeated. This was one of many occasions on which the other Allies left Chiang feeling humiliated and betrayed.[21]

While driving hard bargains with U.S. officials, Chiang's government successfully courted American public opinion. Chiang's wife, Song Meiling (Soong May-ling), was attractive, American educated, fluent in English, and very well connected—one of her two sisters was married to China's richest man, and the other was Sun Yat-sen's widow. She was an effective ambassador for the regime to the United States, helping sell to Americans the image of Chiang as a Christian, democratic reformer and heroic anti-Japanese leader. Madame Chiang addressed the U.S. Congress, only the second woman and the first Chinese to do so. Her speech emphasized the commonality of American and Chinese values and aspirations. She moved spectators to stand up and cheer when she pointedly noted that Japan "in her occupied areas today has greater resources at her command than Germany."[22] Luce-published *Time* magazine, which pictured her on its cover, observed, "The Senate is not in the habit of rising to its feet to applaud; for Madame Chiang, it rose and thundered."[23] Among the American public, interest in and sympathy for China soared. Roosevelt, convinced of China's strategic importance, added his voice in encouraging Americans to support a people who "for four and a half years . . . withstood bombs and starvation and have whipped the invaders time and again in spite of superior Japanese equipment and arms."[24]

The picture most Americans conceived was one of a bravely struggling but outgunned China that deserved as well as needed American help. To American officials, however, the foibles of Chiang's government were increasingly apparent. Commenting on this manufactured view of a proto-democratic Chiang ably leading a strong Chinese resistance against the Japanese, U.S. ambassador to the ROC Clarence Gauss opined, "looking the cold facts in the face, one could only dismiss this as rot."[25] Indeed, KMT governance made a mockery of the ideals the Allies claimed to be fighting for. The same year that Madame Chiang spoke to Congress about shared Sino-U.S. values, a book her generalissimo husband wrote with the assistance of his speech writer was published, apparently in response to an earlier book by communist leader Mao. Titled *China's Destiny*, Chiang's book was hostile toward liberal democracy and anti-Western, blaming imperialism for China's problems. Although the book was compulsory reading for students, military officers, and civil servants in China and sold more than a million copies, the Chinese and U.S. governments suppressed the English translation during the war to avoid exposing the American public to evidence that would undermine the sanitized version of Chiang.

Even among the American officials who worked with Chiang, few comprehended his milieu. Based on their expectations of the alliance, what the Americans saw in Chiang's leadership was corruption, dysfunction, and, in their eyes, irrationality. Even Chiang's chief American adviser Stilwell, who was an experienced China hand, could not understand or at least refused to accept decisions by the generalissimo that addressed domestic political challenges but were less than optimal from the standpoint of aggressively fighting the Japanese. Appointed Chiang's military chief of staff, Stilwell hated Chiang, referring to him as "peanut." Stilwell wanted U.S. Lend-Lease supplies shared with the CCP to strengthen them in the fight against Japan. He also wanted Chiang to reassign the troops enforcing a quarantine of the communists in the north and send them instead into combat against the Japanese. Chiang, however, saw the communists as more adversaries than allies and treated them accordingly. Stilwell urged Chiang to reorganize his forces and commanders with a view toward countering Japanese forces, but these changes would have upset Chiang's calculated positioning of trusted officers to counterbalance less trusted officers.

The series of stinging Chinese defeats in 1944 brought the Stilwell-Chiang rift to a head and more broadly opened a serious breach in the Sino-American alliance. Based on Stilwell's complaints, Roosevelt sent Chiang a message instructing the generalissimo to place Stilwell in command of all Chinese forces, including the communist troops. Chiang replied that he could not work with Stilwell and demanded that Stilwell be relieved. Roosevelt relented and recalled Stilwell, but this was a major step toward the Americans writing off the Nationalist government. The United States eventually gave up relying on Chiang's regime to destroy Japanese forces in China. At the Yalta conference, Roosevelt and Stalin agreed that Soviet forces would attack the Japanese Kwantung Army in Manchuria in exchange for concessions in northern China at Chiang's expense. The capture of the Mariana Islands in July 1944 obviated the need for heavy bomber bases in China. The Chinese claimed they made a crucial contribution to the war effort by keeping more than a million Japanese troops tied down in China and Manchuria. The implication was that larger numbers of Japanese troops deployed in Japan's imperial possessions would have hindered or even prevented Allied victory. In fact, however, the United States was winning the war in the Pacific through control of the sea and the air. In many cases U.S. forces bypassed and isolated Japanese army units. Greater numbers of Japanese troops in overseas battlefields or garrisons would have increased the burden on the Japanese supply chain, which the Americans were gradually destroying, without turning the tide of battle. For Washington, the strategic importance of the Republic of China was waning.

The KMT regime's weaknesses became clearer to Americans immediately after the war as the gloss of wartime propaganda abated. Returning to China on a fact-finding mission for President Truman in 1947, Stilwell's replacement General Albert C. Wedemeyer publicly complained that China lacked "inspirational leadership" and exhibited "apathy and lethargy" and "abject defeatism." General George C. Marshall, who unsuccessfully tried to mediate peace between the Nationalist government and the communists, noted a "popular demand for change in present conditions," and found "no indications that the present Chinese government, with its traditions and methods, could satisfy this popular demand or create conditions which would satisfy the mass of Chinese people."[26]

RESURGENCE OF THE CHINESE COMMUNISTS

In 1937 the Chinese Communist movement faced the real possibility of destruction at the hands of Chiang's forces. The Japanese invasion, however, gave the communists a new lease on life. The CCP's membership grew from 40,000 to 2.7 million between 1937 and 1945. The Party's armed forces, which also numbered 40,000 in 1937, increased to more than 1 million by 1945. The amount of territory under CCP control grew 10-fold, and the population in CCP-administered areas rose from 1.5 million to over 100 million during the war years.[27] Mao was highly productive during this period, thinking through and writing about the application of Marxist-Leninist principles to the particular problems facing China and Chinese Communism. He implemented several practices that would become major features of the future People's Republic of China government, including land reform, a political system based on the mass line, and enforcement of Party orthodoxy by putting individuals though a humiliating process of so-called self-criticism and eventual rehabilitation.

In north China, where the communists had taken refuge, the Japanese conquered the cities along the railway but did not have enough troops to effectively control the vast rural areas behind the front lines and in any case did not consider the communists a serious military threat. Thus the CCP in north China found abundant opportunities to establish camps and carry out political campaigns. The Japanese occupation had the effect of protecting the CCP forces from extermination by Nationalist troops. By 1944 the communists controlled parts of four provinces in China that were nominally under Japanese administration.

Under the United Front that ostensibly made the CCP and the KMT allies, the two main communist armies were officially part of the Nationalist command structure and designated Eighth Route Army and New Fourth Army. In practice they operated independently of Chiang's leadership. Chiang still did not give the CCP legal status, and the CCP refused to allow any KMT troops or officers into the Red Army. The United Front legitimized CCP recruitment of peasants into its forces for the purpose of fighting the Japanese. Once in, these soldiers would receive a steady diet of political indoctrination. The

United Front also enhanced the CCP's prestige, making it appear primarily concerned with China's national interests rather than narrow partisan interests. This earned support for the CCP not only from peasants, but also from Chinese patriots among the groups naturally inclined to oppose communism, such as gentry and merchants.[28] The United Front effectively ended with the New Fourth Army Incident of January 1941, in which a Nationalist Chinese unit and a communist Chinese unit fought each other amidst mutual recriminations. Afterward Chiang kept some 20 divisions of his best troops positioned to quarantine the communists in north China.

The CCP troops enjoyed limited military success. In the Battle of Pingxingguan in September 1937, Eight Route Army troops ambushed a Japanese supply column, wiping out a brigade and capturing a cache of provisions. Emboldened by their increased numbers, and to improve both their physical and political position vis-à-vis the Nationalist armies, the Red Army under the command of Zhu De launched a three-month "Hundred Regiments" campaign in 1940. In these conventional frontal attacks the CCP troops succeeded in shutting down part of the Japanese-held rail line in north China, but at the cost of high Chinese losses. The Japanese retaliated with the vicious "Three Alls" campaign, which cost the CCP about 100,000 troops and reduced the population under communist control in north China from 40 to 25 million.[29] Afterward the Red Army fought more sparingly, employed guerrilla tactics, and mostly attacked Chinese collaborators. Mao admitted that "China's strength alone will not be sufficient, and we shall also have to rely on the support of international forces" to prevail over the Japanese invaders.[30]

The CCP's real success came in the political arena. The communists were infinitely more savvy and effective than Chiang's government at public relations. Chinese villagers saw that in stark contrast to Nationalist soldiers, Red Army troops (in accordance with strict orders from their commanders) generally exhibited orderly behavior and paid for the supplies they took. The communists presented programs for directly improving the lives of the rural working class, which comprised the bulk of China's population. The CCP persuaded millions of Chinese that the Party's primary effort went toward fighting the Japanese invaders, exaggerating in the public's minds both communist activity and Nationalist inactivity. In actuality, after the United States entered the war neither the Nationalist nor the communist forces did much fighting against the Japanese. Sometimes the CCP got inadvertent help from the KMT. For example, the communist message of radical land reform was not playing well in Henan Province before the war. Support for the CCP grew markedly, however, after Chiang's government breached the Yellow River dikes in 1938.[31]

Foreign observers as well, including several influential Americans, began drawing comparisons between Chiang's regime and Mao's communist sanctuary in Yenan that were highly unfavorable to the former. A delegation of U.S. military and foreign service officers, nicknamed "the Dixie Mission," visited the Chinese Communist base in Yenan in July 1944 to assess the capabilities of the communist forces. The Americans were impressed by the efficiency and high morale they found. They recommended greater U.S. assistance for and cooperation with the communists to increase their value in the fight against the Japanese. The military consequences of these contacts amounted to little, as the proposed cooperation programs lacked the support of either Chiang or the new American ambassador, Patrick Hurley. The Dixie Mission did, however, produce reports by John S. Service, one of the American "China hands" later accused of treason in the McCarthyist reaction to the Communist Party's takeover of China in 1949. Service's reports about Yenan and about his interviews with top communist leaders were positive to the point of imbalance. He was correct, however, in pointing out many ways in which communist administration contrasted favorably with that of the Nationalist regime, and in predicting that the communists would eventually win the Chinese Civil War. As historian Immanuel C. Y. Hsü writes, "Mao had in fact created another China in competition with the nationalist government for the supreme power of the Chinese state."[32] Taking advantage of opportunities created by the Sino-Japan War, the Chinese Communists had come a long way since 1937.

THE PACIFIC WAR'S IMPACT ON TAIWAN

Taiwan was a Japanese colony well before the Pacific War. Japan had obtained control of Taiwan as part of the settlement of the First Sino-Japanese War in 1894–1895. Nevertheless, the war years had important effects on Taiwan.[33] The Japanese occupation government intensified its propaganda and indoctrination, intended to instill loyalty toward and respect for Japan and to make the Taiwanese take pride in their opportunity to serve as subjects of the emperor. Some Taiwanese willingly hitched their destinies to that of Asia's new great power. Even as second-class citizens in their own country, many Taiwanese enjoyed enhanced educational and employment prospects through their inclusion in the Japanese empire. Tens of thousands of Taiwanese signed up for service in the Japanese armed forces, some submitting applications written in their own blood. Over 30,000 lost their lives in the war.

The demands of the Pacific War prodded the Japanese to extract greater resources and sacrifices from Taiwan. To compensate for these hardships, the Japanese administration made unprecedented concessions to long-standing Taiwanese desires for a greater role in their own governance. The effect was to accelerate political liberalization in Taiwan. In 1940, the assemblies of most towns and villages were filled by elected Taiwanese representatives. By the end of the war, Taiwan had a few seats in the Diet and the status of a prefecture. Taiwan was already far more economically developed than the Chinese mainland.

These political changes further distanced Taiwan from the mainland and deepened the islanders' sense of accomplishment. Taiwanese pride was matched by Mainlander resentment. Their Chinese cousins saw the Taiwanese as Japanese-brainwashed collaborators who were sitting out the war in relative comfort. The war expanded the political and social rift across the Taiwan Strait that would become disastrously evident when the defeat of Japan brought Taiwan back under Mainland Chinese rule after 50 years of estrangement.

The Second Sino-Japanese War ravaged China and tormented the Chinese people. The political effects on China's postwar relations with Japan would be profound and long lasting. Americans found their wartime partnership with Chiang Kai-shek's government deeply disillusioning. This, too, had important implications for postwar Asia. Yet despite the failures of nationalist leadership, the long list of battles the Chinese forces lost, and the terrible losses incurred by both troops and civilians, as historian Hsi-sheng Ch'i notes, "China's performance in the war sent a clear message to Japan and other potential adversaries that China could become a quagmire even for the strongest possible invaders."[34]

The war severely damaged the Nationalist regime's effort to build an effective and popular government. The war devastated the Chinese economy, gravely undermining the legitimacy of the Nationalist regime. The conflict with Japan led directly to postwar collapses in the agricultural and industrial sectors. The inflation of China's currency in the 1940s was one of the worst cases in history and one of the single greatest causes of loss of confidence in Chiang's mandate to rule.

The Chinese Communists, on the other hand, enjoyed an unlikely reversal of their fortunes. The perceived vigor of their resistance against the Japanese invasion impressed their countrymen. While the Nationalists systematically if unintentionally fostered ill-will, the communists placed great emphasis on winning political support among the masses. The CCP gained experience in agitation, governance and combat during the war, and communist leaders learned much from their mistakes. They would put these lessons to good use soon after the war. In 1964 Mao received a visit from a group of Japanese socialists. They offered an apology for the aggressive war of 1937—1945 against China. Mao reportedly brushed off the apology, telling his guests that Japan's invasion of China made possible the CCP victory in 1949.[35]

CHAPTER 3

Sino-Japan War Expands to Pacific War

THE HISTORICAL BACKGROUND TO PEARL HARBOR

The United States and Japan were two young great powers that became major players in Asia-Pacific geopolitics in the latter half of the nineteenth century. Both began behaving as the more established European great powers of that period: they practiced imperialism, taking control of foreign territories that local governments were too militarily weak to defend. Since Japan was a relatively small and resource-poor great power, the Japanese believed they had a compelling need for colonies. With the Monroe Doctrine, the United States announced it would not accept foreign influence in America's neighborhood. Japan similarly saw the nearby regions of Korea and northeastern China as bearing directly on Japanese security. This is not to justify Japanese imperialism in Korea or China, but simply to recognize that geography and great power rivalry generated an incentive for Tokyo to control these areas, similar to the incentive that has motivated other powerful countries including the United States.

The United States, having fulfilled its Manifest Destiny by expanding (often by ruthless means) from the east to the west coast of North America over the objections of Mexico and numerous Native American tribes, began acquiring foreign possessions as opportunities arose to do so. The United States went to war with Spain partly out of American outrage over reported Spanish atrocities against rebel communities in Cuba and the Philippines. With the defeat of Spain, America obtained a colony in Asia—and U.S. occupation forces replaced the Spanish as targets of a Filipino insurgency. The result was a 14-year conflict beginning in 1899 between U.S. soldiers and Filipino rebel troops and guerrillas. U.S. troops served under commanders who exhibited racist disdain of the Filipinos and encouraged brutal practices. One example was General Jacob Smith, who told his men, "I want no prisoners. I wish you to kill and burn. The more you kill and burn the better it will please me."[1] The Americans reportedly tortured and massacred some of their captives. In an attempt to dry up support for rebel fighters, U.S. forces destroyed villages and relocated their inhabitants into concentration camps, where they were subject to disease and famine. Estimates of the total number of Filipinos who died as a result of the war range from 250,000 to 1 million.

Sustaining a U.S. presence in Asia would require bases in the Pacific. This turned early attention to Hawaii, of which President Grover Cleveland said, "Those islands, on the highway of the Oriental and Australasian traffic, are virtually an outpost of American commerce and the stepping-stone to the growing trade of the Pacific."[2] Cleveland's successor William McKinley annexed Hawaii. This met strong opposition in the U.S. Congress, where many lawmakers condemned it as imperialism.

American interests in Asia centered on the China market, and the chief guiding principle for U.S. policy was the Open Door. Many U.S. leaders in business and government believe sustained American prosperity depended on economic access to Asia. At the turn of the century, the United States saw its economic opportunities in China threatened by the prospect that other powerful states would establish exclusive spheres of influence over various Chinese regions, effectually carving up China into a collage of colonial possessions, each under the economic domination of the colonizing government. To counter this trend, in 1899 U.S. Secretary of State John Hay asked the governments of Britain, France, Germany, Russia, Italy, and Japan to honor an Open Door policy by guaranteeing all nations "equality of treatment for their commerce and navigation"[3] within their respective spheres of influence, rather than maintaining monopolies or exclusive privileges for their own nationals. Maintaining the territorial integrity of Asian nations (with allowances for preexistent European colonization) was another notion associated with the Open Door. The following year Hay announced that all these governments had agreed to the principle, although Japan and Russia openly questioned it. The United States was not defending Chinese sovereignty as much as American economic privileges in China. Washington carried out policies in China typical of an imperialist power, including extraterritoriality, moving U.S. military forces through the country at will, and controlling the Chinese Maritime Customs Department.

Like U.S. imperialism, Japanese imperialism had an idealistic self-image. Japan saw itself as freeing Asia from subjugation by Western countries, which were interested only in extracting and repatriating resources. Japan, by contrast, would help the region achieve economic development and improved quality of life. As an alternative to the selfishness, narrow nationalism, materialism, and decadence that many Japanese associated with Western influence, Japan would promote traditional values and Asian solidarity and cooperation.

The fact that most of Asia was already colonized by the Western powers both limited Japan's access to these areas and left little territory for the building of a Japanese sphere of influence. Wars with China and Russia around the turn of the century gave Japan control of Korea and Taiwan and a strong position in southern Manchuria. These possessions were not enough to free Japan from its deep economic dependence on the other great powers. To expand their empire further than this, the Japanese would have to deal with the Chinese and the other imperialist powers. While the Americans advocated global free trade rather than colonial exclusivity, Japanese statesmen such as Foreign Minister Komura Jutaro (1901–06) concluded that an open competition with the other great powers was not in Japan's best interests, given their advantages over Japan in experience with capitalism and access to raw materials. Rather, Japan needed a colonial hinterland to attain self-sufficiency. The way to achieve this objective was to carve out its own sphere of influence in Asia.[4]

The American government assented to and even welcomed Japan's expansionism in Asia early in the twentieth century, seeing the Japanese as a useful balancer against Russia and a force for progress. U.S. leaders also hoped Japan would help open the region's markets to U.S. business. Prior to the 1930s, Japan's leaders were basically committed to international cooperation and to following the example of the major Western powers. Japan and Britain established the Anglo-Japanese Alliance in 1902. Tokyo joined the League of Nations when it was founded in 1919. A brief period of political liberalism flourished in Japan in the 1920s. Under a government that favored international accommodation rather than confrontation, Tokyo signed the Washington Naval Treaty in February 1922. This established a 3:3:2 ratio for the naval forces of Britain, the United States, and Japan, respectively—the size of Japan's naval forces, measured in capital ship tonnage, was restricted to one-third less than those of the two Western powers. In two other treaties, Japan (and the other signatories) agreed not to make any further imperialist encroachments on China and not to attack another country's colonies.

Americans viewed the Japanese as a modern people and the Koreans as backward. Horace Allen, U.S. minister to Korea, reported to Washington that the Koreans could not govern themselves and that Japanese rule over them should be welcomed for "the establishment of order and the development of commerce."[5] U.S. President Theodore Roosevelt had written to a friend shortly before the Russo-Japanese War, "I should like to see Japan have Korea. She will be a check upon Russia, and she deserves it for what she has done."[6] Roosevelt, to be sure, did not trust Japan. "I have no doubt," he said, "that they include all white men as being people who, on the whole, they dislike, and whose past arrogance they resent. . . . Japan is an Oriental nation, and the individual standard of truthfulness in Japan is low." But Roosevelt loathed the Russians. He therefore wished to avoid the creation of "either a yellow peril or a Slav peril" and hoped "the two powers will fight until both are fairly well exhausted." Seeing growing Russian influence in Manchuria as a violation of the Open Door, many Americans supported Japan in its war with Russia. A *New York Tribune* editorial in 1898 opined, "As Between Russian rule and Japanese rule, a large share of the civilized world would choose the latter every time. Slav-Tartar-Cossack rule means tyranny, ignorance, reaction. Japanese rule means freedom, enlightenment, progress."[7] The war began with a surprise Japanese attack on the Russian fleet in Port Arthur prior to a declaration of war, a foreshadowing of the Pearl Harbor raid. Rather than condemning this attack as sneaky or "dastardly," American observers such as an editorialist for the *New York Times* called it an "enterprising and gallant feat of the Japanese arms."[8] Roosevelt was more than a little pleased with Japan's naval victory over the Russian fleet: "I grew so excited that I myself became almost like a Japanese, and I could not attend to official duties."[9] Roosevelt mediated the postwar settlement, for which he won the Nobel Peace Prize. He brokered a settlement that allowed Russia to retain some ability to balance Japanese power. Russia acceded to Japanese influence over southern Manchuria and Korea and gave Japan the southern half of Sakhalin Island. But the Japanese did not get Vladivostok, any part of Siberia, or reparation payments from Russia, leading to angry demonstrations in Japan that were at least partly anti-American.[10]

Washington subsequently reaffirmed its assent to a Japanese presence in mainland Asia. In the secret Taft-Katsura agreement of July 1905, a memorandum of a discussion in Tokyo between then-U.S. Secretary of War William Howard Taft and Japanese Prime Minister Katsura Taro, the U.S. government accepted Japanese control of Korea, while Japan disavowed any intention to challenge U.S. control over the Philippines. The 1908 Root-Takahira agreement (between U.S. Secretary of State Elihu Root and Japanese ambassador to the United States Takahira Kogoro) recognized Japan's entitlement to control over Korea and Manchuria.

Although Japan accepted the rules of the Western-dominated international system and Washington accepted a limited Japanese empire, U.S.-Japan relations were not without tensions even early in the twentieth century. The basic U.S. plan for a war with Japan, War Plan Orange, dated back to the Theodore Roosevelt Administration. Some Japanese actions appeared to challenge the Open Door. In 1910 Japan and Russia agreed to divide Manchuria into a Russian sphere of control in the north and a Japanese sphere in the south. Two countries the United States hoped would balance each other were now cooperating and in a way that undermined the principle of equal economic access to Asia for all foreign interests. In 1915 Japan's "Twenty-One Demands" made to Chinese President Yuan Shih-kai called on China to accept the Japanese takeover of the German concession in Shandong Province, a privileged Japanese position in Manchuria and Inner Mongolia, and additional Japanese rights in China to the exclusion of the other imperialist powers. A fifth section of the Demands would have given Japan control over Chinese central government policy and China's police forces. Tokyo eventually dropped the fifth section under pressure from Britain and the United States, but Americans saw the Twenty-One Demands as a Japanese attempt to usurp Chinese sovereignty and to close the Open Door. When the British and American governments sent a few thousand soldiers in a limited intervention against the Russian Bolsheviks in 1918, Japan deepened U.S. suspicions by landing 80,000 troops in Siberia, ostensibly to join the anti-Bolshevik effort but principally to maintain Japan's position in Manchuria and if possible drive Russian influence out of Northeast Asia. Even as it acted otherwise, however, Tokyo continued to profess support for the Open Door to help mollify the American government.

World War I afforded Japan the opportunity to take German-controlled territory in Asia. As a latecomer great power, Germany had acquired several island groups in the Pacific that the Germans were now unable to defend. Treaty allies Britain and Japan determined that Japan would inherit control of the former German-held islands north of the equator—the Marshall, Caroline, and Mariana Islands—while Australia and New Zealand would be the custodians of those island groups south of the equator. This made Japan a potential strategic threat to the United States because the Japanese could now build naval bases that would straddle the sea lane between Hawaii, Midway Island, and the Philippines.

If the Americans worried about Japanese imperial ambitions exceeding the desired limits, American racism irritated the Japanese. In 1897, the Hawaiian government (then controlled by Western expatriates) turned away two ships carrying Japanese immigrants, with the Hawaiian foreign minister implying that the Japanese were "dangerous to the community in its moral, sanitary, and economic interests."[11] The Japanese government protested and dispatched a warship in support of its nationals. A few weeks later President William McKinley began the process of formally annexing Hawaii as a U.S. territory, further displeasing Tokyo. The Japanese foreign minister complained that U.S. seizure of Hawaii threatened "the general status quo in the Pacific" and the rights of Japanese nationals living in the islands. In Japan, angry crowds harassed visiting American sailors.[12]

In 1913 the race issue drove bilateral tensions to a level that made war appear possible. By that time there were several tens of thousands of Japanese living on the U.S. west coast. The spark of crisis was a new law in California, the Webb-Heney Alien Land Act of 1913, which prohibited foreigners who were not eligible for U.S. citizenship from owning land in the United States and from leasing it for more than three years. Japanese were ineligible for U.S. citizenship under an 1894 law. The Webb-Heney Act was a rewrite of an earlier proposed law that specifically mentioned the Japanese. Japan followed the issue closely and took deep offense. U.S. Navy commanders recommended sending additional warships to protect the Philippines and Hawaii, but President Woodrow Wilson refused out of fear this would provoke Tokyo. In 1920 California law expanded to prohibit aliens from buying or leasing land in the names of their U.S.-born children, and over the next few years several other states adopted the same restrictions. In the 1922 case *Ozawa v. the United States*, the U.S. Supreme Court held that Japanese nationals did not have a right to obtain U.S. citizenship. The Immigration Act of 1924, known to Japanese as the Exclusion Act, forbade aliens ineligible for citizenship from entering the United States. Many supporters of the law were influenced by Madison Grant's 1916 eugenicist book *The Passing of the Great Race*, which argued that the Nordic race (from northwestern Europe) was superior to others but that America's Nordic-descended peoples were shrinking relative to other races because of immigration and differential reproductive rates. The result, he argued, would be the loss of America's greatness. The law renewed Japanese anger and sparked reactions in Japan, including a mob taking down the flag from the U.S. Embassy, one protestor committing suicide in front of the building, and another trying to kill the U.S. consul in Yokohama.[13]

Sensitive about Western racism and their own national prestige, the Japanese proposed in 1919 that the League of Nations (interwar forerunner of the United Nations) insert into the preamble of its Covenant "the principle of the equality of Nations and the just treatment of their nationals." China's delegate supported the proposal. Wilson, however, opposed it, saying the Covenant already contained the principle of the equality of nations. Japan's proposed amendment passed by an 11–6 vote, but Wilson, who chaired the commission, declared it defeated because the voting had not been unanimous (even though the League had adopted other proposals that passed by a majority rather than a unanimous vote).[14]

DEEPENING RIFT BETWEEN JAPAN AND THE WESTERN POWERS

The worldwide economic crisis beginning in 1929 shook Japan's confidence in the Western international order. Governments desperately tried to save their own economies by manipulating their trade and currency controls despite the risk to other countries or to the international economic system as a whole. Tokyo perceived that the free flow of trade and finance was giving way to the formation of regional economic blocs and that powerful states had become more willing to act unilaterally to protect their interests. The major powers responded to the worldwide economic depression of the 1930s with high tariffs. Japan found that less capital was available from American banks and that the American domestic market was less accessible to Japanese exports. The 1930 Smoot-Hawley Act raised tariffs on imports from Japan by 23 percent. From 1929 to 1931, Japan's foreign trade shrunk by one-half. The global recession had a strong impact on both Japanese domestic politics and Japan's foreign policy orientation. Domestically, many Japanese elites, both civilian and military, turned hostile toward capitalism and liberalism. Japan's brief experiment with liberal government had not uprooted the precursors of fascism. The military retained privileges in Japanese society. The education system taught reverence for both the emperor and the Japanese military. The modernizing Japanese armed forces developed links with the *zaibatsu*, industrial conglomerates. Japanese army officers tended to be conservative and highly dismissive of Western liberalism in its various manifestations, from multiparty politics to freedom of speech to international arms control. Many saw foreign military campaigns as a means of purifying Japan from the effects of what they saw as decadent liberal ideas. With the loss of confidence in the Western political order caused by the global economic crisis of the 1930s, these conservative forces came to the fore. Japan turned from liberalism to nationalism and traditional values, increasing the prestige and relative political power of the military.

Externally, Tokyo became less inclined to accommodate the Western powers while seeking to build up its sphere of influence in Asia.[15] Preference for a liberal economic world order was still a core American value even though Americans had helped bring about the "beggar thy neighbor" international climate of the Great Depression. Given Japan's recent experience, it is understandable that the Japanese did not share this faith in the model the Americans touted. At the London Naval Conference of 1930, the follow-up to the 1922 Washington Naval Conference, Japan demanded a larger ratio of capital ships relative to Britain and the United States. The Japanese refused to sign the treaty that emerged from the second London Conference in 1936, leaving Tokyo free of obligations beginning in 1937. In 1936 the Japanese cabinet adopted the "Fundamental Principles of National Policy," which set a general course of conflict in all directions, envisioning expansion into Southeast Asia and deepening the Japanese position in China, along with improved relations with Germany to counter the Soviet Union.

Events in Manchuria demonstrated the rising influence of militarism in Japan's government and Japanese interest in an expanding and exclusive sphere of influence on the Asian mainland, both worrisome trends for American policymakers. With its victory over Russia in 1905, Japan had won acceptance of a Japanese military presence in Manchuria, called the Kwantung Army (Kantogun in Japanese), to protect Japanese economic interests there. Japan viewed Manchuria as strategically important to maintaining control of Korea. A rail line the Japanese considered vital ran from the port of Dairen (also known as Lüda/Lüshun or Port Arthur) inland to Mukden (now known as Shenyang). The railroad would not only be an important means of transporting troops and supplies in the event of another conflict with the Russians, but it also proved useful in Japan's extraction of resources from Manchuria. Thanks to huge Japanese investments in industry and infrastructure, Manchuria had become a major source of raw materials for Japan and an important market for Japanese products. Most of Japan's coal and soybeans came from Manchuria. Japan had invested more than $1 billion in China as a whole—about the same amount that Britain had invested in China, but a higher proportion of Japan's total foreign investment.[16] The Chinese, however, continued to contest Japan's position in Manchuria. Chinese nationalists had long been calling for boycotts and strikes against Japanese businesses in China. These efforts became more serious as Chiang Kai-shek brought a greater sense of unity to China in the late 1920s. When the local Chinese warlord, Zhang Zuolin

(Chang Tso-lin), professed loyalty to Chiang's central government, Japanese military men assassinated him in 1928. This hardly improved the situation for Japan. Zhang's son, Zhang Xueliang (Chang Hsueh-liang), succeeded him and pledged allegiance to Chiang's Kuomintang in 1928. The younger Zhang was putting pressure on the Japanese by demanding more Chinese rights in Manchuria, refusing to agree to Japanese construction of new railroads and developing a new port that would rival Japanese-controlled Dairen.

Acting contrary to Tokyo's wishes, in September 1931 Kwantung Army officers blew up a section of the railway line near Mukden and blamed the sabotage on the Chinese to create an excuse to drive out Zhang's troops and claim outright control of southern Manchuria. There followed a punitive Japanese campaign against Shanghai, where Chinese rioted and attacked Japanese interests, and Tokyo's withdrawal from the League of Nations and renunciation of the three treaties it signed in 1921–22. In 1932 Japan created a puppet state of "Manchukuo" nominally under the rule of Pu Yi, "the Last Emperor" of the deposed Qing Dynasty. Japanese justified the detachment of Manchuria from China with the argument that neither Chiang nor local officials were capable of carrying out the economic development that Japan could. At home, the military rivaled the civilian leadership in political influence. A group of young naval officers assassinated Prime Minister Inukai Tsuyoshi, who had opposed the military's expansion of its campaign in China, in May 1932. The killers used their trials as platforms to publicly promote their ultranationalist views. In response, judges received tens of thousands of petitions asking that the assassins be pardoned. One group of youths sent the court 11 severed fingers accompanied by an offer to die in the assassins' place.[17]

U.S. officials were not adverse to Japan expanding its influence in China to keep order in a neighboring country (as the United States had recently done by sending troops into several Central American countries) and to check revolutionary forces, particularly Soviet and Chinese communism, that if powerful enough might end the privileges of all foreign businessmen, including Americans, in China.[18] Although the U.S. government said in 1932 it would not recognize the "Manchukuo" regime, U.S. Secretary of State Henry L. Stimson told the Chinese ambassador to the United States that he "had no quarrel with any of Japan's rights in Manchuria."[19] The following year new U.S. Secretary of State Cordell Hull told the U.S. ambassador to Japan that discrimination against U.S. interests in Manchukuo, not infringement on the sovereignty of a foreign people, was the main American concern, and that with Japanese removal of such discrimination "maintaining and promoting goodwill between the United States and Japan" was still possible.[20]

JAPAN'S CHINA QUAGMIRE

The Japanese believed their position in Manchuria was still vulnerable to attack by Soviet forces and from military and political pressure from Chinese nationalists. In 1931–32 they extended the territory under their control to include northern China (parts of the present-day Chinese provinces of Inner Mongolia, Hebei, and Shanxi). Extending its sphere of dominance, however, failed to solve Japan's problem of nagging Chinese opposition and the persistent tension that came with it. An apparently spontaneous clash between Japanese and Republic of China units near the Marco Polo Bridge (Luguoqiao) in July 1937 marked the beginning of full-scale war between the two countries and Japanese expansion into the heart of China in an attempt to destroy Chiang's Kuomintang government. Japan anticipated settling its dispute with China through a brief and decisive military action. In three months, Japanese troops would capture Chiang's capital and shatter his armed forces, forcing the Chinese leader to agree to peace on Japan's terms. Within a year Japanese troops had captured Chiang's capital of Nanking as well as Beijing, Shanghai, and many other cities. Chiang, however, withdrew to China's vast interior and refused to surrender. China was too vast for the Japanese to conquer the entire country. What Japanese termed the "China Incident" turned into a lengthy, inconclusive war. In the meantime, the diversion of resources necessary to fight the unexpectedly long campaign in China prevented Japan from making the investments that would increase economic self-sufficiency. Indeed, Japan became even more dependent on imports from the West to continue the war.[21]

China had become a quagmire for Japan. To keep Manchuria, their buffer for Korea, the Japanese believed they needed to quell the continued resistance from the Nationalist Chinese. This led to Japanese military excursions into other parts of China to secure Manchuria and to force Chiang to accept the loss of increasing amounts of Chinese territory to Japan. The domestic political power of Chiang, however, was not strong enough that he could continue to accede to such demands even had he wanted to. Moreover, the brutality of Japanese military campaigns only deepened the Chinese resistance to bargaining with Tokyo. Japanese forces could control selected parts of China, but not the entire country, so they could never completely defeat China or neutralize all the sanctuaries of their Chinese adversaries.

The quagmire in China was complemented by the vicious cycle of Japan's dependence on the West. As Japan's industrialization progressed, the country's need for a cheap and reliable supply of raw materials became acute. Between 1920 and 1931, the Japanese economy's demand for raw materials tripled, oil imports increased 20-fold, and Japan lost its self-sufficiency in food production. This led to greater reliance on foreign nations the Japanese would come to view as adversaries: the Americans, British, Chinese and Dutch, collectively termed the "ABCD" countries. By 1931, Japan imported from two-thirds to 100 percent of important materials such as oil, iron ore, scrap and pig iron, phosphates, rubber, and lead. The principal suppliers were the United States, China, British-controlled Malaya, Dutch-controlled Indonesia, and Canada.[22] Japan also relied on the Western powers, particularly U.S. banks, for loans to build the infrastructure to economically develop China and make Japan's presence there profitable. America, by contrast, was nearly immune to serious economic coercion. The U.S. War Department had determined that if all imports into the United States ceased for two years, the country would suffer critical shortages only in rubber, manganese, and chromium.[23] The more resources the Japanese put into military production, the less they could produce for export to the lucrative markets of the West, and thus the less buying power Japan had for importing industrial staples such as oil and machine tools. The war in China intensified this dynamic. Paradoxically, by attempting to strengthen itself (through industrialization and the acquisition of colonies to supply resources), Japan increased its need for foreign supplies and markets, deepening its vulnerability to a cutoff of supplies and inviting conflicts with the other great powers.

U.S. ECONOMIC AND MILITARY PRESSURE ON JAPAN

Japan's invasion of China evinced an intention to extend Tokyo's sphere of influence well beyond Manchuria. This was an alarming prospect for Washington. The American vision of liberal global trade, the wellspring of the Open Door policy, clashed with the regional autarchies that Japan and later Germany seemed bent on establishing. The United States believed its own prosperity and national security were premised upon opening world trade to U.S. businesses. In 1938 Japanese Prime Minister Konoe Fumimaro proclaimed a "New Order in East Asia" in which Japan would control China's destiny. Furthermore, his Foreign Minister Arita Hachiro explained to Hull that unlike the United States and Britain, which had access to abundant natural resources, the Japanese needed a hinterland in China to secure Japan's "economic national defense."[24] Previously, the Japanese had professed support for the Open Door even as they violated it through their policies in Manchuria and northern China. Now, however, they ceased paying lip-service to the principle. American officials saw the "Greater East Asia Co-Prosperity Sphere," which Tokyo officially announced in August 1940, as the kind of closed economic bloc that had the potential to seriously undercut U.S. prosperity.

Through the 1930s, Washington expressed disapproval of Japanese encroachment in China but simultaneously declined to militarily confront Japan. Up until late 1941, U.S. Secretary of State Cordell Hull assiduously worked to avoid a strong U.S. policy response to Japanese activities in China, fearing this would provoke even more aggressive Japanese action, possibly including war with the United States. This policy survived years of reports of Japanese brutality against not only Chinese troops but also civilians. When Japanese aircraft sank the U.S. gunboat *Panay* in December 1937 on the Yangzi (Yangtze) River near Nanjing, killing three sailors, the Japanese government signaled its own wish to avoid war with America by quickly apologizing, paying compensation, and punishing several of its military officers. Hull was willing to verbally condemn Japan for its aggression in China but opposed embargoes on vital supplies. This often placed him at odds with other U.S.

officials who favored a more assertive U.S. policy against Japan, such as Stanley Hornbeck, the chief State Department official for Asian affairs. Hornbeck had lived in China but had limited knowledge of Japan. He believed that Japan was a threat to U.S. interests in China but that the Japanese would back down under American pressure. Therefore he advocated a tough policy against Tokyo as the best means of upholding U.S. goals for Asia while preventing war.[25]

The resulting U.S. policy was one of gradually increasing economic and military pressure: cutting supplies of important exports to Japan while fortifying the U.S. military position in the Pacific. Japanese aircraft indiscriminately bombed Canton (Guangzhou), China, in May and June 1938, killing 1,500 civilians. In response, Roosevelt permitted increased military aid to China and called on U.S. businesses to stop selling aircraft and aircraft parts to Japan. In July 1939, Congress abrogated the 1911 Treaty of Commerce and Navigation, restricting Japan's access to U.S. trade and financial services. This dropped the previous American guarantee of Japanese access to U.S. commodities and opened to Washington the option of a trade embargo. In July Roosevelt signed into law the National Defense Act of 1940, which gave the White House authority to declare certain U.S. products vital to national defense and to require licenses for their export. This created another lever for restricting U.S. trade with Japan. July also saw a cutback of U.S. oil and metal exports to Japan. Roosevelt banned all exports of scrap iron and scrap steel to Japan in response to the entry of Japanese troops into northern Indochina in September 1940. With the denial of scrap metal supplies, U.S. trade restrictions attained the potential to seriously affect Japanese military capabilities. Machine tools were another important item the United States supplied to Japan; these exports ceased by the end of 1940. The area of Japan's greatest import vulnerability was oil. This was an era in which the United States dominated the global oil supply, accounting for two-thirds of the world's production, as many of the large reserves in the Middle East were not yet discovered. Japan imported 80 percent of its fuel supplies, and 90 percent of its gasoline, from the United States. Japan's attempts to produce synthetic oil in the late 1930s were disappointing, managing an output of less than 4 percent of production goals.[26] The United States reduced some oil exports to Japan in July. The Dutch also agreed, at Washington's urging, to reduce their oil supplies to the Japanese. Additionally, Roosevelt's pressure on U.S. ship owners early in 1941 to move their ships from the Pacific trade routes to the Atlantic (to help supply Britain) made it more difficult for Japan to import oil.

Several key military moves created another form of pressure on Tokyo. In May 1940, on Roosevelt's orders, the U.S. Navy changed the home port of the U.S. Pacific Fleet from San Diego to Pearl Harbor, 1,500 miles closer to Japan. (James O. Richardson, the fleet commander, complained that this made no sense: because the repair and training facilities at Pearl Harbor were inadequate, the fleet would have to sail to the U.S. west coast if war broke out.[27]) The 1938 Vinson Naval Act and 1940 Two Ocean Naval Expansion

Act began a massive warship-building program (including 18 aircraft carriers) that Japan could not hope to match, with the first new ships to be completed by 1943. In October and November Washington secured approval from Britain and the Netherlands to base U.S. warships in Singapore and the Dutch East Indies (Indonesia). Late in the year Roosevelt strengthened the perception of a U.S.-British military alliance by announcing his intention to supply Britain with weapons. This began a few months later with the passage of the Lend-Lease Act. In March 1941, under orders from Roosevelt not made public, U.S. cruisers and destroyers began making voyages into Japanese territorial waters.

An important element of this campaign was American support for China. America's Open Door policy can easily be misread as an interest in China maintaining its sovereignty against imperialist intrusions. In fact, however, a China that could stand up to the imperialist powers would have put an end to U.S. privileges as well as those of other foreigners. American policymakers wanted China to be strong enough to keep out of a foreign sphere of influence, but not so strong that it would throw out the Open Door. Washington provided modest aid to help the Chinese resist Japan. The American goal was not a Chinese victory per se, but rather to keep Chiang going as a proxy to tie down Japanese forces that might otherwise threaten Western interests in Southeast Asia, and also to deny the Japanese militarists the prestige in their own country that would flow from success in China. In 1933 the U.S. government arranged for reserve Army Air Force officers to help train the Chinese Air Force. The Reconstruction Finance Corporation gave China a $50 million loan to buy foodstuffs and textiles. The U.S. Curtiss-Wright aircraft corporation built a factory in Hangzhou. Tokyo was deeply resentful of U.S. aid to China. Japan's Foreign Office warned in 1934 against "any attempt on the part of China to avail herself of the influence of any other country in order to resist Japan."[28]

Following the Japanese invasion of China proper, although the Neutrality Act of 1937 forbade the U.S. sale of military equipment to countries at war, the American government continued to allow China to buy U.S. weapons. With the outbreak of war in Europe, the possibility of German hegemony over the continent made the specter of a Japan-controlled China even more threatening, as it would isolate the United States and Britain from much of the world. Continuing to encourage China to fight the Japanese was therefore imperative.[29] In August 1941 Roosevelt approved the formation of the American Volunteer Group—better known as "the Flying Tigers." Four months before Pearl Harbor, the U.S. government was helping to arrange for current and reserve U.S. military pilots to fly fighter aircraft against Japanese air forces in China and Burma. In November 1940 the United States approved a loan of $100 million to China for the purchase of armaments.

In 1940 Japan showed no signs of submitting to this economic and military pressure. In July with the status of French-controlled Indochina left unclear by Germany's defeat of France, Japanese forces entered northern Indochina to close a supply road into China. The Japanese also sought to expel Westerners from Shanghai. They successfully pressured Britain to withdraw its troops from the city and to close the Burma Road, another important supply route for Chiang's government. In September 1940 Tokyo forced the French government to allow Japan to establish bases in and move troops through northern Indochina. Japan formally joined the Axis alliance on September 27, 1940. Under the Tripartite Pact, member states would assist "with all political, economic and military means" if any one of them was attacked by "a Power at present not involved in the European War or in the Japanese-Chinese conflict"[30]—that is, the United States. Japan's decision to align itself with Nazi Germany, while alarming to the Western powers, was motivated more by a desire to avoid than to prepare for war against America, as the Japanese hoped this would help force Washington to accept Japan's objectives in Asia by raising the potential costs to the United States (as well as to the Soviet Union) of risking a war with Japan.[31] Similarly, Germany's interest in the alliance was deterring the United States from giving further aid to Britain. Japanese officials assured the U.S. government that Japan's treaty with the Axis powers should not be an issue of concern to America, as Japan did not intend to follow the Germans' lead if they declared war on the United States.

SETTING A COURSE FOR COLLISION

The period that most crucially set Japan and the United States on a collision course for war was July 1941. At an imperial conference convened July 2, Japan's leaders debated over two general strategic options. The first was to attack the USSR now that the Soviets were preoccupied by a German invasion from the west. If successful, this would knock out the Soviet threat to Japan's possessions in China and Manchuria, strengthen Japan's relationship with Germany, and so weaken the position of the European powers in Asia that Tokyo could hope to take over the resource-rich territories of Southeast Asia without having to fight the United States. Attacking to the north had been the preference of the Japanese army. Recently, however, they had learned from hard experience about the capabilities of Soviet troops. Border clashes between Soviets and the Kwantung Army culminated in the Battle of Khalkhyn Gol (also known as the Nomonhan Incident) in May 1939. Under an able commander named Georgi Zhukov, the Soviets won a decisive victory. The Japanese generals now demanded more time to mobilize the additional troops they would need to take on the Red Army. The navy, on the other hand, wanted a commitment to prepare for (but not necessarily fight) a Southeast Asia campaign as a way of ensuring that the fleet got a robust share of funding and resources. Despite misgivings about a war with the Americans, the Japanese navy perceived a need to act decisively before the United States accomplished its naval buildup.

As an interim compromise, the leadership decided to move troops into southern Indochina while the army was preparing for war with the Soviets—in effect, to go south before going north. They concluded this step was necessary to block possible British and American moves to strengthen their influence in the region while Japanese strength was focused on a campaign against the USSR. Japanese leaders took this decision assuming that the Americans and British would condemn but not go to war over Japanese occupation of southern Indochina. At this point, Tokyo was not irrevocably committed to war with the United States.[32] In accordance with the decision, Japanese troops occupied the remaining southern section of Indochina after reaching an agreement with the Vichy French authorities. The Vichy French would ostensibly maintain control of the government, while allowing the basing of Japanese troops, aircraft, and warships in southern Indochina.

Washington read Japan's occupation of southern Indochina in July 1941 as proof that Japan had decided to seize British and Dutch colonies in Southeast Asia, perceiving more resolution and coherence in Tokyo's strategy than actually existed at that time. As an ally of these Western powers and a consumer of the exports of these colonies, the United States had strong interests in preventing Japan from dominating Southeast Asia. In August 1941 the U.S. and British governments agreed on a concerted strategy for deterring Japan from striking the European colonies in Southeast Asia. The British would strengthen their naval presence in Singapore. The Americans would build up their forces in the Philippines, including a strategic bombing capability.[33] U.S. planners assumed that the Philippines would fall to a sustained attack by a determined invader. The U.S. government had already announced its intention to grant the Philippines independence in 1944 and withdraw all American forces by 1946. Now Roosevelt sent B-17 bombers to the Philippines and ordered a program of reinforcing the Philippines' defenses (projected to take several months and far from complete when war broke out). The president federalized the armed forces of the Philippines and reactivated Douglas MacArthur, who had been a Field Marshall in the Philippine Army since retiring from the U.S. Army in 1937, as commander of United States Army Forces in the Far East, headquartered in Manila.

On July 18, Roosevelt met with his cabinet to discuss the U.S. response to the imminent entry of Japanese troops into southern Indochina. Hornbeck and other Japan hard-liners argued that an oil embargo would prevent Japan from striking south: drained by the war in China, Japan could not undertake a large new campaign without massive stockpiling of critical resources, which would be impossible if oil imports from Japan's largest supplier dried up. U.S. ambassador to Japan Joseph Grew, on the other hand, argued that a U.S. oil embargo would drive the Japanese to invade the oil fields of Dutch-controlled Indonesia, which would mean war with the United States. Grew feared "an allout, do-or-die attempt, actually risking national hara-kiri, to make Japan impervious to economic embargoes abroad rather than yield to foreign pressure."[34] The president reflected Grew's view, saying a cutoff of oil to Japan could force the Japanese into aggression in Southeast Asia. The U.S. Navy agreed, as expressed in a July 24 memo to Roosevelt from Chief of Naval

Operations Admiral Harold Stark.[35] Roosevelt ordered the freezing of Japanese assets in the United States, a further reduction of strategic metal exports to Japan, and a *partial* oil sales ban that would apply to U.S. sales of high-octane (aviation grade) fuel to Japan. Britain, China, and the Netherlands quickly followed the U.S. lead and froze Japanese assets under their control.

Assistant Secretary of State Dean Acheson interpreted the guidance liberally and implemented the aviation fuel ban as a virtual oil embargo. By early August, oil shipments to Japan from both the United States and Indonesia had ceased. When Roosevelt discovered what had become of his order, he declined to stop it, perhaps because he feared the appearance of backing down before Tokyo.[36] The Japanese were forced to draw on their stockpiled oil reserves.

These actions confirmed Japanese fears that the so-called ABCD countries were committed to encircling Japan.[37] The oil embargo, as historian Akira Iriye observes, "had a tremendous psychological impact upon the Japanese. The ambivalence and ambiguities in their perception of world events disappeared, replaced by a sense of clear-cut alternatives."[38] The alternative that America hoped the Japanese would choose, cooperation with (and continued economic dependence upon) the Western powers, now appeared less attractive than ever. A Japanese editorialist wrote in September 1941, "As petroleum is an indispensable product in the existence of a modern state and Japan's oil supply is at the mercy of America's whim and pleasure, Japan's only method of survival would be to curry obsequiously to the favor of the United States. But no self-respecting race or nation can tolerate an existence of this kind."[39] If the U.S. oil embargo continued, Japan would run out of oil in less than two years unless it found another source. Without an oil supply, the campaign in China—and more broadly, Japan's quest to be a great power—could not continue. As a high-ranking Japanese navy logistics official wrote later, "The problem was oil. If our reserves were dribbled away, Japan would grow weaker and weaker like a tuberculosis patient gasping along until he dropped dead on the road. A grim and humiliating end." Alternatively, "we could strike boldly and get the oil in the south."[40]

The freeze of assets and oil embargo convinced the Japanese government of the need to break free of economic dependence on the United States. The Japanese army concluded as a result of these developments that going to war against the Soviet Union was not possible in the immediate future because of lack of resources, and that therefore the army had to support the navy's war plan, which offered the possibility of new sources of oil and other vital commodities. Contrary to Hornbeck's argument, while the oil embargo precluded Japanese military action against the USSR, it committed Japan to a campaign in Southeast Asia to capture new oil supplies. Stockpiled reserves were sufficient for this purpose.

Japanese military planners concluded that they could not accomplish the conquest of British and Dutch possessions in Southeast Asia without eliminating American bases in the Philippines. Admiral Yamamoto Isoroku insisted that if Japan was going to fight the United States, the Japanese navy must be allowed to attack the U.S. Pacific Fleet at Pearl Harbor along with supporting army operations in Southeast Asia. To make this possible, Japanese engineers developed shallow-draft torpedoes and armor-piercing bombs expressly for the purpose of striking ships docked in Pearl Harbor.

Shortcomings in U.S. diplomacy helped bring on the Japanese decision to attack American forces. The assumption that U.S. pressure combined with the poor returns from their invasion of China would force the Japanese to conform to American political and economic principles proved erroneous. U.S. policymakers also failed to understand the depth of interservice rivalry in Japan, and that before the oil embargo and freeze of assets, Tokyo was not yet resolved to warring with the West over Southeast Asia. Had Washington been open to a more subtle understanding of the politics inside the Japanese government, the United States could have pursued a policy of selective economic sanctions designed to steer Tokyo away from reaching a consensus for war against Western interests in Asia.[41] The U.S. government also allowed the oil embargo to expand beyond the level ordered by the chief executive at a critical juncture, pushing Tokyo toward the conclusion that war with the West was unavoidable.

THE OUTCOME IS SEALED

In a meeting on September 6 attended by the emperor, Japan's top leaders decided to continue negotiations with the United States until the beginning of October, when they would begin preparations for an attack if they had not reached a satisfactory settlement with Washington. Talks with the United States kept open the possibility, however unexpected, that America would give in to the main Japanese demands: acceding to Japanese expansion in Asia and a return to normal bilateral trade relations. Nomura Kichisaburo, Japanese ambassador to the United States, favored peace with the United States and did not realize that the weight of opinion among the key political and military elites in Tokyo had shifted decisively toward war.[42] Tokyo allowed Nomura and envoy Kurusu Saburo to maintain the appearance that Japan was negotiating in good faith. Striking north was shelved. Tokyo would consider invading the USSR only if the Soviet regime appeared to have collapsed under the blows of the German assault from the west. Instead, Japan would seek a nonaggression agreement with Moscow to ensure peace on the northern flank while Japanese forces attacked Southeast Asia, and to weaken Soviet collusion with Chinese forces.[43] Peace with Japan also (temporarily) suited the Soviets; locked in a desperate struggle against Germany, the Red Army did not have forces to spare for an unprovoked campaign against Japanese Manchuria.

On September 25, Nomura gave Hull a proposal: America would help Japan secure peace with China on terms acceptable to Japan and would cease aiding China, the United States would restore normal trade with Japan, and Japanese troops would remain in Indochina until the war in China was over. Hull responded on October 2 by reiterating the Open Door principles of respect for other countries' territorial integrity, noninterference in their internal affairs, equality of economic opportunities, and political change in the Asia-Pacific only through peaceful means. He also said that "the withdrawal of Japanese troops from China and French Indochina would be most helpful" in demonstrating "Japan's peaceful intentions." Nomura responded that Japan could agree to all these points except Japanese forces leaving China, which he said would not be possible until Chiang no longer threatened Japan's position in Manchuria.[44]

Any chance that Japan would accede to American demands for a withdrawal died in mid-October. Some Japanese leaders, such as Konoe, hoped that the United States would abdicate control of Asia to Japan without war. Increasingly committed to preventing Hitler from achieving a hegemony over Europe, America might conclude it could not take on both Germany and Japan simultaneously. Konoe was also reluctant to start a war with the Western powers when Japan was unable to completely subdue the Chinese. Konoe, who would commit suicide in late 1945 to avoid being tried by the Americans for war crimes, advocated a withdrawal of Japanese forces from China to placate the Americans. At a cabinet meeting, War Minister Tojo Hideki, who was former Kwangtung Army chief of staff, demanded that preparations be made for war since diplomacy had failed. Tojo insisted that withdrawal of Japanese troops from China was nonnegotiable: "there can be no compromise on the stationing of troops in China. . . . If we just acquiesce to the American demand, everything we have achieved in China will be lost. Manchukuo will be endangered and our control of Korea will also be jeopardized." Konoe resigned on October 15, and Tojo became the new prime minister. On November 5, Tojo decreed that the attack plan would proceed unless the United States met Japan's demands by November 25.[45]

Diplomacy continued. Hull and Nomura met secretly 16 times in the months before December 7. On November 20, Nomura proposed to Hull that Japan would withdraw its forces from southern Indochina if the United States would unfreeze Japanese assets, cease aiding China, and supply oil to Japan. This did not come close to addressing American demands. A note Hull delivered to Nomura on November 26, which Tokyo characterized as an ultimatum with terms the Japanese could not accept, demanded that Japan withdraw all of its military and police forces from China (excluding Manchuria) and Indochina in exchange for the United States unfreezing Japanese assets and a return to normal bilateral trade. Hull fully understood that withdrawing from China and Indochina under American pressure would be a humiliating step for Japan. He believed this was necessary to shift the control of Japan's government from military extremists to more moderate politicians with whom the United States could build a constructive U.S.-Japan relationship. The next day Hull, apparently resigned to war, told Stimson (then Secretary of War), "I have washed my hands of it, and it is now in the hands of you and Knox—the army and the navy."[46]

U.S. Treasury official Harry Dexter White, later (and unrelatedly) accused of being a spy for the Soviet Union while working in the U.S. government, formulated an 11th-hour plan that aimed at relaxing bilateral tensions. White's proposal called for a restructuring of the U.S.-Japan relationship, specifically including U.S. economic assistance to Japan in exchange for a Japanese withdrawal from China proper. The objections of various U.S. government agencies, however, combined with Hull's disinterest in the proposal, resulted in its quiet death.[47]

The United States had opposed Japanese expansion into China from the outset, even if Washington was not willing to go to war over it. American officials considered this aggressive policy by a military-dominated Japanese government to be an increasingly serious challenge to fundamental U.S. interests in international great-power cooperation and open global trade. With the additional American perceptions that Hitler's gains in Europe made Japanese control of China more threatening and that Japan was committed to invading Southeast Asia, Washington decided to attempt to force Japan to withdraw from China and Indochina through economic sanctions. These sanctions presented Tokyo with a stark choice: accept a humiliating retreat and continued economic dependence on the West, or drive the West out of Asia and establish an independently viable empire. Given the influence of military men over the government, Tokyo could not accept a withdrawal of its troops from territory in China that they had shed blood to obtain. Japanese businessmen in China insisted they needed these troops for protection. More importantly, the Japanese army would view a withdrawal as a blow both to their prestige and to Japan's aspirations for great power status. Historians have compared the mind-set of these Japanese leaders with that of American presidents who found it politically difficult to pull U.S. forces out of Vietnam in the 1960s, which they saw as an admission that prior American losses in that campaign were in vain.[48]

Few Japanese leaders were optimistic about Japan's chances of defeating the United States. Their hope was that a stunning opening blow against American forces in the Pacific would allow Japan to quickly consolidate a strong position in Asia and convince Washington to negotiate a settlement that would recognize an enlarged Japanese sphere of influence. In the high-level discussion that led to the decision to attack Pearl Harbor, Tojo showed more desperation that confidence when he declared, "You have to plunge into war if there is some chance, however slight, of winning victory." Many, reportedly including Konoe and Yamamoto, were downright pessimistic.[49] A war game in spring 1940 conducted by the navy indicated that conflict with the United States would lead to a protracted war that Japan could not win. But the navy did not share these results with the army or the civilian national leadership.[50] The navy's institutional competition with the army created pressure to maintain preparations for an attack to the south and war with the Western powers. To express doubts about the navy's ability to fulfill this mission would have been tantamount to conceding the battle for resources and prestige to the army.

Nevertheless, the Japanese had what they thought was a feasible plan for a quick defeat of the United States that took advantage of Japanese strengths and of the great distance the Americans had to cover to project naval power into the Western Pacific. The plan anticipated the dispatch of an American fleet in defense of the U.S. possessions Wake Island and the Philippines. Long-range Japanese submarines would follow the U.S. fleet from the time it left port, tracking it and sinking some ships with torpedoes. As it crossed the Pacific, the American ships would suffer more losses in attacks from Japanese aircraft operating from Japanese-held island airfields. Near the Philippines, Japanese cruisers and destroyers would make nighttime torpedo attacks, exploiting the superior night-fighting ability of the Japanese navy. Finally, the weakened U.S. force would face the brunt of the Japanese surface fleet, anchored in its huge battleships.[51] German successes in the war in Europe gave the Japanese additional reason to be optimistic. In the initial months of the Nazi invasion of the Soviet Union, which began in June 1941, Germany appeared headed for a quick victory and dominance of the European continent. With a German declaration of war against the United States expected to follow the outbreak of a U.S.-Japan conflict, the Americans would face a two-front war. A very formidable adversary in the Atlantic theater would divert much of America's resources from the Pacific, greatly easing Japan's task.

The Japanese task force charged with the operation included 6 aircraft carriers, 2 battleships, 2 cruisers, and 11 destroyers. Under the command of Admiral Nagumo Chuichi, the fleet set sail from the Kurile Islands toward Hawaii in great secrecy on November 25. On December 1, an imperial conference convened and formally decided war would begin on midnight of December 8 (December 7 in Hawaii).

On December 6–7, Tokyo sent a 14-part message to Nomura for delivery to Hull. U.S. intelligence intercepted and decoded the first 13 parts by the night of December 6. Tokyo delayed sending the most important part, the 14th, which said Japan had decided to break off talks with the United States. Washington had the 14th part of the message early Sunday morning, but Gen. George C. Marshall did not see it until after returning from his regular horseback ride at 10 A.M. Marshall sent a warning to U.S. military forces in Hawaii to be on alert, but this message did not arrive until after the attack.

Nomura and Kurusu were to deliver Tokyo's message to Hull by 1 P.M. Washington time, just before the attackers struck Pearl Harbor. Because of the delay in the delivery of the last part of the message combined with the time the Japanese embassy staff required to decode, translate, and retype the letter, Nomura and Kurusu did not get the letter to Hull until after he had heard the report of a Japanese air raid on Pearl Harbor. When they met with an angry Hull, Nomura and Kurusu did not yet know about the attack. The memorandum reviewed from Japan's perspective the origins of the crisis and the attempts to resolve it through negotiations, emphasizing that Japan had been reasonable and patient, and the Americans domineering and belligerent.

In Hull's view, the memorandum contained "infamous falsehoods and distortions on a scale so huge I have never imagined until today that any Government on this planet was capable of uttering them."[52] It was not, however, a declaration of war and said nothing about an imminent attack. The key 14th part of the message read, "Obviously it is the intention of the American Government to conspire with Great Britain and other countries to obstruct Japan's efforts toward the establishment of peace through the creation of a new order in East Asia. . . . Thus, the earnest hope of the Japanese Government to adjust Japanese-American relations and to preserve and promote the peace of the Pacific through cooperation with the American Government has finally been lost. . . . [I]t is impossible to reach an agreement through further negotiations."[53] An earlier draft of the message contained a stronger statement—"You will be held responsible for any and all consequences that may arise"—that was removed at the Japanese military's insistence.[54] Thus, even if the Japanese diplomats had delivered the memorandum before the attack, Tokyo would have violated the Hague Convention of 1907, which Japan had ratified in 1911, and which requires a state to declare war prior to opening hostilities. Most importantly, it is unlikely that a timely delivery of the Nomura-Kurusu letter would have affected the readiness of Pearl Harbor before the raid.

NOT SO SURPRISING

The attacks on Oahu were a surprise to the Americans, but war was not. By November, most high-ranking U.S. government officials expected a military conflict with Japan. On November 24, the chief of naval operations warned commanders in the Pacific of "a surprise aggressive movement [by the Japanese] in any direction." On November 27 he wrote, "This dispatch is to be considered a war warning. . . . an aggressive move by Japan is expected within the next few days."[55] Stimson's diary entry of November 25, 1941, noted that Roosevelt expected a Japanese attack as early as December 1 "for the Japanese are notorious for making an attack without warning, and the question was what we should do. The question was how we should maneuver them into the position of firing the first shot without allowing too much danger to ourselves. . . . we realized that in order to have the full support of the American people it was desirable to make sure that the Japanese be the ones to do this so that there should remain no doubt in anyone's mind as to who were the aggressors."[56] Roosevelt had long been suspicious of the Japanese. In 1937 he had asked Admiral William Leahy to investigate whether Japanese crab fishermen were secretly scouting locations for military bases to be employed in a future war with the United States.[57] There is evidence that in connection with the conference between Roosevelt and Churchill in August 1941 that yielded the Atlantic Charter, the two leaders also reached an unpublicized agreement that if Japan attacked British interests in Asia, America would join Britain's war against Japan.[58]

At least some U.S. planners welcomed war with Japan. In October 1940, more than a year before the attack on Pearl Harbor, U.S. Navy intelligence officer Lieutenant Commander Arthur McCollum wrote a classified memorandum for his superiors. McCollum observed that the defeat of Britain would be a serious blow to American security, leaving the United States alone against the combined strength of potential adversaries Germany, Italy, and Japan (the USSR was at that time still officially neutral). Since domestic politics would not allow the United States to enter the war in Europe, America should direct its efforts toward protecting Britain's interests in Asia from the military threat posed by Japan. McCollum recommended eight ways of increasing U.S. pressure on Japan, including basing more U.S. warships and submarines in the western Pacific, maximizing military aid to Japan's foe Nationalist China, and cutting off U.S. and British trade with Japan. "If by these means Japan could be led to commit an overt act of war, so much the better," McCollum wrote. In that case, U.S. forces would be positioned to quickly defeat Japan before concentrating on the European Axis powers. In an entry in his diary, Stimson endorsed the course of action in the McCollum memo.[59]

The American campaign of harassment and coercion against Japan and the expectation of U.S. leaders of an eventual military conflict are certainly inconsistent with the notions of U.S. passivity and shock that most Americans associate with the Pearl Harbor attack. This has moved some analysts to develop the Roosevelt–Pearl Harbor conspiracy thesis. Their argument is that Roosevelt, frustrated by his inability to get Americans to support their country entering the war against Germany, sought a war with Japan as a means of drawing the United States into a fight with the Axis powers. Roosevelt therefore tried to maneuver Japan into attacking the United States. Alerted by intelligence that a Japanese attack on Pearl Harbor was imminent, Roosevelt reputedly kept Pearl Harbor in the dark to ensure the Japanese would go through with the raid.[60]

In my view, however, complacency and underestimation of the opponent are sufficient to explain how Japan caught American forces flatfooted on December 7–8. U.S. military leaders expected a Japanese strike in Southeast Asia; that this presumably inferior country would or could move a large fleet 3,500 miles without being detected and carry out a major air attack on Pearl Harbor was scarcely conceivable. U.S. leaders *did* expect a Japanese strike in the Philippines. Yet when Japanese aircraft raided Clark Air Base on December 8, nine hours after the attack on Pearl Harbor, they similarly found U.S. aircraft parked wingtip-to-wingtip on the ground, facilitating the destruction of half of MacArthur's strategically vital B-17 bomber force.

Despite the embargos, on the day of the attack, Japan had imported from U.S. firms all of its high-octane gasoline; over 90 percent of its copper, trucks, automobiles, and automotive parts; most of its oil and scrap iron; and about half of its motors and machinery. The tanks of the aircraft that bombed Pearl Harbor were filled with U.S.-supplied fuel.[61]

For the Japanese, Pearl Harbor was a brilliant success tactically, but not strategically. The raiders reached their target almost undetected, wreaked serious damage on the warships in port, and escaped with light losses (29 Japanese aircraft destroyed). As Japanese planners hoped and intended, the U.S. Navy was not a serious hindrance to Japanese operations in Southeast Asia in late 1941 and early 1942. The long-term military damage the raid inflicted, however, was limited. The raiders missed the American aircraft carriers, all of which were away from Pearl Harbor during the attack. Japan's aircraft did little damage to the base's infrastructure. The attacking planes spared Pearl Harbor's oil tanks and repair and maintenance facilities, the destruction of which would have delayed an American naval offensive by forcing the U.S. Pacific Fleet to move its staging area back to the U.S. mainland. The sinking of five obsolete battleships (three of which were later raised and returned to service) had little impact on the outcome of a war in which aircraft carriers and submarines played the decisive naval roles. The attack was more than enough, nevertheless, to bring America wholeheartedly into a total war against Japan, a war the Japanese could not win. A previously isolationist-leaning Congress responded to Roosevelt's December 8 call for a declaration of war with an affirmative vote of 82–0 in the Senate and 388–1 in the House of Representatives (uncompromisingly pacifist Jeannette Rankin from Montana was the sole dissenter).

CLASHING IMPERIALISMS

The U.S.-Japan conflict grew out of a clash between two forms of imperialism. The United States promoted the Open Door principle for China to maximize opportunities for U.S. businesses and supported Britain and the Netherlands maintaining their colonies in Southeast Asia. Japan sought an exclusive sphere of influence in Manchuria and northern China and wanted to escape its heavy economic dependence on the Western powers. The United States encouraged a limited Japanese empire while at the same time working to thwart Japan's attempts to break free of reliance on Western-controlled supplies of resources and capital.

Japan failed to achieve its objective through seizing a hinterland in mainland Asia. Continued Chinese resistance and agitation compelled Japanese forces to make deepening commitments to protect their position in China, beginning with Manchuria and growing to include northern China and later most of China's major cities. The Japanese had to keep fighting to safeguard their hinterland, making the hinterland a consumer as much as a provider of resources. Furthermore, the invasion of China increased Japanese economic dependence on the Western countries, especially the United States. The war in Europe led to reduced Japanese access to these supplies, particularly as Axis advances moved the U.S. government to employ trade sanctions in a tougher approach toward Japan. The original proponents of Japan's strategy of seeking economic self-sufficiency had emphasized the need to avoid conflict with

the Western powers until Japan secured a profitable empire.[62] Tokyo disastrously disregarded this counsel.

The Pearl Harbor raid was not without provocation. American policies
played a large role in driving Tokyo to such desperation that it opted to attack
its powerful Pacific competitor. The United States responded to unwanted
Japanese imperialism with a policy of increasing economic and military pressure intended to force Japan to limit its territorial aspirations and to return
to a posture of cooperation with the Western powers. Initially U.S. officials
believed that because of Japan's paucity of resources, Tokyo would eventually
realize it had no other choice. Washington took several steps to strengthen
U.S. military power in the Western Pacific. A campaign of economic coercion
froze Japanese assets in the United States and left Japan in danger of running
out of oil and suffering shortages of other key resources. Washington also
supplied assistance to Chiang Kai-shek to sustain China as a proxy adversary
to bleed Japan's military strength. The United States did not bring on war
with Japan to save the Chinese. It was only the combination of the threat of
Japanese control over China, the specter of a Nazi hegemony in Europe, and
Japanese designs on the Western colonies in Southeast Asia that triggered
serious U.S. economic sanctions against Japan.

Both sides made serious miscalculations. American policymakers expected
until late 1941 that the increase of economic and military pressure on Japan
would force Tokyo to back down rather than lash out at the West. U.S. policies
such as the freeze of Japanese assets and the oil embargo were not intended
to push Japan into attacking the West but nevertheless had exactly that effect.
For their part, Japanese planners gambled that a quick, decisive victory in
Southeast Asia and the Pacific would convince the Americans to submit to
Japanese control over these regions.

The threat of economic strangulation represented by the tightening American trade embargo against Japan, particularly the denial of oil and metal supplies, forced Tokyo into a choice. Japan could, on the one hand, fight to secure
its great power status. Alternatively, the Japanese could choose to give up their
conquered territory and international autonomy, accepting what would have
been the equivalent of suffering a defeat in a major (although not total) war.
With a domestic political climate that could not tolerate an abandonment of
national aspirations, Japanese leaders opted to go to war to consolidate Japan's
position in Asia and expel Western influence.

SHORT-TERM SUCCESS, BUT EVENTUAL DISASTER

The epilogue to the Pearl Harbor attack and the string of Japanese victories that followed in Southeast Asia and the Pacific through early 1942,
including the conquest of the Philippines and Wake Island, was that rather
than concede the Asia-Pacific to Japan, the United States committed itself
to a total war with the objectives of rolling back Japan's overseas empire and
overthrowing its ruling regime. President Franklin D. Roosevelt set the tone

for America's entry into the Pacific War in his speech to Congress asking for a declaration of war on December 8, 1941, calling the attack "unprovoked and dastardly." Tokyo's gamble produced stunning short-term success but eventual disaster. The American economic strength that Japan had found oppressive before the war was then harnessed to the task of defeating the Axis powers. U.S. productivity was sufficient to make an important contribution to winning the war against Germany and to completely overwhelm Japan. Japanese economic capacity was only 10 percent that of the United States.[63] This created a huge differential in the two countries' war-making capacities. Tokyo had the wherewithal to support a short, decisive war against the United States, but could not win a protracted war of attrition. With few natural resources in the home islands, reliance on overseas colonies for raw materials made Japan even more heavily dependent than most countries on vulnerable ocean supply lines, which grew longer as the Japanese empire expanded. The United States successfully exploited this vulnerability with unrestricted submarine warfare. In only its first full year of war, the United States produced many more guns, aircraft, and tanks than all of the Axis powers combined. A single American corporation, Ford, produced more military vehicles and combat aircraft than Italy during the war. Ford's gigantic Willow Run factory in Michigan built a bomber every 63 minutes.[64] American shipyards produced a cargo ship every 12 hours.[65] The United States built 35,000 of a single type of aircraft, the C-47 cargo plane; this was more than all the bomber aircraft of all types built by Germany and Japan combined.

U.S. forces won a naval battle near Midway Island in June 1942 that turned the tide of the war against Japan. Hoping to annihilate the U.S. Pacific Fleet, including the aircraft carriers that were absent from Pearl Harbor, Japan lost 4 of its own carriers, 322 carrier aircraft, and 3,037 killed in action. The Americans lost 1 carrier, 1 destroyer, and 147 aircraft.[66] U.S. forces did not win the battle of Midway because they had superior numbers. They triumphed because of a combination of boldness, good information about the enemy's movements, and sheer luck. But because of their industrial capacity, the Americans could have recovered from the loss of 4 carriers in a single battle. The Japanese could not. After the battle of Midway, Japan completed the construction of only 4 more fleet carriers (the largest size) during the rest of the war. The United States built 22.[67] In the production of major warships, the United States outpaced Japan by a ratio of 16 to 1.[68] Replacing experienced pilots was equally difficult for Japan. About one-third of Japan's naval aviators died in the battle of Midway, with many others injured. After 1942, the United States enjoyed superiority in the air whenever U.S. troops fought the Japanese on the ground. Indeed, the Americans had surplus airpower; the U.S. military's Strategic Bombing Survey in the Pacific theater concluded that U.S. air attacks on Japanese garrisons isolated by the "island hopping" campaign "were often continued longer and in greater weight than was reasonably required or profitable."[69] With no means of resupply or evacuation, these troops were already out of the war, in some cases doomed to starvation.

Some of the bombing in the Pacific War targeted oil refineries, steel mills, production plants, and berthed warships that were already inactive due to a lack of fuel or raw materials because of the interdiction of Japan's maritime supply lines.[70] According to military analyst Martin Van Creveld, "logistics make up as much as nine-tenths of the business of war."[71] In general the Allied countries paid more attention than the Axis countries to logistics and support services. In the Pacific, the Americans had a "tooth to tail" ratio of about 18 support personnel for every combat soldier. For the Japanese the ratio was about one to one.[72] There was an average of four tons of supplies for every American soldier deployed to the Pacific, compared to two pounds for his Japanese counterpart.[73] By one estimate, U.S. forces expended 1,589 rounds of artillery for each Japanese soldier killed.[74] What would be considered luxuries in other armies were standard equipment for American servicemen. The U.S. Navy, for example, deployed a barge that had been converted into a floating ice cream parlor to serve sailors in far-flung seas.[75] Willingness to commit resources to taking care of business in the rear areas paid off in essential but relatively unglamorous activities such as the delivery of supplies and the maintenance of equipment, which in turn determined outcomes on the battlefield.

CHAPTER 4

A Ruthless War

On the night of August 21, 1944, in one of the war's countless tragedies, a submarine sank a merchant vessel carrying 1,660 passengers, half of them children. Only 177, including 56 of the children, survived. One of the survivors was a 13-year-old girl. After rescuing a 4-year-old boy from the water, suffering a shark bite to her leg, and drifting for three thirsty and hungry days atop floating debris, the girl reported, "I saw a bright shining figure in glorious white silken robes walking upon the waves. . . . I couldn't tell if it was Jesus or the Virgin Mary or God Almighty. . . . I understood it was a promise of hope that God was still with us."[1] The next day a passing ship rescued the brave girl and her fellow survivors. Her name was Miyagi Tsuneko. She was a Japanese Christian. The torpedoed ship was *Tsushima Maru*, which was evacuating civilians from Okinawa ahead of the anticipated American attack.[2] The attacking submarine was the USS *Bowfin*, which completed nine war patrols in the Pacific and is now docked in Pearl Harbor, converted into a museum. *Bowfin's* crew was not aware that *Tsushima Maru* was full of children. Such an incident was an inevitable result of the U.S. policy of unrestricted submarine warfare against Japan.

Attacking Japanese merchant ships without first ensuring the safety of their passengers, a contravention of a prewar international treaty to which the United States was a signatory, was only one facet of the unusual level of savagery that characterized the Pacific War. There were unfortunately many more manifestations of ruthlessness, including atrocities against civilians, mistreatment of prisoners of war, and the fiendish activities of the notorious Unit 731. The savagery of the Pacific War was unusual in that some combatants in other theaters of World War II managed to maintain gentlemen's agreements in the midst of combat. In North Africa, for example, both sides respected each other's military field hospitals, which treated all wounded soldiers brought in, whether British or German.[3] The Japanese brutality toward prisoners of war exhibited in the Pacific War contrasted greatly with Japan's conduct in previous wars. The Japanese treated their Russian prisoners from the Russo-Japan War and their German prisoners from World War I well and in accordance with international law. As for the Americans, who fought in both the European and Pacific theaters, and therefore provide a basis for comparison, we can say that they usually accepted the surrenders of German soldiers who wished to give up but largely followed a policy of not taking Japanese prisoners.

WHY AMERICANS FOUGHT, AND WHY THEY FOUGHT RUTHLESSLY

To understand how Americans fought the war, it is useful to understand *why* Americans fought the war. Americans would subsequently interpret their involvement in World War II as part of a moral crusade of the forces of light against the forces of evil, or more concretely as a struggle between liberty and fascism. This contemporary sentiment, however, has lost touch with the spirit of the war years. The United States did not go to war to right the world's wrongs. America did not enter the fight against Germany until the Germans declared war on the United States. Absent Germany's declaration of war, the United States would not have joined the fight against Hitler as a full-fledged combatant until 1942 at the earliest. U.S. isolationism survived the ascension of Hitler to power, *Kristallnacht*,[4] the invasion of Poland and the outbreak of war between Germany and the Western European democracies, the sinking by a German U-boat of the U.S. warship *Reuben James* with the loss of 115 lives, and the stunning initial success of Germany's invasion of the USSR. The United States preferred to stay out of the conflict even when it was clear that Europe was in danger of falling to Hitler's fascism. Indeed, Roosevelt faced strong opposition in his efforts to come to Britain's aid. Similarly, Japanese outrages in China since 1937, including the Nanjing Massacre, the bombing of civilians in Shanghai and other cities, and the sinking of the U.S. patrol boat *Panay* in the Yangtze River near Nanjing, angered Americans but did not move them to go to war.

This isolationism evaporated overnight with the Pearl Harbor attack. For Americans, World War II was mostly a war of revenge in reaction to what was perceived as Japanese treachery. Accordingly, most Americans wanted to fight Japan more than Germany. A poll in 1942 showed 66 percent of Americans thought defeating the Japanese should take priority over defeating the Nazis.[5] An American aviator in the European theater observed during the war, "Like every American who flies to Europe for combat duty, I regretted my failure to get the desired crack at the Jap. I failed to possess any real enmity toward Jerry and sensed a certain repulsion to European bombings where non-combatant Axis life might be involved."[6] Roosevelt eschewed the advice of his top military advisers in ordering American participation in Operation Torch, the invasion of North Africa, in 1942. What drove Roosevelt was the fear that if U.S. forces did not begin fighting the Germans that year, domestic public opinion might align irreversibly behind a "Japan First" policy. Veteran Paul Fussell, who became an English professor and wrote thoughtful memoirs of his own and the national wartime experience, recalls that "to most American soldiers and sailors the United States, at least, was pursuing the war solely to defend itself from the monsters who had bombed Pearl Harbor without warning. . . . the war was about revenge against the Japanese, and the reason the European part had to be finished first was so that maximum attention could be devoted to the real business."[7] Another World War II veteran who became an English professor, Randall Jarrell, wrote in a letter to a friend, "99 of 100 people in the Army haven't the faintest idea what the war's about. Their two strongest motives are (a) nationalism. . . . and (b) race prejudice—they dislike Japanese in the same way, though not as much as, they dislike Negroes."[8] Researchers surveying U.S. servicemen found that 38 to 48 percent expressed a desire to kill Japanese soldiers, while only 5 to 9 percent said they wanted to kill German soldiers.[9] A marine officer recalled, "Killing a Japanese was like killing a rattlesnake. I didn't always have that feeling in Europe about some poor German family man, but I felt with a Jap it was like killing a rattlesnake."[10] Another officer said that "In the last war, I looked at dead Germans and I thought about their wives and children," but with "these [Japanese] bastards, that doesn't even occur."[11]

The fact that Americans were not fighting a moral crusade in the Pacific was in evidence both on the home front and on the battlefield. Anger over the Pearl Harbor attack combined with preexistent racism to condition the conduct of U.S. forces against the Japanese. As Professor John W. Dower points out in his award-winning book *War without Mercy*, Americans portrayed the Japanese, as a people, in various subhuman forms: "as animals, reptiles, or insects . . . monkeys, baboons, gorillas, dogs, mice and rats, vipers and rattlesnakes, cockroaches, vermin"—presented in ways that "virtually demanded extermination."[12] Given the abundant atrocities committed by the Japanese military, this may appear justified. But when discussing Germany, a white nation that similarly committed aggression and atrocities, Americans tended to demonize the Nazis in particular rather than the German people in general. The reason is that wartime Japan evoked deep and age-old Western racial prejudices against Asians. Dower argues that this gave the U.S.-Japan conflict a race-war quality that was missing in the fight among Western Europeans (but visible on the eastern front) and that made the fighting in the Pacific comparatively brutal, with practices such as the killing of prisoners and the collection of enemy body parts becoming routine. It also explains why even some Americans in responsible positions called for the total extermination of the Japanese people.[13]

The Japanese military indoctrinated its troops to fight to the death rather than surrender. Death in battle was glorious, while surrender was cowardly.

Word also quickly spread among the U.S. forces that Japanese soldiers some-times feigned surrender to lure American troops into ambushes. This helps explain why so few Japanese troops were taken prisoner during the war. But the other part of the explanation for why the killing of prisoners or would-be prisoners by the Allied forces became commonplace is simple brutality. Indeed, some units took pride in their reputation for taking no prisoners. At a 1943 meeting of high-ranking U.S. Navy commanders, the recorder noted, "All agree the only way to beat the Japs is to kill them all. They will not sur-render and our troops are taking no chances and are killing them anyway."[14] A June 1945 report by the U.S. Office of War Information noted that Japanese "surrender [was] made difficult by the unwillingness to take prisoners," and consequently some Japanese put considerable thought into ways they could give up without being shot. The famous aviator Charles Lindbergh, who as a civilian observer spent four months in 1944 with U.S. forces in New Guinea, wrote in his diary, "It was freely admitted that some of our soldiers tortured Jap prisoners and were as cruel and barbaric at times as the Japs themselves. Our men think nothing of shooting a Japanese prisoner or a soldier attempting to surrender."[15] Former marine sergeant and Pacific War veteran James Eagle-ton recalls, "In the two years that I was overseas I saw no prisoner ever taken. Once 30 or 40 of them came out with their hands up. They were killed on the spot because we didn't take prisoners." Eagleton said that on another occa-sion a Japanese surrendered to two U.S. soldiers, who presented him to their captain. The captain was angry, saying the soldiers had "ruined our record." According to Eagleton, the captain ordered, "'take this prisoner to battalion headquarters and I will see you at 11:15.' Well, it was eleven o'clock and the headquarters was five miles away. They took him out and killed him."[16]

Marines in the Pacific used their knives to pry out gold teeth from the mouths of dead or dying Japanese soldiers.[17] Collecting the ears or skulls of dead Japanese was commonplace. Such practices were widespread enough in the Pacific Theater even as early as 1942 that the commander of the Pacific Fleet ordered, "No part of the enemy's dead body may be used as a souvenir. Unit commanders will take stern disciplinary action."[18]

For the small number of Japanese military personnel captured during the war (about 35,000[19]), their treatment under Allied captivity generally met the guidelines specified by the Geneva Convention, but abuses were not unknown. Shikimachi Gentaro, a Japanese POW in Singapore after the war, says he "endured two years of harsh treatment at the hands of the Allied forces." His captors were likely motivated by reports of Japanese cruelty toward Allied cap-tives. Shikimachi and his 2,000 fellow prisoners engaged in hard forced labor seven days a week, and "if we disobeyed our captors at all we were beaten with rifles and kicked." According to Shikimachi,

The worst indignity was cleaning the sewers of the town where Chinese, Indians, and Malays lived together. We were told to dredge by hand the dead rats and human excre-ment that flowed down. Or we had to stand up to our chests in excrement to scoop it out. In the cement warehouse, we were forced to run repeatedly through cement powder up to our knees, carrying two sacks of cement. And we weren't allowed to assist anyone who keeled over.[20]

UNRESTRICTED SUBMARINE WARFARE

Ironically, the United States had entered World War I largely in reaction to Germany's practice of unrestricted submarine warfare in the Atlantic, which the U.S. government argued was a violation of international law as well as a threat to American shipping. The United States and Japan had signed an agreement at the London Naval Conference of 1930 that set rules for submarine warfare, including the stipulation that a submarine could not sink or disable a merchant vessel "without having first placed passengers, crew and ship's papers in a place of safety."[21] Such rules, if carried out, would obviously increase the vulnerability of submarines and reduce their effectiveness—a trade-off of combat power for humanitarianism. Some U.S. naval planners did not accept the trade-off. Reacting to results of a war game against Japan, the staff of the U.S. Naval War College recommended to the navy high command in March 1941 that the oceans of Asia be considered war zones in which merchant ships were fair game for unannounced attacks by submarines. The Navy's General Board responded that the war zone idea was a violation of international law and a reversal of a long-standing American position. Navy planners, however, were quietly developing a contingency for unrestricted submarine warfare in the Pacific in the event of war, to the approval of U.S. Chief of Naval Operations Admiral Harold Stark. Previous U.S. policy and the prewar American commitment to observe international norms restricting attacks by submarines did not survive the first day of U.S. entry into the Pacific War. Only about six hours after the Pearl Harbor attack, Stark ordered the U.S. Navy to "execute unrestricted air and submarine warfare against Japan."[22]

Maritime cargo transport was a critical Japanese weakness. Japan's merchant marine fleet, about 6 million tons of shipping when fighting began with the Western powers, was not large enough to deliver sufficient supplies to the vast and far-flung maritime empire the Japanese acquired by 1942. The Japanese employed the merchant fleet inefficiently, dividing the ships among three distinct navy, army, and civilian administrations. Each command used its own ships only for its own needs rather than sharing ships and coordinating schedules. As a consequence, ships sometimes sailed with their holds empty when they could have carried cargo for one of the two other agencies. Furthermore, the Japanese, who believed submarine duty was too tough for comfort-loving Americans to excel in, did little to develop antisubmarine tactics. Japan was late in employing convoys, armed few of its merchant ships, and deployed few escort vessels. World War II combatants learned that smaller aircraft carriers were an effective tool for protecting convoys. Japan employed its first escort carrier only in the last year of the war. The 3 million additional tons of cargo shipping they built during the war covered only a fraction of what they lost.[23]

The submarine service was extremely hazardous. One in five American submariners died in battle, a death rate higher than in any other branch of the U.S. military, including the Marines who stormed the beaches of Japanese-held islands. Moreover, some of the risks U.S. submarine crews took early in the war were negated by faulty torpedoes. The Mark XIV torpedoes that U.S. submarines carried were fast, long ranged, and powerful. Because of the high cost ($10,000 each), the U.S. government's Bureau of Ordinance had never tested the Mark XIV with a live warhead. As a result of design flaws in their detonation mechanism, the torpedoes often failed to explode at the right time. These so-called duds both cheated the American boats of kills and took away their best defense against Japanese destroyers. Complaints from returning submarine captains piled up, but the U.S. Navy hierarchy was slow to respond. The first problem was that the Mark XIV often ran deeper than its set depth, with the result that it was likely to pass completely under the hull of an enemy vessel. A U.S. admiral commanding submarines in Australia who had conducted his own tests reported this problem, which the Bureau of Ordinance initially ignored until forced to carry out its own tests by Admiral Ernest J. King. Additionally, both the magnetic detonator (designed to explode the torpedo under a ship's keel rather than against the often-armored side of its hull) and the traditional contact detonator on the Mark XIV often failed in combat. All of these defects were finally corrected by September 1943, nearly two years into the war.[24]

With reliable torpedoes, more use of radar and sonar, and improved intelligence on Japanese ship movements, the U.S. submariners devastated Japan's merchant shipping fleet in 1944–45. They sank 2.7 million tons of shipping in 1944, more than the combined 1941–43 total of 2.2 million tons. For the entire war, they sank about 5 million tons of gross Japanese merchant shipping. Measured by tonnage, Americans submarines also sank more of the Japanese navy than did U.S. Navy surface ships. U.S. submarines sank 8 carriers, 1 battleship, and 11 cruisers. An American submarine sank the largest aircraft carrier of the war, the 68,000-ton *Shimano*, during the huge ship's first voyage in late 1944.[25]

By the end of 1944 half the Japanese merchant fleet was destroyed, imports were dramatically reduced, and shipments of oil from Indonesia almost completely cut off. Supply shortages began to weigh heavily on Japan's civilian population. Food was strictly rationed. Soldiers based in the home islands got a meager 400 grams of rice per day, while civilians got only 100 grams. New clothing was scarce, and meat, sugar, and soap were rarely available except on the black market. In the winter, the lack of wood or charcoal forced people to forage for material to fuel heating and cooking stoves.[26]

Unrestricted submarine warfare meant, of course, no provision for the safety of the people aboard the targeted ships, whether they were merchant mariners, civilian passengers, or even Allied prisoners of war. In the fall of 1944 alone, some 4,000 of the latter died when U.S. submarines sank their ships.[27]

One of the most tragic cases of Japanese civilian deaths at sea occurred late in the war. The U.S. and Japanese governments had reached an agreement to grant safe passage to Japanese cargo ships involved in the delivery of Red Cross relief packages (picked up in the Soviet port of Nakhodka) to Allied prisoners. As part of the agreement, the Japanese ships would be clearly marked, travel a specified route, and refrain from carrying cargo unrelated to the relief operation. One of these ships was *Awa Maru*, sailing from Singapore home to Japan after delivering Red Cross supplies. The ship was painted green with large white crosses on its side and smoke stack, illuminated at night by spotlights. The ship was packed with a cargo of oil, oil drilling equipment, rubber, tungsten, and tin. This was a violation of the terms of the safe passage agreement. U.S. forces had taken such a toll of Japanese merchant shipping and made cargo voyages so perilous that Japan desperately exploited the prospect of a shipment guaranteed to survive the journey. *Awa Maru* also carried soldiers, officials, diplomats, technicians, and family members—over 2,000 men, women, and children.

The U.S. submarine *Queenfish* spotted *Awa Maru* in the Taiwan Strait on the night of April 1, 1945. The submarine's skipper, Commander Charles E. Loughlin, did not know the Japanese ship was traveling under a safe passage agreement. On three occasions the radio operator of the *Queenfish* had received notification about the sailing of *Awa Maru* under protected status, but he neglected to write it down. During its previous stop in port in Saipan, *Queenfish* collected a stack of classified messages, including an order not to attack *Awa Maru*. Loughlin's subordinates saw the order but did not think it significant enough to pass on to their skipper. The submarine received one more notification after beginning its patrol, but it was so unclearly worded that the crew did not understand it. *Awa Maru* rode unusually low in the water (due to overloading), producing a signature on the *Queenfish*'s radar screen that resembled that of a destroyer or a destroyer escort. It was not zigzagging as was the usual practice for cargo ships, and it was traveling at a relatively high speed. The ship's markings were not clear in the foggy weather. The submarine fired four torpedoes, all of which hit the target. *Awa Maru* sank quickly. *Queenfish*'s crew found only one survivor, from whom they learned about the dead ship and its mission. The Japanese government damned the incident as the "most outrageous act of treachery unparalleled in the world history of the war."[28] This it was not, but the U.S. government took the extraordinary step of promising to compensate Japan after the war. Loughlin was relieved of command and court-martialed. He received a letter of admonition, but stayed in the navy and eventually reached the rank of rear admiral. After Japan's surrender Washington persuaded Tokyo to drop the compensation claims for *Awa Maru* in light of Japanese abuses of U.S. POWs and the heavy economic assistance America would provide postwar Japan. For years afterward many Japanese remained deeply resentful about the episode.

JAPANESE ATROCITIES: CHINA

An awful confluence of factors explains why the Chinese suffered so terribly at the hands of the Japanese armed forces. Japanese troops were subject to the tendency of conquering forces to employ rape as a means not only of sexual gratification, but also of humiliating the adversary. Frustration and anger caused by costly battles, the duration of the campaign, and resistance activities by Chinese civilians worked to increase the occurrence of atrocities. More particularly, Japan's military inculcated brutality among its troops, including a sense of contempt for enemies who had surrendered. Frequent beating and other kinds of harassment were part of the training of Japanese army recruits. Their Bushido ideology taught that a soldier should fight to the death rather than give himself up, which was considered cowardly. This had obvious negative implications for Japanese treatment of Chinese POWs. The Japanese military also partook of a general belief that the Chinese were an inferior, even subhuman, people. Thus the mind-set of the Japanese military was the recipe for atrocity in China. Soldiers who were themselves brutalized and encouraged to behave brutally carried with them feelings of racial superiority over the Chinese and a belief that killing them was a means of serving the emperor. A former Japanese soldier gives a disturbing account of the Japanese attitude and its consequences for Chinese civilians:

Our officers told us we could kill and rape as many of 'the Chinese enemy' as we pleased. There were some of us, however, who did not like the idea, including myself. When we did not join the others in shooting and bayoneting the civilians, we were ridiculed and made fun of. Our troops were holding competitions among themselves to see who could shoot or bayonet to death the most Chinese within a specific time. Eventually, I was persuaded to join them. A sergeant told me with a laugh, 'Killing a Chinese is just like killing a dog! You'll feel nothing! Try it and you'll see!' My first victim was an old Chinese woman. I aimed my rifle at her head. I pressed the trigger. I saw her brains splatter on the brick wall behind her. The other soldiers cheered and encouraged me. After that I killed many Chinese of all ages, even children. I did not feel any remorse. I also raped young girls before killing them. I became involved in the frenzy of killing and everything else that was going on.[29]

Another former Japanese soldier observes, "I looked down on Chinese people and thought, what's wrong with raping Chinese women, since we kill them anyway." The Japanese military organized field brothels for the troops called "comfort stations," but these "were pretty expensive for low-ranking soldiers. . . . So soldiers would just rape women in the villages and cities instead."[30]

Non-Chinese scholars acknowledge that the Japanese invasion killed at least 10 million Chinese civilians (a considerably lower figure than the Chinese claim). *Democide* scholar Rudolph J. Rummel calculates that the Japanese murdered about 4 million Chinese during the war (excluding battlefield deaths), and Chiang's Nationalist government killed an additional 2 million during the same period (plus many more before and after the Sino-Japanese War).[31] Rummel concludes that rather than carrying out mass murder as a policy based on ideology, "Japanese armies and secret police killed defenseless people seemingly as a matter of tactics, expedience, convenience, revenge, recreation, and an utterly amoral disregard for human life and suffering." Japanese occupation forces employed murder

to erase a population supporting anti-Japanese guerrillas, to eliminate witnesses or a distraction (like a crying baby) to a looting or rape in process, to punish enemy soldiers who had surrendered for their cowardice, to avenge forgetting to bow to a Japanese soldier, to squeeze out the maximum labor from Asian or POW laborers at the minimum costs, to liquidate laborers too sick or broken for further toil, to experiment with bacteriological and chemical weapons, to train soldiers in killing, to practice rifle marksmanship or the use of the bayonet, or to revenge [sic] an attack on a soldier . . . or they were killed just for the fun of it.[32]

Although the suffering of the Chinese people reached an early crescendo in the Nanjing Massacre,[33] this incident accounted for only a fraction of the millions of Chinese deaths during the Pacific War. What happened at Nanjing was indicative of the fate of Chinese civilians, albeit in less concentrated form, throughout the war in many other parts of Japanese-occupied China. Smaller towns in the countryside suffered along with large cities such as Nanjing. In Pingdingshan village in Manchuria, for example, the Japanese massacred nearly the entire population of 3,000 in 1932 as a reprisal against partisans.[34] In May 1938, in the village of Yanwo near Xuzhou, Japanese troops killed over 200 civilians on the streets in random acts of violence. Then, more systematically, they gathered young Chinese men into the courtyard of a house. The troops set the buildings around the courtyard ablaze and shot all those who tried to escape. Nearly all of the detainees, more than 600, died.[35]

In an attempt to destroy resistance in north China, the Japanese began a ruthless campaign in 1940 that the Chinese called the "three all's" policy (i.e., "kill all, burn all, loot all")[36]. This involved relocating Chinese peasant communities into guarded encampments and laying waste to everything and everyone outside, presumed to be guerrillas and their supporters. Enomoto Masayo, who as a sergeant participated in the campaign, gives an indication of its viciousness. "We raided a village, but all we found were the abandoned women," he says. "[W]e stripped them naked and made them lie down on top of watermelons. There was no military purpose, just 'Imperial Army comfort.' No enemies around, no information to be gained. So we stripped them and shoved cloth up their vaginas, poured gasoline on them and set them on fire. . . . They weren't spies or anything. Just a message that we'd been in that village."[37]

Some Americans are aware that Chinese villagers assisted U.S. airmen who landed in China after the 1942 Doolittle Raid. Fewer Americans know of the terrible price these Chinese civilians paid. Beginning in May 1942, 100,000 Japanese troops ravaged Zhejiang and Jiangxi Provinces in a four-month reprisal campaign. Along with conventional means of destruction, they used poison gas and released diseases among the Chinese population. Perhaps 250,000 Chinese were killed.[38]

Cruelty by Japanese occupation forces was not limited to China, but appeared throughout the Greater East Asian Co-Prosperity Sphere, even if on a smaller scale. Japanese forces occupying Southeast Asia carried out vengeful policies, including massacres, against ethnic Chinese communities in Singapore and Malaysia. To the Japanese, these overseas Chinese were guilty of supporting the Chinese government and prone to disloyalty toward their new conquerors. During the battle to retake Manila in February and March 1945, the doomed Japanese army and navy garrison turned to raping and massacring the civilian residents. Some 100,000 Manila civilians died in these massacres and in the house-to-house fighting that devastated the city.

Much of the criminal behavior of Japanese forces, including such practices as bayoneting live prisoners (which was supposed to toughen soldiers for battle) and vivisection performed by army surgeons was in accordance with policies dictated by commanders. A former Japanese soldier in China reported that being invited by more senior soldiers to participate in a gang-rape was a gesture of increased personal prestige within the group. "You couldn't turn it down," he said. In other cases, Japanese commanders simply tolerated mayhem by their troops in China. "We had the feeling that in the enemy district we could do anything," said another former soldier. "We were not told officially we could do anything but we learned it from our senior colleagues."[39]

Even where a semblance of military necessity restrained Japanese use of violence, Chinese under the slightest suspicion of aiding the resistance against Japan were subject to arrest. Japanese soldiers routinely tortured Chinese by various means, frequently ending in their captives' deaths. When passing over ground they feared might be mined, Japanese troops forced detained Chinese to walk before them.

To the extent that they were able, the Japanese carried out terror bombing against Chinese city dwellers. The provisional capital of Chongqing (Chungking) suffered 268 air raids, the most of any city during the war. Chinese sources say these attacks killed about 11,900 and wounded 14,700.[40] On one occasion, a three-hour bombing attack resulted in the suffocation of 2,500 people taking shelter in a tunnel. The use of poison gas set Japan apart from the other World War II combatants. Chinese communities suffered more than 1,000 gas attacks. The Chinese claim a death toll of 80,000 to 90,000 from Japanese chemical weapons during the war.[41] Chinese sources claim that the Japanese killed another 270,000 Chinese with biological weapons.[42] These figures are suspect, but the fact that Japanese forces used chemical and biological weapons to kill thousands of Chinese civilians is well established. The Japanese forced millions of Chinese into slave labor. About 41,000 were shipped to Japan, where they were treated hardly better than work animals.[43]

The Chinese refugees displaced by the Japanese invasion constituted the largest forced migration in China's history. A foreign observer said of refugees streaming out of Xuzhou, "On the road to the southwest, a long ribbon of ox carts stretches without interruption. . . . The women and children are on the carts, in the middle of bundles, baskets, sacks, chicks, goats, etc. Many are in tears, the children are crying. The men beat the oxen. Impossible to stop, only to go on. In the middle of all this are incredible numbers of soldiers. To go faster, they pass through the wheat. One would say that there is no air. All is gloom. One breathes only dust."[44] Japanese aircraft frequently attacked columns of refugees, either as a terror tactic or on the assumption that fleeing Chinese soldiers had changed into civilian clothing.

Like Europe's Holocaust, the activities of Unit 731 in Manchuria illustrated what horrors could result when the perceived needs of a ruthless state met up with a captive people considered to have no human rights. In the name of research, the staff of Unit 731 inflicted torturous medical experiments on Chinese prisoners, tested weapons on them, and intentionally infected Chinese communities with diseases. Unit 731 was officially known as the Kwantung Army's "Epidemic Prevention and Water Purification Department"—an Orwellian twist, since Unit 731 actually did the exact opposite. Through methods such as air-dropping infected fleas and contaminating water supplies, Unit 731 staff intentionally spread diseases such as bubonic plague, anthrax, cholera, typhoid, typhus, and dysentery. They also sliced open human subjects, often without anesthesia, to examine organs or test bodily reaction to trauma; froze victims to study the effects of frostbite; burned people to death under observation; and placed people in pressure chambers to observe how much they could withstand before they died.[45] As with the soldiers in the field who committed atrocities, a twisted sense of duty combined with a belief in the racial inferiority of their enemies inured these so-called scientists to their macabre work. Shinozuka Yoshio, who worked in Unit 731, recalls, "I figured if a person can be shot with one bullet, what's wrong with using this person's body as an experiment for developing medical industries? Besides, I had been taught in school that the emperor is the son of God and that we are different from other Asians."[46]

Unit 731 staff commonly referred to their test subjects as *maruta* ("logs"). Former staff member Koshi Sadao further elaborated on the mentality of those who carried out this ghastly work: "We believed that the maruta who were brought by the Kempeitai [military police] would be executed anyway and that it would be better to use them for research which would save our people. At that time there was no feeling that we were doing the wrong thing, although, looking back now, it was horrific."[47]

Lieutenant General Ishii Shiro commanded Unit 731 from 1936 to 1945. When Stalin's armies invaded Manchuria in 1945, Ishii's staff killed their remaining prisoners and dismantled their facilities. After the war, however, U.S. authorities gave Ishii and other 731 leaders immunity from prosecution for war crimes in exchange for the data gained from their research. The justification was that national security needs, and particularly the competition with the Soviets, overruled the demands of justice.[48] Ishii's deputy,

Major General Kitano Masaji, was among those exempted from prosecution and became president of the Japanese pharmaceutical firm Green Cross. By contrast, when the Soviet forces captured Japanese researchers suspected of conducting experiments with humans, the USSR put them on trial for war crimes.[49] It is instructive and disappointing that in the end, America's moral outrage toward the Axis proved negotiable.

JAPANESE MISTREATMENT OF U.S. PRISONERS OF WAR

Japan's treatment of U.S. and other prisoners of war was typically brutal. Japanese soldiers killed many of their prisoners of war in the field, sometimes torturing and mutilating them as well. For the U.S. and other Allied prisoners who made it to the camps, massacres were not uncommon—motivated by revenge, or because sick or injured prisoners had become a burden, or because the captives decided transporting the prisoners was too inconvenient. The Japanese used some Allied prisoners for experiments that often resulted in the harming or death of the prisoners. Physicians at Kyushu University Hospital in 1945, for example, killed eight American POWs through vivisection. The living conditions of Japanese-held POWs were generally deplorable. Rations were insufficient and medical care miniscule. In fairness, in some cases the Japanese captors themselves were also low on supplies. But more importantly, during the Pacific War the Japanese lacked a commitment to humane care of surrendered enemy soldiers. Japan had not ratified the 1929 Geneva Convention on the rights of prisoners of war. Although Tokyo announced in 1942 it would follow the Convention's rules regarding POWs, practice did not live up to the promise. In the view of the Japanese army, troops who allowed themselves to be captured alive were contemptible. POWs had no value beyond their ability to perform useful labor. Of the approximately 95,000 U.S., British, Canadian, Australian, and New Zealand servicemen the Japanese took as prisoners during the war, 28 percent died in captivity. The mortality figure for Americans was 38 percent. By comparison, the death rate of Allied prisoners (excluding Soviets) held by Germany and Italy was 4 percent.[50] In the case of the Sandakan prison camp in Indonesia, which held as many as 2,000 Allied prisoners, only 6 survived until the end of the war.[51]

Prison guards were often prone to violence and cruelty. The Japanese soldiers assigned to guard prisons were often considered unfit for front-line combat duty for various reasons, including insubordination, drunkenness, and even mental deficiency. Some of the guards were Koreans and Taiwanese from the occupied territories, lower in rank and prestige than Japanese army privates. Part of their function was to play the role of subordinates to Japanese enlisted men, absorbing some of the anger the latter felt toward their officers. Both non-Japanese guards and Japanese enlisted men could vent their frustrations on the POWs. A U.S. survivor of the infamous Bataan Death March noted that "the Korean guards were the most abusive. The Japs didn't trust them in battle, so used them as service troops; the Koreans were anxious to get blood on their bayonets; and then they thought they were veterans."[52]

Close to starvation and scourged by malaria and dysentery, about 75,000 U.S. and Filipino defenders who had been driven to Bataan Peninsula surrendered on April 9, 1942, to Japanese forces. The Japanese had not made adequate preparation for moving such a large number of sick and undernourished prisoners to their prison at Camp O'Donnell 65 miles away.

Several hundred Americans and thousands of Filipinos died during the Death March, and thousands more during the first days after arrival at the camp. Japanese guards murdered stragglers. Surviving participants reported that some of the killings were for no apparent reason other than indulgence in cruelty. Such murders were repeated on many other occasions, including the execution of 16 downed U.S. airmen on the day Hirohito's surrender speech was broadcast.

COMFORT WOMEN

Japan used young women to staff its military brothels, which followed the troops abroad and were euphemistically called "comfort stations." The intention was to provide the troops with a regulated sexual outlet as an alternative to uncontrolled raping of local civilians, which Japanese leaders feared would lead to venereal disease among the troops, hostility toward the Japanese by the indigenous population, and the possibility of enemy spies infiltrating private brothels frequented by Japanese soldiers. As the Chinese could attest, the program failed to achieve its original aim of preventing unregulated rapes by Japanese troops.

A limited number of Japanese women worked as prostitutes for the military. They generally serviced higher-ranking officers and enjoyed better working conditions than the non-Japanese women. Their numbers were kept low by the military's belief that Japanese women were needed at home to fulfill the traditional role of mothers.[53] Consequently, most of the comfort women came from Japanese-occupied areas—Koreans, Chinese, other Asians, and a few Westerners. Researchers estimate their number at up to 200,000 women. Some Chinese historians claim the number of Chinese comfort women alone was 200,000.[54]

The women were forcibly abducted or in some cases deceived into signing on by false promises about the nature of the job. Comfort women were virtual sex slaves subject to serial rape and other forms of brutality. A recent report from the International Commission of Jurists in Geneva summarized the plight of these women:

Life at these comfort stations was living hell for the women. They were beaten and tortured in addition to being raped by 15, 20 or 30 soldiers a day and officers by night, day after day, for periods ranging from 3 weeks to 8 years. Living conditions were cramped and shabby. The lives of those who had to follow troops around at battlefronts were put at risk, day after day. Food was usually of poor quality and in short supply. Although medical check-ups by army doctors sometimes took place, many women were afflicted by sexually transmitted diseases.[55]

Wan Aihua, captured by Japanese troops in 1943, reported that she was frequently tortured by beatings and by being suspended from a tree exposed to the burning midday sun. At night she was confined in a cave, where she endured group rapes. Her ordeal left her with permanent scarring and recurring illnesses. Testifying during a 2000 conference about comfort women, Wan said, "My torture was deeper than the sea and I can find no words to express my rage against the Japanese who raped me, beat me and reduced me to an animal."[56]

An anonymous Korean comfort woman remembered, "I was nearly killed several times during my time as a 'comfort woman.' There were some military men who were drunk and were brandishing swords at me while making demands for perverted sex. They drove their swords into the tatami, then demanded sex from me. . . . The threat they were making was obvious—if I didn't cooperate they would stab me."[57]

OKINAWA: INTRA-JAPANESE RUTHLESSNESS

The Battle of Okinawa in 1945 highlighted another facet of the war's ruthlessness: the Japanese military's willingness to employ its own countrymen as cannon fodder. *Kamikaze* (divine wind) suicide pilots were named after typhoons that purportedly saved Japan from Mongol invasion in the thirteenth century.

Organized, large-scale suicide air attacks began in 1944, when the Americans had established a large and growing advantage over the Japanese forces in the quantity of ships and aircraft available for combat as well as increasing operational competence. Japanese aircraft practicing conventional tactics against U.S. ships and other targets were suffering huge losses against the storms of antiaircraft fire produced by ever-abundant American warships and against experienced American fighter pilots. Since the projected life span of Japanese planes and aviators had already grown short (many fliers, rushed into service with little training, were shot down on their first combat mission), suicide tactics offered better chances of success for the sacrifice. Flying an aircraft directly into an American ship was easier to accomplish for a relatively inexperienced pilot than hitting the target with a bomb or torpedo released early enough to give the plane a chance to escape. Peaking during the fight over Okinawa, kamikaze attacks failed to reverse the tide of the conflict but wrought terrible destruction, sinking 34 U.S. Navy ships during the war, damaging 10 times that number and killing nearly 5,000 servicemen.[58]

The Okinawa campaign also demonstrated that Japanese ruthlessness extended to the military's exploitation of civilian communities of Japanese nationals. In March–June 1945, Okinawa was the site of the last major battle of the war and the largest amphibious assault in the Pacific theater. The U.S. invasion force numbered more than half a million. Americans remember Okinawa as a particularly costly battle, with 12,500 U.S. fatalities. The Japanese suffered over 60,000 soldiers killed. For the civilian population the battle was cataclysmic: up to 150,000 died, about a quarter of the island's population.[59] They referred to the battle as the "typhoon of steel." A Japanese infantryman stationed there described Okinawa before the battle as "a whole island shimmering like a gem in a dream world" and lamented that "the whole of this fairy island would be burnt down in the flame of an inferno and turned into a pile of blackened rocks."[60] Okinawa's civilian residents suffered not only from the destruction delivered by enemy forces, but also from mistreatment by their own military. The Japanese armed forces frequently demonstrated during the Pacific War that their lack of regard for civilian life extended to their own people as well as foreigners. This was one of the hallmarks of the battle for Okinawa and its neighboring islands. In effect, rather than seeing themselves as protectors of the public, the Japanese soldiers on Okinawa forced the civilian community to sacrifice itself in the service of the military. On numerous occasions Japanese forces employed Okinawa's civilians as chattel and then sent them to their deaths when they outlived their usefulness.

Asked by a local journalist what he expected of the civilians when the Americans invaded, Japanese General Cho Isamu said that "all the civilians should accept military instructions like soldiers. In other words, each civilian ought to have a fighting spirit to kill ten enemy soldiers and destroy our enemy." Then he warned them, "When the enemy lands and our food supply is cut off, the military is not in a position to provide civilians with food, even if you plead with us that civilians will starve to death. The military's important mission is to win the war. We are not allowed to lose the war to save civilians."[61] Like the Chinese, Okinawa's people were threatened by the forces of their own government as well as those of the enemy. Japanese from the main islands traditionally looked down on and discriminated against the people of the Ryukyu Islands (of which Okinawa is the largest), forcibly annexed by Japan in 1879. Yet the Japanese military also expected the Okinawans to give their lives for the Japanese emperor. They seemingly paid the full price of Japanese citizenship without enjoying the full benefit. Nevertheless, had the war continued long enough for another invasion, Japanese civilians on the main islands of Kyushu and Honshu would have suffered much of the same exploitation that Okinawans endured, as the Japanese government was prepared to execute similar sacrificial policies throughout the country.

The deep-seated prejudice of many mainland Japanese toward Okinawans manifested itself in the Japanese military's distrust of the local population. Before the battle, the military ordered that Okinawans speak only standard Japanese rather than the Okinawan dialect, adding that "those who speak Okinawan will be regarded as spies and receive the appropriate punishment." This resulted in the execution of about 1,000 Okinawans by their own military.[62] A former sergeant who carried out some of these executions for alleged espionage explained that the military needed to take "firm measures" because the civilian residents outnumbered the Japanese troops stationed in the islands. "So if the residents had turned on us and sided with the Americans, we would have been finished right away. . . . I conducted executions in order to keep the civilian residents under our control."[63]

The army feared that Okinawans who surrendered would provide compromising information to the enemy. The military therefore took pains to persuade the civilians not to allow the Americans to capture them. Surrender was disgraceful, the military commanders emphasized. Furthermore, the Americans would torture and murder captive Okinawans. As U.S. forces landed, in communities throughout Okinawa and outlying islands the Japanese army ordered civilians to hand over their food supplies to the troops and passed out grenades to use for suicide to avoid capture. When she received her grenade, Oshiro Sumie remembers, "We were told [the Americans] would cut off our noses and ears, and rape us."[64] Survivor Nakamura Takejiro recalls, "For a long time, the Japanese Imperial Army announced that, on other islands, the women had been raped and killed, and the men were tied at the wrists and tanks were driven over them. The Japanese Imperial Army repeated that again and again, and we believed that announcement completely."[65] "I think we were dreadfully manipulated," says Kinjo Shigeaki, another survivor.[66] Indeed, the propaganda about systematic torture of civilian captives proved a gross distortion. The American soldiers were not angels and committed their share of rape and murder. The U.S. forces, nevertheless, made some effort to persuade Okinawans to surrender and to move them away from the battlefield. Accounts of survivors indicate that most Okinawans who surrendered were treated decently, although the Americans put some of them to work.

The scaremongering had tragic consequences. In the Chibichiri Cave in the center of Okinawa, 140 civilians fearfully awaited the approaching U.S. forces in early April. An 18-year-old girl pleaded to her mother, "Kill me! Don't let them rape me!" The mother obliged the daughter. Other parents followed suit, killing their children and then themselves. Despite entreaties from the Americans outside to surrender, 83 civilians inside the cave killed themselves.[67] In March, civilian teenager Kinjo, his elder brother, two younger siblings, and their mother were part of a group of about 800 residents gathered at the southern end of the island. American forces were nearly upon them, and a bomb exploded nearby. According to Kinjo, this prompted the group to action. "One of the village leaders, a middle-aged man, snapped off a sapling. I gazed at him, wondering what he was doing," Kinjo recalls. "Once he had that stick in his hands, he turned into a madman, striking his wife and children over and over again, bludgeoning them to death. . . . As if by a chain reaction, it spread from one family to the next. . . . People began to raise their hands against their loved ones." Over 300 of this group died in murder-suicides. "Men cut off the heads of their escaping children with sickles and hit their wives with stones while crying bitterly," Kinjo recalls. Kinjo and his brother killed their younger brother and sister. They killed their mother by striking her head with a stone.

Afterward they planned to make a suicide charge, but the Americans captured them alive. Kinjo said. "I couldn't stop crying because of a sadness that I had never experienced before." Kinjo said. "I will never cry like that in my life again." On Zamami, another small island in the Okinawa group, the military commander ordered the elderly and children among the civilian residents to commit suicide before the Americans arrived and forbade the other civilians from harvesting food from the farms. The soldiers killed or allowed to starve those who violated the order.[68] On Geruma Island, 15-year-old Nakamura was with his family when U.S. troops approached. His 20-year-old sister cried, "Kill me now, hurry." His mother strangled his sister with a rope. "I tried to also strangle myself with a rope," Nakamura said, "but I kept breathing. It is really tough to kill yourself." The Americans captured them. A U.S. soldier checked Nakamura for weapons. "Then he gave us candy and cigarettes. That was my first experience on coming out of the cave."[69]

Some overcame their indoctrination, with fortunate results. Nakahodo Shige was then a 16-year-old living in a village in southern Okinawa. She fled with her mother, her two younger brothers, and her uncle's family into a cave to escape the Americans. When they saw a U.S. tank approaching the cave, Nakahodo recalls, her uncle "was about to detonate a grenade he held in his hand. But my mother stood up and grabbed his wrist." Her mother said, "Look at these children with their innocent looks. How can we kill them?" Nakahodo was captured and well-treated by U.S. soldiers. One even bought her a pair of new shoes. "I was overwhelmed by his kindness," she says.[70]

Many civilians died from gunfire, bombs, and shells as they unsuccessfully sought shelter. When they knew or suspected a cave contained Japanese soldiers, U.S. troops often employed tactics such as throwing in explosives, burning the cave out with flamethrowers, or sealing the entrance. Civilians in these caves shared the fate of soldiers.

As the battlefield situation worsened, the Japanese armed forces saw Okinawan civilians as a burden—civilians took up space in caves and consumed scarce food supplies. In many cases, Japanese soldiers took over caves full of sheltering civilians, forcing the civilians back outside to face bullets and shrapnel. In some cases Japanese troops killed civilians who refused orders to vacate caves. Sixteen-year-old Nakajo Mitsutoshi and a group of children were sharing a cave with Japanese soldiers when the group ran short of food. This put the civilians at risk of being murdered. The soldiers

said they were going on a surprise attack mission and took away our food, threatening us with their pistols, but we knew they just wanted to stay alive and get back to the mainland. The next day, they told us they were going to "dispose" of all children under three years of age because they said children would attract enemy attention and Americans would throw explosives into our cave. There were five children under three, including my brother and my niece. . . . When they said they were going to kill the five children, we asked the commander to let us go out of the cave with the children. But he said no. He said we would become spies. He posted guards at the entrance to the cave and would not let us go out. Then four or five soldiers came to us and took away the children from us one by one, including my brother, and gave them the [lethal] injection. . . . Then, the next morning, they said we were the only civilians alive in the area, so they were also going to "dispose" of us before the Americans captured us and crushed us under their tanks. We knew they were going to kill us all just to take our food.[71]

Facing apocalypse, the soldiers overreacted to what they perceived as disloyalty among the populace. Ota Masahide, a 19-year-old pressed into military service during the battle, says "I saw civilians shot by Japanese soldiers when they came out of caves to surrender with their hands raised."[72] American aircraft dropped leaflets encouraging Okinawans to surrender. Possession of one of these leaflets was sufficient cause for execution by the Japanese military. According to Maeda Haru, a Japanese soldier became enraged when her mother, who did not speak the mainland Japanese dialect well, did not understand a question the soldier put to her. The soldier beheaded Maeda's mother. His comrades then stabbed Maeda's younger sister and younger brother, with the latter dying soon thereafter.[73]

The Japanese army mobilized about 2,000 male and female high school students on Okinawa to support the resistance—boys in the Blood and Iron Student Corps, girls as nurses in the Himeyuri (Princess Lily) Student Corps. Half of these youths died in the battle. Generally, the Japanese armed the older boys with rifles and sent them into battle. The younger boys sometimes became suicide bombers, carrying explosive charges and rushing toward U.S. tanks.[74] One Himeyuri nurse was 17-year-old Uehara Tomiko. She cared for wounded in a makeshift hospital set up in a series of caves. Her duties included bringing patients food and water, changing their bandages, cleaning maggots out of wounds, holding down patients undergoing surgery or amputations without anesthesia, and risking her life to go outside the cave to bury bodies and bring in barrels of rice. Himeyuri Corps nurses wore military attire, so when they moved outside of the caves they drew fire from U.S. troops. As the battle continued, food became more scarce and the inhabitants of the cave grew desperately hungry. "They were talking about [eating] amputated arms and legs," she recalls. "Horrible even to imagine. But that's war."[75] On June 18 the Japanese military abruptly dissolved the Himeyuri Corps and ordered the girls to leave the caves in which they had worked. Many died trying to make their way through the battlefields in search of safe haven. Over 200 girls and a few of their teachers served in the Himeyuri Corps; only about 20 survived.[76]

GLIMMERS OF CHIVALRY AMID SAVAGERY

While duly condemning fascist Japan for its aggression and atrocities, it is worth recognizing that even within an institution that inculcated brutality and was embroiled in a ruthless conflict, the decency of some individuals transcended their surroundings. Some of those who fought for Japan demonstrated chivalry and humaneness on the battlefield. A few examples are given here in the interests of balance and of avoiding historical oversimplification or ethnic stereotyping.

During the Bataan Death March, an officer relayed to Col. Imai Takeo orders to shoot any Allied prisoners in his possession. Objecting to the idea, Imai reportedly stalled by demanding a written version of the order. He then set his Filipino and American prisoners free so that he would have no captives to kill.[77]

The company commander of Hirata Yuichi, a Japanese officer in China, ordered him to execute a group of Chinese civilians suspected of passing information to Chinese Communist Party troops. Hirata consulted with his men. One of his sergeants said, "Sir, I can't kill any more Chinese." Under the cover of night, Hirata let the Chinese prisoners escape, risking his own life to save theirs. He later told his commander they had been shot according to orders.[78]

Three days after the attack on Pearl Harbor, Japanese aircraft scored a stunning tactical victory against British naval forces in Asia by sinking the battleship *Prince of Wales* and the battle cruiser[79] *Repulse* in the South China Sea, with the loss of 840 sailors. This was a signal achievement in the history of airpower: the first time aircraft destroyed capital ships that were underway and able to maneuver. Churchill said, "In my whole experience I do not remember any naval blow so heavy or painful as the sinking of the *Prince of Wales* and the *Repulse*."[80] Bert "Yorky" Wynn, a British seaman who was on the deck of the destroyer *Electra* as its crew fished survivors out of the oil-stained ocean, recalled the treatment accorded a Japanese aviator downed near the spot where the *Prince of Wales* had sunk: "As the lads manning the scramble nets beckoned him, I could see he was wearing a leather skullcap and thought he was one of the Walrus [a British seaplane] pilots who'd either been shot down by attacking planes or simply run out of fuel. It was impossible to recognise people by their features because the oil stuck to you like glue; subsequently everyone ended up looking the same. As the lads got him up on deck a shout went out that he was Japanese. Without hesitation he was thrown straight back into the oily depths below." Contrast this ignoble incident with the broad-minded gesture of Japanese pilot Iki Haruki. After participating in the attack that sank *Prince of Wales* and *Repulse,* Iki flew back over the site the next day and dropped a wreath as a memorial to the British sailors who lost their lives.[81]

In 1942, a Dutch C-47 transport plane took off from Java carrying wounded soldiers, a nurse, and several children. They were terrified to observe a Japanese Zero fighter aircraft approach their plane. The nurse and the children pressed close to the windows and waved to the Japanese pilot, hoping he would spare them. The Zero pilot waved and let them go. After the war the nurse tried to learn the identity of the merciful pilot. She contacted the Japanese government, gave the details of the encounter, and asked if Japanese records could supply the answer. It turned out that the Zero pilot was Sakai

Saburo, Japan's highest-scoring fighter ace of the war, credited with shooting down 64 Allied aircraft. Sakai reported that he saw inside the plane a blonde woman with a child, which reminded him of a kind American woman who sometimes taught his class when he was a middle school student in prewar Japan. Although his orders were to destroy any enemy aircraft he saw, Sakai "believed that we should fight a war against soldiers, not civilians. So I decreased my record by one."[82]

In the town of Baofeng in the province of Henan, China, a Japanese lieutenant ordered a sergeant to execute a prisoner of war in March 1945. The sergeant, Uchida Keiji, transported the bound prisoner in a horse-drawn cart toward the edge of town. "Many of the local inhabitants lined the road, watching us with hatred in their eyes. It sent a chill down my spine," recalls Uchida. Unloading the prisoner by a large tree, Uchida conversed with him.

As I asked the prisoner where he was from, how old he was, and why he was captured, I felt compassion for this man, who was my own age. I decided to let him go. My self-justification was that by letting him go I'd be getting the local inhabitants to calm down. This might insure the safety of the Baofeng [Japanese] garrison. I told the prisoner that I was letting him go, so he should never return to this place again. He should go and live a healthy life elsewhere. He wept as he repeated his thanks, "*Xie xie.*" I aimed my rifle at the sky and shot three times and made my way back. When I turned around, the prisoner waved and bowed to me over and over again. Then he ran off like a streak of lightning. When I reached the village, everyone welcomed me with smiles, saying, "Gentleman, thank you for your trouble." I don't know how they had seen what I had done.[83]

Sadly, such cases were the exception rather than the rule during the Pacific War, completely overwhelmed by odious episodes of massacre and rape of civilians, cruelty toward prisoners of war, and disregard for the preexisting rules designed to limit savagery in war. The forms of ruthless wartime conduct noted in this chapter are all too many. Yet there is another that remains to be discussed.

CHAPTER 5

Strategic Bombing in the Pacific War

Contrary to the belief of many Americans today, the deadliest air raid of the war did not strike Hiroshima or Nagasaki. Few Americans know the ferocity of the conventional (nonatomic) bombing campaign against Japan, which did most of the damage and the killing and left only a short list of suitable remaining targets for the A-bombs that became available later. The destruction wreaked on Japan by a U.S. strategic bombing campaign *prior* to the atomic bombs attacks was a Pacific War event of underappreciated importance. To understand its full significance, additional context is useful, including attitudes toward aerial bombardment between the wars and the British and American experience with strategic bombing in Europe prior to the beginning of the bombing campaign against Japan.

By way of definition, in contrast to *tactical* operations, which are attacks on enemy military forces on or near the battlefield, *strategic* operations attack the enemy's ability to wage war—striking behind the front lines, often at the enemy's homeland, at targets such as economic or transportation infrastructure, material resources, the enemy workforce, or the enemy country's will to continue fighting. Strategic bombing may be further subdivided. One type is *precision bombing*, which specifically targets war-related industry, infrastructure, or resources, such as an armaments factory or an oil refinery. Another type is *carpet bombing* (the American term) or *area bombing* (the British term), the indiscriminate bombing of cities, making little effort to avoid residential districts, if not intentionally targeting them. In practice, the distinction could become blurry. Precision bombing was not accurate enough in World War II (nor is it today) to ensure that bombs fell only on military targets and posed no risk to civilians. And if the logic of targeting an adversary's military-related capabilities is pursued far enough, the civilian population eventually becomes a target. This, in fact, is what happened during World War II, reaching an apogee in the U.S.-Japan conflict.

STRATEGIC BOMBING BY JAPAN

Aside from the tactical bombing attack against Pearl Harbor and nearby airfields, which killed 68 civilians (some from stray U.S. antiaircraft rounds), the American homeland was nearly untouched by enemy bombs. Two Japanese Kawanishi "Emily" flying boats returned to Oahu to try to bomb a dock at Pearl Harbor on the night of March 4–5, 1942. They failed, however, to find the harbor, which was obscured by clouds, and consequently dropped their bombs harmlessly on an uninhabited mountain area. In September 1942, a submarine-launched Japanese seaplane twice dropped bombs on western Oregon in hopes of starting larges fires and widespread panic, but the bombs did no significant physical or psychological damage.

A more serious attempt to cause fires and panic involved the launching in 1944 and 1945 of some 9,000 "Fu-Go" balloon bombs from Japan. The balloons, about 10 meters in diameter and carrying antipersonnel and incendiary bombs, were designed to ride jet stream currents to the United States. An estimated 1,000 reached North America, landing in the western United States, Canada, and Mexico. The only known victims of the balloon bombs were a woman and five children killed by the detonation of a balloon they found during an outing in the woods near Bly, Oregon, in May 1945.

Japan was able to carry out terror bombing against Chinese cities, but these raids worked against Japan's overall strategic interests. Instead of forcing the Chinese government to negotiate a settlement with the Japanese, bombing only contributed to Chiang's determination that a compromise with Japan was politically unacceptable.

Beyond the interest in illuminating a lesser-known aspect of the Pacific War, Japan's modest attempts at strategic bombing are worth mentioning to make a point: Japanese bombing of Chinese cities, the effort to start fires on the U.S. mainland, and the generally ruthless conduct of Japanese military operations throughout the Asia-Pacific are sufficient to establish that if Japan had the capability and the resources, its air forces would have conducted a bombing campaign against the American civilian population. Since the Japanese did not have the wherewithal, they left the field to the Americans. It is on the U.S. strategic bombing campaign against Japan that the rest of this chapter will focus.

BACKGROUND: THE INTERWAR YEARS AND THE EUROPEAN THEATER

The interwar years produced two distinct arguments in favor of indiscriminately bombing cities. The first was that tormenting the general population with air raids could drive them to demand that their leaders sought an end to the war. This was termed *terror bombing*, which the Allies later recast as *morale bombing* in discussions of their own bombing policies during the war. The second argument was that the civilian population should be seen as a key component of the enemy's means of war production. If killing or making homeless the employees of an aircraft factory prevented them from going to work, this achieved the goal of halting production just as effectively as destroying the factory. As area bombing grew more destructive, its proponents could add that since destroying a city would also destroy any war-related industry sited therein, area bombing was a more reliable means of shutting down key war-production plants than precision bombing. Italian General Giulio Douhet, probably the most famous of the interwar airpower advocates, argued that destroying the morale of the enemy's civilian population through aerial bombing could by itself win a war. Success in modern warfare, he wrote, "must depend on smashing the material and morale resources of a people caught in a frightful cataclysm which haunts them everywhere without cease until the final collapse of all social organization."[1] Royal Air Force (RAF) Marshall Hugh Trenchard, Britain's strongest prewar airpower advocate, accepted the use of bombers to destroy enemy morale. He said in 1923, "It is on the bomber offensive that we must rely for defense. It is on the destruction of enemy industries and, above all, on the lowering of morale of enemy nationals caused by bombing that ultimate victory rests."[2]

Although experimenting with what might be called terror bombing in some of its colonial counterinsurgencies, the British government in principle opposed the intentional bombing of civilians in the lead-up to World War II, and so did the United States. A commission made up of judges and technical advisers from the United States, Britain, France, Japan, the Netherlands, and Italy met at The Hague from December 1922 to February 1923. They produced a list of rules for air warfare. Although the participating governments never ratified these rules, they provide insight into the norms of the interwar years. The Hague rules of 1923 expressly forbade terror bombing and the intentional bombing of civilians. "Aerial bombardment for the purpose of terrorizing the civilian population, of destroying or damaging private property not of a military character, or of injuring non-combatants is prohibited," reads Article 22. Article 24 says bombing is legitimate only when aimed at military targets. When military targets are in close proximity to civilian dwellings and other buildings, "the aircraft must abstain from bombardment."

In June 1938, British Prime Minister Neville Chamberlain informed the House of Commons that three principles governed RAF bombing policy: intentionally bombing civilians was forbidden, aircraft were to attack only military targets, and aircrews were to make reasonable efforts to avoid bombing civilian areas near military targets. "Whatever be the lengths to which others may go," he said, "His Majesty's Government will never resort to deliberate attack on women and children, and other civilians for purposes of mere terrorism."[3]

In September 1938 the Assembly of the League of Nations unanimously approved a resolution on "Protection of Civilian Populations Against Bombing From the Air in Case of War." The resolution noted that "this practice, for which there is no military necessity and which, as experience shows, only causes needless suffering, is condemned under the recognised principles of international law." Accordingly, the resolution held that "The intentional bombing of civilian populations is illegal; Objectives aimed at from the air must be legitimate military objectives and must be identifiable; [and] Any attack on legitimate military objectives must be carried out in such a way that civilian populations in the neighbourhood are not bombed through negligence."[4]

Britain and the United States were prominent in their prewar condemnation of bombing civilians, which is remarkable considering the policies these countries would pursue during the war. Japan's bombing of Shanghai and other Chinese cities in 1937 shocked the international community, as did the German bombing of the Spanish city of Guernica the same year. These incidents prompted the U.S. State Department to proclaim, "When the methods used in the conduct of these hostilities take the form of ruthless bombing of unfortified localities with the resultant slaughter of civilian populations, and in particular of women and children, public opinion in the United States regards such methods as barbarous. Such acts are in violation of the most elementary principles of those standards of humane conduct." On another occasion, as part of a specific condemnation of Japan, the State Department said, "any bombing of an extensive area wherein there resides a large population engaged in peaceful pursuits is unwarranted and contrary to principles of law and of humanity."[5]

In his famous Quarantine speech of October 1937, Roosevelt lamented that "civilians, including vast numbers of women and children, are being ruthlessly murdered with bombs from the air."[6] Upon the outbreak of war in Europe on September 1, 1939, Roosevelt made this appeal to the warring governments:

The ruthless bombing from the air of civilians in unfortified centers of population during the course of the hostilities which have raged in various quarters of the earth during the past few years, which has resulted in the maiming and in the death of thousands of defenseless men, women, and children, has sickened the hearts of every civilized man and woman, and has profoundly shocked the conscience of humanity. If resort is had to this form of inhuman barbarism during the period of the tragic conflagration with which the world is now confronted, hundreds of thousands of innocent human beings who have no responsibility for, and who are not even remotely participating in, the hostilities which have now broken out, will lose their lives. I am therefore addressing this urgent appeal to every government which may be engaged in hostilities publicly to affirm its determination that its armed forces shall in no event, and under no circumstances, undertake the bombardment from the air of civilian populations or of unfortified cities, upon the understanding that these same rules of warfare will be scrupulously observed by all of their opponents.[7]

As they declared war on Germany, the governments of Britain and France announced on September 2, 1939, that they "have welcomed with deep satisfaction President Roosevelt's appeal on the subject of bombing from the air." The two countries affirmed that they had "sent explicit instructions to the Commanders of their armed forces prohibiting the bombardment, whether from the air, or the sea, or by artillery on land, of any except strictly military objectives in the narrowest sense of the word."[8] Britain's Foreign Office separately reaffirmed, "His Majesty's Government have made it clear that it is no part of their policy to bomb nonmilitary objectives, no matter what the policy of the German Government may be."[9] Even Hitler endorsed this norm, telling Germany's Reichstag, "I will not war against women and children. I have ordered my air force to restrict itself to attacks on military objectives."[10]

WARM-UP: ALLIED BOMBING IN EUROPE

The Allied strategic bombing policy that culminated in the devastating U.S. raids on Japan in 1945 began with the RAF Bomber Command limiting its missions to bombing naval targets, laying mines, and dropping propaganda leaflets in the opening months of the war. The British government was keen to avoid any perception of an aerial attack on civilians. Before May 1940 the RAF did not make a serious effort to target the German homeland. Two factors, however, began to push the British in that direction. One was the alarmingly successful Nazi conquest of Western Europe, especially the quick defeat of France. The other was the early Nazi resort to bombing the cities of their adversaries, despite Hitler's stated commitment. Britain had been willing to play within the rules, but Germany seemed to be flouting them. Churchill said in a speech in January 1940, "We know from what they did in Poland that there is no brutality or bestial massacre of civilians by air bombing which [the Germans] would not readily commit if they thought it was for their advantage."[11]

An RAF bombing campaign of some form was necessary to show both the British public and their foreign allies that Britain was actively fighting the Nazis. Churchill recognized that until the Western Allies could muster the strength to mount a land campaign against occupied Europe, "In no other way at present visible can we hope to overcome the immense military power of Germany." The prime minister did not necessarily have great faith that strategic bombing would fulfill the claims of advocates such as Trenchard. As he said on one occasion in 1942, bombing was "not decisive, but better than doing nothing,"[12] and doing nothing was unacceptable.

On May 15, 1940, reacting to inaccurate media reports of 30,000 killed in the German bombing of Rotterdam, the British government authorized RAF attacks on targets east of the Rhine River, the beginning of limited attacks on German cities. The retaliatory British air raids on Berlin in August and September 1940 were a breakthrough. Bomber Command's shift to attacking cities, nevertheless, remained gradual. Even in the midst of the Blitz later that year, when the British government considered a bombing campaign against German civilians, the Air Staff resisted, saying "nothing would be gained by promiscuous bombing."[13]

While the RAF's main emphasis continued to be precision bombing of military targets, Bomber Command came to realize this campaign was ineffective. The raids on cities were too small to do serious damage, and precision proved unattainable. The chosen solution to Bomber Command's problem was to shift tactics from precision bombing of specific war-related targets to the area bombing of cities. The Douhetian idea had been waiting in the wings. Now out of necessity RAF leaders were ready to make it their principal doctrine. In February 1942 Bomber Command got a new chief: Arthur Harris, who before the war had modified his squadron of cargo aircraft to carry bombs for use against Iraqi rebels and who, while fighting a revolt in Palestine in 1936–39, recommended dropping "one 250-pound or 500-pound bomb in each village that speaks out of turn," because "the only thing the Arab understands is the heavy hand."[14] Harris instructed Bomber Command that "the primary objective of your operations should now be focused on the morale of the enemy civil population and in particular, of industrial workers."[15] He believed it was possible for Bomber Command to win the war by destroying Berlin from the air. He told Churchill in November 1943, "We can wreck Berlin from end to end if the USAAF will come in on it. It will cost us between 400–500 aircraft. It will cost Germany the war."[16] Harris remained committed to area bombing throughout the war, even though technological improvements made precision bombing (even at night) much more feasible for the RAF in the latter stage of the campaign.

With improving navigational techniques and the new four-engine Avro Lancaster bomber, British area bombing proved devastating to German cities. An attack of over 1,000 bombers in May 1942 laid waste to most of Cologne. A calamitous area bombing raid struck Hamburg, Germany's second-largest city, with incendiary bombs in July 1943, killing about 45,000 and destroying half of the city. A series of raids on Berlin took a heavy toll on both the city and the attackers. Area bombing against Germany reached a climax in the February 14–15, 1945, raids on Dresden, a city of great cultural and architectural value that had little military significance and was packed with refugees who had fled advancing Soviet troops. The bombing ignited a massive firestorm and killed an estimated 25,000 to 35,000 (much higher previous estimates reflected Cold War politics, as the Soviet Bloc sought to alienate East Germany from the West). Afterward, even Churchill, who had been a cheerleader of area bombing, concluded that "the destruction of Dresden remains a serious query against the conduct of Allied bombing."[17] From beginning to end, the British experience closely foreshadowed the U.S. strategic bombing campaign against Japan.

As for the American bomber forces in Europe, they seemingly took the high road. U.S. Army Air Force (USAAF) commanders were as desirous as their RAF counterparts to demonstrate that airpower was as potentially decisive a factor in winning wars as ground or naval forces. They perceived that the American public would consider Douhet-style terror bombing of cities as immoral and inhumane. Precision bombing, which promised direct destruction of the enemy's military strength within the norms of a just war, was the United States' basic strategic bombing doctrine. Precision bombing gave pride of place to America's strength in engineering and technology. Another element of the rationale, emphasized in the training of U.S. aircrews, was that bombing the enemy's civilian areas was an ineffective way to try to win a war. It was a better use of resources, rather, to attack targets more directly supportive of the enemy's military strength.[18]

The B-17 bomber and the advanced Norden bombsight promised to make high-altitude, precision bombing feasible. The cliché of the times was that the Norden bombsight used by U.S. bombers was a technological marvel that could drop a bomb into a pickle barrel from an altitude of 20,000 feet. Besides the ability to drop bombs with great accuracy, another premise of the doctrine was that the B-17 "Flying Fortress" could defend itself against enemy fighters. The plane bristled with up to thirteen .50-caliber machine guns positioned to guard against fighter attacks from a variety of angles.

Two years before the Americans began the strategic bombing of Japan in earnest,[19] the U.S. Eighth Air Force brought their principles, doctrines, and equipment to Europe for a baptism of fire. Throughout the war against Germany, the U.S. military officially maintained that American policy was precision bombing of military-related targets and that U.S. air commanders rejected intentionally bombing civilians for both moral and strategic reasons. When the Americans joined the British in the strategic bombing campaign in 1942, the USAAF proposed the approach the British had largely abandoned: bombing in daylight and concentrating on critical cogs in the German war machine such as fighter aircraft plants, ball-bearing factories, submarine bases, and oil refineries—what Harris disparagingly called "panacea targets." Allied commanders decided to let the British and American air forces conduct two mostly independent campaigns. Although they would sometimes cooperate, the RAF generally continued nighttime area bombing of cities, while the Americans would bomb by day, trying to hit specific targets. Dubbed the Combined Bomber Offensive, this approach claimed the advantage of giving the German defenses round-the-clock harassment.

The Americans soon discovered that despite their heavy defensive armament, the B-17 could not adequately protect itself against German fighter aircraft. They also discovered, as had the British before them, the difficulties of achieving precision when dropping bombs under combat conditions. Accuracy was problematic even from lower altitudes. The difficulty increased with altitude, despite the capabilities of the Norden bombsight. Cloud cover often made targets invisible. A navigational error could result in a failure even to land bombs in the intended city. With bombs scattering this wildly, civilian communities near military targets were at risk. U.S. bombs killed thousands of civilians in Nazi-occupied Western Europe. Allied bombing of railway networks before the Normandy invasion, for example, killed 12,000 French and Belgian civilians. Such incidents angered these communities and their governments-in-exile and prompted the British to warn the Eighth Air

Force of the danger of creating hostility among previously friendly populations.

Under the pressures of war, the United States did not always follow its stated policy of attacking only military targets in the European theater, despite the reaffirmations of officials such as USAAF commander Henry H. Arnold that "the Air Corps is committed to a strategy of high-altitude, precision bombing of military objectives" and that the intentional bombing of civilians was "abhorrent to our humanity, our sense of decency." Privately, Arnold told his staff: "the way to stop the killing of civilians is to cause so much damage and destruction and death that the civilians will demand that their government cease fighting. . . . [W]e cannot 'pull our punches' because some of them may get killed."[20] American bombers frequently carried out bombing raids against targets ensconced in urban areas, which guaranteed heavy civilian casualties. In October 1943 the Eighth Air Force bombed the center of Munster. Afterward Arnold directed that when cloud cover made precision attacks unfeasible, as was often the case in late 1943, his bombers should fly their raids under the guidance of radar. In practical terms this was carpet bombing, since the primitive radar then available could at best tell the bomber crew that they were over a district of a certain city, but could not put bombs on a specific target. Other missions were tantamount to so-called morale bombing. In February 1945, for example, almost 1,000 U.S. aircraft bombed central Berlin, killing an estimated 25,000. During the same month Operation Clarion, a series of air raids carried out jointly by U.S. and British air forces, targeted transportation facilities but was also designed to weaken civilian morale by introducing smaller German cities and towns, including those with no direct military value, to the terror of aerial bombing. U.S. bombers joined the RAF in raids intended to shatter public morale in Germany's Balkan allies in November 1943 through April 1944. Thousands of civilians died in the targeted cities, but rather than inducing surrender, the raids engendered deep hostility against the Allies.[21] The USAAF participated in the attack on Dresden, although British planes caused most of the damage. While the Allies condemned the German V-1 and V-2 as unvarnished terror weapons, the Americans produced their own version of the V-1. Called the "Jet Bomb 2" (JB2), it was nearly identical in appearance to its German progenitor. Arnold's staff proposed launching 300 JB2s per day against the Germans, but the war ended before the U.S. flying bomb saw action.[22]

The gap between stated policy and actual performance sometimes created image management challenges for the USAAF, whose commanders paid close attention to the possible impact of media reports on their reputation. With a view toward their postwar goal of an independent air force, they tried to shape their publicity to reinforce the messages that U.S. airpower was playing a prominent role in winning the war, and that the USAAF's way of war was precision bombing. U.S. officials maintained this line despite incidents such as the Dresden raid, which had even Gen. George C. McDonald, intelligence director of U.S. strategic air forces in Europe, complaining internally that

U.S. bombing policy had deteriorated into "homicide." A widely read Associated Press report that cleared censors said the Allied commanders "have made the long-awaited decision to adopt deliberate terror bombing of the great German population centers as a ruthless expedient to hasten Hitler's doom." In response, American officials continued to insist that there was no policy change and that U.S. bombers attacked only military targets. Secretary of War Henry L. Stimson said, "Our policy never has been to inflict terror bombing on civilian populations." USAAF officials reiterated that "civilian populations are not suitable military objectives."[23]

BOMBING JAPAN

The Pacific theater offered Arnold and the USAAF another opportunity to demonstrate the war-winning potential of strategic bombing and the worthiness of the air force to be a separate service. With the activation of the 20th Air Force in April 1944, Arnold felt hard-pressed to show what the bombers could do. He also had to guard his aircraft from appropriation by other American commanders. Both the army and navy argued that they needed heavy bombers to support their respective campaigns. If Arnold did not produce satisfactory results quickly enough, other generals and admirals might be able to wrest control of the heavy bombers for tactical missions. In that case the bomber force would play a mere supporting role in victories for which the army and navy would take the credit.[24] Arnold's determined and urgent pursuit of his service's agenda would strongly affect both strategic and tactical decision-making by the USAAF in the Pacific War.

The workhorse strategic bomber in the Pacific theater would be the new B-29 Superfortress, perhaps the most impressive aircraft of the war. It was designed to operate at 30,000 feet and above, which at that time was an extraordinarily high altitude. It featured a pressurized cabin and remotely operated machine-gun turrets. In contrast, B-17 and B-24 crews had to wear oxygen masks and were exposed to frigid outside temperatures (the waist gunners fired through open windows). The high altitude and speed of the B-29s made it difficult for Japanese antiaircraft guns and interceptors to stop them. Japanese fighters struggled to climb that high and had little fuel remaining afterward for combat maneuvering. Only the highest-caliber Japanese guns could hit a target at 30,000 feet. Anxious to put the B-29 to work, Arnold rushed the aircraft into production and deployment. The result was a spate of accidents stemming from a yet-uncorrected tendency of the plane's engines to catch fire. In a single week in April 1944, five B-29s crashed in India due to engine overheating.[25]

In the American strategic bombing campaign against Japan, carpet bombing became the dominant tactic. U.S. bombers in Europe made little use of incendiaries. About 90 percent of the bombs dropped by the Eighth and Fifteenth Air Forces in Europe were high explosive. Against Japan, by contrast, two-thirds of the bombs delivered by the Twentieth Air Force were incendiaries.[26] American planners began envisioning the carpet bombing of Japanese cities before the Pearl Harbor attack. In November 1941, Marshall threatened that in the event of war American bombers would "set the paper cities of Japan on fire."[27] U.S. military intelligence pointed out that much of Japan's industry was dispersed among small workshops scattered throughout residential and retail areas. By February 1942, two months into the U.S.-Japan war, Arnold's staff had ranked Japanese cities as potential targets based on their "vulnerability to incendiary attack."[28]

Secretary of State Cordell Hull had previously condemned Japanese bombing of civilian areas and particularly "the use of incendiary bombs which inevitably and ruthlessly jeopardize non-military persons and property."[29] Arnold had said, "[The] use of incendiaries against cities is contrary to our national policy of attacking only military objectives."[30] But even as the USAAF was reiterating its official policy of precision bombing against strictly military targets, the American government was developing and improving its capability to fire-bomb Japanese cities. An extraordinary amount of planning and analysis went into the refinement of a practice that officially did not exist.

The M-69 incendiary bomb used against Japanese cities was filled with jellied gasoline—later known as *napalm*—invented during the war as a substitute for magnesium, which was scarce and expensive. The canister was designed to break through the roof of a building. A few seconds later it would ignite and spray burning napalm throughout the inside of the structure. The fiery substance was sticky and difficult to extinguish. Bomb designers wanted confirmation that incendiary bombs would penetrate the roof of a typical Japanese house and create a sufficiently destructive fire. For this purpose they built a mock Japanese neighborhood at Dugway Proving Ground in Utah. With meticulous attention to authenticity, they constructed the houses with the closest available substitutes for *hinoki* and *sugi* wood. The houses had sliding paper screens and were filled with Japanese-style furnishings, including cooking utensils and chopsticks. The researchers traveled to Hawaii to obtain Japanese-style tatami mats. Houses were placed the same distance from each other as on an ordinary Japanese street. After B-29s dropped three types of incendiaries on the houses in tests conducted in 1943, analysts judged the M-69 the most effective.

Planners gave thought to the capabilities of Japanese firefighters, the time of year when wind patterns in Japan would be most favorable to spreading a fire, and the ideal formation in which bombers should fly during their bombing runs to create the largest possible fire. They studied data from Tokyo's 1923 earthquake and fire and from British cities bombed by the Germans. Based on this research, the Committee of Operations Analysts, a group of military officers and prominent civilians with experience in business, industry, and science, submitted a report to Arnold in October 1944 that recommended the USAAF should first target Japanese aircraft production and then undertake carpet bombing against Japan's cities.[31]

INTERSERVICE RIVALRY

In view of the intense rivalry between the U.S. Army and the U.S. Navy for prestige and resources, the U.S. government had divided command of the Pacific theater between them. MacArthur had charge over the Southwest Pacific Area, including the sizable army campaigns in New Guinea, Burma, and the Philippines. Admiral Chester W. Nimitz commanded the Pacific Ocean Area, which involved heavily naval-oriented operations in the central Pacific. In 1944, with MacArthur having reached the Philippines and Nimitz the Marianas, Washington was initially uncertain of the next step in the Pacific campaign. Leadership of U.S. forces in the theater hung in the balance. In discussions of a possible invasion of Japanese-held Taiwan (then commonly known as Formosa), the army insisted MacArthur should be the overall commander, while the navy lobbied for Nimitz. To steal a march on the army, Nimitz presented King with an alternative: instead of Formosa, his forces would invade Iwo Jima and Okinawa. These would be navy-dominant amphibious operations that would rely primarily on Nimitz's marine divisions for ground troops rather than offering an important role to MacArthur's forces, which in any case were committed to fighting in the Philippines.

Arnold helped clinch a decision by siding with the navy. He and the USAAF had supported the navy's preferred strategy of a drive through the central Pacific because this would eventually provide bases in the Marianas for a strategic bombing campaign against the Japanese home islands. With this accomplished, Arnold argued that Iwo Jima in U.S. possession would be useful as a base for fighter escorts, which could rendezvous with longer-range B-29s flying to Japan from more distant bases in the Marianas. Many analysts doubted the feasibility of this idea. Bombing targets on the Japanese island of Honshu were as far as 1,500 miles round-trip from Iwo Jima. A P-51 fighter with added external fuel tanks could make this journey under favorable conditions, but with very little fuel to spare for combat maneuvering or for flying through the high winds that are common over Japan. Arnold, however, was focused on accumulating any possible advantages that might contribute to a successful bombing campaign.

With Arnold and Admirals King and Leahy all in support of an invasion of Iwo Jima, Marshall acceded to the will of this majority of the Joint Chiefs. Planning began in October 1944. Reconnaissance soon revealed a dramatic increase in Japanese construction of fortifications on the island, suggesting American casualties would be much higher than expected at the time the Joint Chiefs made the decision to invade. But the operation went ahead anyway. The invasion force suffered 28,000 total casualties, more than those from the invasions of Guam, Tinian, and Saipan combined (25,000). Nearly 7,000 marines died in the battle for Iwo Jima, which is almost one-third of all the U.S. marines killed in the entire war. Using Iwo Jima as a base for fighter planes to escort B-29s on missions against Japan, which was the justification for capturing Iwo Jima, proved infeasible, as many strategists had foreseen.

P-51s stationed at Iwo Jima flew only 10 escort missions, with poor results, before abandoning the endeavor. Subsequently, an alternative rationale emerged for the invasion of Iwo Jima: the island was needed as an emergency landing site for B-29s that could not make it back to the Marianas due to damage or lack of fuel. It became widely accepted that since B-29s made over 2,000 landings on Iwo Jima during the war, saving the lives of over 20,000 crewmen justified the deaths of nearly 7,000 marines.[32]

Few of these landings, however, were emergencies that would have forced the aircraft to ditch in the ocean if the runway on Iwo Jima was not available (and even in this case, the death of the entire crew was not inevitable). Most B-29 landings on Iwo Jima were for training, operating efficiency, or convenience.[33] The battle of Iwo Jima is thus an illustration of how interservice politics can distort strategic planning, and in this case Arnold was a key player.

The navy-USAAF alliance had its limits. The navy had the opposite worry of Arnold. A navy officer on King's staff noted, "The danger is obvious of our amphibious campaign being turned into one that is auxiliary support to permit the AAF to get into position to win the war."[34] In the spring of 1945, kamikaze attacks on the American ships assembled for the Okinawa campaign were wreaking such mayhem that Nimitz asked for bombing raids on airfields in Kyushu by Marianas-based B-29s. Although the strategic bomber forces in the Pacific were under the direct command of the Joint Chiefs through Arnold rather than Nimitz, as theater commander Nimitz retained the right to commandeer the aircraft in an emergency. Arnold appealed to the Joint Chiefs to allow the B-29s to return to strategic bombing, on the grounds that trying to destroy hidden and dispersed airplanes was a poor use of his bombers. King responded that if the army air forces were not supportive of the navy, the navy might decide to cease shipping supplies to the bomber bases in the Marianas.[35]

WAR COMES TO THE HOME ISLANDS

Before U.S. forces captured the Mariana Islands, China was the only suitable base for heavy bomber raids against the Japanese home islands. In a pitch for resources in 1942, "Flying Tigers" organizer Gen. Claire Chennault claimed that he could defeat Japan with an air force of 12 heavy bombers, 30 medium bombers, and 105 fighters flying from bases in China. Chennault envisioned his fighters destroying Japan's interceptors, allowing the medium bombers to sink Japanese shipping traffic and the heavy bombers to start fires that would incinerate Japanese cities.[36] In retrospect Chennault's proposal seems absurd. Chiang, however, liked a China-based bombing campaign against Japan because it offered him the possibility of making an important contribution to the war effort without requiring him to expend large numbers of his troops or make the kinds of reforms in his command system that his American advisor, Gen. Joseph Stilwell, demanded.[37] Stilwell also argued that if a China-based bombing offensive proved effective,

Japanese forces in China would launch a determined campaign to capture the airfields. Indeed, closing the American air bases in eastern China would be the objective of the second phase of the Japanese "Ichigo" campaign in 1944, which forced some U.S. air units to move further inland. Roosevelt nonetheless accepted the Chiang and Chennault position and directed that a strategic bombing campaign against Japan's home islands and shipping traffic be given high priority. Since the Japanese had cut off the "Burma Road," supplies for the operation came by the costly and difficult method of airlift from India into China over the "Hump" (the Himalayan Mountains). With the bombers forced to fly in their own supplies, it required six round trips over the Hump by a B-29 to bring in enough fuel and bombs for one bomber to fly one combat mission.[38] To build the runways in Chengdu for the B-29s, the Szechuan provincial government required every 100 households in the area to provide 50 laborers, raising a force of 300,000 that worked day and night under armed guard and for extremely meager pay.[39]

Discounting the daring Doolittle Raid of 1942, when 16 medium-range B-25 bombers took off from an aircraft carrier to drop a few bombs on Tokyo and four other cities before trying to land in China, strategic bombing against Japanese forces and targets began in June 1944 with B-29s of XX Bomber Command flying out of bases in India and China. Kyushu was the only one of the main islands of Japan within range of a round-trip B-29 flight; Tokyo was too far. The bombers of the XX managed an average of only one or two sorties per B-29 per month against Japan. They were eventually transferred to new bases in the western Pacific.

Gen. Curtis LeMay took over XX Bomber Command in August. A major general at age 37, LeMay had proved himself a capable and innovative commander with the Eighth Air Force in Europe. LeMay had helped develop formation and bomb-run tactics that made daylight precision bombing more successful. LeMay did not shrink from accompanying his airmen into battle. He led an attack of 146 B-17s against Regensburg, Germany, on August 17, 1943, in which 24 of his aircraft were shot down. He once described how a crewman dropping bombs on German civilians confronts and overcomes his feelings of guilt: "[Y]ou have at least one quick horrid glimpse of a child lying in bed with a whole ton of masonry tumbling down on top of him, or a three-year-old girl wailing for Mutter . . . Mutter . . . because she has burned. Then you have to turn away from the picture if you intend to retain your sanity. And also if you intend to keep doing the work your nation expects of you."[40] On another occasion LeMay remarked that if the Allies had lost the war, he would have been tried as a war criminal.[41]

With the XX, LeMay launched raids against targets in Kyushu, Taiwan, and Japanese-occupied areas of China. These were generally precision-bombing missions, many of which had unimpressive results. An exception was a devastating fire-bombing attack on the docks and warehouses of Hankou (Hankow) in December. The Hankou raid was notable because it was the first major U.S. incendiary bombing attack in the Pacific theater, and because the B-29s dropped their loads from lower altitudes than usual. This raid was a harbinger of what the new year would bring home to the Japanese.

Bases became available in the Marianas Islands in October 1944. In November, XXI Bomber Command began flying missions from Guam, Saipan, and Tinian against Japanese cities, including Tokyo. The unit commander was Gen. Haywood S. Hansell, who was a strong believer in the efficacy of high-altitude, daylight precision bombing against Japan. The bombers flew at high altitudes, usually 30,000 feet, and dropped high-explosive bombs. In the first raids on Japan, Hansell's bomber crews encountered strong winds that disrupted their bombing runs, resulting in few hits on the target. These winds, reaching speeds of close to 200 miles per hour, would remain a chronic problem for high-altitude precision bombing raids over Japan. When flying with the wind, the bombers might pass over the target so quickly that the bombardier had insufficient time to do his job. Flying against the wind, the crews might find themselves moving backward relative to the ground. Clouds over the target area were another common obstacle. Less than 10 percent of the bombs hit their targets.[42]

Despite the poor results achieved during his first month of raids against Japan and calls for him to try carpet bombing, Hansell stuck to precision raids in daylight against specific, military-related targets, primarily aircraft engine factories. Hansell was under pressure to succeed because USAAF commanders in the Pacific were worrying about the perception that U.S. Navy aviation was achieving greater success than the B-29 strategic bombing campaign. That perception could support navy efforts to reassign the bombers to tactical operations under navy direction.

A CHANGE IN TACTICS

Arnold decided to replace Hansell with LeMay, who took command of XXI Bomber Command in January 1945. Initially, LeMay continued to employ precision bombing. The results remained disappointing, chiefly for the same weather-related reasons. LeMay was open-minded about experimenting with new tactics, and he did not allow qualms about harming civilians to prevent the accomplishment of his mission as he saw it. In LeMay's view, "All war is immoral and if you let that bother you, you're not a good soldier."[43] When precision bombing proved unsuccessful, LeMay turned to an alternative tactic for which the groundwork was already in place.

On March 9, LeMay instituted the new approach. His bombers would target four major Japanese cities: Tokyo, Osaka, Nagoya, and Kobe. Instead of high-altitude daylight attacks, they would bomb at night from around 7,000 feet. Japanese interceptor aircraft had much weaker night-fighting abilities than their German counterparts. Instead of high-explosive bombs, the B-29s would carry incendiary bombs and implement the well-tested tactic of firebombing.

Rather than fly in formation, as required for precision bombing, LeMay's aircraft would fly singly, one after another, over the target. Since maintaining an aircraft's place in a formation required constant adjustments to its speed and position, allowing the planes to fly individually used less fuel and therefore freed up more weight that could be devoted to the payload. Dispensing with formation flying also allowed the bombers to pass over the target from a variety of directions, making it harder for the Japanese to concentrate their defenses. LeMay ordered that the B-29s would carry no ammunition for their machine guns, further lightening the planes. These changes allowed for a 65 percent heavier bomb load.[44]

Japanese cities were poorly prepared for what was about to hit them. Radar for tracking enemy aircraft was rare. Interceptor aircraft were in short supply, and Japanese antiaircraft artillery could not stop the bombers whether they were attacking at very high or very low altitudes. The number of well-trained, professional firefighting crews was inadequate, so much responsibility would rest on volunteer part-time firemen. Some residents had dug trenches for shelter in their backyards—useless in a firestorm. At government direction, the people carried out fire drills and recited the "air defense oath of certain victory."[45]

The new tactic debuted with a devastating raid on Tokyo. The aiming point for the raid, the Tokyo suburb of Shitamachi, had a population density of more than 100,000 people per square mile, perhaps the highest in the world. The city's wooden structures burned like firewood. Many buildings with frames constructed of stone or metal became ovens, as their interiors caught fire when sparks entered through shattered windows. The fires formed a marching wall of flame, moving in the direction the wind was blowing, which heated the air in its path. This air was hot enough to kill the people in its midst or to cause flammable materials to burst into flame. Those who escaped from burning buildings were not necessarily safe. Some people's clothing caught fire, ignited by flying sparks. Many jumped into the Sumida River, which winds through Tokyo, for protection, but most of these died. The intense heat reportedly caused some sections of the river to boil. Survivor Tsuchikura Hidezo: "Fire winds with burning particles ran up and down the streets. I watched people, adults and children, running for their lives, dashing madly about like rats. The flames raced after them like living things, striking them down. . . . The whole spectacle with its blinding lights and thundering noise reminded me of the paintings of Purgatory—a real inferno out of the depths of hell itself."[46] The fire-bombing burned 16 square miles of the city. It killed about 84,000, destroyed a quarter of Tokyo's buildings, and left more than 1 million homeless.[47] Tokyo would suffer a total of six incendiary raids during the war. At the end of May half of the city was destroyed, and XXI Bomber Command considered further attacks on Tokyo unnecessary.

In the first 10 days of the campaign that began on March 9, incendiary bombing destroyed 31 square miles of Tokyo, Nagoya, Osaka, and Kobe.

Although precision bombing raids continued against targets such as aircraft plants, arsenals, and oil refineries, most bomber sorties through the end of the war were carpet-bombing attacks on Japanese cities. U.S. bombers eventually destroyed more than 40 percent of the urban area of 66 targeted cities, rendering about one-fourth of Japan's city-dwelling population homeless. U.S. conventional bombing raids killed over 300,000 Japanese civilians, more than the atomic bombings.[48] Losses of bombers to Japanese defenses were not heavy even at the lower altitudes (the loss rate for the B-29s in the first five firebombing missions over Japan was less than 1 percent) and continued to drop through the end of the war. Total losses in the bombing campaign against Japan included 414 B-29s destroyed, more than 2,600 crewmen killed, and 433 wounded. Flying lower also reduced strain on the bombers' engines, increasing the availability of aircraft for combat sorties. Along with the change of tactics, the intensity of bombing dramatically increased. From late 1944 to March 9, 1945, 7,180 tons of bombs fell on Japan. The total for March jumped to 13,800 tons and rose to 42,700 tons in July, the last full month of the war. U.S. commanders planned to step up the pounding to 115,000 tons per month if the war had continued. Ninety-six percent of the bombing of Japan occurred after March 9, 1945. Yet it was so intensive that LeMay's staff estimated the strategic bombing campaign would run out of major targets on September 1, 1945.[49]

In July 1945, LeMay began sending bombers to drop leaflets warning targeted cities of imminent raids. The American commanders judged correctly that Japanese defenses were so weak that these warnings would not significantly increase the risk to U.S. aircrews. The planes dropped some 660,000 leaflets, which read, "In accordance with America's well known humanitarian principles, the American Air Force, which does not wish to injure innocent people, now gives you warning to evacuate . . . and save your lives." In some cases American planes dropped warning leaflets on Japanese cities the day before they were bombed. This was only partly for humanitarian reasons; U.S. psychological warfare experts believed this would help break enemy morale by reinforcing to the Japanese people that their government was powerless to protect them.[50]

As successful as it was at devastating urban areas, the conventional bombing campaign did not break the Japanese population's will to carry on the war, although it eroded the effectiveness of the citizenry to contribute to the war effort by killing and injuring workers and by destroying their homes. The effect of the raids on the Japanese economy was limited by the fact that even prior to the beginning of the massive incendiary raids of March 1945, Japan was on the verge of economic collapse, starved of essential supplies of oil, coal, and iron ore. The postwar United States Strategic Bombing Survey said of "the urban area attacks" on Japan that "in many segments of that economy their effects were duplicative. . . . Japan's economy was in large measure being destroyed twice over, once by cutting off imports, and secondly by air attack."[51]

ETHICAL HIATUS, FORGOTTEN HOLOCAUST

In the case of strategic bombing, rather than World War II inspiring the emergence of a present-day norm, the war saw a dramatic departure by all the major combatants from an existing norm that was later reinstituted. That bombing civilians is bad was not one of the lessons of the war. The world knew this already. Rather, the rules of war were suspended during wartime.

The initial U.S. policy of eschewing the intentional bombing of civilian areas and attacking only targets of military relevance came under severe strain in the European theater. The USAAF moved toward the position that the presence of a war-related target in a city justified the incidental killing of an unlimited number of noncombatant residents—an abandonment of the prewar norm that forbade bombing raids against military targets that would endanger civilians. In the Pacific theater, the distinction between military and nonmilitary targets all but disappeared, and cities themselves were unambiguously targeted. An Army Air Force colonel, commenting on Japanese attempts to organize most of the country's population into a militia to fight the feared American invasion, asserted, "The entire population of Japan is a proper military target. For us, there are no civilians in Japan."[52] Why did Americans take this ethical hiatus from their prewar and postwar norm against bombing civilians? They had a strategic incentive to do it: they thought it would help win or shorten the war. They had no strategic disincentive against doing it: the Japanese were not capable of responding in kind or even of putting up a serious defense against the bombers. Moral and ethical considerations were easily trumped by strategic expediency. As the British public generally accepted that Germans were getting what they deserved for the "Blitz,"[53] Americans saw bombing Japanese cities as just retaliation for Japan's military aggression. Perhaps the most important insight of this episode of the Pacific War is the frailty of moral constraints under the pressure of total war.

The U.S. government's decision to drop atomic bombs on the cities of Hiroshima and Nagasaki has attracted a tremendous amount of attention and discussion over several decades. American carpet bombing of Japanese cities is far less discussed and less well known. Granted, atomic weapons introduced the insidious and frightening scourge of radiation poisoning, which can continue harming the survivors of an atomic blast for years afterward. This began a new era of warfare and gave new urgency to arms control and counterproliferation efforts. Yet in some respects, the U.S. conventional bombing campaign was both quantitatively and qualitatively more significant than the atomic bombings. Conventional bombing did more damage and killed more people than the A-bombs, and killed them just as horribly. LeMay is famously quoted as pointing out, seemingly boastfully, that "we scorched and boiled and baked to death more people in Tokyo on that night of March 9–10 than went up in vapor at Hiroshima and Nagasaki combined." The B-29 attacks prior to Hiroshima also completely broke through the ethical barrier against targeting the civilian inhabitants of an enemy state. Had Tokyo surrendered in July

1945, conventional bombing would have left a powerful historical legacy: that by the end of the war America's economic and technological resources enabled it to mount bombing raids on the Japanese home islands that destroyed whole cities; and that U.S. bombing raids targeted Japan's civilian population for destruction, killing them by the tens of thousands. As it was, this legacy was subsumed by the atomic bombings.

CHAPTER 6

The Atomic Bombs
and the End of the War

Washington's overriding goal after the defeat of Germany was to conclude the Pacific War as quickly as possible and with the least possible sacrifice of American lives, but within the framework of "unconditional surrender," which Roosevelt and Churchill had agreed to in early 1943 and which new U.S. president Truman remained committed to. U.S. leaders would not allow Japan to escape a dismantling of the political system that gave rise to Japan's aggression and atrocities and would demand retribution against those Japanese judged to be war criminals. Ending the war as soon as possible was necessary not only to minimize U.S. casualties, but also because Roosevelt, Marshall, and other American leaders worried about the staying power of the home front.[1] Admiral Ernest J. King spoke for many at the top level when he confided to journalists he was afraid that "the American people will tire of it quickly, and that pressure at home will force a negotiated peace, before the Japs are really licked."[2] The U.S. government pursued all available avenues to expedite Japan's defeat, including strategic bombing, interdiction of Japan's water traffic, planning for an invasion of the Japanese home islands, and research and development of an atomic weapon.

UNCONDITIONAL SURRENDER

The "unconditional surrender" proviso had the advantages of maintaining Allied solidarity (as an assurance none of the Allied governments would break ranks and seek a separate peace with the enemy) and ensuring that the victors would allow no residue of Axis fascism nor ambiguity about its utter defeat to survive into the postwar era. The disadvantage was that it might prolong the war by giving the enemy no incentive to stop fighting. In the Pacific War, the key issue at stake was how the Allied powers planned to treat the emperor, considered a semidivine figure in Japan and the repository of what it meant to be Japanese. As Japanese Prime Minister Suzuki Kantaro said publicly on June 9, 1945, "Should the Emperor system be abolished, [the Japanese people] would lose all reason for existence. 'Unconditional surrender,' therefore, means death to the hundred million; it leaves us no choice but to go on fighting to the last man."[3] If the Japanese felt strongly about the issue, so did Americans. According to a June 1945 Gallup poll, 33 percent of Americans favored executing Hirohito as a war criminal, and another 11 percent thought he should be imprisoned, while only 7 percent supported leaving him on the throne.[4] High-ranking government officials who shared these views included presidential advisor Harry Hopkins, Secretary of State James Byrnes, and Assistant Secretaries of State Dean Acheson and Archibald MacLeish.

Other officials, however, argued that communicating to Japan that it could keep the emperor might hasten Japan's surrender, and that ending the war early was worth a small compromise of the unconditional surrender principle. General Marshall, Admiral Leahy and even Churchill expressed support for this idea. An articulate and credible advocate of this position was Under Secretary of State Joseph Grew, who had been U.S. ambassador to Japan for 10 years and was the U.S. government's top-ranking "Japan hand." In May and June he argued to his superiors that making a concession to Tokyo on preserving Hirohito's status would make a crucial difference in surrender negotiations. Grew said the "greatest obstacle to unconditional surrender by the Japanese is their belief that this would entail the destruction or permanent removal of the Emperor."[5] A committee appointed by Truman, including Grew, Secretary of War Henry Stimson, and Navy Secretary James Forrestal, recommended keeping the emperor. Officials from the State Department and the War Department drafted a statement for possible promulgation during the upcoming summit meeting in Potsdam, Germany. The statement laid out the surrender terms the Allies would offer to Japan. In addition to the demands that would reappear in the Potsdam Proclamation, the draft statement foresaw for postwar Japan a "responsible government of a character representative of the Japanese people. This may include a constitutional monarchy under the present dynasty if it be shown to the complete satisfaction of the world that such a government shall never again aspire to aggression."[6]

Some U.S. officials, however, objected to giving the Japanese a promise that they could keep their emperor. They argued that the cult of emperor-worship had been an integral part of the rise of Japanese fascism, and therefore it was not certain militarism could be completely uprooted from Japan without dismantling the monarchy. There were also grounds for doubting whether the United States would gain anything from making this concession, which might be interpreted as a weakening of American resolve. In a message from Foreign Minister Togo Shigenori to the Japanese ambassador in Moscow in July 1945, which U.S. military intelligence intercepted, decoded, and showed to top U.S. officials, Togo specifically addressed this issue and denied that a U.S. guarantee of the emperor's position would lead Tokyo to surrender.[7] Another important consideration was U.S. public opinion. Byrnes, a former congressman, reminded Truman that the majority of Americans opposed giving Hirohito a free pass and warned of the repercussions of angering the electorate. These factors persuaded Truman not to offer Tokyo a clear commitment regarding the emperor.[8]

THE PLANNED INVASION OF JAPAN

The U.S. military's joint staff planners began in April 1945 to prepare for invasions of Kyushu and the Kanto Plain of Honshu. It was to be an Allied rather than strictly American operation, as several British Commonwealth divisions were also to participate. The Kyushu campaign, Operation Olympic, was scheduled to start in November 1945. The projected date for the landings on Honshu, Operation Coronet, was spring 1946.

The number of casualties U.S. leaders expected to incur in an invasion has been a matter of historical debate. Nevertheless, Truman and his advisors clearly, and with good reason, feared the cost of conquering Japan's home islands would be dear.[9] They saw the ferocity of the battle for Okinawa in April–June 1945 as a harbinger of what lay ahead. About 7,000 U.S. soldiers and nearly 5,000 U.S. sailors died. Most of the Japanese defenders fought to the death. About 66,000 died, although 7,000 were captured, a relatively high percentage for Japanese forces. Contemplating the next step, Truman foresaw the awful possibility of "an Okinawa from one end of Japan to the other."[10] Admiral Leahy suggested that U.S. troops fighting on Kyushu could probably expect the same casualty rate their comrades suffered on Okinawa: about one-third.[11] Andrew Goodpaster, who rose to become the commander of NATO forces in Europe after the war, was a colonel in the War Department Operations Division. Tasked with estimating the cost in U.S. troops of invading Japan, he produced a figure of half a million casualties.[12] Truman and his advisors also evidently took seriously a warning from a commissioned report by Herbert Hoover that as many as 500,000 to 1 million Americans might die in an invasion.[13]

Like the Americans, Japanese army planners thought the Okinawa battle, although a defeat, augured well for Japan's capacity to take a heavy toll against the invaders in the anticipated battle of Kyushu. On Okinawa Japanese defenders with no source of resupply had continued fighting for three months and inflicted heavy casualties on a much larger American invasion force. Kamikaze aircraft battered the attacking fleet. Kyushu would similarly present the Americans with well-prepared defenses, a fight-to-the-death mentality, and punishing kamikaze attacks, but on a much larger scale and under conditions far more favorable to the Japanese. Military leaders hoped that if they defeated the invasion or at least made the Americans pay a high price in blood, the

United States would shrink from further fighting and seek a negotiated peace agreement acceptable to the Japanese. Japan had about two million soldiers in the home islands and 5,000 aircraft set aside for kamikaze attacks. As part of its "Ketsugo" defense plan, Japanese planners hoped that by massing their kamikaze attacks during the crucial hours when the invaders were trying to land soldiers on the beaches and by instructing their pilots to aim for troop transports rather than capital ships, the kamikazes could destroy between one-third and one-half of the attacking soldiers before they reached Japanese soil.[14] The military expected all able-bodied civilians to throw themselves into combat along with the soldiers. The government organized most civilians, from teenagers to middle-aged persons, into a "Patriotic Citizens Fighting Corps" and assigned them support and combat roles with what little weaponry was available. Soldiers instructed them to fight enemy infantrymen with bamboo spears or to carry explosives and make human bomb attacks against American tanks.[15] A government propaganda campaign tried to mobilize support for a "Glorious Death of One Hundred Million."[16] Japanese prison camp commanders also planned to kill Allied prisoners in the event of an invasion of Japan.[17]

By the spring of 1945, many high-level U.S. officials were beginning to believe in the possibility of forcing Japan to surrender without an invasion. The U.S. Defense Department's Joint Intelligence Committee produced a memo on April 18, which argued that "effective air and sea blockade of Japan proper, combined with large-scale strategic bombing, within Allied capabilities" were enough to eventually persuade the Japanese government to "seek an end to hostilities prior to complete destruction of their country."[18] At a June 18 meeting Truman called with the Joint Chiefs and the Secretaries of War and the Navy to review alternatives, the group unanimously agreed that Olympic should proceed, with Coronet to be reviewed later. Bases on Kyushu would be useful, the brass decided, even if subsequent strategy was to finish off Japan by blockade rather than by an invasion of Honshu.[19] But planning for the Allied invasion of Japan did not predestinate its execution. In fact, a division was growing within the U.S. military leadership. Admiral King went along with the need for planning but hoped the Joint Chiefs would eventually reconsider and cancel the plan. The carnage on and around Okinawa, which kamikazes made the bloodiest battle of the war for the U.S. Navy, convinced Nimitz to withdraw his support for Coronet.[20] Predictably, Arnold and Lemay argued that an invasion was unnecessary in view of the success of the bombing campaign, while army generals Marshall and MacArthur maintained that bombing alone could not force a Japanese surrender.[21]

In the summer of 1945, U.S. intelligence discovered the Japanese military had correctly anticipated that the Allies planned an invasion at southern Kyushu and were hurriedly engaged in a massive buildup of forces and defenses there. Allied planning was based on the presumption that the invasion force would need a large advantage in numbers at the point of attack to ensure its success, but the buildup on Kyushu was so large as to give the defenders rough numerical parity with the invaders. MacArthur favored going ahead with the invasion despite the evidence of strengthening defenses on Kyushu. King and Nimitz were preparing to challenge him. The opposition of Nimitz and King, preexistent fears of excessive casualties, and the reduced prospects for a successful campaign in Kyushu made it almost certain that the Joint Chiefs would have reconsidered Operation Olympic before its launch date, possibly canceling it. But all this was to be preempted.

A NEW KIND OF BOMB

Research for the American atomic bomb had begun in October 1941, spurred largely by the fear that Germany would build one first. The original presumption was that the target of the atomic bomb would be Germany, and there is little doubt the United States would have used it against the Germans had it been available in time to fill a perceived need for a final knockout blow. This is important to keep in mind when considering the subsequent claim that the Americans would not have dropped the bomb on other "white people" (a claim that seems more vacuous in light of highly destructive conventional bombing raids such as the Anglo-U.S. firebombing raid in Dresden). While the Germans gave up serious pursuit of an atomic weapon in 1942, that year Enrico Fermi and his assistants engineered the first sustained nuclear reaction at the University of Chicago. The gigantic scientific and industrial effort that became known as the Manhattan Project resulted in a successful test detonation in the New Mexico desert on July 16, 1945. The Manhattan Project employed 120,000 people across the United States and in Canada. It cost $2 billion, a massive investment that created considerable bureaucratic momentum in favor of putting the product to use in the absence of a strong reason to the contrary.

On June 1, an Interim Committee of government officials, scientists, and business leaders unanimously recommended to Truman that he use the bomb as soon as possible as a means of shortening the war. The Committee considered but rejected the ideas of giving the Japanese advance warning about the A-bomb attack or conducting a demonstration explosion for the Japanese over a less populous area than a city. They feared that in response to such a warning the Japanese might move Allied POWs into the target area or make an all-out effort to shoot down the bomber. Furthermore, there was no certainty the bomb would function properly.

The U.S. military produced a list of possible targets for the new weapon. All were cities, because U.S. planners wanted to be able to assess the destructive potential of the bombs over a large area and also wanted to maximize the bombs' shock effect on the Japanese. The list included Kyoto, Hiroshima, Kokura, Nagasaki, Yokohama, and Niigata. Kyoto, the ancient capital, was the Dresden of Japan, a treasury of cultural and religious sites. Stimson had visited the city several times before the war and understood its significance. He prevailed upon Truman not to drop the atomic bomb on Kyoto, arguing that this would create such bitterness among Japanese as to threaten Japan's postwar integration into the U.S. Bloc rather than the Soviet Bloc. Truman agreed, and planners took Kyoto off the list.[22]

DECISIONS IN TOKYO

The Japanese government was deeply factionalized, with the top civilian leaders by the summer of 1945 favoring an early surrender if the Allies would agree to preserve the institution of the emperor, but the military high command insisting on continued resistance. The Japanese officials who favored an early end to the war had to be cautious. Those who openly called for surrender risked offending the military, being labeled disloyal, and being imprisoned or assassinated.

One might hope that in such a circumstance the desire to halt the mounting destruction of Japan's civilian population and cities from conventional bombing would have been the driving force in policymaking. Japanese historian Tsuyoshi Hasegawa, however, characterizes the debate among Japanese elites as centering on the emperor: some wanted to end the war as a way of saving the emperor, while others wanted to fight on in keeping with what they saw as the national spirit, of which the emperor was the embodiment.[23] On June 22, after the loss of Okinawa to U.S. forces, Hirohito instructed his ministers to search for a way to end the war. This was not, it is important to note, a suggestion that Tokyo should surrender, but rather an order to explore opportunities to end the war on terms acceptable to Japan's government. Hirohito continued to support his generals' efforts to prepare for a punishing defense of the home islands against the expected Allied invasion, based on the premise that one more great victory would give Japan a position of strength from which to negotiate peace terms. Some Japanese officials advocated seeking direct negotiations with the United States and gaining clarification from the Allies that they would preserve the monarchy. These officials perceived that the United States and Britain would welcome an early end to the war, that a rivalry for influence in Asia was brewing between the United States and the USSR, and that allowing the war to drag on until the Soviets entered would consolidate Moscow's position in Manchuria contrary to Japanese interests. The Japanese government did not pursue this approach prior to the atomic bombings, however, because of a persistent but futile hope of securing Soviet assistance. Some of Japan's top leaders clung tenaciously to the belief that the Soviet Union might be willing to help Japan obtain more lenient surrender conditions from the other Allied governments. Any incentives the Soviets might have had for doing this were not clear. Relations between Tokyo and Moscow had been tense for decades. The Soviet Union planned to eventually fight Japan at the opportune time. War with Japan, however, did not suit Soviet interests immediately prior to or during the fighting in Europe. Thus Moscow turned down a request from Washington in December 1941 to join the war in the Pacific, citing the neutrality pact with Japan and the need to concentrate on turning back the Nazi invasion.

But with a massive and battle-hardened Red Army left idle by the defeat of Germany, the USSR had the opportunity to make gains in Northeast Asia at the expense of a weakening Japan. Tokyo was greatly concerned throughout the Pacific War with maintaining Soviet neutrality. Moscow entering the war in the Pacific on the side of the Allies would be a strategic catastrophe for the Japanese, opening a new front with a powerful adversary on the back doorstep of an empire that already faced a dire threat from the Americans. Tokyo also feared that short of this step, the Soviets might allow U.S. aircraft to fly from bases in the Russian Far East to attack the Japanese home islands. From 1942 onward the Americans were heavily supplying the Soviet armed forces, potentially giving Washington a strong basis for demanding concessions from the USSR. To avoid antagonizing the Soviets, Japan did not target U.S. armament shipments to the Soviet Union as they crossed the North Pacific Ocean, despite the displeasure of Tokyo's German allies.[24] In March 1944 Japan reached a bilateral fisheries deal favorable to the USSR and agreed to give up oil and coal rights on Sakhalin Island earlier than originally planned. Ideally, Japan wished Moscow would reach a separate peace with the Germans and join the Axis alliance, allowing Germany to concentrate on fighting Japan's enemies, the Western powers. Japanese ambassador to Moscow Sato Naotake attempted unsuccessfully to interest Soviet Foreign Minister Vyacheslav Molotov in this idea in 1944.[25] Tokyo sought and received from Moscow a reaffirmation of the neutrality agreement in May 1943. The Japanese hoped for an extension of the pact before it was scheduled to expire in 1946. In April 1945, however, Moscow formally notified Tokyo that the Soviets intended to let the neutrality agreement expire. Some Japanese leaders called for efforts to negotiate a new treaty, although the Japanese Embassy in Moscow was skeptical. Despite the obviously decreasing utility to the Soviets of maintaining peace with Japan, and despite Moscow's announced intent not to renew the neutrality pact, Tokyo continued in June and July 1945 to try to enlist Soviet diplomatic intervention on Japan's behalf with the other Allied powers. Japan's military leaders also saw the Soviets as potential suppliers of desperately needed oil and aircraft. Indeed, even *after* the Soviets entered the war on August 8 and were fighting Japanese forces in Manchuria, the Japanese army General Staff expressed a hope of "attempting to improve the situation" with the Soviets and of driving a wedge between the USSR and the other Allies.[26]

POTSDAM AND JAPANESE REACTION

In connection with the Potsdam meeting between Truman, Churchill (replaced by new Prime Minister Cement Atlee midway through the conference), and Stalin in July and August 1945, the governments of the United States, Britain, and China released a "Proclamation Defining Terms for Japanese Surrender" on July 25, 1945. This document offered the Japanese a chance to avoid "prompt and utter destruction" by accepting the repeated call for "unconditional surrender of all Japanese armed forces." Terms specifically mentioned were temporary occupation of Japan by Allied forces, reparations, punishment of war criminals, and disarmament, along with the assurance that "we do not intend that the Japanese shall be enslaved as a race or destroyed as a nation." The Proclamation made no explicit mention of the monarchy but stated that Japan's postwar government would be "established in accordance with the freely expressed will of the Japanese people"—implying that Japan could keep the monarchy if this was the public's wish. Time, however, was short; the Proclamation specified, "We shall brook no delay."[27]

Tokyo did not immediately accept the Proclamation. Some top Japanese leaders, including Togo and the emperor, thought the Proclamation included ambiguities worth exploring. Suzuki, however, said at a July 28 press conference that his government considered the Proclamation a repetition of the 1943 Cairo Declaration and would "ignore" it (*mokusatsu*). Tokyo evidently intended to stall for time, continuing to wait for possible assistance from the Soviets (against the advice of Japan's own ambassador to Moscow and many others), rather than to reject the Proclamation outright. During a meeting of the Supreme War Council and the emperor in early August, Togo reaffirmed that Tokyo had not dismissed the Potsdam Proclamation, while acknowledging that foreigners "have imagined that we did."[28] But Washington, not unreasonably, took the report of Suzuki's statement as an official negative response to the Proclamation. So did other Americans, including the editors of the *New York Times*. The paper's headline on July 30, 1945, read, "JAPAN OFFICIALLY TURNS DOWN SURRENDER TERMS ULTIMATUM." Some students of history have seen this as a lost chance for peace, a tragically consequential misunderstanding. Yet if this was an opportunity to end the war, the Japanese government's failure to move quickly to grasp it suggests Tokyo was not yet ready to surrender. Japanese historian Sadao Asada argues that the Japanese government would not have surrendered before the atomic bombings even if the Potsdam Proclamation had guaranteed retention of the emperor.[29]

At the time of the Yalta conference in February 1945, early Soviet entry into the Pacific War appeared highly desirable from the U.S. standpoint. At the urging of the other Allies, Stalin agreed to join the fight two to three months after the defeat of Germany. He also agreed that after Japan was beaten Manchuria would return to Chinese control. In exchange he got agreement from the United States and Britain that the USSR would acquire the Kurile Islands and the southern part of Sakhalin Island, and that Mongolia would be a Soviet satellite state. U.S. leaders recognized that, as with Eastern Europe, the United States was in no position to prevent the USSR from gaining influence over these territories without going to war against the Soviets.[30] After the Potsdam meeting and word that the bomb's test explosion was successful, Truman still wanted the Soviets in the war.[31] Despite the risk of opening the door to greater Soviet influence in postwar Asia, the American leadership still believed that Soviet participation would help save American lives. U.S. leaders hoped but could not be certain that atomic bombings would cause Tokyo to surrender, or, if so, how quickly. Washington already had ample incentive to end the war as soon as possible, but the entry of the Soviets into the fight provided an additional reason.

A prominent postwar criticism of the A-bombings is Gar Alperovitz's thesis that the main reason the Truman Administration used the atomic bomb was to intimidate the Soviet Union and thereby secure American preeminence in the postwar world.[32] The record shows that U.S. officials considered and discussed the Soviet reaction to the atomic bomb. Byrnes, for example, told Truman the atomic capability "might well put us in a position to dictate our own terms at the end of the war."[33] But the U.S.-Soviet relationship was not the primary motivator of the use of atomic bombs against Japan. If some historians see the dropping of the A-bomb as an anti-Soviet act, it was not perceived so at the time. Told about the bomb at Potsdam, Stalin urged Truman to "make good use of it." The American left wing, from commentators in *Nation* and *New Republic* to the American Communist Party, approved of using the bomb even as they maintained a sympathetic view of the Soviet Union and hoped for a cordial postwar U.S.-Soviet relationship.[34]

That Japan was militarily subdued and economically collapsing was not at issue. Admiral Halsey reported on July 28 that the Japanese navy had "ceased to exist."[35] American domination of the sea and airspace surrounding the home islands virtually halted the flow of fuel, food supplies, and industrial raw materials into Japan by mid-1945. Had the war continued beyond August, the situation would have worsened further. On August 11, U.S. heavy bomber forces received a new directive to change their targeting emphasis from incendiary raids on cities to precision raids against Japan's railroad networks. This order resulted from analysis of the recently completed war in Europe that showed the effectiveness of bombing transportation infrastructure as a means of crippling Germany's economy. The likely outcome of such a campaign would have been massive starvation in Japan, as the railroad was the only remaining reliable means of food distribution.[36]

The Americans knew from eavesdropping on Japanese diplomatic messages that surrender was being debated in Tokyo. They also knew, however, that in July those in favor of continuing the war were ascendant. The communications between Tokyo and Japanese diplomats that U.S. intelligence officers intercepted indicated an interest in ending the war, but no interest in surrendering. Similarly, intercepted military communications confirmed that the Japanese were rushing to build up defenses on Kyushu in anticipation of the next great battle.[37] The Japanese had not responded affirmatively to the Potsdam Proclamation. An analysis by U.S. military intelligence in July 1945 concluded, "until the Japanese leaders realize that an invasion cannot be repelled, there is little likelihood that they will accept any peace terms satisfactory to the Allies."[38]

Truman's much-scrutinized decision to use the atomic bomb against Japan was really a decision not to halt or change the course of what was becoming a technical and political juggernaut by the time he assumed the presidency. Committed to an uncompromising victory over a beaten but stubborn enemy, chiefly concerned with saving American lives and shortening the war, and facing the prospect of the bloodiest campaign of the war, Truman welcomed the bomb as an additional means of pressuring Tokyo to give in.

THE ATOMIC RAIDS

On August 6, 1945, just before a B-29 called Enola Gay took off from an airfield on Tinian in Marianas, a chaplain read a prayer asking that God "be with those who brave the heights of Thy Heaven and who carry the battle to our enemies."[39] Despite its unusually heavy load, pilot Col. Paul Tibbets successfully got the bomber off the ground. Enola Gay carried a uranium bomb called "Little Boy." As a precaution, the bomb was not armed when the heavily loaded aircraft took off. A U.S. Navy captain flying with Tibbets's crew assembled the detonator while airborne. Two observation aircraft accompanied the Enola Gay. Detecting only a small number of enemy aircraft, the Japanese elected not to scramble fighters to intercept them, a standard practice to conserve scarce fuel. Tibbets's B-29 dropped the bomb over Hiroshima. The bomb was set to explode several hundred yards above the ground to broaden its effects. Observing the results from his aircraft, Tibbets said the ground below the billowing mushroom cloud looked like "a boiling pot of tar . . . It was black and boiling underneath with a steam haze on top of it."[40] The scene on the outraged ground was worse than the aerial observers could then have imagined. Thousands of corpses appearing as "charred bundles were strewn in the streets, sidewalks, and bridges. . . . Fire broke out all over the city, devouring everything in its path. People walked aimlessly in eerie silence, many black with burns, the skin peeling from their bodies. Others frantically ran to look for their missing loved ones. Thousands of dead bodies floated in the river. . . . Then the black rain fell, soaking everyone with radiation."[41] The blast instantly incinerated those within a half mile of the epicenter. It destroyed about 70,000 buildings and killed roughly 70,000 people outright, with perhaps another 30,000 deaths over the next few months due to radiation exposure.

Carl Spaatz, an experienced USAAF general from the European theater and the new commander of U.S. strategic bomber forces in the Pacific, suggested dropping the second bomb in a visible but less populated area rather than a city, but Washington ordered him to stick to the target list.[42] On August 9, a B-29 named Bock's Car flown by Maj. Charles Sweeney carried the plutonium-fueled "Fat Man" bomb toward the designated target of Kokura. The city was obscured by clouds, so Sweeney diverted to the secondary target, Nagasaki. The second bomb killed another 40,000 instantly, with up to 40,000 more deaths in the following months. "Nagasaki was a big bonfire," remembered bomb survivor Akiko Seitelbach, who later married an American soldier and moved to the United States. "When we ran through the roads between houses still burning on both sides, the scorching heat nearly overwhelmed us. . . . Something was coming toward me. It was a man but he didn't look like a man. He had no hair, his face was swollen to about twice the normal size, and loose skin hung down from his arms and legs like seaweed. He was walking towards me and I was so scared I tried to avoid him. I heard him saying 'Water, water' as he passed me. So I turned around to go to him but he had collapsed, dead."[43]

Dropping two bombs in quick succession was designed to convey the impression that the Americans had many atomic bombs and that their use would become routine if Japan continued the war.[44] Immediately after the Nagasaki bombing, Truman addressed his fellow citizens. After mentioning the Pearl Harbor attack and some of Japan's wartime atrocities (invoking the revenge imperative), Truman said of the atomic bomb, "We have used it in order to shorten the agony of war, in order to save the lives of thousands of young Americans."[45] On August 19, the day after the bombing of Nagasaki, Truman called a halt to further nuclear attacks, reportedly because he did not want another large-scale slaughter of civilians, particularly children.[46]

POLITICAL FALLOUT IN JAPAN

After the first bomb, Hirohito still did not express a desire to accept the Potsdam terms. Rather, the Japanese government more urgently sought an answer from Moscow. Through August 9, meetings in Tokyo of both the six-member Supreme War Council and the 16-member cabinet had been inconclusive.[47] Members of the Supreme War Council split over the questions of whether to surrender and, after Potsdam, what concessions to demand of the Allies in exchange for a Japanese surrender. Togo advocated accepting the Potsdam Proclamation with only one condition, which was that the monarchy should be preserved. He argued that attaching additional conditions would lead the Allies to believe that Japan was rejecting the Proclamation. Others, however, favored adding other terms: no postwar occupation of Japan by foreign troops and allowing the Japanese government rather than the Allies to conduct the disarmament of Japanese forces and war crimes trials for Japanese leaders. War Minister Anami Korechika, a member of both the Supreme War Council and the cabinet, did not accept that Japan should surrender at all. The main spokesman of the hard-line faction, Anami had in April 1945 ordered the arrest of 400 people, including some of high social rank, who were suspected of desiring to end the war.[48]

Soon after the destruction of Hiroshima came another devastating blow. On August 8, the Soviets declared war on Japan and immediately attacked Japanese forces in Manchuria. This not only ended the possibility of a Soviet-mediated armistice, but created the imminent danger of Japan losing its position on the Northeast Asian mainland and then facing invasion from two sides.

The following day came reports that a second massive and unusual explosion had destroyed Nagasaki.

Kido Koichi, Lord Keeper of the Privy Seal, was Hirohito's closest adviser and a liaison between the emperor and the government. At the urging of leaders who wanted a clearer path to surrender, Kido met with Hirohito in the late afternoon of August 9 to urge him to support accepting the Potsdam terms with only one condition. That night, during another meeting of the Supreme War Council with the emperor in attendance, Togo again led those who favored accepting the Proclamation on the condition that it would not "prejudice the prerogatives of His Majesty as a Sovereign Ruler."[49] Anami, in strong opposition and supported by Army Chief of Staff Umezu Yoshijiro, argued that Japan could put up a punishing defense against the invasion and hinted that the army would not accept a decision to surrender. Ignoring Anami's attempt to prolong the discussion, Suzuki asked the emperor to render a decision since the Council was deadlocked. Involving Hirohito in this manner was a highly unusual move. In an abstract sense the emperor was the most powerful figure in the Japanese political system because the authority of the government emanated from him. But he was also above and therefore outside of the government, and thus in practice he had little or no role in actual policymaking. His accustomed function was to approve the decisions made by his ministers, not to issue them himself. Hirohito would later argue that although he was an early supporter of peace, he had to wait for the right moment to assert his view because of the delicacy of his position, lest the perception of impropriety give the militarists an excuse to arrest and isolate him. If so, the moment had arrived. In a prepared speech, Hirohito told his ministers he favored surrender under the single condition that the monarchy be preserved. He mentioned three reasons for his decision that the war must stop: (1) Japanese defenses were not strong enough to prevent a capture of Tokyo; (2) the Japanese race was at risk of extinction; and (3) the enemy was likely to capture the shrines that contained the three sacred imperial relics (a mirror, a sword, and a curved jewel), which symbolized the emperor's legitimacy.[50] Anami and the other military representatives acquiesced, and a cabinet meeting afterward confirmed the decision.

The United States responded on August 11 (received August 12 in Japan) after gaining British, Soviet, and Chinese concurrence. The U.S. answer, something of a compromise and drafted by Byrnes, refused the Japanese demand by asserting that the fate of the monarchy was up to the Allies. "From the moment of surrender," it read, "the authority of the Emperor . . . shall be subject to the Supreme Commander of the Allied Powers." It did not, however, foreclose the possibility of Japan keeping the emperor, and added the vague reassurance that "the ultimate form of the Government of Japan shall be established by the freely expressed will of the Japanese people."[51]

More inconclusive meetings followed in Tokyo. U.S. conventional bombing of Japanese cities continued. By August 14, when Hirohito convened a combined meeting of the Supreme War Council and the cabinet, Japanese scientists had confirmed that the new American weapon was an atomic bomb. Soviet forces were smashing Japanese resistance in Manchuria. The Americans increased the pressure on Japanese leaders by dropping leaflets on Tokyo that reprinted the Japanese response to the Potsdam Proclamation along with the Byrnes Note translated into Japanese. This revealed to the Japanese public that its government was negotiating a surrender, raising the chances the Japanese military would try to sabotage the peacemaking process. At the meeting, Hirohito said, "I have studied the Allied reply and concluded that it virtually acknowledges the position of our note sent a few days ago. I find it quite acceptable."[52] He had decided Japan would surrender, and he called upon the top military leadership to ensure that all units of the Japanese armed forces would comply. He would personally announce the decision in an unprecedented speech to the nation. Late that night NHK radio technicians recorded the emperor's speech, and an aide hid the phonograph recordings in the palace. The cabinet unanimously voted to accept Hirohito's wish, making Tokyo's capitulation official.

It was a bitter pill for the Japanese army to swallow. The same night, even after their superiors ordered them to respect the cabinet's decision, a group of army officers tried to seize the Imperial Palace and prevent the announcement of surrender. The rebel group's leader, Hatanaka Kenji, tried to persuade General Mori Takeshi, commander of the Imperial Guards, to join in the attempted coup. Failing to gain Mori's assent, Hatanaka shot him to death and stole his seal, which he used to sign a fake order to the Eastern District Army Headquarters to join in the takeover of the Imperial Palace. Hatanaka's coconspirators would have assassinated Kido and Suzuki, but could not locate them. Hatanaka also failed to find the phonographs with the emperor's speech, despite a frantic search of the palace. Although he favored fighting on, Anami did not support the coup. Nor did the troops of the Eastern District Army join the insurrection. The next morning their commander, General Tanaka Shizuichi, came to the palace to scold Hatanaka. Realizing he had failed, the would-be coup leader killed himself. Both Tanaka and Anami did the same a few days later.

Tokyo radio broadcast the emperor's surrender speech the next day. It was the first time most of the Japanese people had ever heard their emperor's voice. A few hundred military men and a smaller number of civilians committed suicide immediately afterward. Hirohito sent members of the imperial family traveling to ensure that Japanese military forces abroad obeyed his order to surrender.

On the same day as the surrender broadcast, one of the first acts of U.S.-Japan reconciliation came in Admiral Nimitz's congratulatory message to his forces, which included this admonition: "the use of insulting epithets in connection with the Japanese as a race or individuals does not now become the officers of the United States Navy."[53]

The Soviets, meanwhile, stepped up their offensives in Northeast Asia after getting word that Tokyo was preparing to surrender. The Yalta agreement had promised Moscow the Kuriles without making a precise delineation. Stalin therefore hastened to occupy all of the islands to preclude future challenges.

Soviet commanders intentionally stalled on establishing local cease-fire agreements so their troops could continue to advance as far as possible before the end of the war. Soviet soldiers were still seizing the last of the Kurile Islands on September 5, three days after the formal surrender ceremony in Tokyo Bay.[54]

AMERICAN OPPOSITION TO THE A-BOMBS

As with the general U.S. public, most people involved with the execution of U.S. policy also went along with using the bomb, but there were a few notable exceptions. It is perhaps not surprising that top U.S. Army and Navy leaders would hate a weapon that created the perception that two aerial bombs won the war. MacArthur reportedly opposed the A-bombings, as did Eisenhower. The latter said after the war that he told Stimson in July 1945, "I was against it on two counts. First, the Japanese were ready to surrender and it wasn't necessary to hit them with that awful thing. Second, I hated to see our country be the first to use such a weapon." Even Admiral William F. Halsey, famous for his slogan "Kill Japs, kill Japs, kill more Japs," called the A-bombings "an unnecessary experiment."[55] Admiral Leahy, military chief of staff under both Roosevelt and Truman, wrote after the war, "It is my opinion that the use of this barbarous weapon at Hiroshima and Nagasaki was of no material assistance in our war against Japan. The Japanese were already defeated and ready to surrender because of the effective sea blockade and the successful bombing with conventional weapons. . . . [I]n being the first to use [the atomic bomb], we had adopted an ethical standard common to the barbarians of the Dark Ages. I was not taught to make war in that fashion, and wars cannot be won by destroying women and children."[56] Although the atomic bomb increased the potential capability of strategic air forces, not all USAAF leaders embraced it. After the A-bombing of Hiroshima, Spaatz wrote in his diary, "I have never favored the destruction of cities as such with all inhabitants being killed."[57] Ralph Bard, Under Secretary of the Navy, wrote in a memo dated June 27, 1945, to Stimson:

I have had a feeling that before the bomb is actually used against Japan that Japan should have some preliminary warning for say two or three days in advance of use. The position of the United States as a great humanitarian nation and the fair play attitude of our people generally is responsible in the main for this feeling. During recent weeks I have also had the feeling very definitely that the Japanese government may be searching for some opportunity which they could use as a medium of surrender. . . . I don't see that we have anything in particular to lose in following such a program.[58]

Some of the civilians involved in research and development of the atomic bomb also voiced objections to using it in combat. Their reasons were pragmatic as well as ethical. Nobel Prize winner James Franck led a commission of scientists that in June 1945 recommended to the U.S. government that the bomb not be used against Japan, but rather demonstrated in an uninhabited area before international observers as a first step toward preventing nuclear proliferation. The Franck Report said the long-term consequences of atomic weaponry should take precedence over the short-term military problem of finishing off Japan. "If the United States would be the first to release this new means of indiscriminate destruction upon mankind," said the report, "she would sacrifice public support throughout the world, precipitate the race of armaments, and prejudice the possibility of reaching an international agreement on the future control of such weapons."[59]

Leo Szilard, chief physicist at the Manhattan Project's metallurgical laboratory in Chicago, and 69 of his scientist colleagues signed a "Petition to the President of the United States" in July 1945. They urged that the president refrain from using the bomb against Japan at least until "the terms which will be imposed upon Japan have been made public in detail and Japan knowing these terms has refused to surrender." Even in that case they called for serious deliberation. The basis of the scientists' opposition was couched in terms of national interest: employing the atomic bomb in warfare would launch a new era in which "the cities of the United States as well as the cities of other nations will be in continuous danger of sudden annihilation."[60] The petition made the dubious implication that if America held its atomic weapons in abeyance, other countries would not develop them. An earlier draft of the Szilard petition, signed by 59 scientists but not submitted to the White House, relied more heavily on a moral argument against using the bomb. "The last few years show a marked tendency toward increasing ruthlessness," it read. "At present our Air Forces, striking at the Japanese cities, are using the same methods of warfare which were condemned by American public opinion only a few years ago when applied by the Germans to the cities of England. Our use of atomic bombs in this war would carry the world a long way further on this path of ruthlessness."[61]

It is important to keep these views in proper perspective. The weight of opinion Truman received from his military and political advisors was decisively in favor of using the atomic bomb to bring additional pressure on Japan to surrender as quickly as possible. Some Americans at the time, nevertheless, worried about the ethical and moral ramifications of the new weapon. These sentiments would, of course, become much more pronounced after the war.

GIFT FROM HEAVEN

The issue of the atomic bombs as a cause of Japan's surrender is highly controversial. Clearly, the two hammer blows of early August, the atomic bomb and the entry of the USSR into the war against Japan, forced the surrender decision. The question of the relative weight of these two factors is important but difficult to answer. Some historians argue that the atomic bomb was decisive in breaking the impasse among Japan's top leaders, providing an additional and completely unanticipated shock.[62] Others maintain that Soviet intervention was enough to compel Tokyo's surrender without the atomic bombs.[63] In his surrender speech, along with the abstract observation that "the war situation has developed not necessarily to Japan's advantage, while the general trends of the world have all turned against her interest," the only specific reason Hirohito mentioned for Japan's capitulation was that "the enemy has begun to employ a new and most cruel bomb, the power of which to do damage is, indeed, incalculable."[64] Another Imperial Rescript, however, written specifically for Japan's armed forces and not released until Aug. 17, mentioned the Soviet intervention—"Now that the Soviet Union has entered the war, to continue under the present conditions at home and abroad would only result in further useless damage and eventually endanger the very foundation of the empire's existence"—but not the atomic bomb.[65]

It appears that much of Japan's military leadership, especially the army, remained committed to continuing the fight despite the blockade and the fearsome destruction caused by conventional bombing. They lost hope only when the Soviet shock definitively foreclosed the possibility of success.[66] Of particular interest to Hirohito and many other Japanese leaders privileged by the imperial political system, the Potsdam Proclamation and other Allied statements left open the possibility of retaining the institution of the emperor, while there would be no such expectation if the Soviets conquered Japan, or even if the Soviets won jurisdiction over part of the home islands in a Korea-type divided administration arrangement.

It is also plausible, however, that the bomb provided a critical jolt that helped move Hirohito to instruct his government to surrender sooner than they otherwise might have. After the war, former high-ranking Japanese officials Kido, Yonai, and Chief Cabinet Secretary Sakomizu Hisatsune said the atomic bombings helped the surrender faction prevail over military leaders who wanted to keep fighting through an Allied invasion. Yonai called the bombs "a gift from heaven," and Sakomizu said "The atomic bomb was a golden opportunity given by heaven for Japan to end the war."[67] The claim should not be overstated. Hirohito appeared to have growing doubts from June onward about the likelihood of Japan successfully staving off an Allied invasion, mainly because of shortages of resources needed to supply Japan's defensive forces.[68] He would likely have moved eventually to end the war even without the atomic bomb. And Japan's leaders were already well accustomed to the vulnerability of their cities to destruction by U.S. bombers before August 6. Nevertheless, we should not dismiss the psychological impact of the realization that the Americans had made a technological advance beyond Japan's reach that enabled them to destroy a whole city with a single bomb. This technology also had implications for areas where the Japanese might concentrate troops and equipment to oppose an anticipated enemy invasion.

Moreover, there is an important domestic political angle. Despite the emperor's profession of concern for the Japanese populace, the terrible bombing raids of early 1945, which slaughtered Japanese people by the tens of thousands and against which Japan had no effective defense, had not moved Hirohito to end the war in July. His motivation to save his people might have been less compelling than his motivation to save himself *from* them. Prince Konoe Fumimaro, a former prime minister and one of Hirohito's senior advisers, had implored the emperor in February 1945 to end the war quickly before communist agitation spread among the disgruntled population and led to an overthrow of the government.[69] If he feared the Japanese people would rebel if forced to suffer the privations of war much longer, but also worried that surrender would dangerously weaken his legitimacy in the eyes of his subjects, the atomic bombs helped ease Hirohito out of the dilemma. As the war ended the emperor was beginning to style himself as a blameless, transcendent figure who was distant from the policies of aggression and exploitation but who heroically interceded at the end out of concern for his people—a persona that would help insulate him from both domestic and international criticism.

TROUBLING QUESTIONS

Why did America use the atomic bomb against Japan? The top American leadership cared a great deal about shortening the war, saving American lives, and meeting the expectations of the U.S. public. They also had humanitarian concerns, but these were a relatively low priority, especially in an atmosphere laden with racial prejudice toward the Japanese and a thirst for revenge for the Pearl Harbor attack and Japanese atrocities. The question of why Truman did not try harder to find a way to end the war without using the atomic bomb, raised countless times in the past six decades, is a characteristically postwar question, divorced from the political context of 1945. Months before the Enola Gay dropped Little Boy, U.S. planners were implementing the practice of carpet bombing against enemy cities. Before Hiroshima, conventional bombing had already visited on several Japanese cities devastation comparable to an atomic bombing. The A-bomb made it possible for one B-29 to do what would ordinarily require several hundred. Without the bomb, however, the USAAF was prepared to continue mounting raids of several hundred B-29s against Japan's remaining cities. On August 14, for example, more than a thousand bombers and fighter escorts flew missions against several Japanese targets without the loss of a single U.S. aircraft. After the war the world came to accept a qualitative distinction between nuclear and conventional weapons and developed a strong psychological and political aversion to using nuclear weapons in battle. But the taboo that would attend any contemplation of the use of nuclear weapons today did not exist for American war-fighters in 1945. They saw the A-bomb as a new tool to fit into their ongoing strategic-bombing campaign. Some Americans perceived atomic weapons as a new form of warfare and questioned the wisdom of introducing it, but the U.S. government spent little time or energy agonizing over whether to use it against the enemy. Truman was not looking for reasons to avoid using the bomb. For the president, as much as for Yonai, the bomb was a gift from heaven, a means of pressuring Tokyo to surrender without the need for an invasion.

Critics have argued that the U.S. government should have made more serious efforts to end the war without resorting to atomic bomb attacks. Washington could have pursued diplomacy more vigorously. Perhaps the unconditional surrender stipulation could have been relaxed enough to make it easier for Japan to capitulate earlier, but without forfeiting the Allies' demand for overthrow of Japan's fascist government and a liberalization of the Japanese political system. Given that the (U.S.-dominated) Allied occupation authority ultimately allowed Hirohito to remain on the throne, perhaps offering Tokyo a clear assurance on this point in June or July would have strengthened the pro-surrender faction (although it seems likely the Soviet declaration of war would still have been an additional necessary condition for Tokyo to sue for peace).

Only one week passed between the promulgation of the Potsdam Proclamation and the first A-bomb attack, giving Japanese leaders little time to reach the conclusion Washington hoped for. The Hiroshima bombing and Soviet entry into the war two days later gave Japanese leaders even more to think about. Many have therefore argued that the second bombing on August 9 was unjustifiable overkill. The counterarguments would be that Washington believed, based on Suzuki's July 28 statement, that Tokyo had already rejected the Potsdam Proclamation and that a second bomb would prevent pro-war Japanese leaders from raising doubts about the American ability to create additional atomic explosions. Truman did order an "atomic pause" after the second bomb (there were two more bombs near completion at the time). And as we have seen, even with the combination of two atomic bombs and the declaration of war by the Soviet Union, the decision to surrender was still extremely controversial among the high officials in Tokyo.

Critics of the atomic bombings have also argued that given the effectiveness of conventional bombing and the blockade of supplies in breaking down Japan's economy, continuing these policies would have been sufficient to force Tokyo to surrender within a few months without either the atomic bombs or an invasion.[70] As noted earlier, however, American national leaders worried that the U.S. public was losing its determination to fight the war to its conclusion (i.e., a removal of the militarist Japanese government that had tried to force Western influence out of Asia). Those who make this argument should also understand the human costs on all sides that would have resulted from continuing the war and waiting for the conventional bombing and the blockade to become intolerable for the Japanese government. Every week the war continued meant further deaths and injuries among Allied servicemen.[71] Allied prisoners of war were struggling for survival in Japanese prison camps; more of them, as well, would have died if the war had lasted longer. Conventional bombing, which had already killed tens of thousands of Japanese citizens, would have continued to kill thousands more through the direct effects of bombing and, increasingly, indirectly through starvation caused by the destruction of transportation infrastructure, against which the USAAF planned to increase its raids beginning in August 1945. Deaths through starvation and conventional bombing throughout Japan would have offset the lives saved in Hiroshima and Nagasaki. We might also consider the impact of a longer war on Japan-occupied Asia. Robert Newman calculates that between 250,000 and 400,000 Asians in countries occupied by Japan were dying every month of the war from direct or indirect effects of Japanese rule, including disease and starvation.[72]

If the U.S. government can be criticized for missing a chance to end the war before August, this same criticism is at least as applicable to Tokyo. Despite the growing sense that the war was lost, Japan did not make a clear attempt to surrender before the atomic bombings, which Tokyo could have and should have done. Japan's best opportunity to do so was immediately after receiving the Potsdam Proclamation. Tokyo should have given a quick and clear affirmative response, even if a conditional one, but did not. By dragging out the war, a policy that rested on unrealistic hopes of Soviet mediation and on the fears of elites that they would lose position or prestige, Japanese leaders showed a criminal lack of concern for the hardships of their civilian population. The detachment and arrogance of the Japanese leadership is captured in the government-approved remarks of a commentator broadcast immediately after the emperor's surrender speech on August 15: "We people who invited a situation where we had no choice but to lay down our arms, were unable to live up to the great benevolence of the emperor, but he did not even scold us. . . . In the face of such great benevolence and love, who could not reflect on his own disloyalty."[73]

The survivors of Hiroshima and Nagasaki would no doubt have found it strange that Truman, as expressed in his diary entry two weeks before the Hiroshima bombing, insisted that "the target will be a purely military one" and that "soldiers and sailors are the target and not women and children."[74] Although there were soldiers billeted in and around Hiroshima, there were far more women and children than soldiers among the victims of the blast. Characterizing the city as a "purely military" target is so patently absurd that it appears more likely Truman's statement was the result of self-deception rather than an attempt to manipulate future assessments of his presidency. Truman's statement is perhaps better understood as an epitome of what Americans thought about their own practice of strategic bombing during World War II. The atomic bombings were the culmination of a gradual American acceptance of urban-dwelling civilians as legitimate military targets, a line of thought that emerged in the European theater and reached full flower in the Pacific theater. This departed from the traditional humanitarianism that Americans see as part of their national culture. What most Americans believed, a belief U.S. officials encouraged, was that the United States took the moral high road and avoided targeting civilians, in contrast to the other major power combatants. The outstanding exception to this policy was the atomic bombing of two Japanese cities, but this was explained as a mercy killing that saved the lives of hundreds of thousands of other Japanese as well as Americans by ending the war without an invasion of the Japanese home islands. America believed itself a country that did not bomb civilians, even as it bombed civilians. Thus the United States dropped warning leaflets on some cities but not on others, spared the cultural treasure house of Kyoto but not the cultural treasure house of Dresden, began the war with precision bombing and finished the war with carpet bombing, and burned up Japanese noncombatants in order to save them. Pushed aside during the heat of battle, the undying embers of this contradiction have troubled Americans ever since.

CHAPTER 7

Regime Change in Korea, Japan, and Taiwan

The Pacific War led directly to the American-supervised installment of new governments and changed political systems in South Korea and Japan, and to the change in Taiwan from a Japanese colonial administration to rule by Chiang Kai-shek's Kuomintang regime. This experience permanently altered the history and development of all three countries, propelling them over new territory they might otherwise have never seen, and fundamentally reordering their relations with other Asia-Pacific states. For Taiwan this was yet another change of course in its historical relationship with China, the end-state of which remains unsettled. Most unfortunately, there was continuity in the exploitative character of both the Japanese administration and the ROC military government. For Japan and Korea, the experience represented a test of the strength and resiliency of established social and political patterns in two very old Asian societies against a foreign-imposed agenda. One could emphasize how *little* the world's most powerful country was able to change them. Nevertheless, that the milieu of Japanese and Koreans profoundly shifted as a result of American intervention is undeniable. The present-day character of Japan and South Korea and the nature of the political issues they face owe much to the impact of their few years of U.S. administration after the war. American values and interests wrestled with local conditions to produce unique syntheses. U.S. occupation policy itself was torn between the traditional advocacy of liberal democracy and the short-term but pressing objective of opposing communist expansion; in practice these two considerations sometimes called for nearly opposite approaches.

KOREANS IN WARTIME

Japanese colonialism gave socioeconomic opportunities to some Koreans, including roles in facilitating or enforcing Japan's exploitation of Korea and other occupied areas. Many of the policemen in Korea and Manchuria were Koreans. Koreans also served in the Japanese armed forces. Park (more properly Pak) Chung-hee, a future South Korean president, was a lieutenant in the Japanese army. Lower-ranking Korean officials rounded up young men and women in their districts for Japanese servitude as laborers or so-called comfort women.

If some Koreans advanced under Japanese administration, for most Koreans the colonial experience was overwhelmingly negative. The Japanese did not introduce injustice to Korea. Historically, Korea was a highly stratified and socioeconomically unbalanced country, with the great majority of its population engaged in agricultural labor and living at or near the subsistence level while a small landlord class amassed most of the wealth. Under Japanese rule, however, the overlords were foreigners who viewed and treated Korea as an inferior nation. The Japanese authorities forced Koreans to take Japanese names, worship at Shinto shrines, and profess devotion to the Japanese emperor. Much of the Korean elite class collaborated with the Japanese administration. Those born in less fortunate circumstances were subject to callous exploitation. About two million Koreans worked in Japan during the war in occupations such as agricultural laborers, miners, and factory and construction workers. Typically, they were conscripted involuntarily, often from among the poor or from politically weak clans. They suffered along with the Japanese people as the war came to Japan. An estimated 20,000 to 30,000 Koreans perished immediately in the atomic bombings of Hiroshima and Nagasaki, with perhaps a comparable number dying later of their wounds or exposure to radiation. The Japanese military's sex-slavery program drew more heavily on Koreans than any other nationality, with Korean comfort women probably numbering well over 100,000.[1] As the war went on the Japanese administration moved from encouraging Koreans to join the Japanese armed forces to making all Koreans of military age subject to conscription. Those who refused to serve in the Japanese military faced deportation for slave labor.

The Japanese occupation thus intensified social and political injustice in Korea by adding new forms of mistreatment to the traditional practices. Colonialism also generated tension between, on the one hand, anti-Japanese activists and the mass of ordinary Koreans who suffered under Japanese rule, and on the other hand Koreans who benefited from collaboration with the Japanese. As historian Bruce Cumings writes, "Japan fractured the Korean national psyche, pitting Korean against Korean with consequences that continue down to our time."[2] Division of postwar Korea into zones of U.S. and Soviet influence would deepen this fracture.

The industrial and infrastructure development the Japanese carried out in Korea laid much of the groundwork for the economic growth later exhibited by North Korea (in the first two postwar decades) and especially by South Korea (from the 1970s onward). In the immediate aftermath of the war, however, Korea faced economic disruption. The Japanese had not only made Korea's economy an adjunct of Japan's, they had placed most of Korea's heavy industry in the north while emphasizing the development of agriculture and light industry in the south. Upon their surrender, Japanese forces attempted to destroy some of the industrial infrastructure they had built in northern Korea by flooding mines and sabotaging factories.[3] More seriously, the division of Korea broke the previous synergy by isolating the northern and southern economies from Japan and from each other, contributing to economic stress that would worsen the political instability in the postcolonial south.

PLANS OF THE BIG POWERS

The Cairo Declaration, signed by Roosevelt, Churchill, and Chiang in November 1943, said "Japan will also be expelled from all other territories which she has taken by violence and greed. The aforesaid three great powers, mindful of the enslavement of the people of Korea, are determined that in due course Korea shall become free and independent." This came as a blow to the Koreans, who wished for *immediate* independence. Roosevelt proposed a joint trusteeship of postwar Korea, involving both the U.S. and Soviet governments, leading to eventual independence for Korea. In his discussions with Stalin, Roosevelt said he expected the period of trusteeship over Korea to last 20 to 40 years.[4]

On the night of August 10/11, 1945, a committee designed to coordinate the plans of the State Department and the U.S. military services was hurriedly making plans for taking the surrenders of Japanese troops in Korea and other parts of Asia. A longer-term consideration of the planners was the objective of maximizing postwar American influence vis-à-vis the Soviets, who had already started fighting the Japanese in Korea and occupying Korean territory. The head of the committee gave an assignment to two U.S. Army colonels. One was Dean Rusk, future U.S. Secretary of State under Presidents Kennedy and Johnson. The other was Charles H. Bonesteel, who later became a general and commander of United States Forces in Korea. Rusk and Bonesteel were to select a place to divide Korea into a northern zone, where the Soviets would disarm surrendered Japanese forces, and a southern zone, where the Americans would take this responsibility. Looking at a map, they chose the 38th Parallel. Rusk said later their reasoning was that they wanted the capital of Seoul included in the U.S. zone, but feared the Soviets would not agree if the Americans tried to set the line much further north, knowing there were few U.S. troops available to cover so much Korean territory.[5] Rusk and Bonesteel did not consult Koreans or base their decision on a knowledge of Korean history or culture. The Soviets accepted the proposal, and although it was not the American intention in August 1945, this line became a permanent boundary between two rival states.

THE AMERICAN OCCUPATION IN SOUTH KOREA

With the collapse of Japanese authority, People's Committees sprang up throughout Korea. Yeo Un-hyeong (Lyuh Woon-Hyung), editor of the

Choongang Ilbo newspaper, was one of the Korean leaders who moved to fill the political vacuum. Primarily a Korean nationalist with a Christian background and impeccable anti-Japanese credentials, Yeo was primarily interested in national unification and social justice and was willing to work with both communists and right-wing organizations. He formed the Committee for the Preparation of Korean Independence, to which the Japanese Governor General transferred authority upon Japan's surrender. In September 1945 he announced a new government, the Korean People's Republic, within which he served as vice-premier. A separate organization, the China-based Korean Provisional Government (in exile in China), also claimed the right to govern Korea. An exiled, U.S.-educated Korean nationalist named Syngman Rhee (Yi Seung-man) had led this Provisional Government (until forced out under accusations of embezzlement) and also served as its unofficial representative to the United States, where he became well known as an activist for Korean independence.

American military forces entered a land hungry for independence from foreign rule, a more equitable distribution of wealth and opportunities (including land reform), and a purging of the vestiges of colonialism and collaboration. Two governments vied for recognition, and politics in the south were tumultuous and sometimes violent, with passionate and seemingly irreconcilable positions taken by the far left, moderate left, moderate right and far right.

The Americans were ill-prepared to sort all this out. As a first step to finding their feet, they dismantled the People's Committees, outlawed the Korean People's Republic, and allowed officers of the Provisional Government to enter the country only as private citizens. Forced to resign, Yeo remained active in politics. In the meantime the U.S. military put American officers in local government positions and kept many Japanese officials at their posts into 1946. This hardly addressed Korean demands for change.

The former Allied powers refined their plans for a self-governing, reunified Korea in a December 1945 conference in Moscow. Soviet, U.S., and British representatives envisaged a four-power trusteeship (with China as the fourth) over Korea that would last up to five years. This proposal met with massive and nearly universal disapproval in Korea, expressed in demonstrations throughout the country and strikes by Korean employees of the U.S. military government.[6]

The commander of the American military government, Philippines and Okinawa campaign veteran Gen. John Reed Hodge, quickly discovered a "growing resentment against all Americans. . . . The word pro-American is being added to pro-Jap, national traitor, and collaborator. . . . The Koreans want their independence more than any one thing and want it now. . . . The situation in Korea makes it extremely fertile ground for establishment of Communism. In my opinion Koreans do not want Communism, but the unsettled conditions, the lack of clear cut policies for the future and lack of hope for early national sovereignty by the people may easily push those in US zone to radical leftism, if not raw Communism."[7] Hodge determined that without intervention to the contrary, a leftist revolutionary government would take hold in Korea, which to the Americans meant Korea would become a Soviet satellite state. To prevent southern Korea from going communist, the Americans backed a faction of conservatives to become the new political elites of postwar (as it turned out, South) Korea. By so doing the U.S. authorities put themselves in the position of opposing reforms that, based on American values, most Americans would have considered desirable. At MacArthur's order, the U.S. government flew in Rhee. Although he was 70 years old and had lived outside of Korea since 1912, Rhee had the support of Chiang Kai-shek and some high-level U.S. officials. Unlike many other prominent Korean conservatives, as a consequence of his long exile Rhee was not tainted with Japanese collaboration. The American authorities retained most of the police force that had worked for the Japanese colonial administration. Aligned with the American-empowered conservatives, these police and private right-wing groups carried out a reign of terror against their political enemies. Rhee had tens of thousands imprisoned for political offenses.[8] Hodge and Rhee came to hate each other. Hodge compared Rhee to Chicago gangster Al Capone.[9] Rhee became another Chiang for the Americans, a "friendly dictator" needed as a strategic bulwark but exasperatingly truculent and embarrassingly despotic.

For many Koreans this was too much. In 1947 U.S. officials noted that most Koreans in the southern zone believed they were better off under Japanese than under U.S. occupation.[10] A huge strike by railway workers in September 1946 grew to 300,000 as other groups joined to demonstrate for unification and against what they called continued colonialism. Major rebellions broke out on Cheju island and in the port city of Yeosu in 1948, brutally suppressed by Korean military and police forces with U.S. support. Perhaps 30,000 died in Cheju and 3,000 in Yeosu.[11] A substantial guerrilla warfare campaign, fueled mostly by the grievances of southern Koreans rather than by agitation from the north, troubled the south from 1948 until the outbreak of the Korean War in June 1950. American authorities recognized that the guerrilla war in the south was primarily motivated by southern Koreans' dissatisfaction with the Rhee regime and with the policies of the military occupation.[12]

Hodge tried unsuccessfully to rally national support behind a coalition of the moderate left, represented by Yeo, and the moderate right, represented by former Korean Provisional Government Vice-Premier Kim Kyu-shik. Yeo displeased extremists on both the right and left, and in 1947 a young right-wing activist assassinated him. Kim lacked popular appeal and opposed the trusteeship that was official U.S. policy.

That trusteeship, in fact, was in jeopardy due to an international lack of consensus paralleling the disunity within southern Korea. U.S.-Soviet coordination talks in 1946 and 1947 foundered in the issue of whether groups that opposed trusteeship should be excluded from the interim government. The Soviets favored allowing the participation only of groups that supported trusteeship, among whom were Korean communist organizations. The Americans held that nonsupportive groups should also be eligible, fearing that this was the only way to prevent leftist organizations from dominating the new government. The U.S. and Soviet sides eventually agreed to exclude groups that actively opposed the trusteeship plan.

The Truman administration was never enthusiastic about implementing Roosevelt's vision of a Soviet-American partnership in managing the post-war world. In September 1947 the U.S. government abandoned the Moscow agreements and took the issue of organizing a unified Korean government to the United Nations. In November, against Soviet objections, the UN passed a resolution authorizing a Temporary Commission on Korea (UNTCOK) to administer elections for a Korean government to replace military government. The Soviets refused to cooperate with UNTCOK. UNTCOK went ahead with elections in the southern zone in May and July 1948. These elections selected southern representatives for a National Assembly, leaving vacant seats reserved for representatives from the north. With most of his opponents boycotting the polls, Syngman Rhee was elected president. Later in the year the UN and the United States recognized the government of the Republic of Korea in the south. Except for a few hundred advisors, the U.S. military left the south in mid-1949.

EMERGENCE OF THE KIM REGIME IN THE NORTH

In contrast to the American approach of military government by occupa-tion forces in the south, the Soviets initially worked through the preexistent people's committees in the north. Under relatively low-profile Soviet control, a Provisional People's Committee for North Korea gave way to a Korean People's Committee of North Korea in February 1947. By this time a peace-ful North-South political integration in the near-term was probably impos-sible. The Soviet authorities supported the ascendancy of 33-year-old Kim Il Sung, a recently returned veteran of anti-Japanese guerrilla warfare in Man-churia who had also received Soviet training and the rank of major from the Red Army. With the backing of the Soviets and his former comrades in arms, Kim rose to preeminence in the north, aided by purges and assassinations of his rivals. In contrast to the southern zone, Kim carried out a social revolu-tion. Kim did better than Rhee in meeting Korean demands for land reform, autonomy from the great powers, and uprooting the vestiges of the Japanese colonial system. Kim nationalized industries in the north. The land reform program stripped landlords of their holdings without compensation. It was extremely popular, going a long way toward satisfying a centuries-old desire among the majority of the population by making the peasants masters of the land they worked. Kim's regime enacted other laws to protect the rights of workers and also mandated the equal treatment of women and the abolition of polygamy. Although the Soviets played an important role in shaping the northern zone's new political system and provided substantial economic and military assistance, Rhee was more dependent than Kim on the support of his superpower sponsor for the survival of his government.

While the southern zone was diligently eliminating leftists and consolidating the power of the traditional land-owning (and largely collaborationist) elites, the Soviet-controlled northern zone was working just as hard to purge nonleftists, landlords and collaborators. An estimated 400,000 landlords and others disadvantaged under the new regime in the north fled to the south. The north moved toward totalitarianism, with virtually the entire populace affiliated with one or another state-controlled organization and regularly under surveillance by a massive internal security apparatus. A zealous commitment to rooting out dissent and disloyalty would make Kim's regime notorious for its harsh and large-scale program of punishment for political offenses.

In September 1948 the north announced the establishment of the Democratic People's Republic of Korea, with Kim Il Sung as premier, and at the end of the year the Soviets withdrew their forces.

WHALES CONSTRAIN THE SHRIMP'S MOVEMENTS

Its colonial occupier of 40 years finally gone, Korea had the misfortune of passing from liberation immediately into the context of a zero-sum game between the superpowers. The United States and the Soviet Union had opposing objectives for and interests in Korea. Their own perceived national security interests were the main determinants of both the American and Soviet occupation policies in Korea. In siding with the conservatives in the south, the United States snuffed out the chances of political liberalization in the near term, although one could argue that the denial of southern Korea to a communist government made democratization possible a generation later, while the north continued to wallow in the most miserable political and economic circumstances. It is certainly possible that left on their own, the Koreans would have achieved a better outcome from their standpoint—a united country, with something like the democracy and prosperity of today's South Korea, but without having suffered the terrible and inconclusive war.

Korea was a revolutionary tinderbox at the end of the Japanese occupation because much of the Korean resentment of Japanese colonialism carried over into demands for a restructuring of the traditional arrangement of a small class of elites hoarding power, privilege and wealth at the expense of a poor and excluded majority. The division of Korea into U.S.- and Soviet-administered zones dramatically skewed Korea's development and modern history. Top-down revolutions of a sort did indeed occur in both halves of Korea, but their agenda went in nearly opposite directions. Most significantly, the rival occupations left Korea with two irreconcilable governments, setting up the Korean War, which broke out shortly after U.S. and Soviet troops withdrew. Adding to the instability, the leaders of each of these entities were both anxious to reunify Korea by extinguishing the rival regime.

JAPAN: RECOVERY, RESTRUCTURING, AND REVERSAL

As with the Koreans, the transition from wartime to peacetime was neither quick nor clean for the Japanese. The hardships that developed in the latter part of the war due to the destruction of economic infrastructure and the reduced inflow of supplies from overseas would continue for months to come. As marooned Japanese soldiers went hungry on isolated Pacific islands, demobilized soldiers now appeared on city streets as panhandlers. Large numbers of Japanese were homeless and destitute. In the bigger cities people were starving to death by the hundreds. More than five million Japanese nationals gradually returned from parts of the former Japanese empire, increasing the strain on scarce resources. For many former soldiers, the journey home to civilian life took longer. Both Nationalist and communist forces employed tens of thousands of surrendered Japanese in China for several years after the war. The Americans, British and Dutch did the same with disarmed Japanese soldiers-turned-laborers in various parts of Asia and the Pacific.[13] In violation of the Potsdam Proclamation, which promised that "the Japanese military forces, after being completely disarmed, shall be permitted to return to their homes with the opportunity to lead peaceful and productive lives," the Soviets consigned over 600,000 Japanese prisoners of war to forced labor on projects in Siberia and the Russian Far East.[14]

JAPAN'S AMERICAN MOMENT

MacArthur was Supreme Commander of the Allied Powers (SCAP), the supervisor of the occupation forces. Although representatives from other Allied countries had formal advisory roles and token British and Australian units served in Hiroshima, the United States dominated the "Allied" occupation of Japan. Stalin asked for Soviet representation in the administration of postwar Japan and for American assent to a Soviet occupation zone in the northern part of Hokkaido. The U.S. government rejected both suggestions. In retrospect, American firmness on the latter point clearly spared Japan from becoming another divided postwar state. The United States acquiesced, however, to Soviet possession of all of the Kuriles and to Soviet refusal of any U.S. basing rights in the islands.

MacArthur's official role and the historical circumstances, including an extraordinarily receptive and cooperative host nation, gave him and his staff immense governing powers. MacArthur was in effect the new emperor, and many Japanese gave him similar veneration. Not one to understate the importance of himself or his work, MacArthur often used grandiloquent language, including phrases and ideas from Christianity, when discussing his objectives for Japan. MacArthur said publicly that Japan's "punishment for her sins, which is just beginning, will be long and bitter."[15] Many Japanese were nonetheless relieved to find, contrary to their expectations, that the Americans were not bent on vengeance or unmitigated brutality.

U.S. forces began arriving in Japan in numbers two weeks after Hirohito's surrender announcement. MacArthur's headquarters in Tokyo employed about 3,000 U.S. administrators, a mix of military and civilians. The occupation authorities enjoyed, at Japanese government expense, a colonial expatriate lifestyle of upscale homes, servants, and facilities from which locals were excluded. SCAP intentionally avoiding recruiting Japan hands for important policymaking posts in the occupation government, believing they would be biased toward preserving rather than changing Japanese culture and politics.

The American occupation was attempting something historically unprecedented: a thorough restructuring of Japan's political, economic and education systems and a transformation of public attitudes in a conquered country by a victorious foreign power. The SCAP staff's work was paradoxical. Initially their principal objective was political liberalization, and their agenda for achieving it was more radical than the democracy being practiced in the United States at the time. Yet this democratization, including civil liberties such as freedom of expression, was imposed by a military government that strictly forbade even implicit criticism of the U.S. authorities or their policies. American occupation authorities dictated that what the Japanese had called the Greater East Asia War (*Dai Toa Senso*) be called the Pacific War (*Taiheiyo Senso*). They advised the Japanese media on what themes and ideas their articles, broadcasts and films should promote. The press did not report rapes or assaults involving occupation forces and kept secret the huge occupation costs covered by the Japanese government.[16] In 1946 a U.S. military film crew shot color footage of the wounded and maimed survivors of the atomic bombings in Hiroshima and Nagasaki. The U.S. government quickly classified the film top secret, forbidding public access for three decades.[17]

The American premise was that the causes of Japan's war of aggression were deeply rooted in Japanese institutions and attitudes. These therefore required liberalization. The Americans sent outreach teams to teach democratic practice and civic responsibility to communities throughout Japan. They also imposed a wide swath of reforms. Of necessity the Americans governed Japan through the extant bureaucracy, which they directed through a combination of threats and persuasion. The U.S. authorities instituted new civil and human rights. They redistributed land previously concentrated within a small landlord class. They decentralized the police force and gave local governments more powers relative to the central government. The 1945 Trade Union Law gave workers the unprecedented rights to organize, strike, and bargain collectively. A Labor Standards Law in 1947 guaranteed acceptable working conditions. They liberalized the education curriculum, previously a vehicle for instilling jingoism. The occupation government increased rights for women, giving them the rights to own property and to hold government positions, decriminalizing adultery (previously a crime for women but not for men), and outlawing the practice of contract marriage, under which many Japanese wives had lived like serfs. The Americans ordered the separation of the state and religion, which meant an end to the traditional government recognition of Shinto as the national religion. Initially, reviving Japan as an economic power was not a high priority of the U.S. occupation authorities. Their interest in democratization led them to mandate the breakup of Japan's *zaibatsu* (industrial and banking conglomerates). The public response to democratization was largely positive. Some observers of this period saw the Japanese welcoming a liberalization they had come to thirst for after the oppression of the war years; others saw them following the well-entrenched habit of obeying the authorities of the day, even if the orders had changed. Among the less enthusiastic were Japanese conservatives; their main goals were preserving social stability, retaining the traditional relationship between the emperor and the Japanese people, and reviving the economy. They argued that removal of the militarist clique was sufficient to cure Japan of proneness to aggression.

In the matter of the emperor, however, U.S. policy was conservative rather than reformist. A strong case could be made that Hirohito was a Class A war criminal, or that at minimum he deserved to lose his political position. Even the Imperial Palace suggested to SCAP that Hirohito abdicate. MacArthur immediately rejected the offer. The American administrators had decided that prosecuting or even dethroning the emperor would so enflame the Japanese public as to seriously threaten the work of the occupation, which required local cooperation to achieve success. Furthermore, SCAP determined that Hirohito recast as a supporter of democratization and antimilitarism could help give the American project legitimacy. The American authorities thus became partners in protecting Hirohito from blame or punishment for the war.

Anticipating the problem of widespread rapes of Japanese women by the occupation forces, the Japanese government established a nationwide network of brothels under the auspices of the Recreation and Amusement Association (RAA). The idea was to sacrifice a small number of Japanese women to protect the rest. On August 18, 1945, the Home Ministry instructed the police to prepare facilities and mobilize workers for "comfort stations." The government provided partial funding. Initial recruitment efforts tapped the preexistent sex industry. When the supply of professional prostitutes and geishas proved insufficient, the RAA took in other young women, such as the high school students who had been mobilized to work in armaments factories during the war. Managers also addressed open recruitment advertisements to ordinary women. The Tokyo RAA opened with a stated commitment to "build a breakwater to hold back the raging waves and defend and nurture the purity of our race. . . . [W]e are but offering ourselves for the defense of the national polity."[18] By the end of August, over 1,300 women had signed up for duty in Tokyo alone. By the end of 1945 the RAA had recruited 20,000 Japanese women. The number rose to 70,000, working in hundreds of brothels throughout the country.[19] The price of one session was one dollar, about half the cost of a pack of cigarettes in Japan. In January 1946 the U.S. authorities banned open prostitution. Publicly the reason was concern for women's rights, but unofficially SCAP blamed the RAA for high rates of venereal disease among the occupation troops.[20]

CONSTITUTION AND CONTROVERSIAL TRIALS

One of the occupation's most important events was the promulgation of a new Japanese constitution. A Japanese government commission's attempt to revise the 1889 Prussian-inspired Meiji Constitution disappointed both SCAP and the Japanese public. The commission made few changes and seemed mainly concerned with maintaining the status quo. MacArthur ordered his staff to write a new constitution and gave them only a week to do it. The task fell to 24 American men and women. They represented the range of American political views and abundant legal and administrative experience, but only one was knowledgeable about Japan. Finishing quickly as ordered, they presented their draft constitution, written in English, to the Japanese government's constitutional commission as a fait accompli. The commission requested revising the section on the legislature to make it bicameral rather than unicameral. The Americans agreed, provided members of both houses were popularly elected. In March 1946 the Japanese government, the ostensible author, submitted the revised draft to Diet.

Article 9, the passage prescribing disarmament, was controversial. Some Diet members pointed out that it appeared to deny Japan an armed capacity to defend itself against an aggressor, an inherent right of every country. Ashida Hitoshi, chairman of the House of Representatives' subcommittee on constitutional revision, crafted a solution. The first paragraph opens with added verbage—"Aspiring sincerely to an international peace based on justice and order"—linked to the renunciation of using force. Additional new wording in the second paragraph says it is "to accomplish the aim of the preceding paragraph" that Japan will not maintain military forces. Ashida reasoned that these changes implied Japan renounced maintaining arms for a policy of aggression (which would be inconsistent with a sincere aspiration to international peace), but permitted the country to keep the armaments necessary for legitimate self-defense. SCAP accepted the Ashida revision.[21]

Most of the other revisions recommended by the Diet were minor, and in all but a few cases SCAP permitted them. All the major political parties except the Japan Communist Party (which had also opposed the war) endorsed the new constitution. It passed both Diet houses by an overwhelming majority. It went into effect in May 1947.

Several Allied countries held war crimes tribunals. The Dutch, British, Australians and Chinese each executed more Japanese war criminals than did the United States, which put to death 140. The Soviets executed as many as 3,000, mostly summarily and in secret.[22] The highest-profile of these courts was the Tokyo War Crimes Tribunal (also known as the International Military Tribunal for the Far East), presided over by 11 judges, one from each of the Allied countries involved in the Pacific War. This tribunal lasted from May 1946 to

November 1948, three times the duration of the Nuremberg Tribunal. Of the 28 defendants, 7 were executed, 16 sentenced to life in prison, and 2 to shorter terms. Five died in prison, but the others were released between 1950 and 1958. Although the defendants had legal counsel, critics of the trials say the proceedings were biased in favor of the prosecution. The Tribunal also declined to indict Emperor Hirohito, who at minimum was one of a handful of top wartime Japanese leaders and who arguably could have weighed in decisively on any major policy question during the Pacific War. Both prosecutors and defendants had an interest in deflecting responsibility from the emperor— the prosecution because U.S. officials wanted to co-opt him in their project to reshape Japan, and the defendants because they saw protecting the emperor as their duty. This left more culpability to be borne by his subordinates. The Indian judge Radhabinod Pal was something of a maverick on the bench. He acknowledged that Japanese forces had committed war crimes (a part of Pal's position that present-day Japanese nationalists usually overlook), but questioned the legitimacy of the Tribunal, describing it as an exercise in revenge. Pal said the entire category of Class A war crimes, "crimes against the peace and humanity," was unnecessary and constituted an ex-post-facto law. Pal held that Japan could not be blamed any more than the Western imperialist powers for the war, that the American use of atomic bombs on Japan was comparable to the war crimes of which Japan was accused, and that he favored acquittal of all the Japanese defendants.

IMPACT OF THE COLD WAR

At the risk of oversimplification, the occupation period may be divided into an early phase, during which the main U.S. objective was democratization, and a latter phase, during which the driving interest was strengthening Japan as an American ally in the Cold War. Tensions and latent rivalry with the Soviets were present even before the end of the Pacific War, but in 1947–1948 they came to dominate U.S. foreign policy, framing U.S. activities throughout the globe including plans for postwar Japan. The Americans worried not only about Soviet pressure, but also about the sluggishness of the Japanese economic recovery. Poverty, U.S. officials feared, was a breeding ground for communist agitation. The official change in priorities was discernible from a high-level October 1948 National Security Council memo regarding the U.S. occupation. It made several recommendations "in view of the serious international situation created by the Soviet Union's policy of aggressive expansion." The United States should prepare for the retention of military bases in Japan and expand the national police force, the memo said. The purge of Japanese militarists should be wound up and purged former officials who "held relatively harmless positions" could return to eligibility to hold public office. And Japanese economic recovery should rise to a priority second only to preserving U.S. security interests.[23] The authorities discontinued dismantling of the zaibatsu and relaxed antimonopoly rules. The Diet passed laws in 1949 and 1950 that strengthened state control over the economy, including the creation of a powerful Ministry of International Trade and Industry that would play a large role in Japan's postwar economic success. Politically, the new agenda favored the conservatives, while the space allowed to leftists narrowed. Some Japanese officials purged for their close association with the wartime government were rehabilitated. Among these was Kishi Nobusuke, a cabinet minister during the war who was imprisoned as a suspected Class A war criminal but never went to trial. Released in 1948, he became prime minister in 1957.

The outbreak of the Korean War in June 1950 affected Japan in two important ways. First, it solidified the American commitment to rearming Japan. A Japanese army, euphemistically called the "National Police Reserve," was reestablished in July 1950. The Americans, authors of the constitution that forbade Japan from maintaining armed forces, had changed their thinking on disarmament so drastically that Prime Minister Yoshida Shigeru had to moderate their demands. U.S. officials wanted a Japanese "police" force numbering up to 350,000, but Yoshida held the level at 75,000.[24] A second important consequence of the Korean War was that it provided massive stimulation to Japanese industry, jump-starting Japan's emergence as an economic great power. The United States not only relied heavily on Japan for supplies of war materiel, but also shared technology and managerial and production techniques with the Japanese. This is what Yoshida meant when he called the Korean War "a gift from the gods."[25]

To be sure, the Cold War partnership with the United States also entailed significant costs for Japan. The political left's goal of disarmament and neutrality was irretrievably lost. Even the conservatives who favored the alliance with the United States were nonetheless dismayed at the high cost of host nation support and the large number of bases the Americans expected Japan to provide. The necessity of conforming to the U.S. policy of containing the PRC disappointed members of the Japanese business community who were counting on trade with China.

The U.S. occupation of Japan lasted nearly seven years, from August 1945 to April 1952. It began with a commitment to democratization and demilitarization that made the Americans adversaries of the Japanese conservatives. Postwar Japan saw significant and lasting changes, including land reform, civil liberties, rights for organized labor, abolition of the powerful Home Ministry and national police force, and widespread antimilitarism.[26] The occupation ended, however, with the American authorities having "reversed course" and partnering with the conservatives to support zaibatsu capitalism, the monarchy, a strong state bureaucracy, remilitarization, and hostility toward the political left. The sum of U.S. efforts was to exacerbate a struggle between the left and right. In ultimately supporting the hold of conservatives on elected offices and the bureaucracy, the Americans allowed considerable carry-over in Japanese political practice from the war years to the postwar period. Yet the importance of the political liberalization shepherded by the American occupation, including the changes in the education system that gave voice to a left-leaning agenda, is undeniable. Although institutionally democratized, Japan was ideologically fractured. Conservatives honored the values and aims of the war era, while progressives embraced a liberal or even radical agenda, some going as far as denouncing the monarchy or calling for accommodation with Maoist China.

CHINESE RULE RETURNS TO TAIWAN—DISASTROUSLY

After China lost the Sino-Japanese War, the Chinese government agreed in the May 1895 Treaty of Shimonoseki to permanently cede control of Taiwan to the Japanese. China's Qing Dynasty government had ruled the Chinese-settled areas of Taiwan since 1683, but Taiwan was a province of China only for the last 10 years before the handover to the Japanese. Mainland officials fled the island amidst the anger and resentment of Chinese residents. The Taiwanese tried to declare independence before the arrival of the Japanese and mounted many uprisings afterward, but they gradually shifted toward working within the Japanese-run political system for greater Taiwanese rights and autonomy. While the principal goal of the Japanese authorities was to orient Taiwan toward serving the needs of the Japanese economy, and while the status and opportunities of Taiwanese were inferior to those of Japanese expatriates, the island and many of its people enjoyed benefits from association with Asia's most modern country, including economic development and improvements in sanitation, infrastructure and public order. Taiwan's standard of living surpassed that of any province on the Chinese mainland. The Japanese colonial experience fostered the emergence of Taiwanese nationalism, overcoming much of the communalism that had previously divided various groups of Chinese on Taiwan. Equally importantly, Taiwan's people believed their struggle for rights under the Japanese occupation, often at great personal risk or sacrifice, had lifted them to a standard of political development above that of their mainland cousins. While they generally welcomed the return of mainland Chinese rule after Japan's defeat, the Taiwanese expected Chiang Kai-shek's government to accommodate their relatively high levels of education and political maturity.

If anything, however, mainland Chinese troops and officials were inclined to look down on Taiwan. Mainlanders already tended to view the Taiwanese as semiferal Chinese whose ancestors had unfathomably chosen to leave the center of civilization to live in barbarian territory. Furthermore, the Chinese were well aware that the Japanese had tried to brainwash the Taiwanese to think of themselves as subjects of the Japanese emperor rather than members of the Chinese nation. It was easy for mainlanders to see the Taiwanese as collaborators who had sat out the war in relative comfort and even helped the Japanese in their war effort (more than 80,000 Taiwanese served as soldiers or sailors in the Japanese armed forces, and another 126,000 as civilian employees of the

Japanese military).[27] This while the mainland had suffered terribly under the Japanese invasion and still faced the final chapter in the Chinese Civil War.

Many Taiwanese were shocked at the appearance and behavior of the ROC troops that began landing on Taiwan in October 1945. These soldiers generally came from the countryside of provinces much poorer than Taiwan. They were uneducated, unhygienic, poorly disciplined, and bewildered by much of the modern technology they saw on Taiwan. They continued on Taiwan their standard practice of finding sustenance by stealing or looting what they needed from the local community. A foreign diplomat noted that the soldiers "had overrun schools, temples and hospitals at Taipei" and that "Any building occupied by KMT troops becomes a mere shell." A major hospital, for example, was "stripped of its equipment and all metal fixtures, including doorknobs. Many of the wooden doors, door-frames and stair banisters were used by the soldiers to feed cooking fires built on the concrete floors."[28] The usual locust-like behavior of the common KMT soldiery was compounded by the attitude of their officers that the time had come for Taiwan to contribute its resources to the rebuilding of the mainland. Some officers organized large-scale carpet-bagging operations using captured Japanese trucks to clean out buildings and private homes and transport the goods to the docks for shipment to the mainland. This practice started with Japanese-owned houses but spread to those owned by Taiwanese. Taiwan's people expected the new ROC government would help them reclaim property taken by the Japanese colonialists. Instead, the incoming administration confiscated this property as war booty. The newly arrived authorities also dismantled industry and infrastructure and shipped it to China, from whole factories to small items such as pieces of pipe and wire. Some of this resource transfer was official policy, but many of the KMT officials involved took the opportunity to enrich themselves by keeping what they seized or arranging for it to be sold off in Shanghai. From the standpoint of the Taiwanese, what was clear was that the new Chinese administration was mostly interested in extracting the island's wealth.

The political development of Taiwan's people got as little respect from the ROC leadership as their property rights. Instead of organizing a provincial government on Taiwan, Chiang put the island under a military government, an arrangement typically implemented in conquered enemy territory. The first governor-general was Chen Yi, who ironically could be classed as a Japanese collaborator because of his strong ties to Japan and cooperation with Japanese authorities during the war on the mainland. Chen presided over an administration that was demonstrably corrupt and ineffective. Mainlanders dominated the high-ranking positions in government, business and education and earned higher salaries than their Taiwanese counterparts. These mainlanders in turn frequently hired their friends and relatives to staff positions under their purview. The government's rationale was that elite posts required fluent Mandarin speakers (Taiwanese spoke a different Chinese dialect) who were not tainted by

Japanese collaboration. Chen favored a heavily state-controlled economy over the free market. Government monopolies regulated most major goods and services. These created ample opportunities for mainland officials to reap illicit profits through the manipulation of price and availability, diversion of supplies to the black market, and the sale of licenses. The crime rate soared and public health plummeted relative to the Japanese colonial period. A precipitous fall in rice production combined with excessive shipments of rice to the mainland created food shortages.

Taiwanese were soon comparing the new ROC administration unfavorably to the former Japanese colonial government. A common local aphorism of the time was "Dogs go and pigs come." The Japanese were like watchdogs: frightening, but at least they kept order. The mainlander authorities, on the other hand, provided no such service while voraciously consuming Taiwanese property. By 1947 Taiwanese resentment toward the authorities from the mainland was so deep that a small incident could trigger a spontaneous insurrection. That incident occurred on February 27, when two officers from the Monopoly Bureau confronted a widow selling cigarettes in a Taipei park. They seized her supplies and cash, and one of the officers struck her with his pistol. A crowd sympathetic to the woman gathered and menaced the officers. They shot a bystander and escaped. Demonstrations sprang up the next day, giving the episode and its aftermath the name "2-2-8 Incident" (for February 28). Word spread and more Taiwanese took to the streets, attacking mainlanders and government buildings. Government security forces on Taiwan, reduced to a minimum as the fight against the communists in China absorbed manpower, could not hold off the crowds. Taiwanese townspeople took over the island's nine largest cities, with local communities forming committees to carry out the basic functions of government. The strength of the uprising forced Chen to open negotiations with a hastily organized committee of prominent Taiwanese. They demanded not only punishment of the Monopoly Bureau men and other offending officials, but also civil liberties, economic reforms, and more autonomy for Taiwan within the ROC political structure. On the mainland, Chiang saw the uprising as a betrayal from within during a national emergency (the armed struggle between KMT and CCP forces). He dispatched troops and police to reassert central government authority on Taiwan. These reinforcements arrived during the second week of March and immediately began a violent and often indiscriminate crackdown, involving not only random shootings but also rape, robbery and looting. Within days these forces put down the uprising, but they continued to hunt down and execute (often summarily) Taiwanese intelligentsia and suspected political activists. Those who had criticized the authorities, volunteered public service during the hiatus of ROC governance, or previously crossed a government official were particularly at risk, but many of the victims were unfortunate bystanders.[29] Estimates of the number of Taiwanese killed during the 2-2-8 Incident range from 8,000 to over 20,000. The extent of the retribution was initially suppressed and not thoroughly investigated by the Taiwan government until 1995, after political liberalization and under the presidency of Lee Teng-hui, who was of Taiwanese ancestry. The 2–2-8 Incident remains a touchstone of Taiwanese resentment against mainlander rule, which reinforces resistance against unification with China.

What followed was four decades of authoritarian governance under a single-party Leninist system. Defeated on the mainland, the entire ROC central government relocated to Taiwan in 1949. Chiang Kai-shek forced on the majority Taiwanese population his vision of Taiwan as a staging area for the recapture of the mainland, suppressing dissent (often brutally) through a massive public security apparatus led by his son and future successor Chiang Ching-kuo. Fortunately for Taiwan the economic picture was less bleak. A successful land reform program in the 1950s greatly improved the standard of living for Taiwan's farmers. Later an export-led economic development strategy resulted in rapid growth, kept Taiwan more prosperous than the tumultuous mainland, and set the stage for eventual democratization.

The end of the Pacific War thrust upon Taiwan a change of government that initially proved disastrous and left a deep scar on Taiwan's ethnically divided society (if Taiwanese and mainlanders can be considered distinct ethnic groups, which is controversial). The mainland and Taiwan had diverged greatly during the period of Japanese occupation, which spanned from the premodern to the modern era in China and kept Taiwan isolated from the 1911 Revolution, rule by warlords, Chiang's Northern Expedition to nominally unify China, the early rounds of the Chinese Civil War, and the terrible ordeal of the Japanese invasion. Taiwan meanwhile became more developed, both economically and politically, and more cosmopolitan. The expectations that mainlanders and Taiwanese had of each other upon their reunion in 1945 were impossible to meet. This is not to justify the poor governance displayed by the newly arrived ROC authorities, which fit a pattern that contributed to their failure on the mainland.

There were echoes of the Pacific War in Taiwan's external environment during the Cold War. As we have seen, the Japanese invasion contributed to the Chinese Communist Party forces' ultimate victory on the mainland. That outcome left Chiang Kai-shek virtually abandoned by the Americans, who were frustrated over his perceived intransigence, and awaiting the PRC invasion of his last stronghold on Taiwan intended to finish the Chinese Civil War. But the outbreak of the Korean War was a "gift from the gods" for Chiang as much as for Japan. Viewing the Korean War as part of an aggressive global offensive by the communist powers, Washington determined it could not allow an additional communist breakthrough elsewhere in Asia. Truman announced that the U.S. Seventh Fleet would protect Taiwan from an invasion by the People's Liberation Army. In 1955 the United States established a mutual defense treaty with the ROC on Taiwan, a pact that lasted until the U.S. de-recognition of the ROC in favor of the PRC in 1979. America thus returned to its wartime role as Chiang's strategic partner. Washington found this postwar iteration similarly aggravating, although from the U.S. standpoint the problem shifted from trying to get Chiang to fight (the Japanese) to trying to restrain him from fighting (the communists on the mainland).

BEGINNING OF A DIFFICULT JOURNEY

The end of the war brought dramatic, wrenching changes in these three Northeast Asian societies. These changes help set them on a path that would see Japan, South Korea and Taiwan emerge as relatively prosperous democracies by the end of the Cold War. This path, however, would be tortuous and often sorrowful, particularly for South Korea and Taiwan.

Regime change was one of the challenges that victory in the Pacific War brought to the United States, now the undisputed dominant power of the Asia-Pacific region. In both Korea and Japan American officials felt compelled to choose between the perennial principle of promoting democracy and the short-term objective of preventing the emergence of a government that might cooperate with America's enemies. Through most of the Cold War, South Korea and Taiwan would continue to test American ability to balance support for an important ally with pressure on authoritarian leaders to liberalize in accord with U.S. political values.

CHAPTER 8

Pacific War *Rashomon*

Rashomon is a 1950 film by famed Japanese director Kurosawa Akira based on an early twentieth-century Japanese short story. In the film, four main characters—a samurai, his wife, a robber, and a woodcutter—give differing and self-serving accounts of an incident in the countryside that leaves the samurai dead (he gives his testimony through a spiritual medium) and his wife raped. The story has become a metaphor for the difficulty of finding out the truth through human intermediaries. Even when the subject is a factual event, storytellers are inherently subjective and prone to offering biased interpretations.

Something of a *Rashomon* effect among some of the key participants in the Pacific War is apparent in their differing interpretations of important aspects of the war. Most Americans believe the conflict began suddenly with the Japanese raid on Pearl Harbor, which they consider aggressive, unprovoked, and treacherous. This view largely ignores a key component of the history we reviewed earlier: the decades of American policy in Asia before the Pearl Harbor attack, including America's own imperialist enterprise and efforts to control and coerce Japan. It is an unbalanced and selective view of history that paints America as innocent and peaceful prior to the Japanese attack. This view justifies the harsh punishment America subsequently meted out to the Japanese. It also supports the strong postwar role the United States has taken in attempting to manage international affairs in the Asia-Pacific region. In Japan we can similarly find in the right-wing nationalist outlook, which holds considerable sway within the long-ruling Liberal Democratic Party, an interpretation of the U.S.-Japan conflict that displays selective memory and lack of balance. In this rendering Japan's actions were justifiable: the Japanese tried to liberate Asia from Western colonialism, while it was the Americans who were scheming and self-servingly imperialistic. The view purveyed by the Chinese Communist Party (CCP) government of China offers yet another distinctly different angle on the conflict. Here China's brave and purportedly effective resistance against a patently evil Japanese invasion and occupation is made a key plank in the legitimacy of the current ruling regime and sets a shrill tone for China-Japan relations in the early twenty-first century. The Rashomon effect arising from competing interpretations of the Pacific War is at the heart of important political disputes in present-day Northeast Asia. To reprise the themes described in the introduction of this book, we will see in the competing interpretations of the war among the societies of the three major Northeast Asian states that each of these interpretations is self-serving, each was encouraged by the country's respective wartime government, and each is reflective of the country's political circumstances during and after the war.

PEARL HARBOR: THE OFT-TOLD STORY

The belief that Japan's attack on Pearl Harbor was unprovoked is widely established in the United States, having persisted through the decades since Roosevelt's famous speech of December 8, 1941. President George W. Bush said in 2003, for example, that "America was attacked without warning and without provocation" at Pearl Harbor.[1] Other public officials such as Speaker of the House Nancy Pelosi, U.S. Secretary of Veterans Affairs R. James Nicholson and Senator Bob Dole have also called the Pearl Harbor raid "unprovoked" or "without provocation."[2] Several governors recently found occasion to label the attack "unprovoked" or "without provocation," with some proclaiming Pearl Harbor commemoration days for their states. These include New Jersey Acting Governor Richard Codey, California Governor Gray Davis, Alaska Governor Frank Murkowski, Ohio Governor Ted Strickland, Mississippi Governor Haley Barbour, Wisconsin Governor Jim Doyle, and South Carolina Governor Mark Sanford.[3] Commentators such as syndicated columnists Cal Thomas and Michelle Malkin, former Speaker of the House Newt Gingrich, and radio talk-show hosts Rush Limbaugh and Barbara Simpson are among those who have repeated the notion, which is still widely believed among the U.S. public.[4]

Bitterness about the attack on Pearl Harbor still runs deep in American society. It appears, usually in controlled and restrained ways, on the expected commemorative occasions. Some unplanned events, however, trigger spontaneous and raw emotional outbursts. In February 2001 the Pearl Harbor–based U.S. Navy submarine *Greeneville* was carrying civilian guests during a demonstration cruise off the coast of Oahu. In the area was the Japanese fishing vessel *Ehime Maru*, operated by a Japanese vocational high school for students training to be commercial fishermen. While surfacing, the submarine struck the *Ehime Maru*, cutting a gash in the rear of its hull. The Japanese vessel immediately sank with the loss of nine crew members. Four of the victims were high school students. In the days that followed the tragedy, some called for the U.S. government to apologize to Japan for the accident and to pay for raising the sunken ship. Oahu resident Don Mitchell wrote to the *Honolulu Star Bulletin* with a comment on the issue. "Where is Japan's apology for Pearl Harbor, the Rape of Nanking, the Bataan Death March?" wrote Mitchell. "Did they attempt to raise the *Arizona* to recover the bodies of the 1,100 or so of our American men who are entombed there? In addition, the sinking of the *Ehime Maru* was an accident. Pearl Harbor was a planned, vicious and unprovoked attack."[5]

The widespread view that the attack was unprovoked suggests that no justification for it is to be found in U.S. Asia policy prior to December 7, 1941. The surprise of the strike was all the greater because the United States was an innocent victim, with a clear conscience and therefore no reason to keep its guard up. Hence the tremendous shock of the "sneak attack." A 1991 *Newsweek* retrospective opined that as a result of the Pearl Harbor attack, America was "shaken to the bottom of its soul, its geopolitical innocence in ruins."[6] By implication, the United States was "geopolitically innocent" because it paid little attention to foreign affairs and, to the extent it had an Asia policy, inoffensive. Academic Ira Chernus sees the growth of a Pearl Harbor "myth," according to which "America was asleep on Dec. 7, 1941. . . . The nation lay tucked between clean white sheets early on the Lord's day, the same as it ever was: naïve and innocent, isolated from the world."[7] Evidence in support of Chernus' observation is abundant. Many Americans believe, like editorialist Ruth Talovich, that prior to the attack "Japan controlled China, Korea, Mongolia and other parts of Asia with unquestioned military force," while "America was confined to one place by President James Monroe with his 'stay in this hemisphere' isolationist doctrine." But the attack "changed all that. We became a major international power and the doctrine became past tense."[8] While drawing parallels with the September 11, 2001, terrorist attacks, Bush said of Pearl Harbor in a March 2005 speech, "a sudden attack on the United States launched our country into a global conflict and began a period of serious reflection on America's place in the world. The bombing of Pearl Harbor taught America that unopposed tyranny, even on faraway continents, could draw our country into a struggle for our own survival."[9] Bush implies here that America got attacked because of inattention to outside events—for failing to "oppose tyranny"—and that the attack marked a change from U.S. uninvolvement to involvement in foreign affairs. Again, there is little recognition that U.S. Asia policy might have been a factor in Japan's decision to attack.

As Chernus alluded to, American retellings of the story of the Pearl Harbor attack almost invariably include the description of servicemen half-asleep on a peaceful Sunday morning, suddenly jarred by explosions, smoke, and destruction into the realization that a new war was upon them. As one author puts it in a typical passage, "One moment they were getting out of bed, putting on their clothes, eating breakfast, and thinking of the usual routines of Sunday. The next, they were under savage attack."[10] That the attack took place in the relaxed paradise of Hawaii reinforces the sense of shock and makes the

Japanese raiders appear all the more monstrous. This scene acts as a perfect symbolic microcosm of the larger point that many commentators make: while the United States was failing to pay attention, the distant forces of aggression and oppression had grown large enough to reach across the seas, and being evil they were naturally disposed to target America's way of life. The United States seems to have done nothing to bring on this attack except respond appropriately to Japanese aggression in Asia with verbal condemnation and economic sanctions.

American commentators, including authors of history books written for young people, frequently leave the impression America had no influence over events in Asia prior to the war. Joy Hakim's *A History of Us* describes the lead-up to the Pearl Harbor attack this way:

In Japan, a military dictatorship took control of the nation and began stomping on its neighbors. . . . They thought they needed more room for their growing population. They began by attacking China with a ferocity that is still hard to believe. In a massive campaign of terror, millions of civilians were tortured and killed. Just as in Germany, the Japanese rulers told the people they were a superior race and destined to rule others. . . . In Asia, Japan has earlier occupied Manchuria (in 1931) and other parts of China (in 1937), and has just invaded French Indochina . . . in July 1941. Japan is also threatening Thailand, the Philippines, and other Pacific nations. The United States sends letters to Japan objecting to this aggressive behavior, and finally imposes a total trade embargo and freezes Japanese funds in U.S. banks.[11]

The attack follows: "On Sunday morning ships were lined up in the harbor; their crews were having breakfast, or relaxing, or sleeping." A description of the raid on Pearl Harbor follows, ending with the conclusion, "It is an astonishing act of aggression."[12]

The situation is starkly simplified in black and white terms in Robert Leckie's *The Story of World War II:* "Tojo's plan was to put half the population of the world under Japanese control" in a campaign of "conquering and looting." The only mentions of U.S. interaction with Japan are "America began protesting against Japan's continued presence in China" and "President Roosevelt would not agree to Japan's remaining in China." Of the raid, Leckie says, "Church bells were ringing when, at five minutes before eight, Battleship Row suddenly became ablaze with fire and thunder." Leckie twice characterizes the raid as a "sneak attack" and judges that "This was treachery unrivaled in modern history."[13]

In *V Is for Victory: America Remembers World War II* by Kathleen Krull, the section on the prelude to Pearl Harbor explains that because it "was undergoing a population explosion" and "dominated by military leaders," Japan invaded China.

During a decade of Japanese aggression against China, over 10 million Chinese people died in what has been called the 'forgotten Holocaust.' . . . By the fall of 1941, relations between the United States and Japan had reached an impasse. Japan had moved further into China and then into French-occupied Indochina. The United States retaliated by halting trade with Japan—a devastating economic blow. When the United States called for Japan to withdraw, Japanese leaders regarded this as an insult.

Then the author moves on to the Pearl Harbor attack: "At 7:55 A.M., American servicemen at Pearl Harbor were eating breakfast or still sleeping."[14]

Alan Axelrod's *Complete Idiot's Guide to American History* says nothing about U.S. policy in Asia prior to Pearl Harbor, but it does mention Japanese invasions of Manchuria and China and Japan's alliance with Germany. From there the text cuts directly to December 7: "At 7:50 on that quiet Sunday morning, Japanese aircraft struck without warning."[15]

In the *Children's Encyclopedia of American History* by David C. King, the explanation for the attack on Pearl Harbor consists of the following: (1) a small section on "The Bombing of Shanghai," featuring the famous photo of a blackened, crying baby in the bombed-out railway station, with the following text—"Japan's war of conquest in China seemed more remote to Americans than the aggression in Europe. However, when the Japanese bombed the city of Shanghai in 1937, Americans were shocked by the newsreels and news photos showing the first full-scale air attacks on a populated city"—and (2) a passage reading, "The Roosevelt Administration was worried about the Japanese. Japan had joined the Axis powers, Germany and Italy, in September 1940; all three Axis powers had agreed to declare war on America if it went to war with any of them. Fears about an invasion on the West Coast were realized in part when the Japanese attacked Pearl Harbor." The author does not discuss U.S. Asia policy or pressure on Japan, yet devotes a paragraph of space to the theory that Roosevelt knew the attack was coming.[16]

There are, of course, many English-language histories that examine the lead-up to war between Japan and the United States with appropriate depth and balance. The point is that many of the more popular and accessible histories tend to oversimplify the issue in ways that reinforce the dubious theme of American innocence.

THE VIEW FROM ACROSS THE PACIFIC

For Americans, the war in the Pacific was to dismantle an empire that would lock away much of the Asia-Pacific region from the liberal world economic order favored by the United States and to uproot the militarist government that was the author of this aggressive Japanese imperial project. The Pearl Harbor attack confirmed in the American mind that fascist Japan was both uncivilized and a dire threat to U.S. interests. Most Japanese, of course, have a different view of the U.S.-Japan conflict. If asked today what led to the outbreak of war between Japan and the United States, the average Japanese will respond something like this: the Japanese presence in

China caused U.S.-Japan tensions; the United States imposed an oil embargo against Japan; and this left Japan with no choice but to go to war, leading to the attack on Pearl Harbor.

Like their American counterparts, today's ordinary Japanese know little about the war. In particular, Japanese textbooks have generally provided very scanty coverage of the brutality of Japan's forces toward prisoners of war, forced laborers and conquered peoples. It was not until the late 1980s that Japanese textbooks began to cover Japanese war crimes such as the recruitment and employment of so-called comfort women from other Asian countries. Japanese teachers have done little by way of lecture and class-room discussion to extend this coverage. Indeed, many teachers over the years have intentionally limited or avoided discussion of the Pacific War with their students because it is a sensitive topic. Lack of knowledge about the war and other important historical events is all too common among the younger generations of many countries. Japanese youths, however, face something of an asymmetry of ignorance. People in Asia-Pacific countries *other than* Japan tend to know a fair amount about Japan's invasions and cruel occupation policies. Many a Japanese college student studying abroad has undergone the shock of learning the extent of Japan's wartime atrocities during a classroom discussion amidst non-Japanese students already familiar with the events.

What Japanese typically know best about the war is the U.S. strategic bombing campaign against Japan, particularly the atomic bombing attacks on Hiroshima and Nagasaki. As a consequence, Japanese are more accustomed to thinking of their country as a victim of the war than an aggressor—so much so that many Japanese feel they have the credentials to speak boldly as advocates of peace and nonviolence. In a 2003 memorial service for the Hiroshima victims, Mayor Akiba Tadatoshi decried the proliferation of nuclear weapons, declaring that "The chief cause is U.S. nuclear policy that . . . appears to worship nuclear weapons as God." The conclusion of a 2005 *Asahi Shimbun* editorial on the anniversary of the U.S. firebombing of Tokyo noted that Japanese "understand the anger of Iraqi residents who are being subjected 60 years later to the same tactics." Japan's wartime victimization seems to qualify these commentators to occupy the moral high ground.[17]

Many of the thousands of Japanese who visit the *U.S.S. Arizona* Memorial in Pearl Harbor express shock and a sudden realization of the relationship between the Pearl Harbor attack and the atomic bombings (a link that is relatively easily made in the minds of Americans). Japanese scholar Yagu-chi Yujin, who has studied the experience of these Japanese visitors, reports that common reactions are shame, embarrassment and a desire to apologize. Japanese visitors to the Memorial "connect the dots," says *Arizona* Memorial chief historian Daniel Martinez. "They knew Pearl Harbor was an event of the Pacific War. But they're not used to thinking of Japan as the aggressor, the attacker."[18]

THE JAPANESE RIGHT WING ACCENTUATES
THE POSITIVE

The officially promoted Japanese wartime view of the outbreak of trans-Pacific war was in its most important respects nearly a mirror-image of the American view: Japan's expansion was well-intentioned and mutually beneficial—it would throw out Western imperialism, accelerate regional development, and promulgate what the Japanese believed were constructive values; by contrast, Western imperialism was greedy and oppressive; and finally, the Americans forced Japan to go to war in its own self-defense. In his declaration of war on December 8, 1941, Hirohito first condemned the Chinese for "failing to comprehend the true intentions of our Empire, and recklessly courting trouble." While Japan offered "neighborly intercourse and cooperation," he said, China "disturbed the peace of East Asia and compelled our Empire to take up arms" with its "fratricidal opposition." Next he blamed the United States and Britain for supporting Chiang's regime, for making "military preparations on all sides of our Empire to challenge us," and for "a direct severance of economic relations, menacing gravely the existence of our Empire." He concluded that "our Empire for its existence and self-defense has no other recourse but to appeal to arms and to crush every obstacle in its path."[19]

Some of these themes carried over into Hirohito's surrender speech (called the *Gyokuon-hoso*, or "jewel voice broadcast") of August 15, 1945, which contains many key assertions that still serve as the basis for the Japanese nationalist position in the twenty first century. Many Americans have heard that Hirohito spoke of "enduring the unendurable" and, knowing nothing more about the content of the speech, assume that its general tone is shame and contrition. That assumption, however, is mistaken. Rather, the tone is best described as self-righteous. Hirohito's speech explained that since "the war situation has not necessarily turned favorable, and the great tendencies of the world also are not an advantage to us," he was taking "an extraordinary measure" of informing the Allies that his government "accepts their Joint Proclamation." This is the closest Hirohito came to saying that Japan was surrendering. He expressed sympathy for the suffering of his people. To continue the war, he said solipsistically, "Not only would ultimately invite the ruin of our race, but in turn it would destroy also the civilization of humankind." Hirohito recounted the reasons why Japan "declared war on" (not attacked) the United States and Britain: "for both the self-existence of the Empire and the stability of East Asia." He denied that Japan was an aggressor, pointing out that "to do anything like disregard the sovereignty or violate the territory of another State has not at any time been my purpose." Rather, his aim was the "emancipation of East Asia."[20] The key points of the speech, then, are as follows: (1) Japan went to war in defense of peace and justice in Asia—to relieve Western threats against Japan and to clear Western imperialism from the region; and (2) the emperor performed an act of great benevolence for the Japanese people and for all humanity by bringing about peace.

After the war, a pragmatic form of pacifism swept Japan. Postwar generations internalized the notion that war had been disastrous for Japan and led to the horrible atomic bombings. But in conservative circles Hirohito's interpretation also persisted: that Japanese imperialism was essentially benevolent, that the West was the aggressor, and that the experience confirmed the rectitude of the emperor system. Unlike postwar Germany, which strove vigorously to delegitimize the ideology and policies of the former Nazi regime, Japan did not make a great effort to air the war crimes of the fascist era and tolerated a conservative minority that clung to a romanticized version of Japan's role in the conflict. Japan's conservative postwar governments had strong and extensive ties to the wartime government. These politicians and their partners in business and the bureaucracy had an interest in exonerating the Japanese political and economic system and its elite classes, with the exception of a small number of scapegoats. The U.S. government had a hand in this outcome. The Americans shared the interest of Japanese conservatives in closeting the issue of Japanese war guilt because ensuring that Japan became a strong Cold War ally became the highest-priority objective.[21] The occupation's quick shift in emphasis from democratization to anticommunism reduced the pressure to purge the conservatives associated with the wartime regime and to marginalize their ideology. For individuals such as Kishi, "reverse course" was a reversal of their fortunes. The ramifications are still being felt. Kishi's grandson Abe Shinzo served briefly as Prime Minister in 2006-07. Soon after taking office, Abe said of the Japanese leaders convicted by the Allied tribunal that it was "ridiculous" to consider them war criminals.[22] The Japan Socialist Party and the Japan Communist Party were more willing to confront their country's wartime misdeeds, but their influence was limited with the conservative Liberal Democratic Party's dominance of Japanese politics.

The conservative view of Japan's role in the Pacific War has not overcome the aversion toward militarism and jingoism that most Japanese developed after the war. Beginning in the 1990s, however, Japan's political environment became more hospitable to the conservative view. Japanese have adopted a more hard-headed attitude toward international relations, losing confidence in the ability of multilateral treaties and institutions to protect them from looming threats such as North Korean missiles and an increasingly powerful China. Japanese born after the end of the war are less inclined than their forebears to accept the need for restrictions and penance because of the sins of the wartime generation.

Japanese liberals such as historian Ienaga Saburo attempted to raise public awareness of their government's darker deeds during the Pacific War. Ienaga was at the forefront of the battle some Japanese waged to educate schoolchildren about the awful consequences of fascist rule during the Pacific War period. Over a period of nearly three decades, Ienaga fought court battles against the Japanese government over its demands that he revise parts of his textbook manuscripts that dealt candidly with Japanese atrocities during the war. Ienaga endured death threats and harassment at his home by right-wing activists, but the courts ruled in his favor on some of his grievances. Such efforts led to the inclusion of unsavory events in the history books. For example, a textbook used by 41 percent of Japanese middle schools in 1998 mentions the Nanjing Massacre despite very brief treatment of the China Incident: "The fighting spread from northern China into central China, and at the end of the year the Japanese Army occupied the capital Nanjing. In the process it killed an estimated 200,000 people, including women and children."[23]

Conservatives counterattacked. Complaining of a "masochistic" anti-Japanese bias and the influence of the "Tokyo War Crimes Trial view of history," Fujioka Nobukatsu, a professor of education at Tokyo University, cofounded the Association for the Advancement of A Liberalist View of History (Jiyushugi Shikan Kenkyukai) in 1995 and the Society for Creating New History Textbooks (Atarashi Kyokasho wo Tsukurukai; hereafter Tsukuru-kai) in 1996. "We have been taught that our country was a villain in the war," he said. "I discovered that our history education is wrong."[24] Fujioka argued that there was no Nanjing Massacre and that there is no evidence the Japanese government forced comfort women into sexual slavery. Several editions of the conservative *New History Textbook* reflected the view that the story should downplay the atrocities and cast a positive light on Japan's aims during the Pacific War. The book drew widespread international criticism, particularly from China and South Korea, although its impact was limited by the fact that few Japanese schools adopted it. Textbooks produced or endorsed by Tsukurukai remain on the fringe of Japan's education system. Less than 1 percent of Japanese junior high school students were using them in 2005.[25] The significance of the so-called patriotic textbooks, however, is less in their readership than in their political backing. Both Abe and Japan's former minister of education, Nakayama Nariaki, are part of a group including over 100 Diet members that committed themselves in 1997 to promote nationalistic textbook revisions. The Ministry of Education itself has allegedly intervened to pressure textbook publishers to remove or dilute references to the Nanjing Massacre or the comfort women.[26] "Why should Japan be the only country that should teach kids—12- to 15-year-old kids—bad things about itself?" said Kanji Nishio, a leader of the Create New History group. "I think it is ridiculous, and very sad and tragic that Japan cannot write its own patriotic history. We lost the war, and a fantasy was born that by talking bad about yourself, you can strengthen your position. I call that masochistic."[27]

Even leaving aside the impact of these conservative-oriented textbooks, the Pacific War coverage of mainstream textbooks is dubiously weighted. By the late 1990s the textbooks used by the vast majority of Japanese students covered the comfort women and the Nanjing Massacre. References to these unsavory subjects markedly decreased, however, in mainstream textbooks in 2001.[28] From the 1980s through the present decade, discussion of the suffering the Japanese government caused to other Asian countries and to Okinawans increased. The dominant theme, nevertheless, remained the same: the suffering the war brought to the Japanese people, or Japan as Pacific War victim. In a recent survey, among Japanese junior high school students asked to name the most important subject of study to further the goal of promoting peace, more than twice as many named the atomic bombings of Hiroshima and Nagasaki as named Japanese aggression in Asia.[29]

Even if their knowledge of the war is relatively shallow, more than half of Japan's population believes their government committed aggression against Asia in the fascist era and that contemporary Japanese leaders should accept greater responsibility for Japan's past war crimes.[30] Thus the nationalist position is best understood as a minority, albeit a numerous and vocal one with many powerful sympathizers. Among the most visible nationalists are the committed activists.

There are about a thousand *uyoku dantai* ("right-wing groups") in Japan with an uncertain total membership of probably between 10,000 and 20,000. Their *gaisensha*, trucks or vans fitted with loudspeakers blasting nationalistic music and commentary, appear frequently in Japan's cities. These groups have differing agenda, but most share an emphasis on patriotism, loyalty to the emperor system, a disdain for communism, and hostility toward what they see as an anti-Japan bias in the educational system. A variety of outlets continue to disseminate the conservative message. Controversies over historical events such as the Nanjing Massacre give conservatives opportunities to voice their views. Some commercial films have purveyed the message through the cinema. About six million Japanese annually visit the Yasukuni Shrine, which is a bastion of right-wing sentiment. The Nanjing Massacre, perhaps the Japanese wartime atrocity best known throughout the world, is a primary historical battleground between Japanese conservatives and their critics both inside and outside Japan. The story was not widely known among the Japanese population until the 1980s. A 1999 symposium sponsored by the Association for the Advancement of a Liberalist View of History called the Nanjing Massacre "the biggest lie of the twentieth century." In 2000, another right-wing organization planned a conference in the semipublic Osaka International Peace Center that also took as its theme the assertion that the Nanjing Massacre was "the biggest lie of the twentieth century." The Chinese Foreign Ministry lodged an official protest with Tokyo. The Japanese government responded that it could not obstruct a legal private event.[31] Those who deny that a massacre took place at Nanjing argue that documentary evidence does not support the higher estimates of Chinese casualties in the area after the fall of the city. The numbers are indeed subject to some interpretation, pieced together from various accounts of eyewitnesses and relatives as well as population and burial records. Japanese historian Hata Ikuhiko, for example, estimates the number of Chinese killed at around 40,000.[32] Defenders of the Japanese conquerors of Nanjing also argue that fleeing Chinese troops shed their uniforms and changed into civilian clothes; since they were not really civilians, those subsequently killed should not count as victims of a massacre. This argument amounts to a kind of historical plea-bargain, as it still saddles Japanese troops with responsibility for executing Chinese prisoners and deserters.

The sense that national honor is on the line can bring a fanatical conviction to beliefs about events such as the Nanjing Massacre. Matsuoka Tamaki is a Japanese primary school teacher turned Nanjing Massacre researcher who has interviewed scores of both Japanese and Chinese in a quest to prove to her compatriots that the horror stories are true. She reports that after the publication of her first book about the Nanjing Massacre, she received over 1,500 threatening email messages. She fears reprisals from Japanese right-wing activists. "When I am walking on the street," she says, "I look back all the time to see whether someone is following me or if a car is rushing towards me. I never stand in the first row when waiting for Metro trains to avoid being pushed onto the tracks."[33] Such fears are not paranoid. In 1988 Motoshima Hitoshi, mayor of Nagasaki, said publicly he believed Hirohito was responsible for the war. Right-wing activists came to Nagasaki to condemn Motoshima from loudspeaker trucks. In 1990 one shot the mayor in the back, although Motoshima survived and recovered.

The top grossing domestically made Japanese commercial film of 1998 was *Pride: The Fateful Moment*. The film presents Tojo as a heroic figure, the Pacific War as primarily a Japanese crusade to liberate their fellow Asians from Western colonialism, and the Tokyo war crimes trials as a corrupt farce. The film's opening scene has Tojo explaining the decision to attack Pearl Harbor: "The government tried its best to stabilize the relationship with the United States, but our efforts were in vain. If this empire yields to their demands, it means the loss of our imperial dignity and will result in endangering the existence of the empire." The next scene shows crowds of Indians cheering as the Japanese-trained Indian National Army marches in New Delhi on India's independence day in 1947. Among the onlookers is a Japanese veteran, joyful to see the realization of what he fought for. The film's main point is that Japanese should take pride in what their government and military forces tried to do during the Pacific War.[34] A 2001 Japanese film titled *Merdeka* (the Bahasa Indonesian word for "independence") controversially characterized Japanese troops who seized control of Indonesia from Dutch administrators as liberators. Indonesia's ambassador to Japan formally requested that the film's makers delete the opening scene, which depicts an elderly Indonesian woman kneeling down and kissing the feet of an arriving Japanese officer in 1942 Java. Kase Hideaki, who headed production of *Merdeka*, maintained that "Indonesians are very, very pro-Japanese," as are "people of Myanmar, the Malaysians, Filipinos and . . . Taiwanese."[35] But Syahri Sakidin, an official at the Indonesian Embassy in Tokyo, told journalists, "We never, never considered the Japanese a savior from colonial power."[36] In 2007 Japan screened the film *For Those We Love*, a sympathetic portrayal of the kamikaze suicide pilots. Tokyo Governor Ishihara Shintaro, an outspoken nationalist, wrote the story for the film. While promoting his Japan-friendly film about the

Nanjing Massacre, director Mizushima Satoru said Japanese leaders convicted and hanged for war crimes "resemble Jesus Christ who was nailed to the cross in order to bear the sins of the world." He also compared them to the title characters of the film *The Seven Samurai* (like *Rashomon*, directed by Kurosawa), who heroically helped a farming village defend itself against a large group of bandits.[37]

Japanese weekly news magazines, which are influential despite some similarities with American tabloid periodicals, regularly carry articles that support the theme of a historically well-meaning Japan picked on by malicious foreigners. Even Japanese manga (comic books) are a vehicle for apologist views of the Pacific War. Manga that defend Japanese wartime policies toward China and Korea are enjoying a boom in popularity. *Introduction to China* denies that Japanese committed atrocities in China during the war. Through the experiences of its main characters, *Hate Korea: A Comic* concludes that "Japan built the South Korea of today."[38] Both of these best-selling books reprise the negative Japanese stereotypes of Chinese and Koreans that contributed to cruel treatment of these peoples by Japanese occupation forces.

It would be easier to dismiss the Japanese equivalent of Holocaust deniers as the lunatic fringe of Japanese society if there were not regular public statements by prominent Japanese questioning whether Japan behaved wrongly during the war. One of the most famous cases was in 1994, when Nagano Shigeto, newly appointed Justice Minister and former Chief of Staff of the Japanese army, characterized the Pacific War as a Japanese attempt to liberate Asia and called the Nanjing Massacre a "fabrication." Nagano's remarks caused an outcry in Japan as well as in China and Korea, forcing Nagano to resign after only 10 days in office. Criticized for not taking swifter action against Nagano, Japanese Prime Minister Hata Tsutomu sent a letter of apology to Chinese Premier Li Peng. More recently Ishihara, co-author of the controversial 1989 book *The Japan that Can Say No*, said in 2003 that Koreans chose to be annexed by Japan and that Japanese colonialism "was carried out in the most developed and humane manner."[39] Ishihara is even less inclined to apologize to the Americans, insisting that the U.S.-Japan conflict was justified as self-defense and as a means of liberating Asians from colonialism. Prime Minister Hosokawa Moihiro told reporters in August 1993, "I understand the Asia-Pacific War to have been a war of aggression and a mistake." Ishihara, then a Diet member, was among those who challenged him. "The attitude that losers were bad and victors were good is ridiculous," said Ishihara. "The United States has not apologized after losing in Vietnam. . . . Any apologies should be mutual."[40] Minister of Education Nakayama asserted in 2005, "There was no such term as 'comfort women for military forces' back then," which Korean and Chinese observers viewed as a denial of the well-established fact that the Japanese military forcibly recruited female sex workers from occupied Asian countries.[41] In June 2007 about 100 Diet members endorsed the conclusion of a study led by Nakayama that only 20,000 people died in Nanjing and the massacre was an anti-Japanese myth.[42]

Some Japanese perceive a nationalist resurgence that threatens freedom of expression in Japan. The chairman of the Japan Newspaper Publishers and Editors Association said in 2006 that because of right-wing intimidation, "Speech and journalism in this country are facing an extremely difficult situation."[43] In December 2006, Japan's Diet passed a bill upgrading the status of the office overseeing the armed forces from an agency to a ministry and another bill requiring that Japan's education system instill in students a "love of country." At minimum, these were retreats from Japan's postwar antimilitarism. Japanese conservatives had long argued that the 1947 education law dating from the U.S. occupation over-emphasized individual liberties and thereby contributed to a decline in both discipline and patriotism among Japanese youths. Opposition politicians countered that using the schools to promote patriotism was reminiscent of the fascist era. The state has punished several hundred teachers in recent years for offenses such as refusing to stand for the raising of the national flag or the singing of *Kimigayo*, a song associated with the militarism of the war years and only in 1999 designated by the Diet as Japan's national anthem. One of those who has refused to stand or sing when the song plays at public gatherings is Nezu Kimiko, a junior high school teacher, who says "They are trying to weed us out of society. The pacifists, the people who oppose nationalism in Japan. We are gradually being silenced. . . . I feel as if freedom to question authority is being quashed just as it was during the war years." In one case in 2004, a 65-year-old retired teacher pointed out to the members of the audience at a high school graduation ceremony their constitutional right to remain seated during the playing of Kimigayo. Prosecutors recommended an eight-month jail sentence, but the former teacher got off with a ¥200,000 ($1,800) fine. Besides fines and reprimands, another form of punishment has been sending the offending teachers through a "retraining program" requiring them to attend a lecture and write a report. In July 2007 the Tokyo District Court ruled against a group of 130 teachers who challenged the "retraining" on the grounds that it violated of their freedom of conscience.[44]

RELIGIOUS SHRINE WITH A POLITICAL MESSAGE

The Yasukuni Shinto Shrine in Tokyo was built in 1869, originally to pay respect to soldiers killed in Japan's civil war to reassert the authority of the emperor over the Tokugawa Shogunate, a clan-based military dictatorship. It now honors the souls of all those killed in military service for Japan since 1853, a total of two and a half million individuals. The number includes thousands of Koreans and Taiwanese. In 1978 the shrine added the names of over 1,000 convicted war criminals from the Pacific War era, including 14 Class-A criminals such as Tojo. Along with the souls of the dead, Yasukuni is a depository of the right-wing interpretation of the U.S.-Japan conflict. The Web site for the shrine observes that the Military Tribunal for the Far East [concluded] that Japan fought a war of aggression. Can we say that this view is correct? . . . We cannot help but feel that the possibility of ulterior motives has not been discounted. Isn't it a fact that the West with its military power invaded and ruled over much of Asia and Africa and that this was the start of East-West relations? . . . Japan's dream of building a Great East Asia was necessitated by history and it was sought after by the countries of Asia. . . . We cannot overlook the intent of those who wish to tarnish the good name of the noble souls of Yasukuni.[45]

According to a pamphlet published by the shrine, which calls the war criminals "Showa martyrs" (*Showa* refers to the reign of Hirohito), they were "cruelly executed because they were falsely accused as 'war criminals' in a one-sided tribunal held in form only at the hands of the Allied Forces . . . that fought against Japan."[46]

Yasukuni also operates the Yushukan Museum of modern Japanese military history. Through museum artifacts, text and video presentations, the museum offers an interpretation of Japan's wartime history with two strong, clear themes: the glorification of the Japanese military and emperor worship.[47]

As background to the war, the museum notes that "Western powers encroached on Asia," and specifically that Admiral Matthew Perry forced a treaty with "inequitable terms" on Japan. Western sailors in Japan "demanded and sometimes stole supplies." Japanese troops in China, on the other hand, "were respected by the residents of Peking . . . for their military prowess and discipline, in contrast to Russian troops, who looted wherever they went." The Sino-Japan conflict resulted from "anti-Japanese harassment and terrorism" against Japanese residents in China from "nationalistic and xenophobic" Chinese who violated "existing international agreements." A previous commentary on the Nanjing Massacre noted that Japanese soldiers were ordered not to commit "unlawful acts," that Chinese soldiers should have surrendered instead of fighting to defend the city, and that after Japanese troops captured Nanjing its "residents were once again able to live their lives in peace." Presumably because of severe criticism, this commentary had been changed when I visited in March 2007 to read as follows: "After the Japanese surrounded Nanjing in December 1937, Gen. Matsui Iwane distributed maps to his men with foreign settlements and the Safety Zone marked in red ink. Matsui told them that they were to maintain strict military discipline and that anyone committing unlawful acts would be severely punished. The defeated Chinese rushed to Xiaguan [a district of Nanjing], and they were completely destroyed. The Chinese soldiers disguised in civilian clothes were severely prosecuted." This is all Yushukan says about the Massacre. On the outbreak of conflict with the United States, Yushukan says the United States forced Japan into "a war for [Japan's] survival and self-defense" in order to help America shed the lingering effects of the Great Depression: "the U.S. economy made a complete recovery once the Americans entered the war." According to the museum, Roosevelt sought to maneuver Japan into striking first by insisting that Japanese forces withdraw from China, an impossible demand for Japan to meet because of its many legitimate interests in China and Manchuria.

The museum goes on to blame the United States for "prolonging the war": the "Japanese were willing to negotiate," but the United States "had no interest in bringing the war to an early end." Oddly, the museum's commentary reads that "Prime Minister Suzuki announced his intention to ignore the [Potsdam] Declaration, providing the Allies with an excuse to continue their offensive campaign against Japan." The Allies are blamed for continuing the war after Suzuki refused the opportunity to surrender and thereby end the war early. A large hanging banner displays a heroic quotation from Hirohito: "Saddened by the loss of the precious lives of so many of my people, I ended the war. It mattered not what became of me." Pointing out that "the Japanese people's source of strength was their reverence for the emperor and Shinto," the museum criticizes the postwar occupation authorities for attempting "to dilute that strength" by outlawing state support of Shinto, reforming the education system, and writing a new constitution for Japan. Finally, Yushukan commentary credits Japan with inspiring postwar decolonization movements by "advancing" the ideals of "racial equality and self-determination" and by "awakening" the "desire for independence" from "the colonizers who had been defeated by Japan." The museum does not get around to mentioning Japanese invasions and exploitation of several countries in Asia, the killing of civilians in Nanjing, any other war crimes by Japanese forces, the hatred the Japanese engendered in the countries they occupied, or the willingness of the Japanese government to let its people endure months of firebombing before it was sufficiently "saddened" to end the war.

Yushukan is disturbing not only for its refusal to acknowledge that there was anything bad about twentieth-century Japanese militarism, but also for its lack of commitment to the democratic values that most outsiders assume are by now deeply entrenched in Japan. A few extremists have violently opposed those values. In 2006 an indebted and unemployed member of a right-wing group sought a glorious death by attempting ritual suicide after starting a fire that destroyed the house of the mother of Kato Koichi, a Diet member. Kato had criticized Prime Minister Koizumi's visits to the Yasukuni Shrine. Kato's mother was away from the house at the time of the fire and the rightist arsonist survived his suicide attempt to face prosecution. During the same year, a story in the *Nikkei* business newspaper said Hirohito had stopped visiting Yasukuni because of the enshrinement of convicted war criminals. Angered by the story, a right-wing activist threw a Molotov cocktail (which failed to ignite) at the Nikkei Corporation's Tokyo headquarters. After his arrest, police quoted the man as saying, "I intended to give a warning to the newspaper, which aimed at manipulating public opinion over the Yasukuni issue by using the emperor, whom I worship as a god."[48]

Such acts are few and isolated, but the ideology they represent has formidable support. Okudaira Yasuhiro, professor emeritus of Tokyo University, says the influence of Yasukuni is "appalling. It shows the strength of groups who are trying to diminish the changes made in the postwar era. We take the democratization of Japan for granted, but it is increasingly being called into question."[49] Japan's neighbors, as well, have seen Yasukuni as a litmus test for Japan's ability or inability to fully transcend the militarist era. During Prime Minister Koizumi Junichiro's tenure (2001–2006), his visits to the shrine became the single most salient issue in Sino-Japanese political relations. Koreans felt equally strongly; Koizumi's 2001 shrine visit prompted a group of 20 young Koreans to gather at the symbolic site of Independence Gate in Seoul and chop off the tips of the little fingers as part of an anti-Japan protest.[50]

CHINESE VIEWS OF THE WAR

We can find yet another perspective on the Pacific War, and thus see the Rashomon effect deepened, by considering the Chinese viewpoint on what they call the Anti-Japan War (*Kang Ri Zhanzheng*) or the Second Sino-Japanese War (the first being the Sino-Japanese War of 1894–95, which Japan won and which resulted in Japanese colonization of Korea and Taiwan). Not surprisingly, the Chinese do not accept the conservative Japanese position that Japan's expansionism into other parts of Asia meant liberation from Western imperialism, greater opportunity for economic development, and cultural rejuvenation. From the standpoint of the Chinese government, as conveyed through Chinese media, the Second World War was "a life-and-death struggle between the countries and people that loved peace and justice and the ruthless enemies of human civilization," with Japan in the latter category. Nor do Chinese believe the other powers forced Japan to fight out of self-defense. "The widely known fact," says a representative Xinhua News Service commentary, "is that Japan launched the brutal aggression war against its Asian neighboring countries and Japanese aggressors made abundant atrocities on Asian people."[51]

Up to this point most Americans could agree. Where Chinese and Americans part company is on the issue of who won the Pacific War. Americans consider the battles in China as having been peripheral, despite the large numbers of troops involved, to the successful and primarily U.S. effort to force Japan's surrender by destroying the Japanese Navy, capturing islands in the Pacific, and inflicting punishment on the Japanese homeland through bombing and a cutoff of supplies. As we learned earlier, the communists followed basically the same approach as the Nationalists: fighting the Japanese sparingly in order to preserve their strength for the final round of the Chinese Civil War.

According to the People's Republic of China, however, China, and more specifically the Chinese Communist Party forces, won the war. Much the same as occurs in the United States, the frequent references the Chinese government and media make to their country's role in the Pacific War are not only analytically sloppy, but sloppy in the direction of self-aggrandizement and promoting national pride. "History has proved that a weak China defeated a strong Japan, and the miraculous victory was thanks to the CCP,"[52] goes the line that Chinese state-run media and officials have repeated countless times. The same message is delivered in the classroom. At a prominent high school in Shanghai, a teacher recently pointed out in a lecture that "America's attitude toward the Japanese invasion of China stopped at empty moral criticism." Students learn from both lectures and textbooks that the main reason for the defeat of Japan was Chinese resistance led by the Chinese Communist Party. As a textbook put it, "The fundamental reason for the victory is that the Chinese Communist Party became the core power that united the nation."[53] Chinese textbooks neglect to credit the United States not only for its military aid to China, but more importantly for rolling back Japan's Pacific empire and directly attacking the Japanese home islands to force the surrender that liberated China. The CCP also long argued that Chinese communist forces did the hard fighting while Chiang's Nationalists sat unpatriotically on the sidelines. This belief was widely accepted after the war both inside and outside of China and remains widespread today, a testament to a highly successful CCP public relations campaign.

Chinese historians make claims that are more sophisticated and circumspect. Chinese professor Peng Xunhou asserts, more defensively than boastfully, that "China should not be written out of the World Anti-Fascist victory story." The case made by Chinese historians relies on counterfactuals: Chinese resistance tied down large numbers of Japanese troops that otherwise would have fought in Southeast Asia or the Soviet Union, changing the course of the war. Li Jijun of China's Academy of Military Science argues that the war in China slowed and weakened the Japanese campaign in Southeast Asia, buying time for the Allies in their struggle against Hitler in Europe. "Without Chinese resistance," he says, "it would have been almost impossible to implement the 'Europe first' strategy." Peng argues that China tied down the Japanese army, preventing a Japanese conquest of the Soviet Union and "the possible convergence of the two strongest fascist countries in the Middle East."[54]

Yet even these claims are problematic. Japan still had more than six million troops at the time of surrender. Manpower was perhaps less an issue than logistics. Keeping a large invasion force supplied over great distances was a Herculean challenge for any of the major Pacific War combatants, and particularly for Japan with its limited resources and industrial capacity. India, for example, was some 3,000 miles from the Japanese home islands. Even with more troops available, seizing and holding India would never have been feasible for Japan. What about the Chinese contribution with regard to Japanese campaigns in Southeast Asia or possibly the Soviet Union? Chinese resistance did not prevent Japan from conquering Southeast Asia. Japanese forces controlled most of Southeast Asia from the early months of the Pacific War, including Indonesia, the largest country in the region, as well as Indochina, Malaysia and Singapore. How the relatively rapid British and Dutch collapse and mass surrender in Southeast Asia in 1942 aided the defeat of Germany, as Li alleges, is not clear. In any case, it was the Soviets who did the heavy lifting in Europe. Did the war in China prevent a Japanese invasion of the Russian Far East and thereby make it possible for the Soviets to focus on and defeat the German invasion in the west? There are several reasons for doubting this claim. First, the Japanese had reasons other than the war in China for deciding not to invade the USSR, chief among them the jarring defeat they suffered at the hands of Soviet forces in the Khalkhin Gol battles of May and July 1939. Second, Stalin did indeed redeploy capable Red Army Siberian divisions from the east to the western front beginning in late 1941, where they helped the Soviets fight off the assault on Moscow and win the decisive battle of Stalingrad, because he concluded that the likelihood of a Japanese attack on the Russian Far East was low. But Stalin's decision to move the Siberian divisions was not based simply on the fact that the Kwantung Army was busy fighting in China, which had been the case since 1937. Probably more important factors were the Soviet-Japanese neutrality pact of April 1941 and the intelligence from master Soviet spy Richard Sorge in August 1941 that the Japanese intended to strike south rather than north. Finally, it is uncertain that a Japanese invasion of the Russian Far East, even in conjunction with a German invasion from the west, would have succeeded. The Soviet Union proved unconquerable by the Germans, who fielded the most capable combat forces of the war,[55] largely because the invaders could not meet the extremely formidable logistical demands that grew more imposing the further the attackers advanced. Russia may well have swallowed up a Japanese invasion force as well.

China's spin on World War II history is transparently linked to the current agenda of the CCP. Chinese Communist Party history, within which the Anti-Japan War figures prominently, is heavily politicized and instrumentally employed in China. It is not only a major basis for the CCP's authority to rule China, but also a source of corporate myths and lessons for the training of Party and government functionaries.[56] A major point in the CCP's case for its own legitimacy to rule China is that the Communist Party has resisted foreign intrusion and reclaimed the Chinese sovereignty that preceding Chinese governments lost. Upholding the CCP's reputation for heroic patriotism is even more important now that China has all but abandoned communism as a practical policy goal. Independent of the stimulus from Japan, in the 1980s the Chinese government began moving toward building up an alternate pillar for the legitimacy of CCP rule: patriotism. This led to greater emphasis on nationalistic content in the education system. The Anti-Japan War became the most important touchstone of modern Chinese history.[57] It represented the culmination of the themes of foreign intrusion, Chinese suffering, and eventual triumph led by the CCP. As part of the package, the KMT was rehabilitated from a group of capitalist collaborators to partners in the cause of preserving China from a dire threat. Beijing was increasingly appreciative of the postwar KMT's role on Taiwan as advocate of the "one-China" principle against a newly unleashed movement for Taiwan independence. Japan now became the focal point of China's historical enmity. Chinese commentary in various forms discussed Japanese atrocities in great depth and thoroughly demonized wartime Japan. Chinese war movies portrayed the Japanese more negatively than before. PRC officials, media and textbooks were previously quiet about the Nanjing Massacre. The loss of the Nationalist capital represented an embarrassing defeat by the Japanese. It also drew attention, undesirable from the standpoint of the CCP, to the role Chiang's forces played in the war. In some cases Chinese officials quashed plans of Chinese historians to organize conferences about the Massacre. That changed, however, in the 1980s. In 1985 China completed a large memorial to the Nanjing Massacre, with other memorials and museums springing up in other cities. As He Yinan, a political science professor at Seton Hall University, observes, the simple interpretation of the Anti-Japan War as a struggle between cruel, destructive Japanese invaders and heroic, long-suffering Chinese has the effect of glossing over China's failures or shortcomings (such as cases of collaboration with the enemy) and shifting much of the blame for postwar China's socioeconomic backwardness onto the Japanese, and thereby "evad[ing] many sensitive issues that might hurt national self-respect or the Party's prestige."[58]

Chinese learn a story of the war that includes several key Japanese atrocities. The Nanjing Massacre, with the official Chinese figure of 300,000 victims, heads this list. Another episode well known in China is the contest between two junior Japanese officers to chop off the heads of Chinese. In the Chinese version of the story, the victims of these beheadings were noncombatants. The story has its origins in a series of articles in the *Tokyo Nichi-Nichi Simbun* in 1937, which followed a purported race between two Japanese army Lieutenants, Mukai Toshiaki and Noda Tsuyoshi, to be the first to kill 100 of the enemy using a samurai sword. According to the reports, when these two sword-swinging superheroes met to compare scores, Noda had 105 kills, and Mukai 106. Since there was no way to determine who had first reached the target of 100, the two officers agreed to start afresh with a new goal of 150 kills. The articles are full of jingoistic improbabilities and were apparently fabricated. They also indicate that the reported victims were Chinese soldiers at the front lines or in camps. One of the articles specified that Noda and Mukai agreed as part of the contest not to hack any Chinese who were attempting to flee. After the war these newspaper articles came to the attention of Tokyo War Crimes Tribunal prosecutors. The Chinese government had Mukai and Noda extradited from Japan and executed them in 1948.[59]

Some Chinese educators realize and regret that politics has distorted the curriculum. They understand a compromise is necessary and hope for eventual change. Says Ge Jianxiong, director of the Institute of Chinese Historical Geography at Fudan University in Shanghai and an advisor to the government on history textbooks, "Quite frankly, in China there are some areas, very sensitive subjects, where it is impossible to tell people the truth. . . . In China, history is still used as a political tool, and at the high school level, we still must follow the doctrine." Shanghai Normal University historian and textbook author Su Zhiliang tries to strike a balance. "I must take a practical approach," he says. "I want my students to learn, and I've put out the best book that I can. In 10 years, perhaps, China will be a much more open country."[60] Pu Zhiqiang, a Chinese lawyer who specializes in politically sensitive cases, rises above instinctive nationalism when he asks, "Is Japan's clumsy effort to cover up history in its textbooks any worse than the gaping omissions and biased blather in Chinese textbooks? . . . [I]f we look honestly at ourselves—at the massacres and invasions strewn through Chinese history, or just at the suppression of protesters in recent times—and if we compare the behavior of the Japanese military with that of our own soldiers, there is not much to distinguish China from Japan."[61] This point is not lost on the Japanese who are the targets of Chinese criticism. "There is a tendency toward this in any country, but the Chinese textbooks are extreme in the way they uniformly convey the 'our country is correct' perspective," Japanese Foreign Minister Machimura Nobutaka said during a particularly rough period of Sino-Japanese relations in 2005.[62]

Although Taiwan is mostly ethnic Chinese, it has no interest in glorifying the CCP. Since its democratization it has also scraped the protective varnish from the history of Chiang Kai-shek, who ruled Taiwan with an iron hand between his flight in defeat from mainland China until his death in 1975. But at a 2007 commemoration in Taiwan of the 70th anniversary of the Marco Polo Bridge Incident, then-candidate and future ROC President Ma Ying-jeou repeated the notion that "Because of the [Chinese soldiers'] high spirits, rural China was able to defeat the industrialized Japan."[63] Ma's intent, no doubt, was to express his ethnic Chinese pride and to honor Taiwan veterans rather than to teach a history lesson, but he taught a history lesson nevertheless, and a demonstrably wrong one: China did not defeat Japan, and largely because "spirit" did *not* compensate for the opponent's "industrial" advantages. What is interesting here is that Ma finds it politically useful to reinforce a myth supportive of the regime that represents Taiwan's greatest security threat and that maintains the kind of authoritative and often brutal system of governance that Taiwan has rejected.

The Chinese claim to have "suffered the heaviest national sacrifice" in World War II with 35 million Chinese killed, nearly 31 million of them civilians.[64] The Chinese, however, do not have an influential constituency in the United States making top-grossing films or otherwise publicizing their historical grievances. Chinese often express disappointment that Germany's slaughter of European Jews is so much better known internationally than Japan's slaughter of Chinese.[65] Those Chinese who lament that their own version of the Holocaust is little-known outside of China would not be pleased with the results of a survey I conducted among 47 people of various ages in my community. The sample size is relatively low, but I believe the results are broadly representative of Americans as a whole. If anything one would expect Honolulu residents to have a higher awareness of Asian affairs than the U.S. mainland. I asked respondents to estimate the number of Chinese World War II military and civilian deaths. Only eight out of the 34 respondents who ventured guesses believed that a million or more Chinese civilians died in the war. The highest estimate was 12 million total Chinese deaths, far below what the Chinese claim. Respondents in their twenties made lower estimates of Chinese war fatalities than respondents 30 and older. Only two of the 14 in this younger group offered guesses of the number of Chinese civilian deaths that exceeded 100,000, and the highest figure was 500,000. Americans are unfamiliar with China's wartime ordeal, and the trend is toward even greater ignorance among the rising generation.

The Chinese are trying to reverse this trend in their part of a three-way cinematic *Rashomon* on the topic of Nanjing. In 2006 China announced plans to make a major film about the Nanjing Massacre, with the Nanjing-based Jiangsu Cultural Industry Group providing most of the funding. The film's director said he hoped the film would be "just like *Schindler's List*."[66] The American director Bill Guttentag offered his take in the critically acclaimed 2007 documentary *Nanking*, which portrayed the Japanese attackers as criminal and depraved, the Chinese as massively victimized and a group of Western expatriates as heroic. Apparently in response, veteran Japanese movie director Mizushima announced in a January 2007 news conference his plan to make a film called *The Truth About Nanjing*. His supporters include members of the Diet's upper house and Ishihara. Mizushima said "history is being distorted" by "anti-Japan propaganda. . . . That would not only put shame on the Japanese people but also disgrace those who fought in the war, which is unacceptable."[67]

COMPETING SELF-JUSTIFICATIONS

Japanese and Americans differ on what led to the conflict between their countries. Chinese have a particular view of how the war was won. Of the three views of the Pacific War discussed in this chapter, the Japanese conservative nationalist interpretation has attracted the most criticism and is arguably the most objectionable. American and Chinese interpretations of the war, however, contain distortions of their own that are less contested domestically.

Neither the conservative Japanese interpretation that glorifies Japan's policies during the Pacific War nor the Japan-as-victim mentality resonates with the common American view that Japanese aggression was the cause of the U.S.-Japan conflict and, ultimately, of the destruction Japan suffered. Rather, in American eyes, Japan got what it deserved. The common American understanding of the origin of the U.S.-Japan conflict is based on a degree of historical ignorance and contortion. This version of the story emphasizes U.S. innocence and the lack of provocation for the "treacherous" raid on Pearl Harbor. America appears mostly detached from Asia other than standing up for the rights of the downtrodden Chinese against a militarist bully. Such a view serves to shift blame and guilt for the U.S.-Japan conflict to the Japanese. Our review of history, however, showed that the United States was neither innocent nor inattentive. From the beginning of the century, the United

States was deeply involved in Asia, trying to mold both regional politics and the rules of great-power interaction into forms that would be favorable to U.S. interests. By any reasonable definition, the United States was an imperialist power in Asia. Furthermore, prior to the war Washington supported the colonialism of its Western allies and, to a limited extent, Japan. Japan's behavior as a colonial power in Asia in the twentieth century, distinguished by its routine brutality and frequent depravity, was worse than America's. But the differences between the two great powers were not as great as many Americans believe. The United States' record is blemished by the harshness of its conquest of the Philippines. American business interests in Asia and their political supporters at home demonstrated no less avarice than their counterparts in other strong states. Americans like to think of their country as a benign hegemon that helps its conquered territories progress economically and politically, while the other imperialist powers have tended to be cruel and exploitative. But as some peoples have discovered, American domination could have a brutal edge. If the Americans meant well, one could say the same of many Japanese imperialists who talked of liberating Asia, extending to it a mutually beneficial economic relationship, and sharing with their neighbors the values Japan venerated.

If the American view of the lead-up to Pearl Harbor justifies the United States and makes Tokyo the villain, we can find this same distortive tendency in Japan. The right-wing Japanese view over-corrects for the mainstream American view that saddles Japan with too much responsibility for the outbreak of the war. The interpretation offered by Japanese conservatives indeed encourages Japanese to feel pride about their country's policies during the fascist period. Japan, it appears, expanded out of necessity and benefited areas within its sphere of influence economically and culturally. When forced into war by Western pressure, according to this interpretation, Japan sought to extricate not only itself, but the entire region from the oppression of Western imperialism. For this Japan suffered a martyr's fate, her cities devastated by bombing and her leaders prosecuted to satisfy a victor's justice. Such an understanding of Japan's twentieth-century history may boost national pride, but at a high cost. Japanese who overlook the exploitative nature of Japanese imperialism and deny or ignore its atrocities are not serving well their country's interest in promoting a healing of historical wounds between Japan and its neighbors. More subtly, the glorification of Japan's militarist recent past is potentially corrosive of Japanese democracy because of the close association between militarism and emperor worship and because right-wing activists have often resorted to extralegal tactics to attempt to curtail their opponents' right to free expression.

The Chinese, it must be said, do much to keep the Japanese on the defensive and thus make it more difficult for Japan to transcend the scandal of historical whitewashing. The Chinese clearly have motives for keeping the old wounds bleeding—to reaffirm the CCP's monopoly over domestic political power, to pressure Japan to make economic and other concessions in its relationship with China, and to suppress Japanese aspirations to regional and global political leadership. Redressing China's myths about the Second Sino-Japanese War is exceedingly difficult when the result might challenge that most basic of political interests: the legitimacy of the regime. In China, the state largely controls discussions of history and politics, so open inquiry in sensitive areas that touch on the regime's current agenda is almost impossible and the emergence of a dominant corporate interpretation is to be expected. It is perhaps more surprising to find that a substantially distorted view of history has a large following in Japan and the United States, which allow much freer political discussion.

These contending views of the war support the different domestic and political circumstances of the three societies. From the standpoint of the United States, an innocent and traditionally isolationist America was reluctantly thrust into a purportedly new role of global leadership outside the Western Hemisphere as a response to a gross injustice by an imperialist aggressor. The importance of American policies attempting to contain Japan in support of Western colonies in Asia is relatively little known among Americans. Chinese similarly see the war as a just crusade against aggression, but with China instead of America playing the leading role in the victory. As the war demonstrated for Americans a U.S. birthright to preside over Asia, for the Chinese it served as the proving ground for the CCP's mandate to rule China, settling a domestic issue that preceded the Japanese invasion. For Japanese nationalists, the intrusion of the powerful and well-endowed United States forced Japan out of its natural and deserved role of regional leadership and destroyed the noble project of expelling Western colonialism and helping Asia develop economically. Japan became a victim of one of history's greatest war crimes in the process, only to be condemned afterward in a victor's justice. Japan's reintegration into the international community after the war as an important U.S. ally did not require a renunciation of the romanticized view of Japanese wartime behavior and the emperor system because in their moment of greatest influence over the Japanese political system the Americans decided to rehabilitate rather than disenfranchise conservative Japanese elites. In each of these cases, large segments of society continue to hold to the notions that were promulgated as part of the wartime propaganda of their own governments. The intense nationalist atmosphere of war is conducive to effective indoctrination of the public by political elites. But as we will see in subsequent chapters, the interaction between government and society since the end of the war has not been limited to the state manipulating the masses.

CHAPTER 9

"Comfort Women" Discomfiture

In 2005, Japanese education minister Nakayama Nariaki defended the deletion of references to the comfort women from Japanese history textbooks by raising the trivial argument that *jugun ianfu* ("military comfort women") was not the term commonly used during the war. In a perfect illustration of why Japan has gained so little from the many apologies by Japanese officials, a spokesman for the South Korea Foreign Ministry shot back, "This completely negates the Japanese government's 1993 announcement that it will remember the problem of comfort women for a long time and never repeat the same mistake again."[1]

The international community generally accepts that the Japanese military engaged in sexual slavery during the war; that the number of so-called comfort women was around 200,000; and that they were mostly Korean and Chinese but also included young women from the Philippines and Taiwan, and a smaller number of Europeans. Most observers outside Japan who know about the issue also believe Japan has been unjustifiably reluctant to admit to the responsibility of the wartime government for the comfort women program and to pay compensation to the surviving former comfort women. Reputable organizations not directly involved in the issue have repeatedly affirmed these criticisms. A 1996 report on the comfort women issue by Radhika Coomaraswamy, a special rapporteur appointed by the United Nations Commission on Human Rights (UNCHR), concluded, "The Special Rapporteur is absolutely convinced that most of the women kept at the comfort stations were taken against their will, that the Japanese Imperial Army initiated, regulated and controlled the vast network of comfort stations, and that the Government of Japan is responsible for the comfort stations. . . . [and] should be prepared to assume responsibility for what this implies under international law."[2] In a

1998 report on sexual slavery in wartime, UNCHR Special Rapportuer Gay McDougall concluded that on the comfort women issue "the Japanese Government remains liable for grave violations of human rights and humanitarian law, violations that amount in their totality to crimes against humanity." McDougall rejected "the Japanese Government's argument that Japan has already settled all claims from the Second World War through peace treaties and reparations agreements following the war," pointing out the "failure until very recently of the Japanese Government to admit the extent of the Japanese military's direct involvement in the establishment and maintenance of these rape centres."[3] More recently, a 2007 report by the U.S. Congressional Research Service concluded that "the evidence is clear that the Japanese government and military directly created the comfort women system" and that "there appears to have been little of a genuinely voluntarily nature to the system."[4] The same year, the United Nations Committee Against Torture criticized Japan for "the inadequate remedies for the victims of sexual violence, including in particular survivors of Japan's military sexual slavery practices during World War II."[5] A large number of Japanese agree that their government should take greater responsibility for the exploitation of the comfort women and pay the survivors compensation.

The comfort women issue was brewing in Korea through the 1980s. Although Korean former comfort women were subject to a traditional social stigmatization and were therefore inclined to keep quiet about their ordeal, a more progressive political environment and a growing feminist movement encouraged them to speak out. The issue exploded in August 1991 when one of them broke her silence. Kim Hak-sun surmounted the social obstacles and publicly told her story, drawing increased attention to the issue from both Koreans and the Japanese. In December of that year Kim became one of the plaintiffs in the first class-action lawsuit on behalf of comfort women in the Japanese courts. As part of its defense, the Japanese government claimed that documents substantiating involvement by the military did not exist. This moved Japanese historian Yoshimi Yoshiaki to search the library of the National Institute for Defense Studies, where in January 1992 he found five documents linking the Japanese military to the recruitment of comfort women and the operation of the brothels. The *Asahi Shimbun* reported his findings, forcing an embarrassed government to admit that "the deep involvement by the Forces of the time cannot be denied" and to promise that "the facts will continue to be investigated." Many more relevant documents soon surfaced. In 2007, for example, a group of Japanese historians said they found documents within the archive of evidence from the Tokyo War Crimes Tribunal that demonstrated the Japanese military had forced local women to work in brothels that the military set up in Indonesia, China, and Vietnam.[6]

A few days after the *Asahi Simbun* published its story, Prime Minister Miyazawa Kiichi apologized during a visit to Seoul. His apology was strong, but Koreans considered it personal rather than official and were dissatisfied that it came with no promise of financial compensation. Yoshimi's revelations helped prompt an investigation by the Japanese government into the wartime comfort women program. In 1993 Chief Cabinet Secretary Kono Yohei read a statement summarizing and reacting to the results of that investigation. What became known as the "Kono Statement" acknowledged that "in many cases [the women] were recruited against their own will" and that they "suffered immeasurable pain and incurable physical and psychological wounds." As for responsibility for this harm, Kono said the "Japanese military was, directly or indirectly, involved in the establishment and management of the comfort stations and the transfer of comfort women. The recruitment of the comfort women was conducted mainly by private recruiters who acted in response to the request of the military. . . . [A]t times, administrative/military personnel directly took part in the recruitments." Kono thus places some of the blame on the Japanese military, but a greater share on the "private recruiters." The Statement offers an apology: "The Government of Japan would like to take this opportunity once again to extend its sincere apologies and remorse to all those, irrespective of place of origin, who suffered immeasurable pain and incurable physical and psychological wounds as comfort women."[7] The Kono Statement was and remains controversial among the Japanese ruling elite. Many opposed it because they believe the Japanese military did not practice forcible recruitment, or because they worry it will open the door to compensation claims, or both. The comfort women and their supporters rightly saw it as a victory because it marked the Japanese government's first admission of wrongdoing by its military. It was, they hoped, an important step toward the objective that they desire and the Japanese conservatives fear. That objective, however, proved elusive. Korean, Chinese, Filipina, Taiwanese, and Dutch former comfort women filed nine lawsuits in the Japanese courts in the 1990s. All were dismissed (in one case, a higher court overturned a district court's ruling in favor of compensating the plaintiffs). Additional lawsuits filed this decade are still in process at this writing.

The issue has settled into a stalemate that appears exasperating to both sides. As the Japanese government points out, Japanese leaders offered apologies for the comfort women program on many occasions since the Kono Statement. Japan has contributed over $16 million in financial assistance to the comfort women. Most of the history textbooks used in Japanese high schools mention the comfort women.[8] Yet the victims and their supporters are still unsatisfied, not only because of the compensation issue but also because it is all too apparent that part of Japan remains defiantly grudging and resistant.

An unsuccessful Japanese attempt to put the issue to rest was the Asian Women's Fund (AWF). Germany established a fund in 2000 for compensating former slave laborers of the Nazi regime. The fund totaled more than 5 billion euros, provided by the German government and German corporations, and quickly processed tens of thousands of claims. In the case of the comfort women, by contrast, the Japanese preferred the characteristic tactic of oblique compensation, offering the victim a gift while avoiding the acceptance of direct responsibility for the offense. In 1994, Tokyo addressed demands for compensation by proposing to spend $1 billion over 10 years on the affected countries in the form of student exchanges, cultural programs, and training. This produced crowds of angry Koreans hurling eggs at the Japanese Embassy. Tokyo tried a different approach in 1995, creating the AWF, which would collect private donations and distribute compensation to former comfort women. Japanese officials hoped the fund would satisfy demands that the government address the issue, but the government itself would not provide the money lest Tokyo undermine its position that the window for claiming war reparations was closed. The Japanese government did, however, fund a separate AWF payment program for welfare services (distinct from the privately supplied "atonement" funds, or war crime compensation). The victims understood the political nuances. Yang Mi-kang, spokeswoman for the Korea Council for Women Drafted for Military Sexual Slavery in Japan, called the Asian Women's Fund "a scheme of the World War II aggressor, Japan, to avoid legal responsibilities for its actions."[9] Most of those eligible refused to take money from the AWF before its closure in 2007, arguing that the Japanese government was trying to evade responsibility. Others wanted to accept the money but came under pressure to decline. Some of these women took payments secretly. The governments of South Korea and Taiwan established alternative funds for their nationals to encourage them not to take Japanese money. Seven Korean women who accepted AWF payouts in 1997 attracted severe criticism from some of their countrymen, who said Japan had carried out a second rape by buying off its victims.[10]

THE JAPANESE NATIONALIST VIEW

Outsiders wonder why the Japanese continue to generate ill-will toward themselves by fighting this losing and ignoble campaign. The explanation is that many Japanese do not accept the conventional wisdom regarding the comfort women that is prevalent outside Japan. Japanese nationalists and other apologists consistently make several points in defense of the wartime Japanese government with regard to the comfort women issue. Following is a summary of their position.[11]

The Japanese armed forces did not forcibly recruit comfort women. The Japanese military's involvement in the comfort women program was limited to granting approval, building facilities, establishing regulations, and carrying out inspections of the brothels. The military did not seize girls and young women and send them against their will to the brothels. Indeed, the War Ministry warned its personnel to guard against unscrupulous recruiting methods tantamount to kidnapping by private brokers because this would tarnish the prestige of the armed forces. The document found by Yoshimi and published by the *Asahi Shimbun* in 1992 to substantiate the military's complicity in the comfort women program proves that the military's "involvement had benevolent intentions," says Korean Studies Professor Nishioka Tsutomu. "[T]he military was involved in recruiting comfort women, but only by attempting to prevent private brokers from engaging in immoral behavior and claiming they were acting on behalf of the military."[12] The comfort women program is often and erroneously conflated with the Female Volunteer Corps, which recruited large numbers of Korean girls for labor but not prostitution. The notion of forcible recruitment by Japanese authorities is a myth that relies heavily on an account by Yoshida Seiji in his 1983 book *Watashi no Senso Hanzai* (*My War Crime*) that was later discredited. Because of prevalent poverty, the income of prostitution became attractive to many young women, so there was no need for the military to forcibly recruit them. History professor Nakamura Akira argues that "the majority of these women began to serve as comfort women on their own. Or they became prostitutes to pay back their parents' debt. Those were the days when even in Japan women in poor families were sold to prostitution houses."[13]

According to the Japanese nationalist view, the Japanese military did not systematically mistreat the comfort women. The comfort women were not only paid, but their pay was much higher than that of the soldiers they serviced. Komori Yoshihisa, a veteran conservative journalist and *Sankei Shimbun* editor, argues, "I know for a fact that some of those women were making lots and lots of money and built houses back home; remitted money back home to their loved ones. They were getting paid more than generals."[14] One Korean comfort woman named Mun Ok-sun reputedly earned ¥26,145 during three years of service in a brothel in Burma. At the time the annual salary for a Japanese lieutenant general was ¥5,800, and ¥1,000 could purchase a small house in Korea.[15] The comfort women earned higher pay to compensate for the dangers of being located at or near the battlefield. Nonetheless, 95 percent of them returned home alive. Comfort women received medical care and had the rights to time off and recreation. They could and did refuse customers who were drunk or badly behaved. The popular manga artist Kobayashi Yoshinori's Pacific War series *On War* depicts the comfort women as willing, well-paid, and even domineering over their soldier clients and officer supervisors.

Japan's military brothel system should not be singled out for condemnation. All countries have struggled with the matter of meeting the sexual demands of soldiers. Even the United States has sanctioned the establishment of brothels for its soldiers deployed overseas, such as during the postwar occupation of Japan. Although South Koreans strongly criticize Japan for the wartime prostitution of Korean women, before their country's economic take-off, the postwar South Korean government supported sex tourism to Korea as a means of gaining revenue from abroad.[16] Japan approached the problem in an organized and regulated way, motivated by the objectives of controlling sexually transmitted disease among the troops, preventing troops from raping the local women, and strengthening morale. Comfort stations were the battlefield counterpart to civilian brothels, which were tolerated in Japan at the time and not outlawed until 1958. Many of the comfort women were Japanese, so this was not a role reserved for conquered peoples. Historian Hata Ikuhiko has argued that the number of comfort women was only around 10,000 to 20,000 and that 40 percent of them were Japanese, with Chinese and Koreans comprising only 30 percent and 20 percent, respectively.[17]

The comfort women issue is a myth manufactured by groups seeking to shame Japan. The Koreans themselves did not raise the issue until prompted by anti-Japanese *Japanese* beginning in the 1980s. The origin of the comfort women as a postwar political problem is found in the activities of Japanese left-wing activists, who in some cases went to Korea to encourage Korean grievance groups to find women who would claim to be victims. The cooperation of these two groups sharing an interest in embarrassing the Japanese government—leftist Japanese and Koreans with a grudge against Japan and/or seeking payouts from Japan—gave impetus to the comfort women issue. The first of the former comfort women to attain public prominence, Kim Hak-sun, was actually sold into prostitution by her destitute family. The *Asahi Simbun* had a secret agenda in breaking the story in 1991 of Kim going public with her experience. The author of the article was Uemura Takashi, whose mother-in-law Yang Sun-in was a leader of the organization in Korea that Kim first contacted with her story. So Uemura got an important scoop, and Yang got publicity that would build momentum for a potentially successful outcome in Kim's lawsuit. Many of the testimonies of surviving comfort women are dubious. The women have told significantly differing versions of their stories, suggesting the stories have been embellished or fabricated. The Japanese government has worsened the situation by continuously apologizing to the Koreans and Chinese rather than challenging the assertion that the Japanese military systematically abused the comfort women. The South Korean government privately assured Tokyo that once Japan admitted official involvement in the comfort women program, the issue would be dropped. On this basis Japan released the Kono Statement. The Koreans, however, reneged on their promise and supported demands for more apologies and for compensation.

Some of these views can be found among high-ranking government officials. As alluded to earlier, their public statements in this vein undercut the ceremonial apologies. These views also operate behind the scenes, as in the case of a controversial television program. To publicize the issues of sexual slavery and biological warfare by Japan during the war, in 2000 Violence Against Women in War Japan Network (VAWW-Net) and other groups sponsored a mock "Women's International War Crimes Tribunal" that included legal experts from several countries, women's rights activists, and surviving comfort women. The tribunal's judges found Hirohito guilty of war crimes. In 2001 NHK, the state-run Japan Broadcasting Corporation, aired a program about the women's tribunal called *How Is War to Be Judged?* on its educational channel. Tribunal participants were furious with what they saw as a bias in the program against the tribunal and its findings. In July 2001 VAWW-Net sued NHK for violating their agreement on how the program would present the tribunal and for making substantial changes without consulting the tribunal organizers. The program's producer said NHK censored the program in response to pressure from Abe, then deputy cabinet secretary, and another high official. Other participants confirmed the removal of original material that would have further incriminated and embarrassed the Japanese government (including the guilty verdict against Hirohito), as well as the late insertion of a commentary by the conservative historian Hata, who as usual denied military involvement in the comfort women program and ridiculed the tribunal. In January 2007 Tokyo's High Court ruled in favor of VAWW-Net and ordered NHK to pay compensation.[18]

The issue flared brightly again with the ascension of Abe to the post of prime minister. Abe was already well known for asserting that the misdeeds of the Japanese military during the war have been exaggerated. A group of 120 Diet members from Abe's LDP called on the new prime minister to retract the Kono statement. Conservatives were disappointed by Abe's conciliatory approach to China, which might have given him further motivation to defend the wartime regime in which his grandfather was a cabinet minister.[19] In March 2007 Abe in his new capacity made several additional statements that suggested he took issue with the Kono Statement. He said there was "no evidence of coercion" by the military in the recruitment of comfort women. "The testimony that the Japanese military hunted women as sex slaves is completely fabricated. No other evidence supports such testimony," Abe said.[20] The Japanese government followed Abe's remarks with a statement referring to a study in the 1990s. "Among the materials it discovered," said the statement, the study "did not come across any that directly show that the military or authorities so-called forcibly led away" recruits for the brothels.[21] Fellow LDP politician Nakayama Nariaki, one of the advocates of throwing out the Kono Statement, elaborated: "Some say it is useful to compare the brothels to college cafeterias run by private companies, who recruit their own staff, procure foodstuffs and set prices. . . . To say that women were forced by the Japanese military into service is off the mark. The issue must be reconsidered, based on truth, for the sake of Japanese honor."[22]

With his domestic popularity sinking (for unrelated reasons) and his international reputation hurt by what outsiders saw as comfort women denial, Abe backed down and said he accepted the Kono Statement. The U.S. ambassador had reportedly warned the Japanese government that the United States could not support Japan's efforts to press North Korea for more information on its Japanese abductees unless Japan stopped denying that its government forced young women into the comfort women program.[23] Abe's retreat was too late to stop the momentum for a condemnatory resolution by the U.S. Congress and did little to salve the irritation of old wounds in China and Korea.

DILEMMAS FOR THE KOREAN, CHINESE, AND U.S. GOVERNMENTS

The Korean government has struggled with the dilemma of meeting the demands of domestic public opinion while preserving the working relationship with Japan that is important to South Korean prosperity. In 1993 South Korean President Kim Young-sam sought to position Seoul as taking a principled stand while at the same time keeping the way clear for strengthening relations with Japan. Kim said Seoul would not ask Japan for compensation but urged the Japanese government to continue to investigate the comfort women issue and make public its findings. The South Korean government began making its own payments to former Korean comfort women.

In another example, the Kim Dae-jung Administration maintained a seemingly uncompromising rhetorical stand with statements such as "a true future-oriented and mutually beneficial relationship between Korea and Japan can be achieved only if Japan recognizes past history and remorsefully reflects on its deeds."[24] Kim, however, tried in 1998 to smooth over the issue by dropping the official South Korean demand for Japanese compensation and offering another round of funds from his own government to pay the comfort women (about $23,000 per victim). Kim hoped to settle the larger history issue through a general apology for the colonization of Korea from the Japanese government, which Prime Minister Obuchi Keizo provided in October. Afterward Kim said that he considered the comfort women issue closed and that his country's 1965 normalization agreement Japan precluded claims for compensation.[25] This has not settled the issue for the Korean public. Former Korean comfort women and their supporters have demonstrated outside the Japanese Embassy in Seoul every Wednesday at noon since 1992.

Like South Korea, changes in China beginning in the Deng reform era of the 1980s were also conducive to airing the story of the comfort women. Chinese not only became more familiar with the concept of human rights, they also became more sensitive to their victimization by Japan during the war, largely at the urging of the Chinese government. On the comfort women issue in particular, important stimuli were the example of Korean former comfort women seeking compensation from Japan, continued statements from Japanese nationalists downplaying Japanese wartime misbehavior, and the cooperation of sympathetic Japanese lawyers and activist groups with the Chinese. In 1994 a group called the Chinese War Victims Lawyers' Research Committee had organized 280 Japanese lawyers willing to help Chinese seek redress through the Japanese courts.[26]

Chinese plaintiffs in Japanese courts, however, have been no more successful than Korean plaintiffs. Between June 1995 and March 2007, Chinese plaintiffs filed 27 suits seeking compensation for harm they suffered as a result of Japan's wartime policies. These were not only comfort women, but also forced laborers, victims of Japanese bombing and Unit 731 activities, and people harmed by abandoned Japanese chemical weapons. While the victims successfully proved they were harmed, until 2002 the courts dismissed these cases on the basis of either too much time having intervened or state immunity. After 2001 Japanese courts stopped allowing the "time limitation" defense. From 2003 onward the courts in some cases also rejected the state immunity defense. In a March 2005 case, however, the Tokyo High Court accepted the government's argument that Chinese had abandoned their right to claim war damages from Japan as a result of the Treaty of Peace between Japan and the Republic of China that Tokyo signed with Chiang Kai-shek's government on Taiwan in 1952, a treaty explicitly nullified by the 1972 Japan-China normalization agreement. That 1972 agreement became the basis for an important judgment in April 2007.

Japan's Supreme Court dismissed claims for compensation by former Chinese comfort women and former Chinese slave laborers in two separate cases, ruling that these individuals lost their rights to seek compensation as a result of Beijing's renunciation of reparations claims. Although the premises have shifted, the important point is that the Japanese judiciary has declined to seriously challenge the government's position that private citizens from China or Korea cannot be empowered to sue for wartime damages.

The Chinese government's role has been ambivalent. Through the 1990s Chinese history textbooks did not even mention the Chinese comfort women. China's most publicized scholar on the comfort women issue is Professor Su Zhiliang of Shanghai Normal University, who has claimed that Chinese comfort women alone numbered 200,000.[27] Su led an effort to give the issue coverage in textbooks used in Shanghai in the middle of the following decade, but it remained absent from most other Chinese textbooks. Nor was there a memorial to the Chinese comfort women, while there were plenty of memorials throughout the country to other Chinese victims of Japanese aggression.[28] Public pressure forced Beijing first to stop obstructing and then to offer verbal support to the plaintiffs. The state allowed private Chinese activists and scholars to publicize Japanese atrocities against China, and it permitted the formation of support groups for war victims seeking compensation from Japan. The officially sanctioned Chinese media have frequently discussed the comfort women program as an atrocity and an example of the Japanese government's incomplete rehabilitation. To quote a typical passage from the *People's Daily:* "The Comfort Women system carried out by the Japanese army during the Second World War was the ugliest, filthiest, darkest sexual slave system in human history of the 20th century."[29] Chinese officials are very sensitive to Japanese self-justifications on this issue. In 2005, for example, Nakayama as education minister read and endorsed what he said was a comment on the comfort women by a female Japanese student: "it was an occupation they could do with pride if you think they soothed the unstable minds of men on the battleground and provided them rest and a certain order."[30] Chinese Foreign Ministry spokesman Liu Jianchao responded quickly, saying of Nakayama, "The Japanese cabinet member has once again made such utterly shameless remarks, which we feel indignant [about] and strongly condemn. Such comments have hurt the feelings of the people in the victimized countries. The Japanese government should take the responsibility to strictly restrain the words and deeds of relevant persons."[31]

Beijing has not interfered with Chinese citizens seeking redress from Japan, but neither has it been substantially supportive.[32] Initially the Chinese government did not grant the former comfort women permission to travel to Japan for court cases or criticized them after they returned to China.[33] In 1995, the Chinese Foreign Ministry announced the Chinese government's position that the 1972 China-Japan Joint Communique—which said, "The Government of the People's Republic of China . . . renounces its demand for war reparation from Japan"—does not preclude individual Chinese citizens from claiming compensation from Japan for war-related damages. Thenceforth the Chinese government took the position that its citizens had the right to sue the Japanese government and Japanese firms in Japanese courts.[34] But given many opportunities to comment on Japanese responsiveness to the comfort women issue and particularly on lawsuits brought by or on behalf of Chinese former comfort women in Japanese courts, the Chinese Foreign Ministry has consistently stopped short of demanding that Japan pay compensation and instead made only general statements such as, "We request the Japanese government to listen to the just appeal of the international community, properly and earnestly handle the issue left over from history in an attitude responsible for history."[35] Beijing has also quashed the idea, frequently raised by the Chinese public, of protesting through boycotts of Japanese products. Chinese war victims attempting to sue for compensation through the Chinese courts have had their cases rejected, and the Chinese government unlike Seoul has never made payouts to its own former comfort women from public funds.

Like South Korea, Beijing seeks a balance between meeting the expectations of public opinion and preserving the important relationship with Japan. The Chinese government avoids raising the issue in meetings between Chinese and Japanese officials. It appears that Beijing wants to avoid a Japanese accusation that the Chinese are angling to renege on their promise that the government will not seek reparation payments. Beijing also clearly does not want to make its own payments to Chinese victims. Perhaps, as well, the subject is too uncomfortable or humiliating, even compared to the other forms of victimization Chinese people have suffered.[36]

The United States has comparatively weak and cross-cutting interests in the comfort women issue. On one hand, as a self-appointed global human rights monitor and as leader of the coalition that fought against Japan and characterized Japan's military policies as criminal, America sympathizes with the women Japan victimized. On the other hand, Japan is a key U.S. ally and supporter of the U.S. political agenda in Asia. The U.S. State Department has taken a restrained public position on the issue, making only mild statements urging Japan to deal forthrightly with the consequences of its historical behavior. The U.S. judicial branch has been noninterventionist. A group of 15 former comfort women from several countries attempted in 2000 to sue Japan through the U.S. court system under the auspices of the U.S. Alien Tort Statute. The case twice went to the U.S. Supreme Court, which ultimately ruled in 2006 that the issue in question was primarily political and therefore jurisdiction belonged to the U.S. executive branch.

The strongest U.S. response has come from the Congress. Most Americans sided against Japan over the comfort women and by the 1990s some members of Congress were becoming interested in the possibility of weighing in on the issue. Observers in Korea and China saw significance in an official condemnation of Japanese stonewalling over the comfort women issue from the United States, a country that did not have a constituency of victims and was a close ally of Japan. After several years of effort by its supporters, a Congressional resolution calling on the Japanese government to take greater responsibility for victimizing the comfort women was moving toward realization in 2006 until it suddenly suffered procedural death—the proposed resolution was left off the calendar that determined when proposed legislation went to the floor for a vote. Despite the urging of 25 Congressional co-sponsors, House Speaker Dennis Hastert and House Majority Leader John Boehner apparently succumbed to the Bush Administration's argument that antagonizing a key strategic ally is against American interests. To reinforce this argument, the Japanese government was reportedly paying a lobbying firm headed by retired Congressman Bob Michel $60,000 per month to dissuade Congress from highlighting Japanese war crimes.[37]

Abe's evasive statements in spring 2007, however, finally clinched success for the resolution. Its principal sponsor, Congressman Mike Honda of California, is of Japanese ancestry and spent part of his early youth in an internment camp in Colorado. Honda said previous apologies, including the Kono statement and Abe's damage control, fell short of "a formal, official and unambiguous" recognition by the Japanese government "that these women were coerced into sexual slavery by the Japanese Imperial Army before and during World War II."[38] Rep. Tom Tancredo, one of the measure's opponents, asked "how many times we expect a government to apologize for the sins of an imperial government of the past. Asking the Japanese government to take historical responsibility for atrocities of the defunct imperial-era government is somewhat counterproductive and unfair to the people of Japan."[39] The issue for Americans, however, was not Tokyo's apologies, but its denials. Rep. Tom Lantos, Chairman of the House Foreign Affairs Committee, said, "Those who posit that all of the comfort women were happily complicit and acting of their own accord simply do not understand the meaning of the word 'rape.'"[40]

Before the vote, a full-page advertisement appeared in the June 14, 2007 issue of the *Washington Post* listing five so-called facts about the comfort women program, including the main thrust of the apologist position: (1) None of the documents found proves that the Japanese military forced women to work as prostitutes, only that the military tried to prevent forcible abduction. (2) Japanese authorities punished Korean recruiters who kidnapped women. (3) The case of a rogue Japanese Army unit in Indonesia that made sex slaves of Dutch women was an aberration. When higher ranking officers discovered this comfort station, they closed it and punished the perpetrators. (4) The comfort women who supplied testimony to the U.S. Congress did not, when they first told their stories, implicate Japanese military or other Japanese government personnel in their kidnappings. They later embellished their stories. (5) The comfort women were well-paid professional prostitutes in a military brothel system similar to those established by the armed forces of other countries, including U.S. occupation forces in Japan. The advertisement concluded by citing Hata's claim that 40 percent of the comfort women were Japanese and asserting that the House resolution's accusation of massive sexual slavery by the Japanese military is erroneous. Appended to the advertisement were the names of 44 Diet members plus others identified as political commentators, professors and journalists. Although most of the undersigned Diet members were from the conservative LDP, 13 were from the liberal and left-leaning Democratic Party of Japan.

The ad did not prevent the passage of House Resolution 121 in July 2007. The resolution says the Japanese government "should formally acknowledge, apologize, and accept historical responsibility in a clear and unequivocal manner for its Imperial Armed Forces' coercion of young women into sexual slavery," should "clearly and publicly refute" denials that this occurred, and "should educate current and future generations about this horrible crime." (The resolution did not call for payment of the victims.)[41]

The main reaction from Japan was dismay. A *Yomiuri Shimbun* editorialist remarked, "The resolution was made without verifying the facts and smacks of cheap rhetoric. It makes us doubt the intelligence of U.S. lawmakers."[42]

AGGRIEVED SOCIETIES VERSUS DEFENSIVE STATE

There is still considerable uncertainty about the comfort women program. The numbers of women involved are difficult to verify, and the proportion of the different nationalities is disputed. While Hata says the largest ethnic group was Japanese, the Chinese claim there were "at least 200,000 Chinese women." Many sources repeat the statistic that 80 percent of the comfort women were Korean.[43] Which was the typical comfort woman: the one who volunteered knowing what she was getting into, was well-paid, and benefited from military rules preventing abusive treatment, or the one who was either forced or tricked into a cruel sexual enslavement? The scantiness of data allows for a great deal of interpretive leeway by the groups making contending claims. The issue is so emotional and politicized that even if it were forthcoming, the power of compelling new evidence to change or moderate established views is questionable. Each of the two sides (Japan vs. Korea-China-Taiwan, since the latter three can be conflated) is convinced the other is acting in bad faith, concerned with narrow national self-interests rather than in attaining truth or justice.

The comfort women issue is a vehicle for the Koreans and Chinese to pursue their profound and unrequited sense of victimization by the Japanese. The plight of the former comfort women taps into deep societal reservoirs of discontent about the invasion of China and the colonization of Korea. For

Japan, the issue is threatening in two ways. First, it revives the danger of Japanese liability for postnormalization reparation payments. Second, it is an affront to national honor. This sentiment is especially acute for the more conservative Japanese who believe in and desire a high degree of continuity from twentieth to twenty-first century Japan.

The Japanese government and part of Japanese society take the position consistent with the general nationalist view that Japan's wartime policies do not deserve being singled out for condemnation. The positions of the Chinese and Koreans seeking compensation from Tokyo are consistent with their premise that the war was primarily about their suffering under Japanese aggression. For them victory is not defined by the victimization of Japan's population as a result of the war or by the defeat and overthrow of the fascist political system in Japan, but by their yet-unanswered demand for official Japanese restitution.

This is largely an issue driven by the Korean and Chinese publics. The Chinese and South Korean governments, keenly aware of the value of a constructive relationship with Japan, appear to be less interested than their constituents in seeking justice for the victims. On occasion Seoul and Beijing may wish nearly as much as Tokyo to shelve the matter. Given the emotional gravity of the issue, it is not politically possible for the national leaders to take the position at home that the overall relationship with the government representing Asia's largest and most technologically advanced economy outweighs the interests of the individuals with claims against Japan. Significantly, this is as much a problem for the authoritarian Chinese government as for the democratically elected South Korean government. If the political elite is often able to shape mainstream public perceptions about international affairs, this is a case in which national leaders are forced to fulfill the expectations dictated by the public's view of the war.

CHAPTER 10

China and the "History Card"

China is often accused of "playing the history card" by referring to the Pacific War in support of arguments that Japan should make greater economic concessions to China, or that Japan should not increase its defense spending, or that Japan does not deserve a permanent seat in the United Nations Security Council. Political analysts see China playing this card not only with Tokyo and with the international community as a group, but even with Japan's ally the United States. Aspiring to leadership of its part of the world and viewing Japan as a potential rival, Beijing would prefer that the United States join with China in constraining Japanese power, not encourage Japan to take a more active regional and global role in international security issues. Hence the reminders that the Americans were once partners with China in opposing Japanese expansionism. In recent years China has also played up stories of the U.S. Flying Tigers and of Chinese peasants assisting downed American fliers. In 2005, for example, a memorial hall honoring the Flying Tigers opened in Zhijiang in Hunan Province, and in 2007 the Chinese Xinhua News Agency announced plans to build a park in Kunming to honor the Flying Tigers who volunteered "to help China drive out invading Japanese troops."[1]

Employing history as a political tool, Chinese leaders have found it to be powerful but not always compliant. Invoking history has released a flood of nationalistic indignation from a Chinese society deeply embittered by and still highly emotional over the Japan invasion of last century. The leadership's attempt to harness public opinion has led to unintended and even undesirable public input into the management of China's relationship with Japan. If this has made Japan policy one of the most democratized aspects of Chinese

Communist Party rule, it has also kept China and Japan from achieving a real rapprochement in spite of their healthy economic relationship.

EARLY POSTWAR SUPPRESSION OF HISTORY

Contending interpretations of the Pacific War did not become a major issue in postwar relations between China and Japan until the 1980s. In the early postwar decades, rather than cultivate a sense of grievance, the Chinese government and media tried to smooth over the rancor of the Anti-Japanese War. China had ideological, strategic and economic reasons to reach out to Japan across the communist-anticommunist divide. The CCP leadership hoped to encourage the Japanese people to join China in a socialist revolution. In the late 1960s, tensions between China and the Soviet Union and the growing possibility of a thaw in Sino-U.S. relations provided additional incentive for the Chinese to position themselves for an improved relationship with Japan. The rebuilt and resurgent Japanese economy was an attractive potential partner to China, which needed expertise, technology, capital, and markets for Chinese goods.

Consequently, official Chinese historiography emphasized the glory of victory over Japan, but did not cultivate hatred of the Japanese. Chinese officialdom was careful to distinguish between the decent Japanese masses and the few evil militarists responsible for the war and its crimes. The Japanese people as a whole, the Party taught, were victims of the war along with the Chinese people. The emphasis was on the victory led by the CCP. The prevailing political climate in the Mao years held that delving deeply into the suffering of the Chinese people during the war was inappropriate because it could breed discouragement and defeatism and because it smacked of "bourgeois humanitarianism."[2] The state did not promote research into Japanese war crimes and did not make public potentially contentious history-related issues such as the treatment of the Pacific War in Japanese textbooks.

Despite considerable interest among the Japanese people in upgrading economic and cultural exchange with China, Tokyo was constrained in the early postwar years by the containment policy of its important ally the United States and by the large faction of Japanese politicians who were sympathetic toward the Kuomintang-ruled Republic of China on Taiwan. The surprising American diplomatic breakthrough with China, however, allowed Japan to follow suit. Anxious to move ahead with economic cooperation and strategic coordination, the Chinese wanted normal relations with Japan badly enough to bargain away the history issue. During the exchanges attending the Sino-Japan normalization in 1972, Chinese Premier Zhou En-lai accepted a weak semi-apology from Japanese Prime Minister Tanaka Kakuei (who called the war an "unfortunate period" that had caused his country "deep reflection"). Beijing tacitly agreed that responsibility for the war rested with a handful of key individuals from Japan's fascist government. Despite claiming that Japan's invasion and occupation of China caused up to US$50 billion in direct and indirect damages, China exempted Japan from reparation payments, with the understanding that Japan would generously aid China's economic construction thereafter. Deng Xiaoping later explained China's attitude: "Frankly speaking, Japan is indebted to China more than any other nation in the world. At the time of diplomatic normalization, we did not raise any demand for war reparations. . . . I think Japan should make much greater contributions in order to assist China's development."[3] China would eventually be disappointed by Japan's "contributions," but the first years after the normalization saw something of a "honeymoon" in Japan-China relations. The Chinese government continued to suppress discussion in China of Japanese war crimes. Chinese authorities and media ignored the debate within Japan about how to remember the war and what Japanese students should learn about it. Yet there remained a dissonance between the Chinese government's Japan policy and the quiet dissatisfaction of a large number of Chinese whose families the Japanese invasion had scarred. As scholar He Yinan writes, "Beijing attempt[ed] to create an illusion of Sino-Japanese friendship in the 1970s without first settling the historical account."[4]

By the early 1980s new conditions were replacing those that were conducive to the honeymoon. Chinese elites became worried about Japan's military buildup and the possibility of a revival of militarism if the Japanese did not acknowledge the full extent of their war crimes. They also desired to extract greater economic assistance from Japan. Even more important was the new domestic environment. The damage and disruption of the Cultural Revolution (1966–1969, with vestiges continuing until the arrest of the ultra-leftist Gang of Four in 1976) had greatly reduced the CCP's prestige in China. The Party was searching for an alternative ideology to unify the country and mobilize support for the modernization campaign. Furthermore, the reform program of newly emergent paramount leader Deng had many conservative domestic opponents because of the increases in unemployment, inflation, crime and corruption that were the downside of economic liberalization. The approach Party leaders chose to deal with these problems owed much to media reports out of Japan in June 1982 discussing new developments in an old issue.

THE 1982 TEXTBOOK CONTROVERSY

Japanese schools choose their history textbooks from a list of books approved by the Ministry of Education. Authors hoping to make the list must have submitted their manuscripts to the ministry for review. The current textbook authorization system began in 1947 at the order of the U.S. occupation government, which wanted the schools to have a choice of textbooks written by independent scholars. Both liberals and conservatives in Japan have seen history textbooks as a crucial ideological battleground because of their potential impact on impressionable youth who represent the country's future. The Ministry of Education came under the pressure of both liberals who wanted a more frank acknowledgement of Japan's war crimes and conservatives who wanted textbooks to pass through a so-called patriotism filter. Liberals believed it was essential for Japanese citizens to understand the destruction their country had inflicted on other Asians and the terrible consequences that resulted from Japanese fascism. Conservatives saw this as a leftist or foreign-inspired attempt to discredit the traditional Japanese social and political order with a view toward promoting a communist revolution. In January 1982 the LDP demanded that Japanese schools should "cultivate the Japanese spirit and foster national pride."[5]

On June 26 and 27 at least four major Japanese newspapers reported that the Ministry of Education had ordered a revision in textbooks being prepared for use the following year. The Ministry reportedly wanted the passage noting that Japanese forces "invaded and plundered" (*shinryaku*) north China changed to "entered and assaulted" (*shinko*) or "advanced into" (*shinshutsu*). Other reports soon followed that the Ministry sought to remove Nanjing Massacre casualty figures and to disparage the Korean independence movement during the Japanese occupation. The truthfulness of these reports came into question, and in September the *Asahi Shimbun* and *Sankei Shimbun* printed retractions.[6] These mattered little, as the incident had already caused important shifts in both Chinese domestic politics and China-Japan relations.

This became the first major diplomatic row between China and Japan since their normalization of relations. Chinese criticism began in the summer of 1982—apparently after considerable deliberation, since nearly a month passed between the first Chinese media acknowledgement (without commentary) of the story in June and the first protests by Chinese officials in July. These officials and their media organs accused Japan of attempting a dangerous and unacceptable distortion of history, called on the Japanese government to correct the mistake, and rejected the Japanese defense that textbooks were written by private scholars rather than the government.[7] Japanese Prime Minister Suzuki Zenko, who visited China in September to celebrate the tenth anniversary of the normalization of relations, was among the Japanese officials forced to endure harangues over the textbook issue and more broadly the history issue from their Chinese counterparts. In August Miyazawa Kiichi, then Japan's Chief Cabinet Secretary, made a public statement noting that China and South Korea "have been criticizing some descriptions in Japanese textbooks." He offered the assurance that "From the perspective of building friendship and goodwill with neighboring countries, Japan will pay due attention to these criticisms and make corrections at the Government's responsibility."[8]

The 1982 textbook controversy marked the beginning of the history issue as an open dispute in Sino-Japan relations. As Chinese elites knew, liberals and conservatives in Japan had been battling over interpretations of the Pacific War for years prior to 1982. The Chinese might have reached the conclusion that the influence of Japanese conservatives had proven more of a threat than previously hoped, and that the time had come for China to change from a stance of passively waiting for jingoism to die out to one of active intervention. That has become the conventional wisdom for many Chinese, such as Zhang Xianwen, director of the Center for the History of Republican China at Nanjing University. As Zhang puts it, "We have decided to fight back and force Japan to admit its responsibility" because "the Japanese right is becoming stronger and stronger, and they have denied causing the war in Asia."[9] It seems at least as likely, however, that the driving factor was Chinese domestic politics, particularly the need for a new way to use history to galvanize the disillusioned masses and deflect criticism from the ruling regime.[10] Within weeks of the textbook controversy, the CCP began to move toward a new education program and a new spin on the Anti-Japan War.

PATRIOTISM AND VICTIMIZATION

Radical Maoism had torn the country apart during the Cultural Revolution. The relevance of socialism itself was endangered by the market-oriented economic reforms that began in the late 1970s. The government promoted so-called patriotic education as a means of shoring up the Party's mandate to rule. Gradually patriotism replaced communist ideology as the main source of the CCP's legitimacy.[11] In the 1950s China had begun a program of "five loves education," one of the loves being love of country. That program soon gave way to a focus on Maoist ideology, but in the mid-1980s it returned. The Party also introduced a new perspective on the historical period within which the war fell, characterized by scholar Peter Hays Gries as a "victimization narrative."[12] This stressed foreign aggression and the harm and humiliation it had caused China. A particular feature was greater discussion of Japanese atrocities against the Chinese. The message was that past backwardness left China vulnerable to malicious foreign powers. Economic development, however, would bring strength, security, and respect. National indignation should therefore motivate the people to work for a restoration of the power and prestige to which the Chinese believe they are destined.

Chinese media gave increased attention to Japanese war crimes committed in China. Several large museums dedicated to the war appeared: the Memorial Hall for the Victims of the Nanjing Massacre, built in Nanjing in 1985 and expanded twice since then; the Memorial Hall of the People's Anti-Japan War, which opened in 1987 in Beijing; and Shenyang's September 18 (the date of the Mukden Incident in 1931) History Museum in 1992. Equally importantly, the greater openness of the post-Mao reform era and the Chinese government's willingness to allow discussion of Japanese atrocities provided opportunities for forces in Chinese society—scholars, activists, lawyers and media—to conduct research into this topic, form advocacy groups, raise awareness through the media, and launch legal and political campaigns seeking redress.

Lifting the suppression on stories of victimization brought a catharsis from the Chinese people. The Nanjing Massacre museum got up to a million visitors a year. Chinese historians revealed details of specific atrocities. Victims (comfort women, forced laborers, harmed by discarded chemical weapons, etc.) and activists began a "redress movement" (*suopei yundong*) to attempt to win compensation through the Japanese courts. The movement gained momentum when Japanese lawyers visiting China to gather information formed alliances with Chinese history activists. The Chinese media enthusiastically covered these activities, which were also among their most popular stories. The media coverage expanded knowledge of these stories of victimization from local to regional and from regional to national. Chinese society created pressure on the Chinese government. Private activists lobbied the government for changes related to the history issue. Activists have sponsored grassroots movements during this decade, for example, to demand that the Chinese government establish national holidays to commemorate important wartime events such as the start of the Japanese invasion and the beginning of the Nanjing Massacre. These movements won support from the media and some regional office holders but met resistance from Beijing.[13]

This dynamic has great significance for Chinese domestic politics, but even greater import for China-Japan relations. Beijing's wish is to play the history card selectively depending upon the official Chinese attitude toward the overall bilateral relationship—whether China is basically satisfied or dissatisfied, and whether Beijing is in complaining or reconciliation mode. In 1991, for example, the Chinese government cancelled a commemoration of the Nanjing Massacre that would have coincided with a visit by Japanese Prime Minister Kaifu Toshiki. Strong public demand for government action in defense of national honor and dignity, however, is often irresistible even for China's authoritarian, one-party state. By the 1990s popular nationalism had become a major political force in China. It does not always accord with the agenda of the Chinese leadership. Chinese citizens fired with nationalistic fervor questioned why Beijing waived reparations payments upon normalization of relations with Japan; the famous dissident Fang Lizhi was among them.[14] The Foreign Ministry's 1995 announcement that Chinese citizens had the right to file private lawsuits against the Japanese government resulted from public pressure. Chinese authorities sometimes try to suppress activities that are likely to produce national outrage at times unwanted by the government. The CCP, for example, ordered cadres not to encourage compensation claims against Japan prior to the emperor's visit to China in 1992. In the two recent flare-ups of public outrage over the disputed Senkaku / Diaoyutai Islands, the government tried to stop demonstrations by students and activists. Authorities also restricted demonstrations planned for Prime Minister Hashimoto Ryutaro's visit to China in Sept 1997. The history issue is able to mobilize Chinese society to impact Sino-Japan relations in ways not controlled by the Chinese government.

The *official* Chinese Japan-bashing campaign apparently peaked in 1998. In October of that year Japanese Prime Minister Obuchi Keizo gave South Korean President Kim Dae-jung a written apology for Japan's invasion of Korea, with Kim responding that he considered the history issue between

Korea and Japan settled. The following month Chinese President Jiang Zemin visited Japan hoping to get a similar written apology. The Chinese saw the summit as an opportunity for a breakthrough in Sino-Japan relations, comparable to the normalization of bilateral relations in 1972, if Japan could satisfy Chinese expectations on the history issue. Tokyo, however, disappointed the Chinese. The apology contained in the Japanese part of the joint statement was relatively weak, avoiding the unambiguous Japanese term with the connotation of responsibility. Japan's statements on the Taiwan issue also failed to please China. While in Japan, Jiang displayed China's dissatisfaction by lecturing his hosts about the need for greater penitence from Japan with regard to its Pacific War baggage. Jiang's tough approach backfired. Much of the Japanese public not only judged Jiang to be a rude guest, but became convinced that the Chinese government was cynically over-using the history issue as a political weapon to bind Japan in a permanently subordinate position. Sensing that bashing Japan over war crimes had become counterproductive, Beijing thereafter scaled back its rhetoric on the subject. In the meetings with Japanese leaders in 2000–2002, Chinese Premier Zhu Rongji and future Vice-President Zeng Qinghong avoided strong criticism over the history issue and instead emphasized the value of cooperation. With Hu Jintao and Koizumi Junichiro leading new administrations, the Chinese focused on the modest goal of getting the Japanese prime minister to stop visiting Yasukuni, making this a precondition to further bilateral summit meetings. In 2002–03, some Chinese intellectuals proposed new thinking toward Japan: leaving aside historical grievances and concentrating on forging a relationship with Japan that suits China's current strategic interests. The argument had merit, but public reaction was so negative as to deter Chinese leaders from carrying the idea forward.

Indeed, while Beijing moved to cut back on Japan-bashing in favor of stabilizing the relationship, the Chinese public remained more interested in pursuing its grudge against Japan. The increased attention to Japanese wartime outrages against China created a climate among the Chinese people of animosity toward Japan and heightened sensitivity to any further perceived offenses. This climate was conducive to episodes of focused hostility, of which there were several in the decades of the 1990s and the 2000s, some spontaneous and clearly unwelcomed by the Chinese government.

The Chinese public is quick to interpret Sino-Japan relations through the lens of twentieth-century history. A photo of Chinese actress Zhao Wei that appeared on a magazine cover in 2001 enraged many Chinese. Zhao was wearing a dress that displayed a stylized Japanese rising sun flag with the Chinese characters for the words *hygiene, health, happiness,* and *peace* printed around the flag's edges. Since the flag is associated with Japanese militarism, Zhao was accused of insensitivity toward the feelings of Chinese who had suffered during the Japanese invasion. The outcry was so great that Zhao responded with a public apology. Nevertheless, while Zhao was performing at a concert in Hunan a few days later, a man attacked her onstage and splashed excrement on her. The man's grandparents had reportedly died in the war. He later said, "As a famous Chinese person, [Zhao] should have been aware of such an important event in Chinese history."[15]

Japanese automaker Toyota placed advertisements in the Chinese magazine *Auto Fan* in 2003 that drew national attention for their perceived subtext of Japanese national superiority. The first ad, which was for the Toyota Prado (unfortunately transliterated in Chinese as *Badao*, which means "domineering"), depicted two traditional Chinese carved-stone lions bowing and saluting a passing Prado, with a caption reading, "You cannot but respect Badao." Not only are the stone lions a common symbol of China, but some Chinese saw an allusion to the lions at the entrance of the Marco Polo Bridge, the site where Japan launched its invasion of China proper in 1937. The other ad showed a Toyota Land Cruiser towing a broken-down Chinese military truck through mountainous country. In December 2003 Toyota apologized for and discontinued the two advertisements, saying they "are solely commercial and contain no other intention."[16]

The Chinese authorities appealed for calm and civility during the 2004 Asian Cup soccer tournament hosted by China, but history-driven hostility followed the Japanese contingent. Countless anti-Japan banners made reference to war crimes. After a game in Chongqing Chinese rioters surrounded the Japanese team's bus. As Japan played the Chinese team in the final match, Chinese fans inundated the visitors with nonstop jeering. Japan won the game 3–1, causing a riot among Chinese spectators that thousands of Chinese security personnel struggled to contain. Japanese fans were trapped in the stadium for several hours and hundreds of angry Chinese protested outside the hotel where the Japanese players were staying.

In the economic sphere of the relationship, Chinese share their leadership's belief that given both Japan's aggressions against China and the magnanimity of Beijing in waiving reparations, Japan should be extraordinarily generous in its economic exchanges with China. In the inevitable trade disputes between large economies such as those of Japan and China, Chinese tend to assume that the burden is on Japan to give ground. Chinese commonly speak of the success of Japanese products penetrating the China market as a new form of invasion. The frequent call for anti-Japanese boycotts from private Chinese citizens harks back to similar tactics in the 1930s protesting Japanese encroachment on Chinese territory.[17]

Chinese sensitivity is particularly high near anniversaries of major events of the second Sino-Japan War. If a perceived affront from Japan falls within one of these time periods, the Chinese response will typically be even greater. In September 2003, Chinese media reported police were investigating an incident involving Japanese tourists. Some 380 visiting Japanese businessmen, employees of a construction company based in Osaka, reportedly engaged in a three-day orgy with several hundred Chinese prostitutes in a luxury hotel in Zhuhai. The episode coincided with the anniversary of the 1931 Mukden Incident. The Zhuhai orgy drew widespread public attention and provoked strong anti-Japanese sentiment in China. A Foreign Ministry official said the "odious" incident "harmed the feelings of Chinese people and also seriously harmed Japan's international image." Another incident soon followed. At the end of October, four Japanese exchange students and a Japanese professor participating in a cultural festival at Northwest China University in Xian performed a ribald dance while wearing red brassieres over their T-shirts and paper cups representing genitalia. The Chinese spectators deemed the act obscene and humiliating. Word of the incident spread quickly, creating a furor that undoubtedly got a running start from the other recent Japan-related controversies. Chinese students assaulted two Japanese students in their dormitory, prompting Chinese police to move all the foreign students out of the dormitory and into a hotel. As many as 1,000 Chinese students protested on the campus and then marched downtown. The Chinese MOFA called in a Japanese embassy official to protest, and the students composed a public apology.[18]

A pattern has developed: an unforeseen incident that fuels anti-Japanese sentiment comes to the attention of the Chinese public. This leads to strong expressions of public outrage through the media, street demonstrations, the Internet, and petition drives. The pressure moves the Chinese government to lodge a strong, public protest with Japan.

JAPAN'S RESPONSES

The rise of anti-Japanese sentiment in China was reciprocated. Public opinion polls administered by the prime minister's office show that a solid majority of Japanese had favorable feelings toward China until the Tiananmen Incident of 1989. Thereafter negative feelings rose sharply and remained high through the 1990s. In 2005, 63 percent of respondents expressed a negative view of China, compared to only 32 percent reporting a positive view.[19] Japanese like other observers saw the crushing of protestors in and around Tiananmen Square as a disappointing reminder that the CCP retained a brutal authoritarian core despite the market-oriented economic reforms that drew so much positive attention through the 1980s. Japanese also became more concerned in the 1990s that their authoritarian neighbor not only nurtured anti-Japan sentiment, but was also building up its conventional military power. Yet, again reminiscent of China, these political misgivings did not prevent Japan from maintaining a strong economic relationship with China. Indeed, only a year after Tiananmen, Japan broke ranks with the Western powers and discontinued the punitive economic sanctions against China.

Japan has been willing to accommodate China in some respects on the history issue, but in other areas the Japanese stand their ground. Japanese were showing clear signs of guilt fatigue by the 1990s. Most Japanese by that time had been born after the war and knew Japan as a democratic, anti-militarist country that participated enthusiastically in efforts to strengthen international norms and to assist developing countries. Furthermore, among increasing numbers of Japanese, sympathy for the victimized Chinese was giving way to resentment. Many Japanese believed, with considerable merit, that the Chinese government was promoting anti-Japanese sentiment through the Chinese media and education system, while ignoring Japanese economic assistance to China and the pacific character of Japanese foreign policy in the six decades since the war. Japanese observers also noted that Chinese history is selective. Chinese textbooks do not discuss the dark side of Maoist policies such as the purge of landlords, the Great Leap Forward or the Great Proletarian Cultural Revolution, which resulted in the deaths of substantially more Chinese than did the Japanese invasion.

Several prime ministers and other officials and even the emperor have apologized to China (as well as to Korea and other countries) about the war. These obviously have not satisfied the Chinese. There are two reasons why. First, as we have seen, statements and activities by Japanese conservatives often undercut the apologies, and effectively invalidate them in the minds of foreign observers. As Prime Minister Murayama Tomiichi offered an apology on the 50th anniversary of the war's end, for example, nine cabinet members were symbolically visiting the Yasukuni Shrine, and under the pressure of conservatives an accompanying Diet resolution omitted the so-called apology phrase of Murayama's statement. One Japanese nationalist pressure group that has opposed Diet resolutions apologizing for or criticizing Japan's wartime behavior says, "Such a resolution would be unique in world history and Japan would become the only nation to accept responsibility for a war as a criminal nation." This would "wound the honor of the state and the Japanese people, profane the spirits of the war dead martyred in a national calamity, and would deal a grievous blow to the future of the nation and the Japanese people."[20] Nationalist activists collected 4.5 million signatures opposing the proposed Diet resolution in 1995. Japanese veterans often express the view that if the war is de-legitimized, the meaning and heroism of their comrades' deaths will be lost, a prospect they cannot accept.

The second reason why the intended audiences are not satisfied by Japanese apologies is the specific wording. Japanese apologies in the 1970s and 1980s used the word *hansei* (regret or remorse), a relatively weak expression that might apply to something minor. Beginning in the 1990s Japanese prime ministers used the word *owabi*, which means "apologize." But Japanese officials have resisted using the word Chinese and Koreans want to hear: *shazai*, which is the appropriate term for an official apology for a grave offense. Thus, while many Japanese believe Japan has apologized enough and should stop, Chinese tend to believe Japan has not yet sincerely apologized.

As we saw in connection with the comfort women, Tokyo fears opening the potential financial floodgates to the claims for private individuals seeking compensation for harm they or their relatives suffered during the war. Another group that falls into this category are former forced laborers. Their lawsuits in Japanese courts over the past two decades have been no more successful than those of the former comfort women, and for similar reasons. In addition to reaffirming the position that the 1972 China-Japan Joint Communique closed the possibility of reparations claims by Chinese individuals as well as their government, in 2007 the Japanese Supreme Court dismissed two cases involving a total of 48 Chinese plaintiffs seeking compensation for forced wartime labor because they exceeded a 20-year statute of limitations.

In 1999 Tokyo committed to take responsibility for and pay the costs of removing the estimated 700,000 (Japanese estimate) to 2 million (Chinese estimate) chemical weapons shells Japan abandoned in China during the war, plus storage containers full of still-lethal chemicals. Progress in the location and removal of these abandoned weapons and chemicals, which have harmed an estimated 2,000 Chinese since the end of the war, has been slow because they are buried in multiple, unknown sites spread over several Chinese provinces. In August 2003, a construction project in Heilongjiang dug up Japanese-dumped chemical weapons, resulting in the death of one worker and harm to 44 others. More than a million Chinese Internet users endorsed a demand that Japan immediately apologize and pay compensation. The Chinese government made its first strong denunciation of Japan for moving too slowly to remove its abandoned chemical weapons. After a delay that further angered the Chinese, Tokyo offered a cash payment for "costs related to the disposal of chemical weapons" rather than compensation.[21] Considerable Japanese effort to find and remove these deadly munitions has bought Tokyo little goodwill, as Chinese generally feel Japan has moved too slowly and grudgingly.

A history-related irritant to China that would be far easier for the Japanese to neutralize is the recent tradition of prime ministerial visits to the Yasukuni Shrine. Although it involves neither financial implications nor technical challenges, the Japanese have found it difficult to discontinue this practice for domestic political reasons. Several Japanese prime ministers visited the Yasukuni Shrine prior to 1985 without drawing criticism from China's state-controlled media. Japanese Prime Minister Nakasone Yasuhiro's 1985 visit to Yasukuni prompted an anti-Japanese demonstration by Chinese students, rare up to that time but commonplace since then. The dispute over Nakasone's Shrine visit in 1985 led to an informal bilateral agreement that the Japanese prime minister, foreign minister and cabinet chief secretary would stay away from Yasukuni, but that Beijing would tolerate visits to the Shine by other Japanese officials.[22] This held up until Prime Minister Hashimoto Ryutaro visit Yasukuni in 1996. Despite explicit requests from the top Chinese leadership not to do so, Prime Minister Koizumi Junichiro visited the Yasukuni Shrine every year during his tenure as prime minister from 2001 to 2006. Chinese leaders identified Koizumi's visits to Yasukuni as the single greatest obstacle to improved Sino-Japanese relations. Chinese Foreign Minister Li Zhaoxing complained in November 2005, "If a German leader went and worshipped Hitler, worshipped the Nazis, how would the European people look at this? Would this hurt their feelings? . . . Yet Japanese leaders are worshipping these war criminals that harmed so many Chinese people."[23] But the shrine visits pleased Koizumi's conservative supporters, and he consistently maintained that outsiders had no right to dictate how Japanese honor their war dead. Koizumi said repeatedly his purpose in going to the shrine is to pray for peace. Confronted with the argument that his visits to the shrine imply that he condones the actions of convicted war criminals, Koizumi responds with an attitude that is prevalent in Japanese culture: "Why keep blaming the dead for the crimes they committed when they were alive? I don't think it befits Japanese thinking not to forgive people even after their death."[24] According to Shinto doctrine, spirits are purged of sin at the time of enshrinement.

Both outsiders and Japanese have debated possible compromises. One proposal is to de-shrine the war criminals and move them to a less prominent shrine, while continuing the practice of symbolic visits to Yasukuni by high Japanese officials. The Japanese government, however, counters that it has no authority to impose this change upon this shrine, and Yasukuni's Shinto priests insist that an enshrinement cannot be undone. Another idea is to establish an alternative, secular war memorial, one that implies no glorification of war criminals, which could replace Yasukuni as the site of high-profile visits. The families of Japanese war dead reject this idea, saying Yasukuni should remain the focal point of commemoration. Koizumi's successors seemed to finally find a way to defuse the issue. Abe Shinzo had visited Yasukuni Shrine a few months before becoming prime minister. Upon taking up the office in September 2006, Abe followed a policy of ambiguity that seemed to satisfy both the Japanese public (which was divided over the issue of prime ministerial Yasukuni visits) and the Chinese. He said he would not publicly comment on whether or not he intended to visit the Shrine. Japan's next Prime Minister, Fukuda Yasuo, went even further, promising that he would not visit Yasukuni and that he placed a high priority on improving Japan's relationship with China.

2005: A BAD YEAR

What happened in 2005 exemplified well the dynamic of the history issue in this decade's Sino-Japan relations. On March 21 a United Nations report supported granting a greater decision-making role to countries such as Japan that are major financial contributors to the UN. This sparked adverse reaction in China, including an Internet petition campaign to oppose Japan gaining a permanent seat in the UN Security Council. In early April, while Chinese were still agitated over the UN issue, Japan's Ministry of Education announced its list of approved textbooks. Reports of more whitewashing of history in the textbooks caused anti-Japanese demonstrations to break out in at least 30 Chinese cities. The protests continued for three weeks. In some cases the protesters sought out and damaged Japanese-made cars and Japanese businesses. The Japanese ambassador to China demanded that Chinese authorities do more to ensure the safety of Japanese nationals in China. In Beijing thousands marched on the Japanese Embassy to hurl rocks and bottles. Protestors in Shanghai marched to the Japanese consulate, damaging

Japanese-associated shops and Japanese cars along the way. Then they splattered the consulate's walls with eggs and paint. Expressing a sentiment typical of the protestors, one participating Chinese student said, "China must stand up for its rights and stop being soft on Japan."[25]

The reaction of Chinese authorities indicated they felt compelled to allow the populace to blow off some anti-Japanese steam, but at the same time they were committed to keeping the protests contained. The authorities initially tolerated the protests. In some cases they provided buses to transport protestors to and from rally sites. Police allowed the crowds to vandalize the Japanese Embassy and consulates. After letting the public indulge its rage, however, the government moved to rein in the protests. The state deployed larger numbers of police, who began telling the crowds to disperse. University campuses organized seminars about Sino-Japan relations. The media carried appeals for stability and cut back on inflammatory stories about Japan.[26]

There was an echo of these demonstrations in Japan, which saw a few cases of Japanese, angry about what was happening in China, sending threats to Chinese diplomats and damaging Chinese-linked buildings in Japan. The Japanese government asked the Chinese government to apologize and pay for the damage caused to Japanese property in China, but Beijing refused. "The Chinese government has never done anything for which it has to apologize to the Japanese people," said Foreign Minister Li Zhaoxing. "The problem now is that the Japanese government has done a series of things that have hurt the feelings of the Chinese people on the Taiwan issue, some international issues and especially the treatment of history."[27] Chinese Vice Foreign Minister Wu Dawei said in April 2005 that the bilateral relationship was in the midst of "the most serious difficulties since China and Japan normalized their relations in 1972."[28]

Koizumi had begun a strong push for permanent Japanese membership in the UN Security Council in late 2004. The Council's permanent membership had not changed since the end of World War II and was limited to the five major Allied powers: the United Kingdom, Russia, France, China, and the United States. The Chinese government had long opposed Japanese membership. Admitting Japan would raise Tokyo's global leadership profile, signal Japan's rehabilitation in the eyes of the international community, strengthen the subgroup of Security Council states that frequently disagrees with China's positions on international security issues, and end China's tenure as the sole representative of Asia among the permanent members. Rather than themselves openly opposing Japan's campaign for a permanent seat, Chinese leaders had been following the familiar course of letting other countries (such as South Korea) take the lead on a contentious international issue while China maintained the flow of economic benefits from Japan. But the three weeks of demonstrations and the 30 million Chinese names on an Internet petition opposing Japan's Security Council bid evidently forced Beijing to take a stronger and more public stand. On April 13, 2005, while visiting India, Chinese Premier Wen Jiabao announced that China was opposed to Japan gaining a permanent seat in the UN Security Council. In China's view, he said, the history issue disqualified Japan. "Only a country that respects history, takes responsibility for history and wins over the trust of peoples in Asia and the world at large can take greater responsibilities in the international community," he explained.[29]

In sum, spontaneous outbursts of anti-Japan sentiment among Chinese already sensitized to the issue, only partly triggered by a controversial Japanese action, forced the Chinese government to take unplanned steps and to suffer undesired damage to Japan-China relations. Beijing played a delicate game, trying to appease its public enough to avoid being accused of unpatriotism, while at the same time staking out limits to the protests with a view toward limiting the bilateral damage. These events renewed the wish of both governments that the other side would make the necessary changes enabling the relationship to transcend the history issue.

THE EFFECT OF THE HISTORY ISSUE ON SINO-JAPANESE RELATIONS

The history issue obviously raises bilateral tensions and is a major impediment to improved political relations. As in other regions that have suffered a recent and major war, the history issue warps the bilateral relationship. From Japan's point of view, the Chinese intentionally neglect Japan's exemplary record of peaceful and constructive international citizenship over the last six decades, including a massive amount of assistance to China's economic development. Japan also has legitimate grounds for concern about the rapid buildup and modernization of the Chinese armed forces and asks why such a unilateral military increase is necessary when China faces no apparent threat (certainly not from Japan, with its small force, very limited budget, and unique constitutional constraints on the use of force). From the Chinese standpoint, China is the historical victim and Japan the historical aggressor. Therefore, Japanese complaints about growing Chinese military power are patently absurd and presumably a smokescreen for a Japanese right-wing agenda to limit China's strength while Japan rearms.

International security assessments consider not only capabilities, but also intentions. Japanese intentions appear potentially hostile to the Chinese because of what Japan did last century and because some Japanese today refuse to condemn what Japan did. Chinese intentions appear hostile to the Japanese because China displays a level of anti-Japan sentiment that to the Japanese seems irrationally dismissive of Japan's postwar transformation. This perceived mutual hostility can feed a security dilemma: one country's attempts to protect itself look threatening to another state, causing a tragic downward spiral of action and counteraction toward a conflict neither state wants.

The history issue worsens bilateral disputes. For example, the disputed Senkaku/Diaoyutai Islands, although very small and uninhabited, take on an exaggerated importance because they fall into the historical Kang Ri

Zhanzheng context of Japan seizing Chinese territory. The activities of private Chinese who object to Japan's claims to ownership of the Senkaku / Diaoyutai Islands led to an increased presence of Japanese security forces there and prompted a Diet resolution reaffirming Japan's position. Consequently, it is not difficult to imagine an incident between Chinese and Japanese security units near the islands that would have dangerous potential for further escalation. Were it not for the Pacific War history issue the Chinese and Japanese publics probably would not even be aware of the disputed islands.

The history issue can have a tangible effect on Sino-Japan relations in the form of lost trade opportunities. Anti-Japanese protests in China, which sometimes involve the destruction of property that the angry crowds associate with Japan, affect Japanese decisions about the costs of doing business with China. During consideration of proposals for new high-speed mass transit systems in China, which saw the Japanese Shinkansen (Bullet Train) competing against European firms, a Chinese official confirmed that Chinese displeasure with Japan over the history issue would be a factor in the selection.[30]

China-Japan relations are often described as a marvel for the stark contrast between the thriving economic relationship and the troubled, seemingly intractable political relationship. Japan has been an important market for Chinese goods, a source of investment capital and technical expertise, and a provider of low-interest loans. Bilateral trade surpassed $200 billion in 2006 and continues to grow rapidly. The political aspect threatens but has not destroyed the economic aspect of the relationship; indeed, the economic ties seem to provide a "safety net" that prevents the overall relationship from plunging into irreparable deterioration. Along with the simmering rivalry between two major regional states, the history issue contributes mightily to the pressure on this net and has the potential to break through it.

RIDING THE TIGER OF HISTORY

The Chinese government first suppressed popular sentiment about the war against Japan. This sentiment, initially latent and unorganized, held that Japan committed outrages against the Chinese that were of such an odious character and on so a great scale that the Chinese people required a full airing of what happened to them as well as sincere penitence and compensation from the Japanese government. But the CCP saw such an exhumation as inconsistent with the Party's program for nation-building and with its Japan policy. In the early postwar years, seeking an upgraded relationship with Japan, China played the history card by declining to play it. This, as the Japanese understood, was a substantial concession. The Chinese government essentially let bygones by bygones for the purposes of Sino-Japan relations, not holding the postwar Japanese government or people responsible for the aggression of the fascist period. The agreement to forego reparations typified this approach.

Later, under new leadership and amidst changed domestic conditions, the CCP altered its policy on dealing with wartime history by employing the theme of national victimization at the hands of Japan as a means of galvaniz-ing national unity and support for Deng's economic development strategy. This had consequences for China's relationship with Japan that clearly went beyond Beijing's wishes. Having encouraged the growth of popular Chinese nationalism, the state could not completely control it. Since the 1980s the Chinese government has struggled to limit the damage to bilateral relations while at the same time avoid appearing to the Chinese people to be weak in the face of foreign challenges. Throwing the history card onto the table at home has forced Beijing to do the same internationally even when Chinese leaders preferred not to.

China's postwar relationship with Japan clearly illustrates two of the ana-lytical dimensions that recur in this study. The first is the variability of a community's understanding of the meaning of the war in light of the political circumstances of the day. While the Party's view of the war as an affirmation of its own worthiness to lead China has not changed, the place of Japanese atrocities in this official narrative has shifted from peripheral to central. The second relevant analytical dimension is the interaction between state and soci-ety. In China's Japan policy we see a government both attempting to manage history and bowing to the expectations of a history-conscious mass public.

Invoking history is useful at both the domestic level and the international level. China's experience with the history card, however, demonstrates two hazards. First, sometimes regime or national interests call for playing the card differently for the two audiences, and it is not always possible to keep these two arenas compartmentalized. With the continued opening of China and increasing access of Chinese citizens to the Internet, cell phones and other communications technology, the days of keeping the public in the dark are clearly past. To satisfy both the demands of popular nationalism and the need for a healthy economic relationship with Japan, the Chinese government may wish to play up its indignation over the war among its own people while play-ing it down in interactions with the Japanese. Awareness of this inconsistency is displeasing to both groups. To uphold the most immediate and pressing objective of regime security, the government cannot afford to run too far afoul of public opinion. A recurring theme of modern Chinese history is the swiftness with which public anger toward foreigners can turn to anger against the government for failing to uphold China's interests and dignity against affronts from abroad.

Chinese leaders have discovered that invoking history in support of today's political battles is akin to riding a tiger. Once energized, mass nationalism is not completely controllable and can sometimes force national policymak-ers to act against their own preferences. Chinese leaders might believe that the national interest is best served by the kind of moderation that recom-mended officially waiving demands for reparations or putting a stop to some planned anti-Japanese protests. To an emotionally charged citizenry, however, this looks like pusillanimity. Thus, the leadership can appeal to nationalist sentiment to gain support for domestic policies or to increase its bargaining power on bilateral issues, but does so at its own peril. Pulling the nationalist lever may in the end force the government to choose between suffering a loss of legitimacy at home and excessively damaging a relationship with another country.

With its limited territory and resources and a middling and gradually shrinking population, Japan has apparently peaked as an economic major power and a strategic middle power. China is surpassing Japan economically and has the potential to go on to achieve superpower status. With its relative power growing and its strategic situation increasingly favorable, China might choose to feel less threatened by Japan and therefore less alarmed by the unwillingness of some Japanese to adopt China's interpretation of the Pacific War. Alternatively, as their relative power grows the Chinese might become more expectant that Japan adopts China's outlook on this and other questions.

CHAPTER 11

U.S.-Japan Relations

As we have seen, wartime Japan had an authoritarian political system with a militarist ethos and a particular aversion to Western liberal values. Tokyo sought security through a sphere of influence to be established by invading and brutalizing neighboring countries. It was old-fashioned imperialism, the seizure of foreign territory to be reoriented under the Japanese government's direct or indirect control toward feeding Japan's growth and prosperity. The Japanese perceived America as a threatening strategic and ideological hegemon, and Americans themselves as repulsive and demonic creatures. At the end Japan seriously contemplated national suicide as preferable to the destruction of the fascist state that the government of the day said represented traditional Japanese values.

For its part, the United States saw Japan as a powerful but politically and culturally backward adversary, a rabid dog terrorizing the Asia-Pacific region, a modern avatar of the Golden Horde. Japan represented a rival empire that rejected the enlightened liberal values of which the Americans liked to think of themselves as the defenders. A sense of vengeance for the Pearl Harbor attack and for Japanese atrocities gave the American war against Japan an unusual intensity and savagery. In the fight against amply "evil" Nazi Germany, the American armed forces generally accepted surrenders on the battlefield and insisted that USAAF bombing policy was to target enemy military assets rather than enemy cities. These niceties were unceremoniously dropped in the bitter combat of the Pacific theater. The U.S. leadership took the decision to practice unrestricted submarine warfare against Japan with no hand-wringing. The United States was committed to winning a total war (including the overthrow of the enemy government) against Japan, wanted to do it as quickly as possible, and believed the Japanese had forfeited the protections of the laws of war the international community had developed and agreed to before the conflict began.

The earlier chapters on the ruthlessness of the Pacific War and the U.S. bombing campaign against Japan made clear the brutality with which both sides prosecuted the war. U.S.-Japan enmity was between the two societies, not just the two governments, and it was racial as well as political—the Japanese seeing the Americans as depraved devils and the Americans viewing the Japanese as vermin. In view of this brutality, the existential nature of the conflict, the depth of mutual hatred and contempt, and the vast cultural, philosophical and systemic differences between Japan and America, what followed was amazing. After a mostly benevolent seven-year U.S. occupation, the two countries formed a close and enduring postwar partnership that would inspire terms such as "Amerippon."[1]

On December 7, 1964, Hirohito presented Gen. Curtis LeMay, who was retiring as the U.S. Air Force Chief of Staff, with the Grand Cordon of the Order of the Rising Sun, First Class, an extremely prestigious award and the second-highest available from the Japanese government. Officially, the basis of the award was LeMay's contribution to the postwar defense of Japan. To be sure, Hirohito had as great an interest in putting the past to rest as any Japanese leader alive. Nevertheless, this was an astonishing event. That the ceremony took place on the anniversary of Pearl Harbor is ironic enough. That the symbolic head of the Japanese state should honor the architect of the indiscriminate bombing of Japanese cities less than 20 years later, and 4 years after Japanese took to the streets in massive protests against Japan's postwar alliance with the United States, was stunning. Many Japanese understandably protested LeMay's award, but this episode encapsulated the remarkable reconciliation between the two Pacific War adversaries.

THE U.S.-JAPAN ALLIANCE

Occupied Japan presented U.S. policymakers with a quandary. As we have seen, the Cold War required a discontinuation of the radical democratization that Americans counted on to prevent the reemergence of a powerful and fascist Japan that could pose a challenge to U.S. interests in Asia. Furthermore, American officials understood that the occupation risked becoming counterproductive if it went on too long. The Japanese public was growing tired of American supervision, and leftist activists played on this discontent in their call for Japan to distance itself from America and to accommodate the rise of communism in Asia. At the same time, however, U.S. officials doubted the depth of Japan's commitment to liberal democracy. Echoing an assertion about Japan's "national character" that was a common theme of U.S. wartime propaganda, Truman's Secretary of State Dean Acheson said postwar Japan was prone to backsliding because "the Japanese are communal people long accustomed to passive acceptance of leadership and subordination of individual interests to the state's."[2] That meant the apparent enthusiasm with which the Japanese embraced democratic values and institutions under American leadership did not preclude their equally enthusiastic support of a resurgent authoritarian regime, and even an alliance with China or the Soviet Union, after the Americans departed. Thus, either continuing or discontinuing the occupation risked failure of the project to ensure Japanese support for the U.S.-led security order in postwar Asia. U.S. policymakers, even those within the State Department, were divided over getting out of Japan quickly versus staying indefinitely. The U.S. military, in any case, was not prepared to give up its bases in Japan.[3] With the Chinese Communist Party's conquest of mainland China in 1949 and the outbreak of the Korean War in 1950, a partnership with Japan was crucial to U.S. plans. Strategically, Japan was an "unsinkable aircraft carrier." Economically, it represented one of the world's centers of industrial power. The U.S. Bloc could not abide losing it to the Communist Bloc.

The rearmament of Japan posed a similar dilemma. With memories of the Pacific War still fresh, the potential danger created by rebuilding the Japanese military was not lost on American elites, a substantial proportion of whom would have believed a few years prior that Japan could never again be trusted with any capability stronger than a domestic police force. The fear of a rearmed Japan, however, quickly collided with Cold War exigencies. Americans perceived that communism was on the offensive in Asia, especially after the outbreak of the Korean War, and that U.S. conventional forces were undersized. After rapidly demobilizing military personnel with the end of World War II, the U.S. government reinstituted the draft in 1948 and expanded it in 1951. American planners concluded that at minimum, Japan needed more forces to ensure its own defense while large numbers of U.S. troops were required in Korea.

The security treaty was an effort to address these dilemmas. John Foster Dulles, appointed by Truman to direct the crafting of the U.S.-Japan peace treaty, explained his intention that the alliance would constrain Japan from military policies against U.S. wishes: "Japan will base its security not merely upon a national Japanese defense force but upon collective defense which would involve such a combination with [the armed forces of] others . . . that a national war of revenge would be materially impossible."[4]

Two treaties signed in September 1951—the Treaty of Peace with Japan (or San Francisco Peace Treaty) and the U.S.-Japan Security Treaty—provided for a permanent residual occupation aimed at making a formally independent Japan both strong and compliant. The Peace Treaty specified the withdrawal of occupation forces within 90 days, but provided for "the stationing or retention of foreign armed forces in Japanese territory under . . . bilateral or multilateral agreements." The Security Treaty gave Japan's explicit agreement that U.S. forces would remain in Japan, while Japan would "increasingly assume responsibility for its own defense against direct and indirect aggression, always avoiding any armament which could be an offensive threat or serve other than to promote peace and security." The treaty said further that U.S. forces in Japan "may be utilized" to defend Japan, to deploy elsewhere "in the Far East," or to intervene against "internal riots and disturbances in Japan."[5] The Americans would keep their bases in Japan and use them as they wished, while Japan would rearm within limits the Americans set. Later Tokyo would come under U.S. pressure not only to strengthen its armed forces but also to expand its military activities beyond Japanese shores. America has even shared advanced military technology with Japan, including the AEGIS naval defense system and licensed production of a version of the F-16 (Japan's FS-X) when it was the most advanced U.S. fighter aircraft in service.

The alliance with the United States was controversial in Japan from the outset. Conservatives supported maintaining small Japanese armed forces, but with the United States shouldering the main responsibility for defending Japan so the Japanese could concentrate their resources on economic development. Socialists and other groups on the political left (including the Communist Party, which was legal in Japan throughout the Cold War) opposed alliance with the United States, arguing that this could drag Japan into a war. They favored a neutral Japan with a passive foreign policy, which they said would avoid conflicts with China or the USSR.

In 1951, Prime Minister Yoshida Shigeru and other Japanese elites accepted that an unequal treaty was necessary to get the Americans to end the occupation. Thereafter, the rise of the Liberal Democratic Party (LDP) would act as a bulwark of support for the alliance against the Socialists for most of the postwar period. The popularity of the Japan Socialist Party motivated the two major conservative parties to merge in 1955 into the LDP. The new party captured the government that year and remained the ruling party until 1993. It implemented a policy of alignment with the United States and gradual, limited rearmament.

Relying heavily on the United States for the defense of Japan had several advantages for the Japanese. They could avoid the economic drain of a large military budget. Japan for many years running has spent only about 1 percent of its gross domestic product on defense, one of the lowest levels in the world and easily the lowest in Northeast Asia. This also reduces the possibility of a resurgence of militarism, which some Japanese, particularly on the political left, fear is a genuine danger. Finally, an under-armed Japan dependent on the U.S. military helps assure the neighboring countries with which Japan seeks expanded trade that there is no need to worry about an imperialist relapse. Still, to speak openly of the U.S. military presence "containing" Japan along with the communist powers was bad form, as it could offend Japanese nationalist sensibilities. In 1990 Gen. Henry C. Stackpole, commander of U.S. Marines in Japan, made a public reference to the containment aspect of the alliance. "No one wants a rearmed, resurgent Japan, so we are a cap in the bottle, if you will," Stackpole said. "[I]f we were to pull out of the U.S.-Japan Security Treaty, it would be a destabilizing factor in Asia."[6] His comments attracted criticism both from the Japanese press and from Washington. Speaking this way during closed-door discussions with China, however, was a different matter. During the Nixon era, Washington played on Chinese fears of a militarily resurgent Japan to gain China's assent to the U.S.-Japan defense arrangement as insurance against a fully independent and rearmed Japan.[7]

While clinging to the relationship, Japan has frequently and tenaciously struggled to keep to its own agenda where it disagreed with American goals and policies. Through most of the Cold War Tokyo tried to get what it wanted from the security relationship (a strong American commitment to defend Japan) while at the same time trying to avoid what the Americans wanted: Japan's assistance in the Cold War, which for Japan meant the risk of being trapped into participating in a regional conflict. Beginning in the 1950s U.S. officials pushed Japan to make a stronger military contribution toward what Washington called the alliance's common goals. During the Korean conflict, Japanese minesweepers helped clear Korean harbors and Japanese transportation experts with experience in Korea served as advisors to the American military.[8] But the Americans wanted more. Both the LDP and the Japan Socialist Party resisted. Under U.S. pressure Yoshida raised the manpower of the National Police Reserve to 110,000 in 1951, but this was only one-third the number the Americans asked for. Although Australia, Thailand, and the Philippines were among the states that joined the Southeast Asia Treaty Organization, an abortive attempt by the Eisenhower administration to stop the spread of communism in Asia, Japan was not.

The end of the occupation did not quell Japanese complaints that their partnership with the United States was unequal. Even the conservatives held this view, while the left wanted to end the alliance outright. Issues such as crimes committed by U.S. servicemen, large amounts of land appropriated for military installations, GIs taking Japanese women home as "war brides," the relatively low pay earned by Japanese working for the Americans, and prostitution near military bases rankled Japanese society. Japanese weariness with the American military presence in their country spiked with news of a 1957 incident in which U.S. soldier William S. Girard shot and killed a Japanese woman from short range while she collected spent brass bullet casings from a gunnery practice range in Japan. The Girard case became a cause célèbre in U.S.-Japan relations. Japanese demanded that the U.S. government hand Girard over to a Japanese court for prosecution. To the displeasure of the onlooking U.S. public, Washington agreed to extradite Girard on the condition that the Japanese court would try him on a reduced charge. Girard got a three-year suspended sentence from the court and returned home demoted and disgraced. The U.S. government paid the dead woman's husband $1,748.32 in compensation. While provoking anger among the Japanese, Girard's case drew complaints from American society about Japanese ingratitude.[9]

With anti-Americanism apparently pushing Japan toward a break from the United States, the two governments opened negotiations for a new security treaty that would revise the terms of the alliance. In negotiations with the Eisenhower administration over revision of the security treaty, Japanese

Prime Minister Kishi Nobusuke said a new treaty more accommodating to Japan would help conservatives, who favored a continuing close U.S.-Japan relationship, fight off the Socialists. The revised treaty removed a previous provision that U.S. forces could intervene in a Japanese domestic crisis. The treaty could be cancelled by either side after 10 years, and it required U.S. consultation with Japan before bringing in nuclear weapons or using Japanese bases to fight a conflict outside Japan. Prior to passage of the revised treaty, Kishi and Washington reached a secret agreement that U.S. nuclear weapons would be allowed "transit" through bases in Japan, while the Japanese government would continue to affirm in public that there were no nuclear weapons in Japan.[10] Despite the concessions, the Socialists opposed the treaty on the grounds that the presence of American forces in Japan was "imperialism" and violated the constitution and that U.S. bases increased the possibility of Japan being dragged into a war. Other groups, including most of Japan's major newspapers, thought the treaty did not go far enough in redressing the inequality of the partnership. The LDP rammed the new treaty through the Diet in a midnight session during which boycotting Socialist legislators were absent. In the streets outside, millions participated in protests that left one student dead and hundreds of both protestors and police injured. The controversy led to the resignation of Kishi. A planned Eisenhower visit to Japan was cancelled.

Another period of Japanese restiveness with the alliance came with the deepening of U.S. military intervention in Indochina—ironic since the ultimate objective of the American war in Vietnam was to secure Japan (on American terms, of course). The idea that communism in Southeast Asia was a danger to Japan began during the Truman administration. In a 1954 press conference Eisenhower explained the centrality of Japan in what would become known as the "domino theory." He compared the advance of communism through individual adjoining countries to "a row of dominoes. . . . [Y]ou knock over the first one, and what will happen to the last one is a certainty that it will go over very rapidly. . . . It takes away, in its economic aspects, that region that Japan must have as a trading area or Japan, in turn, will have only one place to go—that is, toward the Communist areas in order to live." The consequences, Eisenhower said, would be "just incalculable to the free world."[11] Japan, with its potential capacity, was the final, great domino that could shift the global strategic balance if it joined the Communist Bloc. The struggle in Vietnam between the Vietminh-controlled north and the anticommunist government in the south mattered to Americans because of the implications for Japan.

Tokyo's material support for the war in Vietnam was limited to providing radios and medical supplies. American leaders wanted Japan to send troops to join the fight, as U.S. ally South Korea did. Tokyo, however, did not share Washington's commitment to the war in Indochina or the American fear of how China might behave if South Vietnam fell to a communist government. Japan wanted to do business with the North Vietnamese, not fight them. The war was unpopular among the Japanese public, which largely sympathized with the attempt by the Vietnamese to win autonomy from Western great powers. Japanese viewed with great dismay reports of the destruction the American military wrought among Vietnamese noncombatants through aerial bombing of cities and rural pacification campaigns. Many Japanese disapproved of the Americans using their bases in Japan to prosecute the war, particularly the bombing missions by aircraft flying from Okinawa. In 1968 support among Japanese for maintaining the security agreement with the United States fell to 20 percent.[12] During the same year Secretary of State Dean Rusk expressed similar dissatisfaction from the other side. Complaining to the U.S. ambassador to Japan about "this intolerable Japanese attitude," Rusk said, "It is almost more than flesh and spirit can bear to have Japan whining about Okinawa while we are losing several hundred killed each month in behalf of our common security in the Pacific."[13]

It was not until the 1980s that the Japanese public became comfortable enough with U.S.-Japan defense cooperation for Japanese leaders to speak of the relationship as an "alliance" and of Japan as an "unsinkable aircraft carrier."[14] This was because Japanese support for a strong Self Defense Force and for greater security cooperation with the United States rose in the 1970s due to the U.S.-China rapprochement, Japan's fear of abandonment by the United States after the 1969 Nixon Doctrine (which said America's friends could count on the American nuclear umbrella but should supply their own manpower for defense), and an increase in the perceived Soviet threat.

Many observers concluded the Soviet threat was the glue that held the alliance together. Some international relations scholars, particularly those of the Realist school, predicted that Japan would move away from its reliance on the United States for its defense and fully rearm itself after the end of the Cold War. According to Realist thinking, the international system conditions national governments to constantly fear for their security, to consider all other states potential adversaries, and to avoid leaving themselves vulnerable. In the words of the leading Neorealist thinker of the time, Kenneth Waltz, Japan represented "a structural anomaly" because it had the economic strength of a great power yet chose to rely on the United States for its defense. Between 1945 and 1990 Realists could explain this as a case of cooperation against a greater common enemy, the Soviet Union. But the Soviet abdication of its superpower status should have weakened the unnatural bond between the two countries that had been such bitter Pacific War enemies. Scholar Christopher Layne asserted that in response to the post–Cold War shift in the structure of international politics from bipolarity (with the United States and the USSR as rival bloc-leaders) to unipolarity (with the United States left as the sole superpower), "Japan is measuring itself for a great power role" and the U.S.-Japan relationship was likely to move from close defense cooperation to increased tensions and possible conflict. Waltz predicted that "uncomfortable dependencies and perceived vulnerabilities will lead Japan to acquire greater military capabilities" including nuclear weapons, which would spell the end of the U.S.-Japan defense arrangement.[15]

In fact, however, Japanese support for the alliance has grown since the end of the Cold War. In the early 1990s Japanese elites became more interested in the United Nations and other multilateral institutions as important vehicles for achieving Japanese security. This worried U.S. officials that the U.S.-Japan alliance was losing its centrality in Japanese strategic planning. Furthermore, Japanese support in the event of a regional crisis such as a U.S.-North Korea confrontation was uncertain. Observers pointed out that such a conflict might end the alliance, as America would not tolerate Gulf War-like Japanese noninvolvement while U.S. forces went into harm's way in Japan's own neighborhood. A highly publicized 1995 rape case involving three U.S. servicemen in Okinawa created additional pressure for the two governments to rearticulate the aims and modalities of the bilateral security arrangement. Chinese missile exercises intended to intimidate Taiwan in 1995 and 1996 increased Japan's sense of insecurity and the perceived value of the alliance with the United States. With these events as background and many observers describing the alliance as drifting or in crisis, the 1997 Revised Guidelines for U.S.-Japan Defense Cooperation seemed to rejuvenate the relationship. Specifically, it addressed a key American concern by clarifying the support Japan would offer American forces engaged in a regional military operation. Japan's 2005 National Defense Program Outline further aligned Tokyo with the U.S. strategic agenda by identifying North Korea, China and terrorism as security concerns and by supporting an antimissile defense system.

The relationship continues to display points of friction. One of these is the long-standing issue of host nation support—getting the Japanese government to pay more of the costs of the U.S. bases that defend and contain Japan. In September 1990 the U.S. Congress threatened to withdraw Japan-based U.S. forces unless the Japanese paid substantially more in host nation support. Three months later Tokyo announced that it would raise Japan's contribution from 40 percent to 50 percent of the costs of maintaining the bases. In a similar vein, in 1991 many U.S. politicians severely criticized Japan's lack of military support for the American-led coalition that would drive invading Iraqi forces out of Kuwait. They derided Japan, which relied on the Persian Gulf for most of its oil supply, as a wealthy free-rider. This criticism eventually shamed Tokyo into contributing $13 billion, which the Diet did not approve until after the conflict had ended. Some U.S. critics remained unsatisfied, pointing out that Japan was giving money while other countries gave their soldiers' blood.

On the other side, some Japanese continue to object to the defense partnership. Recently a group of Japanese citizens, opponents of revising Article 9 and of what they perceive as excessive Japanese subservience to the United States, have employed the indirect approach of suing the Japanese government for failing to compensate Japanese civilians for the harm they suffered in the conventional U.S. bombing raids against Tokyo during the war. Nagai Kinichi, one of the plaintiffs, saw his teenage sister killed in an American incendiary raid. "I look at the current cabinet and see a bunch of young politicians who have no understanding of war and the pain it can cause," Nagai explained. "They are happy to follow the U.S. government blindly and revise the constitution but are not aware of the consequences. That is why this suit had to be filed."[16]

THE PACIFIC WAR AND POSTWAR BILATERAL ECONOMIC RELATIONS

The U.S.-Japan postwar economic relationship is linked to the Pacific War in two ways. First, the outcome of the war—including a seriously disrupted Japanese economy and U.S. authorities gaining responsibility for governing Japan—led to an American policy of playing midwife to a Japanese economic recovery to prevent Japan from falling prey to communism. Second, American elites have often viewed postwar U.S.-Japan trade disputes within the context of the Pacific War, calling Japanese trade policy a continuation or replay of the war through different means.

As part of the project of rebuilding Japan as a robust U.S. ally, the United States temporarily nurtured Japan's economic development. America would help Japan gain economic access to Southeast Asia, an issue the two countries had gone to war over a few years earlier. Washington accepted that in order to prosper (and thereby stave off communist agitation), the Japanese needed trade with Southeast Asia to compensate for economic opportunities missed by Tokyo adhering to the trade embargo against China. Other Asian countries were more interested in getting reparations from Japan than in buying Japanese products. In accordance with American advice, Japan paid reparations and gave financial aid to Southeast Asia to settle compensation claims, helping to reestablish economic ties. In many cases Japanese pay-outs carried the condition that recipients would use them to purchase Japanese products or services. The more substantial stimulus to Japanese economic recovery, however, came from Japan's trade with the United States. America not only provided technical assistance, but also opened U.S. markets to Japanese exports while tolerating Japanese barriers to American products. Like the Korean War, the Vietnam War proved a boon for Japan, bringing manufacturing orders and an influx of advanced technology.

Japanese chafed under the restrictions against trading with China, a policy called for by the U.S. Bloc's initial Cold War strategy and specified by the Coordinating Committee for Multilateral Export Controls, of which Japan was a member along with the United States, Western Europe, and Australia. Trade with China had support within Japan from the entire ideological spectrum. In 1953, the Diet unanimously passed a resolution calling for greater trade with China. Strategic considerations as well as economic self-interest dictated Japan's desire to do business with the PRC. Japanese leaders believed the American approach of an economic embargo against China was wrongheaded. Separating China from the Soviet Union would be more effectively achieved by opening a channel of economic exchange with the Chinese. Tokyo persistently lobbied for a relaxation of this policy. Many American officials saw the Japanese attitude as treasonous or immoral. After vigorous internal debate, the U.S. government allowed Japan to begin limited trade with China starting in 1949 as a means of stimulating Japanese economic development. The Eisenhower administration allowed Japan to reach trade agreements with China that were ostensibly private rather than official. By 1965, China was Japan's fourth-largest trading partner.[17] This sore point with the Americans grew more sore as the volume of Japan-China trade increased.

Until 1965 Japan suffered a trade deficit with the United States. The Eisenhower and Kennedy administrations struggled to encourage Americans to buy more goods imported from Japan. In the 1970s, however, with Japan's economy not only recovered but threatening many American industries, the economic relationship reverted to a competitive character more typical of international relations. U.S.-Japan trade disputes, some quite acrimonious, mainly involved Washington alleging Japanese protectionism against U.S. products. Two of the "Nixon shocks" in the summer of 1971 were economic policy moves that hurt Japanese exports to the United States: (1) suspending the convertibility of the U.S. dollar to gold, which led to appreciation of the Japanese currency against the dollar; and (2) the imposition of a 10 percent surcharge on foreign goods imported into the United States. The other Nixon shock exacted a measure of revenge for Japan's trade with China. Without prior consultation of the Japanese government, Nixon made a surprise public announcement in July 1971 that he planned to visit the PRC, signaling an American move to improve Sino-U.S. relations. Trade disputes continued into the 1980s even as the United States became economically dependent on Japan, which purchased U.S. Treasury bonds and thereby allowed Americans to maintain their standard of living despite massive national debt. Americans harbored fears of Japan outperforming and even dominating the United States economically by a combination of efficiency and ruthlessness until the 1990s, when the United States staged an economic resurgence while Japan went into a prolonged recession.

Some Americans have placed U.S.-Japan trade relations within the context of the Pacific War, revealing a direct carryover of political residue. As U.S.-Japan trade tensions rose in the 1970s, Maurice Stans, Secretary of the Treasury and a close friend of President Nixon, said, "The Japanese are still fighting the war, only now instead of a shooting war it is an economic war. Their immediate intention is to try to dominate the Pacific and then perhaps the world."[18] In a 1985 article in the *New York Times Magazine*, the well-known journalist Theodore H. White said the question of "who finally won the war fifty years before" was at stake in Japan's "trade offensive," which White described as similar to the Greater East Asia Co-Prosperity Sphere but this time on a global scale.[19] In 1992 the U.S. press reported that Japanese Prime Minister Miyazawa Kiichi had criticized American workers as lacking a "work ethic." This assertion was demonstrably false based on comparative productivity figures. Nevertheless, U.S. Senator Ernest F. Hollings responded with the small-minded and disturbing observation that the atomic bomb was "made in America by lazy and illiterate Americans, and tested in Japan."[20] The interpretation of postwar events as part of a supposedly unfinished Pacific War was common in the Japan-bashing genre that encompassed many books in the 1980s and early 1990s as well as blockbuster films such as *Rising Sun* (1993) and *Black Rain* (1989). The war clearly provided a handy set of historical metaphors and interpretations. Beyond that, it is not clear that the experience of a having recently fought a war against each other made these U.S.-Japan trade disputes more likely to occur or even more bitter.

OKINAWA'S PERPETUAL SACRIFICE

Ironically, the pre-Japanese Ryukyu kingdom of which Okinawa was a part had a tradition of pacifism and disarmament. This changed with the Pacific War and its aftermath. After capturing Okinawa with terrible destruction and loss of military and civilian life, the Americans quickly covered Okinawa with bases, forcibly expropriating the land they wanted from local communities. For the United States government Okinawa has been a strategic gem. The war's end made it unnecessary as a staging area for the invasion of the main islands of Japan, but its proximity to Korea, Taiwan and China gave it lasting value as a U.S. military outpost. Japan wants U.S. military protection but not the headaches caused by the interface between American troops and Japanese society. For mainland Japanese, exiling most of the bases to Okinawa largely resolves this dilemma. The losers in this bargain are the Okinawans, most of whom want at least a partial reduction of the military infrastructure and population on their island. In the Japanese game of *go*, a stone placed on the board as a sacrifice to block the opponent's progress is called a *suteishi*. The Okinawan people see themselves as a permanent suteishi, having first paid a terrible price as part of Tokyo's last-ditch attempt to deter an Allied invasion of the main islands, and being forced since then to endure an extended American occupation and militarization so extensive that no Okinawan community is far from a U.S. base or installation. Over the last 20 years, surveys administered by the *Okinawa Times* have consistently indicated that about 75 percent of Okinawa residents want a gradual withdrawal of the U.S. bases, while 10 to 15 percent desire immediate withdrawal. The preference for a gradual withdrawal is mostly based on the belief that communities need time between the announcement of withdrawal from a base and the actual evacuation to plan for the massive job of cleaning up and converting abandoned bases for local civilian development.[21]

Despite their victimization by Japanese forces during the war, Okinawans were treated as a conquered people under U.S. administration. Compensation for seized land was low. Wages earned by Okinawans working for the U.S. government were also low compared to what Filipinos and mainland Japanese earned. It was plainly visible that Americans living on Okinawa had a dramatically more affluent lifestyle than the local people. Okinawans also believed the police and the courts were relatively lenient toward Americans involved in criminal or legal disputes. In 1952 the Japanese government in effect sacrificed Okinawa by agreeing to continued American control over the island as a concession that made possible the end of U.S. occupation of the Japanese mainland. The United States Civil Administration of the Ryukyu Islands tried to cultivate a sense of Ryukyuan nationalism by sponsoring radio programs on Ryukyuan history and encouraging the use of a distinct Ryukyuan flag and national anthem. The aim was to dampen Okinawan interest in reunifying with mainland Japan.[22] Nevertheless, from the early days of occupation a majority of Okinawans favored reversion to Japanese rule. They hoped this would make them masters over their island's affairs through the democratic process and lead to a downsizing of the U.S. military presence. After a massive protest campaign on Okinawa, the U.S. and Japanese governments agreed on the reversion of Okinawa to Japanese rule in 1972. The U.S. military bases, however, remained in place and under American control. In February 1995, the Nye Report said the United States intended to retain its military position in Asia, including the Okinawa bases, for another 20 years. This signaled a halt to the policy of drawdown begun by the Bush (Sr.) administration, which had given hope to the Okinawans who favored phasing out the bases.

The suffering of Okinawans during the war remains a sensitive and controversial issue in Japan. A 1993 opinion poll showed that only 6.2 percent of Okinawans thought the fighting over Okinawa was "an unavoidable battle necessary for the defense of the fatherland," while 87.5 percent thought it was "a reckless battle which sacrificed countless Okinawan lives."[23] The underlying sentiment is Okinawan resentment over neglect, discrimination and exploitation by mainland Japanese. The specific issue that draws out the Okinawan-Japanese historical divide is the question of how to remember the suicides of Okinawan civilians during the battle. The dispute is whether the civilian suicides among Okinawans were, as conservative nationalists argue, heroic and noble (*jiketsu*), inspired by and affirming their Japanese patriotism; or, as many Okinawans believe, meaningless and ignominious deaths (*inujini*), reflecting pressure and disinformation by the Japanese military.[24] Japanese who campaign for a sanitized version of Japan's conduct during the Pacific War have gone so far as to argue that Okinawans seeking postwar compensation payments from their government fabricated the idea that Japanese troops murdered islanders or forced them to commit suicide.

In an intra-Japanese component of the textbook flap during the 1980s it was clear that the Japanese central government did not accept what many Okinawans testified about Japanese army atrocities against their civilian countrymen on the islands. The Japanese Education Ministry textbook reviewers deleted the following passage from a proposed 1982 history textbook: "About 800 civilians of Okinawa Prefecture were murdered by the Japanese troops on grounds that they hindered the fighting." The Ministry claimed the figure came from sources that could not be confirmed, but a Ministry official also reportedly said, "It is inconceivable that Japanese could do such a thing to other Japanese."[25] The impulse to whitewash the Okinawa chapter of the Pacific War has persisted to recent years. In April 2007, a few months after the passage of a law mandating that education should promote patriotism, the Ministry of Education's screening panel directed the publishers of history textbooks submitted for the required vetting to remove statements that blamed the Japanese military for instigating suicides among Okinawan civilians. Such references had been in Japanese textbooks since the 1980s. One passage to which the Ministry objected read, "The Japanese army gave hand grenades to residents, making them commit mass suicide and kill each other." Revised passages read, "Mass suicides and killings took place among the residents using hand grenades given them by the Japanese Army," or with the words "by the Japanese Army" deleted.[26] The Ministry took the position that it was "not clear that the Japanese Army coerced or ordered the mass suicides."[27] Okinawans, however, thought the recollections of their elderly neighbors and relatives made the Japanese army's complicity abundantly clear. In September over 110,000 people participated in a rally in Ginowan protesting the proposed textbook revisions. Over the next few weeks, most of the municipal governments on Okinawa as well as the Okinawa Prefectural Assembly passed measures calling on the Ministry of Education to restore the original passages indicating the military's responsibility for civilian suicides. The Municipal Assembly of Tomigusuku said the Ministry's demand for revisions "den[ied] the historical facts" and "can never be accepted by the people of Okinawa Prefecture." Tokashiki's Municipal Assembly asserted, "It is an undeniable fact that 'mass suicides' could not have occurred were it not for an order, coercion, manipulation or other acts by the Japanese military."[28] Private activist groups also organized protests and collected over 100,000 signatures in opposition to the Ministry's attempted sanitization. In December the Ministry of Education agreed to restore watered-down references to the Japanese military's "involvement" in the mass suicides.

Okinawans complain that they bear a disproportionate share of the burden of hosting U.S. bases. While the Okinawa Prefecture constitutes less than 1 percent of Japan's land area, three-quarters of all the Japanese territory occupied by the U.S. military is on Okinawa or its nearby islands. Military bases cover 20 percent of Okinawa. The bases reduce the quality of life for residents. Nakasone Fujiko, a former junior high school teacher on Okinawa, reported that "Students in schools around the U.S. Air Force Base at Kadena . . . lose an average of two years during their 12 years of education due to class interruptions resulting from the constant high level of noise caused by military aircraft flying overhead. The physical problems they suffer include nervousness and an inability to concentrate, hearing loss, headaches and stomach aches." An Okinawan public health study also found that babies in the community near the Kadena Air Base have the lowest average birth weights in Japan.[29]

Another cost is environmental degradation, including permanent destruction of the original features of large parts of the island in order to build facilities such as airfields and practice ranges, and contamination of the land caused by fuel, chemicals and expended ordnance. Under the current arrangement, when the United States eventually vacates its bases it is not legally obligated to restore the land to its original condition.

Okinawa suffers from economic underdevelopment. It is Japan's poorest prefecture, with only 70 percent of the per capita income of mainland Japan and relatively high unemployment. The bases bring some economic benefit to Okinawa, but they also inhibit normal and well-rounded economic development. Okinawa's economy has largely been a collection of service industries that feed off the bases. The American military presence has been an obstacle to civilian infrastructure, a detriment to the island's tourism potential, and a destroyer of farmland.

Then there are the direct and immediate dangers of living near American bases. Between 1972 and 1997, there were 127 cases of death or destruction caused by mishaps involving U.S. aircraft, 137 brush fires started by U.S. military drills, and 12 Okinawans murdered by Americans. According to Okinawa prefectural government statistics, U.S. forces and their dependents committed nearly 300,000 crimes between 1972 and 2001, including 531 "brutal crimes" (more serious than "assaults," which are counted separately).[30] American officials argue that statistically, their troops in Okinawa are not crime-prone. U.S. troops in Okinawa commit fewer crimes than U.S. troops stationed in the United States. Despite the fact that they are preponderantly young males, Okinawa-based U.S. military personnel commit crimes at only half the rate of the local Okinawan population. That is not necessarily the impression of Okinawans or mainland Japanese, especially when opinion leaders such as House of Councilors member Inoue Satoshi say that American troops commit sexual assault at a rate 22 times higher than the general Japanese population.[31] Antibase activists also argue that many of the sex crimes of Americans in Okinawa are unreported because of the stigma that hangs over rape victims.

Okinawans were still fuming over the implications of the Nye Report when, in September 1995, a U.S. sailor and two Marines kidnapped and raped a 12-year-old Okinawan girl. The incident sparked an explosion of outrage among Okinawans and a crisis for Tokyo and Washington. American officials quickly implemented their practiced damage-control technique of emphasizing that the Okinawa bases help keep Japan and the region secure. But Okinawans maintained the pressure. They protested for months, including a gathering of 85,000 in October, for a partial or complete removal of the U.S. bases. Admiral Richard C. Macke, the commander of U.S. forces in the Pacific, said of the incident a few weeks later, "I think that it was absolutely stupid. . . . For the price they paid to rent the car they could have had a girl." Both the Japanese and U.S. governments cringed at the remark. A Japanese Foreign Ministry spokesman said, "The remarks by Admiral Macke are most inappropriate in view of the terrible incident that took place in Okinawa." U.S. Defense Secretary William J. Perry quickly sacked Macke. Perry explained that in view of "our valued relations with Japan and Okinawa," Macke's insensitivity constituted a "lapse of judgment . . . so serious that he would be unable to perform effectively his duties as Commander in Chief of U.S. Forces in the Pacific."[32]

Japan's Land Acquisition Law, which after 1972 dictated the terms for compensating Okinawan landowners whose land the Americans expropriated, required that every five years landowners or a local official sign an affirmation of consent. After the protests over the 1995 rape incident, Okinawa Governor Ota Masahide refused to sign on behalf of the owners. This presented the central government with the possibility that American bases would be illegally occupying the land beneath them. The prime minister sued Ota, and both the Fukuoka High Court and the Supreme Court ruled in favor of the central government. Then the Diet changed the law to allow the central government to sign on behalf of the landowners. Public opinion, however, could not be legislated away. In a nonbinding plebiscite held on Okinawa in September 1996, 89 percent voted in favor of reducing the American bases, although only 60 percent of Okinawa's registered voters participated.

The uproar over the 1995 case forced the Japanese and U.S. governments to promise a realignment of U.S. forces on Okinawa. U.S. officials came to believe that even though it involved a permanent partial reduction of American forces on Okinawa, the realignment was necessary to relieve the pressure of local antibase sentiment. The island seemed to be one major accident or incident away from demanding the closure of all American bases including the Kadena air base, which U.S. defense officials consider vitally important. An official committee recommended in 1996 closing the Marines' Futenma Air Station in the crowded city of Ginowan and building a new heliport (an artificial island that would rest on piles or float on pontoons) off the coast of a less heavily populated area of Okinawa to the north near the city of Nago. *After* the completion of the new facility, 8,000 Marines and their dependents would move from Okinawa to Guam, an actual reduction of resident U.S. forces. Nago's residents were cool to the idea. They pointed out that the new Marine heliport would threaten a coral reef that provides a habitat for the dugong and the sea turtle, both endangered and protected species. A petition signed by more than half of Nago's eligible voters demanded a local referendum on the issue. Despite heavy lobbying by the central government in favor of building the heliport, the nonbinding referendum held in 1997 in Nago returned a majority opposed to the proposal. Governor Ota backed the result and said the Futenma base should be moved to mainland Japan or to the United States. He overruled the Nago City government, which had approved of the heliport plan. Tokyo retaliated by cutting the flow of funds to Okinawa and denigrating Ota, which contributed to his defeat in the next gubernatorial election in November 1998. Tokyo promised the new Okinawa government a large infusion of money through construction projects, a scarcely disguised payoff for the island's tolerance of the American bases.[33]

Planning for the heliport went forward, but ran into problems. The projected size and expense of the project grew. It was doubtful that it could pass a legitimate environmental impact assessment. Protestors disrupted initial survey drilling work. In 2005 Tokyo dropped the floundering project. The Japanese and U.S. governments agreed on a new proposal. Instead of being built completely offshore over a coral reef, the new facility would be an airfield lying partly within the confines of the Marines' Camp Schwab, a base located at the tip of the Henoko Peninsula (also near Nago), with an extension built from the base out into the shallow water immediately offshore. The mayors of Nago and other northern Okinawan cities supported the latest proposal, representing the view that the base relocation within Okinawa is desirable for the money and jobs it will bring to Okinawa's economy. Okinawa Governor Nakaima Hirokazu, however, who took office in 2006, sought to adjust the position of the new runway in Henoko Bay, threatening to sidetrack the first step in the envisioned chain of events. In the latter years of the Bush administration, Washington became frustrated with the inability of Japanese officials to implement the deal.[34]

As of this writing, the new airfield was scheduled for completion in 2014, with the plan subject to the results of an environmental impact study in August 2009. Tokyo was still trying to persuade Nago residents to accept the new base in their area to replace Futenma. The 8,000 Marines' billets slated for transfer to Guam remained on Okinawa. Nothing had substantially changed more than a decade after the announcement of the realignment plan. U.S. military commanders still find it impossible to completely eliminate criminal acts by U.S. servicemen against the townspeople, and every act carries a disproportionately large political impact, revitalizing the opposition movement. In February 2008 Japanese police arrested a U.S. Marine suspected of raping a 14-year-old girl. He admitted kissing her against her will but denied the rape charge. The girl later dropped the charge and the police released the Marine, but not before a new round of public protests, including a rally that drew a crowd of 6,000 despite rain, and expressions of frustration by Okinawan officials. The U.S. military put its personnel under a curfew for several days while they rode out the storm. Although it took place on the Japanese mainland rather than Okinawa, an incident the following month reprised the theme of crime-prone American servicemen. After a taxi driver was found stabbed to death near the U.S. naval base at Yokosuka, Japanese police charged with murder a 22-year-old AWOL U.S. sailor whose credit card they found in the taxi. (One can imagine what Macke might say about the assailant's "stupidity" in this case.)

Okinawa's treatment certainly demonstrates a subordination of local democracy to the central government's national security strategy. Unfortunately for the Okinawans, addressing their concerns about the U.S. bases suits the interests of neither Washington nor Tokyo. In important respects their situation has changed little since the last days of the Pacific War.

AN ABNORMAL BUT RESILIENT RELATIONSHIP

Japan and the United States are today two powerful actors in the Asia-Pacific region, Japan primarily through its economic strength and America through both its economic and military capabilities. They share strong trade and investment ties and a highly cooperative political relationship. One might conclude that in the main, Japan and the United States have transcended the legacy of the Pacific War. This is true in the sense that the profound animosity of the war years did not prevent these two countries from establishing close and mutually dependent relations afterward. The impact of the war on today's Japan-U.S. relations could be further discounted by focusing on some important continuities from the prewar era. Japan is one of history's best illustrations of what has been called "the Phoenix factor."[35] Despite suffering devastation in a major war, countries with a strong intellectual infrastructure are able to recover with remarkable speed. Typically, such a country's level of economic development two decades after the conflict has reached the trend line established prior to the conflict, in effect erasing the long-term economic effects of the war. The foreign policies of both the United States and Japan also exhibit considerable continuity if viewed from a long-term perspective. In a very broad sense, the United States in the postwar era has pursued a Japan policy similar to that before the war: getting the Japanese to support a political and economic order in Asia that upholds U.S. interests. Victory over Japan in the Pacific War positioned the United States to pursue that objective through more direct control and influence over Japanese policies. Tokyo has returned to its prewar grand strategy of cooperation with the preeminent Western power. Japan is more deeply enmeshed in the Western-sponsored international order than before the war: relying on its erstwhile enemy the United States for its national defense, often following the U.S. lead in its foreign policy, and illustrating as much as any other country on earth the strength of American postwar soft power. As America was a growing Pacific power before the war, the conflict with Japan accelerated this process. Secretary of the Navy James Forrestal boasted in 1946 that "China is now our eastern frontier."[36] For the Japanese, that meant the war they fought to expel the United States from the Western Pacific and East Asia had the ultimate effect of greatly strengthening America's Asia-Pacific influence. But equally ironically, the postwar found the U.S. government helping to reestablish Japan's economic penetration of Asia.

The war's impact on today's U.S.-Japan relations, nonetheless, should not be underestimated. Its legacy is apparent in two areas. First, in addition to the questions and disputes common to any dyad of large countries, the war bequeathed to the U.S.-Japan relationship a unique set of issues directly related to the war and its outcome. These include the status of U.S. military installations in Japan and differing opinions on how the atomic bombings should be remembered. Second, and no less importantly, the war fundamentally altered the basis of U.S.-Japan relations. In the absence of the Pacific

War, Japan and America might have been unambiguous rivals in recent decades. Without the war, Japan and the United States would never have become so close, and it is unlikely they would have stayed so close for so long. Japanese leaders would not and politically could not have voluntarily surrendered responsibility for national defense to a foreign power, with tens of thousands of foreign troops and dozens of major bases in Japan as part of the bargain. Only defeat in a total war could bring about this scenario. But having survived almost the worst and most feared fate that can befall a state, and learning that the Americans for their own reasons wanted Japan to be prosperous and secure, the Japanese continued the partnership even after regaining their capability to do otherwise. This choice, too, owed much to the legacy of the war. The Japanese understood that as a result of the ill will toward themselves they had created in Asia, partial reliance on the United States remained the best course for securing Japan. It is a normal relationship within an abnormal relationship. Japanese leaders have continually pressed for more control over their country's destiny and resisted U.S. pressure to implement policies they disliked, even at the risk of straining the alliance. They have been more successful than the apparent asymmetry of the relationship would seem to allow. As East Asian security affairs scholar Mike M. Mochizuki observes, "What is remarkable is how much autonomy Japan was able to exercise despite its profound security and economic dependence on the United States."[37] Where it could not prevail, Tokyo has concluded that the loss of independence Japan must suffer to maintain the security arrangement is better than abandonment.

For the Americans, the choice has been whether to treat Japan as a reforming ex-criminal or an unsinkable aircraft carrier. The needs of the present, specifically the postwar security environment, outweighed the unfinished business of the past. Having determined to base their policy on the unsinkable aircraft carrier view of Japan (with its concomitant containment aspect), U.S. government officials have had little interest in dwelling on Japan's wartime criminality. As with the Chinese, some private American citizens have tried to seek redress from Japan for Pacific War crimes. Like the Chinese, they did not find their own government to be a strong advocate for their cause. In 1999 former American POWs sued for compensation from Japan through the Northern California District Court. They amply demonstrated mistreatment by their Japanese captors during forced labor. They nonetheless lost their case, with the presiding judge Vaughn R. Walker making the bizarre argument that "the immeasurable bounty of life for themselves [the plaintiffs] and their posterity in a free society and in a more peaceful world services the debt."[38]

Bilateral disputes have been frequent and sometimes serious. They have not, however, broken up the relationship. Through the end of the first decade of the twenty-first century, mainstream politicians in both countries remained committed to the alliance, and on most important international issues Tokyo and Washington continued to take the same positions.

In terms of this book's main analytical themes, what is perhaps the most striking feature of the postwar U.S.-Japan relationship is the primacy of the international political environment. Ideologically, the American occupation authorities would have preferred to continue the liberalization program in Japan, but they discontinued it for the strategic reason that rehabilitating conservatism appeared the more effective path for strengthening Japan against the threat of communism. This saddled the Japanese government with the continuous challenge of managing the pressure from those quarters of Japanese society that had drawn the lessons from the war that Japan should not rearm, ally with the United States or have anything to do with nuclear weapons. Some of Tokyo's policies remain in permanent conflict with the wishes of vocal but insufficiently powerful segments of the Japanese public including peace and antinuclear activists and most of the people of Okinawa.

While the U.S.-Japan postwar reconciliation suited the interests of both countries in an environment that remained unstable and threatening, the idiosyncrasies of the American worldview were supportive. This surely was one of those occasions that might justify journalist James Reston's contention that a strength of the American people is that "we have no memory."[39] The attempt to build a liberal democracy in a country like 1945 Japan and the assumption that this would lead to more peaceful international relations in Asia exhibited an audacious idealism. Not all victors would have dealt this way with a conquered country. In retrospect, the self-interested magnanimity of postwar U.S. Japan policy stands as one of the greatest successes in the history of American foreign relations: producing a remarkably durable alliance from the ashes of an unusually bitter war, and providing an environment in which Japan could reach its potential in prosperity, democracy and international citizenship. This success, however, depended upon an international environment that compelled the United States to rehabilitate, strengthen, and harness Japan in support of American interests in Asia; and upon the ruling political party in Japan concluding that allying with the United States was to Japan's advantage. Fighting a major war against each other does not generally create a basis for a strong political bond between two states. The norm is more the opposite, as illustrated by Japan-China relations after the war. With so many peculiarities involved, the postwar U.S.-Japan relationship is not an easily replicable model for postconflict reconciliation.

CHAPTER 12

Atomic Rancor between America and Japan

Both American and Japanese audiences enjoyed the Japanese monster movie *Godzilla*, which debuted in 1954 (and led to many sequels). Superficially, this shared experience seemed an example of cross-cultural commonality and the progress of the postwar reconciliation process. The outwardly frivolous film, however, featured a core political allegory that was easily overlooked by American audiences but clear to Japanese filmgoers. The monster is awakened by U.S. nuclear bomb tests, he breathes radioactive fire, and he lays waste to urban Japan—that is, the monster of nuclear destruction brought into the world by America is threatening Japan again. Furthermore, one could easily infer a warning to Japan to resist being drawn into the Cold War by its nuclear-armed ally. American editors removed some of the more overt anti-nuclear references (and added scenes introducing a major new character, an American reporter) for the version of the film released in the United States. They cut the Japanese version's first scene, in which a bright flash emerging from the ocean destroys a Japanese fishing boat in an unmistakable allusion to the *Lucky Dragon* incident that had occurred earlier in the year. *Godzilla* was pure escapism for Americans, but not for Japanese. Nuclear weaponry was a subject on which the two societies did not see eye-to-eye.

The postwar partnership between the U.S. and Japanese governments is remarkable not because it extinguished the rancor left over from the war, but rather because it has succeeded despite that rancor. On no issue is the sense of an unsettled grievance between the two societies more evident than the divergence of attitudes toward the atomic bombings. An exchange in 1994 was one of many occasions when this long-simmering dispute flashed into public view, revealing the distance between Japanese and American positions and the strength of the emotions underlying both. On that occasion the U.S. press quoted Nagasaki Mayor Motoshima Hitoshi as saying that "Pearl Harbor was not as cruel as the atomic bombing. The atom bomb wiped out everything: people in church, children in kindergarten, even their dogs and cats. Pearl Harbor was terrible, but not as bad as that." Americans sent in responses, most of them in angry disagreement with Motoshima. One letter writer who identified himself as a World War II veteran from Michigan wrote, "When the Japanese assassins bombed Pearl Harbor, your ambassador was in Washington bowing and smirking, assuring my government that Japan wanted to be friends. . . . Before the A-bomb was dropped, your government was warned many times to surrender or be bombed. It was not a sneak attack. . . . It is the belief of most Americans that Japan owes reparations to America of hundreds of billions of dollars."[1]

WHAT AMERICANS REMEMBER ABOUT THE ATOMIC BOMBS

As we saw earlier, at the time of the A-bombings most Americans approved of using the new weapon on Japanese cities, although a considerable minority had misgivings. This, after all, was an unmistakable departure from the precision bombing that Americans generally understood to be official U.S. policy. As with the Dresden raid, the controversy grew stronger after the war with the return of peacetime sensibilities. The early postwar view of most Americans was that Truman ordered the bombings of Hiroshima and Nagasaki to force an intransigent Japanese government to surrender and thereby preclude the need for a bloody Allied invasion of Japan to end the war. In this view the bombings were justified because on balance they saved lives, Japanese as well as American, and hastened the building of a peaceful and democratic Japan. The episode is therefore a proud rather than a troubling or shameful moment in American history—a technological triumph yielding immediate and important political benefits, and another affirmation that what is good for America is good for the world.

In the 1960s a wave of historiography arose challenging that view. These historians argued that the bombings were unjustified for the reasons discussed earlier in this book: Japan was thoroughly beaten and wanted to surrender by mid-1945; use of atomic weapons against cities was the epitome of an indiscriminate attack on civilians; and the Truman administration must have had an ignoble motive other than military necessity for dropping the bombs, such as racial hatred, a desire to intimidate the Soviets, or the need to justify the high costs of the Manhattan Project. This view was prominent by the 1980s and is widely accepted by Americans of Generation X and thereafter. In fact, revisionist criticisms of the A-bomb attacks are among the few remaining items in the rapidly shrinking pool of American public knowledge about the Pacific War. Stanford University military historian Victor Davis Hanson lamented in 2005 that "American textbooks discuss World War II . . . as if the war was essentially the Japanese internment and Hiroshima."[2] Nuclear

Regulatory Commission historian J. Samuel Walker concluded in 1990 after an extensive review of the scholarly literature that the revisionist view was winning out: "The consensus among scholars is that the bomb was not needed to avoid an invasion of Japan and to end the war within a relatively short time. It is clear that alternatives to the bomb existed and that Truman and his advisers knew it."[3]

Nevertheless, the traditional view is heavily represented even in newer general-interest books found in American libraries. In my own local library, for example, I found that Alan Axelrod's *The Complete Idiot's Guide to American History* says "At this time, the Allies were planning the final invasion of Japan, which, based on the bloody experience of 'island hopping,' was expected to add perhaps a million more deaths to the Allied toll. President Truman therefore authorized the use of the terrible new weapon against Japan."[4] In his youth-oriented book *First Facts About U.S. History*, author David C. King writes, "It was up to President Harry S. Truman whether to use the new weapon against Japan. Truman believed that it would end the war quickly. A warning was sent to the Japanese government. When no reply was received, an atomic bomb was dropped on the city of Hiroshima on August 6, 1945. A second bomb was dropped on Nagasaki three days later. The explosions leveled the cities, claiming at least 200,000 lives and forcing Japan to surrender."[5] As Sherry Marker's *Illustrated History of the United States* tells the story, "It seemed quite possible that Japan would not surrender (despite the all-out firestorm bombing of Japanese cities) unless invaded and utterly destroyed. An invasion of Japan would be terribly costly in American lives, and Truman authorized use of the atomic bomb."[6] The textbook for my daughter's seventh-grade social studies class reads, "The United States and its allies gradually destroyed Japan's ability to wage war. In August 1945, the United States dropped atomic bombs on the Japanese cities of Hiroshima and Nagasaki. Faced with the destruction caused by this new superweapon and the threat of more attacks, Japan quickly surrendered."[7] The implication seems to be that the bomb persuaded Tokyo to surrender and thus spared both sides further losses, which conforms perfectly to the traditional view.

THE JAPANESE VIEW

The atomic bombings place the Japanese in the role of victims of a highly consequential massacre. Like other episodes from the war, the number of casualties was large, and their fate was gruesome. Unlike other grim wartime episodes, however, Hiroshima and Nagasaki could be seen not only as events from a completed war, but also as the opening acts of the new Cold War and of the nuclear era, with its continuing threat of another nuclear attack. Thus the A-bomb victims carry the additional burden of involuntary martyrdom, having demonstrated by their suffering the frightful effects of nuclear weapons used in anger and thus making themselves a point of reference in an ongoing struggle. Their story will remain pertinent to present-day political discussions as long as nuclear weapons exist. The Japanese find positive meaning in the hope that the world's revulsion toward what happened in the two bombed cities will contribute to eventual global denuclearization, so that Japanese suffering will have prevented others from similar suffering. This would help those affected by Hiroshima and Nagasaki to attain a sense of closure. Unfortunately, the day that humanity can confidently declare that nuclear weapons have been permanently eradicated is unforeseeable.

The victimization represented by the atomic bombings resonates in Japan with both right-wing nationalists and antinuclear / antimilitary activists, ideological opposites. Nationalists employ the story of the A-bombings to deflect attention from the harm Japan did to other Asians, the Japan-as-victim notion crowding out Japan-as-aggressor. According to Japanese historian Asada Sadao, emphasis on the A-bombings "accords with Japanese unwillingness to come to grips with their responsibility for the war and its consequences."[8] For the left, the atomic attacks were the culmination of the ruin brought on Japan by a militarist government. The bombings serve as the strongest possible warning that Japan should never again take even a single step down that path. Additionally, the A-bombs give credence and concreteness to the agenda of antinuclear activists everywhere, while bestowing a unique authority on Japanese activists.[9]

The mainstream of Japanese opinion cannot accept the common American view that the atomic bombings were justified. Japanese Defense Minister Kyuma Fumio, who was not known as an apologist for the United States, substantiated this in July 2007. Kyuma said of the atomic bombings, "My understanding is that it ended the war and that it couldn't be helped. I don't hold a grudge against the United States." This produced an outcry among the Japanese public, particularly *Hibakusha* (see below) and antinuclear activist groups. Hatakeyama Hiroko, vice-secretary of the Hiroshima Prefecture Confederation of A- and H-Bomb Sufferers, said "Kyuma makes it out as if the people who died because of the atomic bombs had to have died. . . . it makes me so sad I'm at a loss for words."[10] The furor forced Prime Minister Abe Shinzo to fire Kyuma.

Many Americans seem content with the assertion that responsibility for the atomic bombings rests with the wartime Japanese government, Tokyo having brought due retaliation for Japanese outrages at places such as Pearl Harbor, Bataan, Manila, and Nanjing. Japanese people such as Motoshima, however, decry the implicit idea that "because of . . . aggression and atrocities committed by the Japanese, there is no need to reflect upon the fact that an unprecedented weapon of mass destruction was used on a community of non-combatants."[11] From this standpoint, the criminality of the Japanese government during the war cannot justify crimes committed against Japanese civilians. Specifically, the Japanese do not accept the equivalency of the Pearl Harbor attack with the atomic bombings. They would be quick to point out that the A-bombs killed far greater numbers of people than the Pearl Harbor raid; that the victims were primarily civilians and the target was a city, while

Pearl Harbor was a military base and most of the casualties were soldiers and sailors; that the A-bombings had longer-term effects, with radiation poisoning harming or killing many survivors long after the attack; and that the atomic bombs had a far more profoundly negative impact on history because they set a precedent for the use of a cataclysmic new kind of weapon.

The Japanese are highly receptive to arguments that considerations other than quickly bringing the Pacific War to an end motivated the atomic bombings. The idea that the U.S. government used the atomic bomb against Japan to intimidate the Soviets is much more widely accepted in Japan than in the United States. Many Japanese saw in the Indochina conflict, and particularly reports of brutality by U.S. soldiers, evidence of what they viewed as American racism toward Asians. This bolstered the notion that American racism was a prime cause of the A-bombings.[12]

The physical heart of the Japanese antinuclear movement is Hiroshima Peace Memorial Park, a complex of parkland, memorials, and museums located at the epicenter of the Hiroshima A-bomb attack. The Park gets about 150,000 visitors per year. The emphasis, not surprisingly, is heavily on the suffering of the Japanese victims of the bombings: photographs, paintings, and testimonials of the death and destruction wrought by the bomb. The complex includes the famous skeletal dome of the Hiroshima Prefectural Industrial Promotion Hall, left in its bomb-damaged state as a relic of the attack. Kiroku Hanai, a liberal Japanese journalist, reported being "stunned" by his first visit to the memorial in 2007: "One exhibit showed a middle-school student, with skin hanging from his body due to extensive burns, sucking on pus oozing from nail-less fingers to try to slake his thirst. A painting showed a group of female students and their teacher, all naked after the blast blew off their clothes, walking aimlessly among the rubble."[13] The park is the site of an annual commemorative ceremony on the anniversary of the bombing. The ceremony features a speech by Hiroshima's mayor condemning the A-bomb raids and calling for progress toward global peace and international nuclear disarmament. Anti-U.S. overtones are inescapable. During the 2007 ceremony, for example, Mayor Akiba Tadatoshi demanded that Japan "protect its pacifist constitution which it should be proud of, and clearly say 'no' to antiquated and wrong U.S. policies."[14]

IMPACT ON POSTWAR JAPANESE POLICY

"Japan is different from other countries in that it has suffered a nuclear attack," said Abe in 2006.[15] Indeed, the atomic bombings have had a significant impact on policymaking in postwar Japan. Japan's terrible and tragic "difference" yielded a constraint as powerful in its own way as Article 9.

Survivors of the A-bombings of Hiroshima and Nagasaki are termed *Hibakusha* (explosion victims). About 250,000 are still alive, and the organizations that represent them form a powerful pressure group that often gets a hearing from the media and from politicians. Until recent years the *Hibakusha* rarely spoke publicly about their experience, finding it too painful to revisit or fearing discrimination from other Japanese who might consider them contaminated. Many *Hibakusha* and their children have claimed that their status has reduced their marriage and employment prospects. The Japanese seem to view them with equal measures of sympathy and fear. Although *Hibakusha* who register with the government are eligible for special benefits, some have declined this opportunity in order to avoid stigmatization.[16]

A 1954 incident deepened Japan's antinuclear commitment. The 23-member crew of the tragically unlucky Japanese fishing boat *Daigo Fukuryu Maru* (*Lucky Dragon 5*) suffered contamination from the fallout created by a U.S. hydrogen bomb test at Bikini Atoll. The ship was operating outside a U.S.-declared danger zone, but the blast was more than twice as powerful as expected and sent radioactive fallout into areas that scientists thought would be safe. The ship's crew fell ill, and one died within a few months. This triggered a widespread outpouring of antinuclear and anti-American sentiment in Japan. The Japanese press dubbed the incident a "second Hiroshima." U.S.-Japan relations were severely strained. Washington eventually apologized and paid Japan $2 million in compensation. Japanese antinuclear activists collected 30 million signatures on a petition to ban nuclear tests. In 1955 a World Conference Against Atomic and Hydrogen Bombs convened in Hiroshima.[17]

Prime Minister Sato Eisaku announced in 1967 that Japan would abide by "three Non-Nuclear Principles of not possessing, not producing and not permitting the introduction of nuclear weapons, in line with Japan's Peace Constitution."[18] His successors have reiterated Sato's policy. Japan ratified the Nuclear Nonproliferation Treaty in 1976, joining as a nonnuclear-weapons state pledging not to manufacture or acquire nuclear weapons. Japan's nonnuclear principles posed a possible difficulty for the Japan-U.S. alliance if they prevented U.S. ships and aircraft carrying nuclear weapons from using bases in Japan. Tokyo and Washington secretly agreed, however, that the temporary presence in Japanese territory of transiting American nuclear weapons did not violate Japan's nonnuclear pledge. Although publicly declaring that it did not keep nuclear weapons in Japan, the U.S. government secretly stored them on the islands of Okinawa, Iwo Jima, and Chichi Jima.[19] By the early 1980s, the Japanese public knew of the arrangement. A former American ambassador to Japan revealed that U.S. submarines carrying nuclear weapons, with the knowledge of the Japanese government, routinely entered ports in Japan and Okinawa.[20] The press also reported that an American vessel used as a storage site for nuclear weapons was anchored off the shore of a U.S. Marine Air Station at Iwakuni from 1959 to 1966, again with official Japanese knowledge. Many Japanese saw the presence of American nuclear weapons in Japan as a betrayal by their own leaders.

Nuclear propulsion is a separate issue from nuclear weapons. Japan is not averse to nuclear energy, operating 53 nuclear power plants. Nevertheless, many Japanese have objected to the presence of nuclear-powered U.S. warships. In 2005, the only U.S. aircraft carrier home-ported in Japan was the conventionally powered USS *Kitty Hawk*, based at Yokosuka. With the *Kitty Hawk's* retirement approaching, the mayor of Yokosuka conveyed his city's wish that the U.S. Navy would not replace it with a nuclear-powered carrier. The U.S. ambassador announced that the city's wishes were impossible to fulfill and that the new carrier would be one of the nuclear-powered *Nimitz*-class vessels. Clearly, where the alliance clashes with the Japanese public's wishes to remain nonnuclear, the alliance wins out.

Japanese antinuclear activists have watched with alarm as Japanese elites have begun publicly discussing the once-unthinkable notion of a nuclear-armed Japan. There has never been any doubt that Japan has the technological sophistication to produce nuclear weapons. Japan's stockpiling of plutonium and its space program provide the foundations for a fuel supply and a delivery system. For some Japanese, North Korea and China provide the strategic rationale. Fiercely anti-Japanese North Korea has a ballistic missile program, the potential of which was dramatically illustrated by the launch of a missile that overflew Japan in 1998. North Korean interest in a nuclear weapons program that could someday furnish the payload for such a missile is amply evident in two crises in the 1990s and the 2000s, culminating in a nuclear test detonation in 2006. The Japanese are keenly aware that China, already a nuclear weapons state, is carrying out a large and rapid upgrade of its conventional military forces. In 2002 Ozawa Ichiro, leader of the opposition Liberal Party, said that in response to a rising Chinese threat "it would be so easy for us to produce nuclear warheads—we have plutonium at nuclear power plants in Japan, enough to make several thousand such warheads."[21] (Ozawa later said he was not advocating Japan going nuclear, but rather pointing out that Chinese policy could lead to such an outcome.) After North Korea's nuclear weapons test, LDP Policy Research Council Chairman Nakagawa Shoichi said, "We need to find a way to prevent Japan from coming under attack. There is an argument that nuclear weapons are one such option. . . . [w]e need to have active discussions." A 2007 survey of LDP candidates for the upcoming Diet upper house election showed that one-third favored Japan reconsidering its policy against possessing nuclear weapons.[22]

CONTROVERSIAL AMERICAN COMMEMORATIONS

The Japanese have observed A-bomb commemorations in the United States and weighed in where they thought necessary. There were two prominent cases that arose around the 50th anniversary of the war's end. In late 1994 the U.S. Postal Service revealed a plan to introduce a stamp in 1995 depicting the atomic mushroom cloud with the notation, "Atomic bombs hasten war's end, August 1945." The proposed stamp created an outcry in Japan that included the media, the mayors of Hiroshima and Nagasaki, and other political figures. The umbrella Japan Confederation of Atomic and Hydrogen Bomb Victims Organizations declared, "The planned stamp is an insult . . . to the hundreds of thousands of people who were thrown into the hell created by the two A-bombs while they were still alive, and were miserably killed like insects. . . . The U.S. government should admit that its two atomic attacks on Hiroshima and Nagasaki were atrocious acts violating international law and apologize."[23] The Postal Service cancelled the stamp.

The Smithsonian Enola Gay controversy demonstrated that emotions about the atomic bombings ran as high among Americans as among the Japanese. Although this was largely an intellectual squabble among Americans, Japanese looked on, intervened, and sorrowed at the ultimate outcome. The Smithsonian Institution's Air and Space Museum planned an exhibit in 1995 on the end of the war, featuring part of the Enola Gay bomber, plus other artifacts, photos, and text commemorating the bombing of Hiroshima. Much of the presentation was to focus on the suffering of the bombing's victims. One section of the exhibit was to feature photos of casualties and videotaped testimonies of bombing survivors describing their experiences. The exhibit organizers' aim of generating reflection on the human consequences of the decision to drop the bomb was a departure from the Air and Space Museum's typical approach, which was to celebrate technological achievements. Director Martin Harwit, who had been involved in U.S. nuclear tests in the Pacific islands while serving in the army in the 1950s, had expressed antinuclear inclinations and had also said he disliked the museum's "World War II gallery we have now, which portrays the heroism of the airmen but neglects to mention in any real sense the misery of war." An article in *Air Force Magazine* in 1994 revealed the museum's plans. Subsequent press reports reproduced passages from the draft text that would accompany the exhibit. Critics said it was an unbalanced presentation that emphasized Japanese victimization and courage while portraying the Americans as belligerent. One infamous line of the draft text read, "For most Americans . . . it was a war of vengeance. For most Japanese, it was a war to defend their unique culture against Western imperialism."[24]

This was to be another episode of a larger cultural clash taking place in America between two camps that knew each other well. The broader domestic context was a conservative backlash against the counterculture movement of the 1960s and its perceived erosion of traditional patriotism and moral values. These conservatives were sensitive to so-called revisionist history that cast American behavior in a negative light. In particular, American veterans had strong views on the commemoration of the war and the atomic bombings. An American veteran who was a POW in Japan at the war's end said he saw a note posted in his camp, signed by Japanese Premier Tojo, proclaiming that guards would kill all prisoners if Allied troops invaded Japan. "That's why all of us who were prisoners in Japan—or were headed for it to probably die in the invasion—revere the *Enola Gay*. It saved our lives."[25] America in turn revered World War II veterans, so their views carried great weight with Congress.

The reports about the proposed content of the exhibit mobilized veterans groups and other critics who complained that the presentation was revisionist propaganda. The exhibit, they argued, neglected to point out the brutality of Japanese military behavior during the war, overemphasized the suffering of bomb victims, and failed to make the point that using the atomic bomb saved many Japanese and American lives. The Air Force Association called the proposed exhibit "a slap in the face to all Americans who fought in World War II" and said it "treats Japan and the U.S. as if their participation in the war were morally equivalent." It called on the museum to "display [the Enola Gay] in a patriotic manner that will instill pride in the viewer for . . . ending World War II without the need for an invasion of Japan and without the additional invasion-related casualties."[26] The exhibit's designers revised the proposed text several times, but the changes failed to satisfy the critics. In September 1994 the U.S. Senate unanimously passed a resolution that extolled the role of the Enola Gay in "helping to bring World War II to a merciful end" and opined that the museum "should reflect appropriate sensitivity" toward U.S. veterans. It criticized the revised text of the planned exhibit as "revisionist," "unbalanced" and "offensive."[27] In January 1995, 81 members of Congress demanded the resignation of Harwit. The Smithsonian cancelled the exhibit that month and fired Harwit in April.

A stripped-down Enola Gay exhibit opened in June. This featured the forward section of the fuselage and other parts of the aircraft with a relatively brief historical commentary that noted the atomic bombings led to Japan's surrender, making unnecessary an invasion that American leaders expected would result in "very heavy casualties" on both sides. In July three protestors poured blood and ashes on the aircraft, forcing the closure of the exhibit for part of a day. The display continued for three years and drew four million visitors.

In 2003 a new chapter of the controversy commenced as the Air and Space Museum planned to put the entire restored Enola Gay on display in a new museum annex near Dulles International Airport. A Japanese survivor of the bombing objected to putting the aircraft in a museum. "For us, the *Enola Gay* equals the atomic bomb," he said. "Displaying the plane is not only an insult to us but also glorifies the bombing."[28] Peace and antinuclear activists demanded that the museum politicize the exhibit by posting text near the aircraft detailing the number of deaths caused by the atomic bombing. An American academic argued, "You wouldn't display a slave ship solely as a model of technological advancement."[29] The new exhibit, however, was devoid of political commentary. A brief explanatory sign noted only technical information and the fact that the plane "dropped the first atomic weapon used in combat on Hiroshima, Japan." On the exhibit's opening day in December 2003, it attracted a protesting crowd of A-bomb survivors and peace activists, one of whom threw a bottle of red paint at the aircraft.

A DIFFERENT APOLOGY ISSUE

If the Chinese and Koreans have an apology issue with Japan, the Japanese have one with the Americans. According to Asada, the Japanese "feel that for the mistake of starting the Pacific War they have already taken their punishment and are thus absolved while the American side remains unrepentant for the atomic holocaust."[30] Japanese officials have in various settings apologized for their Pacific War aggression, but there has been no comparable apology from Washington for the A-bombs.

If the atomic bombs remain a sore spot for the Japanese, Americans feel similarly about the Pearl Harbor attack. Bilateral discussion of either one of these issues often brings in the other. In 1991, the upcoming 50th anniversary of the Pearl Harbor attack raised the possibility of dual U.S. and Japanese apologies to demonstrate complete reconciliation. There were several attempted steps in this direction, but the dual apology did not occur. In May, *Rashomon* director Kurosawa Akira's film *Rhapsody in August* began screening in Japan. The film follows four Japanese children learning about the atomic bombing of Nagasaki that killed their grandfather. The children visit the spot where he died and learn that other countries have donated memorials to the bombing—but not the United States. The film also features the children's half-American cousin from Hawaii, played by Richard Gere, traveling to Nagasaki and expressing remorse over the bombing. But in the eyes of most of his countrymen, Gere spoke out of turn. Western critics assailed the film as an unbalanced political statement because it focused on Japanese suffering without explaining the Japanese aggression that led to the attack. Kurosawa seemed surprised by the criticism.[31]

In August, the mayor of Honolulu invited Japanese officials to participate in a Pearl Harbor commemoration. The invitation was conditioned on the Japanese delegation's willingness to offer an apology for the Pacific War. The Japanese government's Deputy Chief Cabinet Secretary Ishihara Nobuo officially responded with a refusal, saying that "the entire world is responsible for the war."[32] In a televised interview in early December, President George Bush addressed the issue of an American apology for the atomic bombings. "No apology is required," he said. Bush defended Truman for making "a tough, calculating decision, and it was right." The Japanese press reported Bush's comments, which drew renewed condemnation from Hibakusha groups and offended many Diet members.[33] A few days later, Japanese Foreign Minister Watanabe Michio sent a message to the U.S. public in an interview with the *Washington Post*. "We feel a deep remorse," he said, "about the unbearable suffering and sorrow Japan inflicted on the American people and the peoples of Asia." He added that Japan was not seeking an American apology for the atomic bombings.[34] The Japanese Foreign Ministry evidently felt a concession was necessary to contain the anticipated spike in anti-Japan feelings accompanying the Pearl Harbor anniversary, especially in light of the Ishihara statement. Not surprisingly, many Japanese thought Watanabe's one-sided apology was unfair. Bush's refusal to apologize halted further consideration of a statement of apology from the Diet that month.

The Pearl Harbor linkage came up again in 1994, when Emperor Akihito toured the United States. He originally planned to visit the USS *Arizona*

Memorial at Pearl Harbor during his trip. Some Diet members, however, complained that the Pearl Harbor visit was inappropriate since no American president had either visited the Hiroshima Peace Memorial Park or apologized for the A-bombings. Akihito's office consequently deleted Pearl Harbor from the emperor's itinerary.

President Bill Clinton, who was noted for the large number of official apologies offered during his presidency (including one for the internment of Japanese-Americans and another to American nuclear industry workers exposed to radiation), declined to give the A-bomb victims what they wanted. In 1995 he said, "The United States owes no apology to Japan for having dropped the atomic bombs on Hiroshima and Nagasaki."[35] George W. Bush did not apologize either. Abe's government said it would not seek an apology from the United States because America was an ally committed to defend Japan. That did not stop continued Japanese demands for a U.S. apology in 2007, including one from Liberal Party chief Ozawa and another from the city of Usa, in a resolution unanimously adopted by its municipal assembly.

SHINING A-BOMB, CRUEL A-BOMB, FORGOTTEN FIREBOMB

Consistent with a theme we have seen throughout this study, both Americans and the Japanese have developed views of the atomic bombings that are strongly self-serving. Summarizing the different views of the A-bomb in the two societies, scholars Laura Hein and Mark Selden conclude that to Americans the bomb is a "shining example of American decisiveness, moral certitude, and technological ingenuity in the service of the nation." To the Japanese, on the other hand, the bomb is "the symbol of both national defeat by a cruel and powerful foe and stoic endurance." They add that "American commemorations of the bombings leave out Japanese victims, whereas Japanese ones leave out the victims of Japanese aggression."[36] The decision to drop the atomic bombs is as great a controversy within the United States as between the United States and Japan, allowing the Japanese to form coalitions with like-minded American activists in the pursuit of their agenda, just as sympathetic Japanese have cooperated with Chinese Pacific War victims in their attempts to influence a different war-related debate in Japan.

This is also another case of tension between Japanese society and its government on a war-related issue. The strong and emotional antinuclear sentiment of much of the Japanese public complicates the necessarily more cold-blooded and pragmatic Japanese government's attempts to manage the alliance relationship with the United States.

As we saw previously, U.S. conventional bombing of Japan caused more destruction and loss of life than the two atomic attacks. Yet there is a huge disparity in knowledge and discussion of the A-bombings versus the conventional campaign. Put simply, most Americans know about Hiroshima but don't know about the incendiary raids. There is a similar imbalance in Japan. One

Japanese writer observed in 1968 that during the 22 years since the end of the war, there were four stories in the major Japanese newspaper *Asahi Shimbun* about the conventional air raid on Tokyo. In contrast, there were about 400 stories in the same paper about the A-bombing of Hiroshima.[37] If we could separate out the conventional bombing campaign as a distinct event, we might conclude that it is possible for two societies to virtually forget a wrenching and divisive issue that could otherwise have obstructed the development of their relationship. This, however, is a special case. The atomic bombing issue has apparently subsumed the firebombing issue, the former taking precedence because of its pertinence to the ongoing debate about nuclear disarmament. As historian Jeffery Roberts has observed, "Moral attacks on the Hiroshima decision . . . seem to have less to do with the Pacific War than with the dawn of the nuclear age. For many people, to oppose the bombing of Hiroshima and Nagasaki is to oppose nuclear weapons generally, and the possibility of a third world war especially."[38] Perhaps, then, the legacy of the Pacific War firebombing is not so much suppressed as deflected. It might have played a more prominent role in postwar U.S.-Japan relations had Tokyo surrendered in July instead of August 1945.

CHAPTER 13

Conclusion

What happened in the Pacific War? It was a war in which conduct that is shocking by today's standards was routine. Murder and other mistreatment of prisoners of war and the wholesale slaughter of civilians were commonplace. A militarist-dominated Japan got bogged down in China. Tokyo tried to consolidate its great-power status and autonomy from the Western powers by driving them from Asia and seizing their colonies, leading to the desperate gamble of the Pearl Harbor attack. Japan briefly enlarged its empire but then lost everything. All the people and lands fought over suffered terribly, notably the Chinese and Okinawans. The United States marshaled its vast industrial and technological capabilities, while laying aside previous ethical restraints, to defeat and displace Japan. Governments were changed out in Korea, Taiwan, and Japan, with China soon to follow.

UNSETTLED CLAIMS AND SEISMIC SHIFTS

What are the war's political legacies? They fall into two general categories. The first might be called *unsettled claims*. These involve one party demanding redress from another for a grievance related to the war. Here we find the comfort women issue, lawsuits against the Japanese government by former forced laborers or by Chinese harmed by leftover chemical weapons, condemnation of Japanese nationalists for their self-beautifying interpretations of history, the Yasukuni Shrine controversy, Okinawan opposition to U.S. military bases, and the disagreement between many Americans and most Japanese over whether the atomic bombings were justified.

A second category of Pacific War legacies could be called *seismic shifts*. These are major changes in the geopolitical landscape of the Asia-Pacific region resulting from the war. We have become so accustomed to some of these postwar conditions that we no longer think about their origins. If we did, our appreciation of the impact of the Pacific War on today's world would increase. Several features of the postwar world stand out as political seismic shifts wrought by the war.

First is the rule of the Chinese Communist Party over China. As we saw, the Japanese invasion helped facilitate the eventual CCP victory. It deflected KMT military pressure on the communists that otherwise might have destroyed them as an organized political actor. Without the burden of the Anti-Japanese War, the KMT might have been more effective at nation building as well as keeping itself in power. With the war, however, the CCP forces gained a refuge in northern China, where they refined their political and guerrilla warfare skills and successfully cultivated a popular image as a patriotic movement that was a viable challenger to the KMT regime. Imagine how dramatically different our world would be today if Chiang Kai-shek's party had survived and overcome the communist challenge, China underwent some kind of political liberalization under KMT rule by the 1990s, and the China of today had a political system more like that of Taiwan than that of the People's Republic of China.

Second is the division of the Korean Peninsula. However unintentional, the U.S.-proposed plan in the last days of the Pacific War to divide Korea into American and Soviet zones for the purposes of accepting Japanese surrenders and keeping public order had the effect of dooming Korea to long-term separation. In this sense the Korean War, lingering inter-Korean tensions, the U.S.-ROK alliance, and the two crises over North Korea's nuclear weapons program are part of the legacy of the Pacific War.

A third seismic shift is Japan's transformation from traditional great power to "civilian great power."[1] After the war Tokyo turned away from imperialism and sought security under the U.S. defensive umbrella. Domestically, the war and its immediate aftermath had a long-term unsettling effect on Japan's politics. Japan's conservative wing suffered severe setback with the militarist government's defeat in the war and U.S.-forced political liberalization, only to be rehabilitated by the American authorities as they oriented Japan for Cold War serviceability. This promoted a seemingly unsustainable polarization in Japan between two contending camps. One is antimilitarist, critical of the wartime political system and government for bringing disaster upon Japan, and opposed to a "normal" Japan that departs from Article 9. The other is nationalist, favors using sanitized history to promote pride in Japan, and believes the country should shed the unique restrictions on its military capabilities and policies. This ferment is additional reason to marvel at the longevity of the postwar Japanese status quo of a constrained military (with no right of collective defense, no nuclear weapons, intentionally limited force-projection capability, and an informal cap of about 1 percent of GDP on defense spending) and the alliance with the United States.

Fourth, America's postwar attachment to the Republic of China on Taiwan is largely a heritage of the wartime alliance with Chiang Kai-shek. Washington's decision to oppose further Japanese expansion and the consequent U.S.-China alliance, undergirded by a well-established American paternalism toward China, ensured that the wartime generation in the United States imbibed a favorable view of China as pro-Western and pro-democratic, with Chiang's wife Soong Mei-ling serving as an effective spokeswoman. Nationalist China became the depository of American hopes for China, later inherited by Taiwan as "free China" after the devastating "loss" of mainland China to communist forces. That political bond, more than the strategic and economic rationales that faded after the Cold War, formed a basis of continuing U.S. support for the Taipei government (although it was strained after 2001 by Taiwan President Chen Shui-bian's overuse of the presumed American commitment as cover for his de-Sinification agenda).

Finally, a permanently internationalist and militarily forward-deployed United States is an important feature of the geopolitical world that stems from the war. World War II as a whole created a postwar bipartisan consensus in the United States that there is no security in isolation—that problems abroad, if left unchecked, can threaten vital Americans interests. It is difficult to separate the European component of the war from the Pacific component in this respect. It was from the European theater that postwar American leaders drew the Munich analogy that the failure of peace-loving governments to stand up to aggression only encourages further aggression. Nevertheless, it was from the Pacific theater that fascism reached across one of the great oceans to strike U.S. territory. The war spawned America's so-called global cop role. Prior to the attack on Pearl Harbor, most Americans were not willing to intervene to prevent Europe from falling to Hitler or to stop Japanese atrocities in China. Now U.S. intervention in foreign affairs is commonplace, even when the stakes are seemingly lower. A network of overseas bases far more extensive than existed before the war now facilitates these interventions.

Perhaps worthy of an honorable mention in the seismic shifts category is the Soviet seizure of the Kurile Islands at the end of the war. This not only resulted in the expulsion of 17,000 Japanese residents, it also created an intractable obstacle in postwar relations between Japan and the USSR/Russia. Japan disputes Russian ownership of the southern Kuriles (Kunashiri, Etorofu, Shikotan, and the Habomai islets), which the Japanese call the Northern Territories. According to the Yalta agreement, "The Kurile Islands shall be handed over to the Soviet Union." The later Potsdam Proclamation was more ambiguous. It did not specifically mention the Kuriles, while allowing that postwar Japan would retain ownership of "such minor islands as we determine." According to the 1951 Treaty of San Francisco, Japan renounced any claim to "the Kurile Islands,"[2] but the Soviets refused to sign the treaty and the Japanese government took the position that the Northern Territories are not technically part of the Kuriles. During the Cold War, Washington sided with the Japanese—or, some scholars have argued, obstructed a Japan-Soviet rapprochement by encouraging Tokyo to maintain demands the Soviets could not accept.[3]

The position of the Russian government, strongly supported by most of the Russian people, is that Russia gained ownership of the entire Kurile group as a result of the war. In 2006, Russian President Vladimir Putin offered to give Japan Shikotan and the Habomai islets (totaling only 6 percent of the Northern Territories) if Tokyo would drop its claims to the larger islands of Kunashiri and Etorofu. This was unacceptable to the Japanese leadership, since most of the Japanese public demands the eventual return of all four parts of the Northern Territories.

Failure to settle the dispute has blocked the conclusion of a peace treaty between Russia and Japan since the end of the war. The deadlock has prevented progress in Japan-Russian relations, keeping bilateral economic cooperation far below its potential. Both sides stand to gain much from improved trade and investment links, as Russians yearn for Japanese capital to aid in the development of the Russian Far East, while Russia could serve as a major oil supplier to Japan. The bilateral atmosphere worsened in August 2006 when Russian coast guard personnel killed a Japanese fisherman and arrested three others accused of poaching crab near the Habomai group.

As Russia has grown stronger in the latter part of the decade, the prospect of Moscow making further concessions, such as offering to return Kunashiri or Etorofu to Japan, has become more remote. The Russian government also announced in 2006 that it plans to make major infrastructure improvements to encourage larger numbers of Russian citizens to reside on the islands. This investment will make it harder for the Russians to consider handing any of the territory over to Japan. Remarkably, the Soviet seizure of the Kuriles has had a negative effect on postwar Japan-Russia relations that approaches in magnitude the effect of the Japanese invasion of China on postwar China-Japan relations.

HISTORY AND POLITICS

This book underscores an important point for the general study of global affairs: history matters in international relations. Some theories of international politics emphasize the material basis of interstate behavior. Neorealism holds that a country's relative capabilities, particularly its military capability, determine the character of its policies toward other countries. In contrast, a theory such as constructivism holds that the foundation of interstate relationships is ideational, with governments deciding how to treat each other based on whether they seem to follow socially derived rules.[4] My study supports the indispensability of ideational factors to a thorough understanding of world politics. The experience of the Pacific War has clearly affected international behavior such as Japan's postwar security policy, the Asia-Pacific region's attitudes toward American military power in Asia, China's policy toward Japan, and the U.S.-Japan alliance. History matters for Neorealists as well. Even where national governments are focused on their own survival and on worst-case military scenarios involving their potential adversaries, they consider intentions in addition to capabilities. Assessments of intentions are based largely on historical track records.

As important as it is, history is also malleable, for better or worse. The political winds have made the commemoration of victimization inconsistent, almost faddish. The Japanese children killed in the atomic bombings are regularly and internationally memorialized, but the Japanese children killed in conventional air raids or in ships sunk by American submarines are not. China's government first kept quiet about the wartime slaughter of its civilian population but now makes considerable efforts to publicize it. The stories of abuse of the comfort women, long hidden, now elicit sympathy from most quarters but denial from some.

Events may be factual, but their meaning, interpretation, and significance are subjective constructs. This means governments and societies can choose to let go of divisive and antagonizing historical interpretations and to emphasize themes that are uniting and pacifying. It is equally true, however, that history offers a collection of politically relevant notions that one group may draw from to support an argument or claim against another. This brings us to the question of the relationship between history and today's political actors. As we have seen through various cases surveyed in this book, there are at least three aspects of the relationship. The first is political actors as products of history. Every nation partakes of certain widely accepted historical interpretations that serve as part of the foundation of a national outlook and core national values. These interpretations dictate some of the policy preferences of both the national leadership and the society over which it rules: that is, our nation always follows Behavior X and never Behavior Y because it is part of our identity established by our (interpretation of) history. Other nations may have different preferences based on different but equally deeply rooted historical interpretations, raising the possibility of a clash between two nations following conflicting policies, each backed by a national consensus that to do otherwise would be unthinkable.

The second relationship between history and political actors we have observed is government or other political actors instrumentally controlling history. They do not necessarily believe or care about a particular historical interpretation but welcome and employ it as a means to support a separate and perhaps hidden agenda. In this case elites promote domestic or international awareness of a carefully managed historical interpretation that strengthens the elites' bargaining position. Since the goal is short-term gain, the long-term danger of bequeathing to society a jerry-rigged history with flawed lessons is not given due regard.

A third aspect of the history-actor relationship is that of history constraining elites. Deeply held historical interpretations within society create expectations that elites do not necessarily share but feel compelled to fulfill. These historically derived expectations become a burden to policymakers, forcing them to compromise their preferred courses of action. The common trade-off is between, on the one hand, strengthening or preserving an important bilateral relationship that suits the national economic or strategic interest, and on the other hand, mollifying the demands of public opinion in order to retain domestic legitimacy.

We have seen each of these phenomena at work in various times and places. Both government and society in Korea and Japan, for example, seem to believe deeply in highly contrasting interpretations of the Japanese colonial period in Korea, including specific aspects such as the comfort women issue. These differences continue to hamper postwar bilateral relations. An even more menacing manifestation of the phenomenon of governments as products of history appears in the Taiwan Strait. Convinced of the lesson they have drawn from their history that a divided China cannot be a great power, the Chinese say they will go to war to prevent Taiwan's independence. Many people on Taiwan, and the island's government from 2000 to 2008, believed equally strongly in a historical interpretation demonstrating that Taiwan is not part of China. The second scenario, the instrumental use of history by governments for narrow, immediate political purposes, is evident in the George W. Bush administration's use of doctored analogies from the European and Pacific theaters of World War II in defense of the invasion and occupation of Iraq, which began in March 2003. Historians have frequently criticized Bush and his top advisors for distorting history in their speeches about the Iraq operation.[5] (I will add my own criticism below.) Finally, we have seen the phenomenon of history as a constraint on policymakers in the case of China-Japan relations, with PRC leaders who wanted to improve relations with Japan forced to meet the demands of the historically aware Chinese public for a more confrontational approach to Tokyo.

Attempts by government to use history to manipulate public opinion are perhaps comparable to a man trying to move a large boulder. If the boulder rests on level ground, the man can only with great difficulty start and keep the boulder rolling. Similarly, the government's rhetoric will have little effect if it does not resonate with the public's predispositions. If, conversely, the government presents the public with an interpretation of history that meets their expectations and fulfills their wishes, mobilizing the public is far easier. In this case the boulder is perched on a downhill grade and requires only a nudge to get it started. A problem arises when the man decides he wants to stop the downhill-rolling boulder or change its direction. His only chance may be to step in front of the boulder and try to block it with his shoulder, but by so doing he puts himself at risk of the boulder crushing him. Since historical issues involve the very serious and emotional matter of national honor, the perception of failure to live up to perceived duties can quickly imperil a government's legitimacy.

BOGUS HISTORICAL LESSONS

This study makes clear that issues left over from the Pacific War are still at play in the relations between Northeast Asian countries. A final reason why your time reading this book has been well spent is that the Pacific War is part of present-day political discourse in another way: as a fount of purported "lessons" that offer guidance in dealing with today's problems. The Pearl Harbor attack, for instance, has become one of the touchstones of American history, a stand-alone event that transcends its context. It can crop up even in a relatively mundane setting. During the 2007 season, the University of Alabama football team lost two consecutive games to what it considered weaker opponents. Coach Nick Saban said afterward that his team suffered a shock comparable to the September 11 terror attacks or the raid on Pearl Harbor. "Pearl Harbor got us ready, you know, for World War II, or whatever, and that was a catastrophic event. I don't think anybody in this room would have bet that we would have lost back-to-back games to Mississippi State and ULM [University of Louisiana-Monroe]," Saban said.[6]

Pacific War allusions are more serious when they appear in ongoing national policy debates. President George Bush Sr. invoked Pearl Harbor as a justification for Operation Desert Storm in 1991. "The seeds of Pearl Harbor were sown back in 1919," he said, "when a victorious America decided that in the absence of a threatening enemy abroad, we should turn all of our energies inward. That notion of isolationism flew escort for the very bombers that attacked our men 50 years ago [at Pearl Harbor]. . . . [T]o believe that turning our backs on the world would improve our lot here at home, is to ignore the tragic lessons of the 20th century." He went on to describe the operation to drive Iraqi forces out of Kuwait as "affirm[ing] the values cherished by the heroes of the Harbor."[7] The elder Bush suggested that American isolation was responsible for the Japanese attack on Pearl Harbor. That is clearly wrong, as we have seen. It was the experience with Hitler, not Japan, that gave rise to the lesson that "isolationism leads to an expanded war." But the United States was not inattentive or unengaged in Asia. Rather, the Japanese attacked Pearl Harbor because of U.S. pressure on Japan and because the United States had military bases in Philippines.

Another Bush also alluded to the Pacific War in connection with another war against Iraq. As he spoke at a naval air station in San Diego in 2005 on the anniversary of the defeat of Japan, President George W. Bush's administration was consumed by the floundering U.S. occupation of Iraq and looking for ways to maintain support for it. Bush gravitated to the topic of what the Pacific War teaches us about the Iraq War. "President Roosevelt. . . . knew that the best way to bring peace and stability to the region was by bringing freedom to Japan," Bush said. "With every step toward freedom, the Japanese became a valued member of the world community, a force for peace and stability in the region, and a trusted and reliable ally of the United States of America."[8] In this speech Bush makes the U.S.-Japan war sound like it fit the same pattern. But the intimated similarities between the two cases do not survive close inspection.

The Iraq War was an elective war for the United States, allegedly part of the neoconservative grand strategy of taking advantage of America's unparalleled global power to transform the Middle East into a stable and tranquil region by democratizing its major states. It is grossly misleading, however, to imply that the Pacific War was an elective war for America, motivated by a desire to liberalize Japan. It would have been more accurate to say that President Roosevelt tried to bring peace and stability to the region by using economic and military levers to attempt to dissuade the Japanese from challenging the colonial positions of the Western powers in Asia.

In a speech to American veterans in 2007, the younger Bush contended that "the militarists of Japan . . . were driven by a merciless vision for the proper ordering of humanity. They killed Americans because we stood in the way of their attempt to force their ideology on others." Of the U.S. occupation, Bush said,

In the aftermath of Japan's surrender, many thought it naïve to help the Japanese transform themselves into a democracy. . . . Some said Japanese culture was inherently incompatible with democracy. . . . Other critics said that Americans were imposing their ideals on the Japanese. . . . Other critics argued that democracy could not succeed in Japan because the national religion—Shinto—was too fanatical and rooted in the Emperor. . . . You know, the experts sometimes get it wrong.[9]

Bush argues here that since the American project in postwar Japan had its doubters but was ultimately successful, we can expect that the same will be true of Iraq, and thus we should not be deterred by critics of the U.S. occupation of Iraq. Leaving aside the lack of cogency in Bush's argument, his statement is also dangerously deceptive in that it leaves out what Japan and Iraq do *not* have in common. Japan was an unusually cohesive, homogeneous, and orderly society that generally accepted the U.S. administration as a legitimate authority. In contrast, Iraq in 2007 was characterized by a remarkably fractious polity and a high degree of public disorder. Furthermore, many Iraqis did not accept the U.S. occupation or the American-backed government as legitimate. These differences between Japan and Iraq were in the very areas crucial to the success or failure of an occupation.

The primary interest of these two presidents as well as countless other leaders in government and other fields is not to present accurate, complete, and balanced interpretations of history, but rather to win short-term political battles. This tendency of human political behavior is not likely to change. Our only defense against vulnerability to this kind of attempted manipulation is to gain knowledge, with priority given to that which is most worth knowing. A foundational historical event such as the Pacific War is surely high on that list.

Notes

CHAPTER 1: INTRODUCTION

1. Associated Press, "Remains of WWII Pilot Found in Koolaus to Be Buried," *Honolulu Advertiser*, July 20, 2007, http://the.honoluluadvertiser.com/article/2007/Jul/20/br/br2567180943.html, accessed July 23, 2007.

2. "The 10 Worst Dates in Hawaii's History," broadcast June 16, 2006, KITV Oceanic Cable channel 16, 9:55 P.M.; William Safire, *Safire's Political Dictionary* (New York: Oxford University Press, 2008), p. 666.

3. Gregg K. Kakesako, "WWII Veterans Spread Praise," *Honolulu Star-Bulletin*, September 4, 2005, 1; Thomas Fargo, remarks at Pearl Harbor, December 7, 2003, http://www.pacom.mil/speeches/sst2003/031210dec7.shtml, accessed September 13, 2005.

4. John A. Krout, *United States History From 1865*, 20th ed. (New York: Harper-Collins, 1991), 277–281; Sherry Marker, *Illustrated History of the United States* (Greenwich, CT: Bison Books, 1988), 138–140.

5. David C. King, *Children's Encyclopedia of American History* (New York: DK Publishing House, 2003), 176, 180; Alan Axelrod, *The Complete Idiot's Guide to American History* (New York: Alpha Books, 1996), 248.

6. Roger Ebert, "Ebert's Review of Pearl Harbor," May 25, 2001, http://www.freerepublic.com/forum/a3b0ee1252547.htm, accessed March 12, 2008.

7. Ian Waldron-Mantgani, "Pearl Harbor," June 2001, The UK Critic online, http://www.ukcritic.com/pearlharbor.html, accessed Aug. 25, 2005.

8. Lisa Takeuchi Cullen, "Make Love Not War," July 9, 2001, TIMEasia.com, http://www.time.com/time/asia/arts/printout/0,9788,166755,00.html, accessed August 25, 2005.

9. An exception was the 1978 documentary about the grim fighting between the Soviets and the Nazis on the eastern front titled *The Unknown War.*

10. Jay Matthews, "Students Don't Know Much About WW II Except the Internment Camps," *Washington Post*, May 28, 2004, posted on History News Network, http://hnn.roundup/entries/5397.html, accessed September 6, 2005.

11. Anders Henriksson, "Do Students Care About History?" History News Network, [no date], http://hnn.us/articles/594.html, accessed September 30, 2005.

12. Chris Hasting and Julie Henry, "D-Day—As Kids Remember It (Prepare Yourself)," *The Sunday Telegraph* (London), May 30, 2004, available online at http://hnn.us/roundup/entries/5462.html, accessed Aug. 26, 2005.

13. Natalya Loseva, "The Fourth Generation," April 25, 2005, Russia Profile.org, http://russiaprofile.org/culture/article.wbp?article-id=EA111594-FC3D-4D5F-A925-49B80904FADD, accessed August 30, 2005.

14. "President Commemorates 60th Anniversary of V-J Day," White House press release, August 30, 2005, http://www.whitehouse.gov/news/releases/2005/08/200508 30-1.html, accessed September 6, 2005.

15. Tom Brokaw, *The Greatest Generation* (New York: Random House, 1998).

16. Stephen E. Ambrose, *Citizen Soldiers: The U.S. Army from the Normandy Beaches to the Bulge to the Surrender of Germany; June 7, 1944 to May 7, 1945* (New York: Simon and Schuster, 1997), 473; interview with Ambrose posted on the Web site kidsread.com, http://www.kidsreads.com/features/0522-wwii.asp, accessed June 24, 2005.

17. George H. W. Bush, "Remarks on Signing the Proclamation Commemorating the 50th Anniversary of World War II, June 4, 1992," Bush Presidential Library Web site, http://bushlibrary.tamu.edu/research/papers/1992/92060400.html, accessed November 15, 2006.

18. Maurice Halbwachs, *On Collective Memory* (Chicago: University of Chicago Press, 1992); Barry Schwartz, "The Social Context of Commemoration: A Study in Collective Memory," *Social Forces* 61 (1982): 374–402; Schwartz, "Social Change and Collective Memory: The Democratization of George Washington," *American Sociological Review* 56 (1991): 221–36; Robert N. Bellah, Richard Madsen, William M. Sullivan, Ann Swidler, and Steven M. Tipton, *Habits of the Heart* (New York: Harper and Row, 1985), 152–155.

19. George Archibald, "Textbooks Flunk Test," *The Washington Times*, March 28, 2004, 2.

20. Ernest Renan, "Qu'est-ce qu'une nation?" *Oeuvres complètes de Ernest Renan*, Vol. I, ed. Henriette Psichari, 891 (Paris: Calmann-Lévy, 1947 [1882]); translated by and quoted in Arash Abizadeh, "Historical Truth, National Myths and Liberal Democracy: On the Coherence of Liberal Nationalism," *The Journal of Political Philosophy* 12, No. 3 (2004): 292.

CHAPTER 2: CHINA'S ORDEAL

1. Stephen MacKinnon, "Refugee Flight at the Onset of the Anti-Japanese War," in *Scars of War: Impact of Warfare on Modern China*, ed. Diana Lary and Stephen Mackinnon, 118–134 (Vancouver: University of British Columbia Press, 2001).

2. Brian Crozier, *The Man Who Lost China* (New York: Charles Scribner's Sons, 1976), 10.

3. Christopher Thorne, *The Issue of War* (New York: Oxford University Press, 1985), 60.

4. Jonathan D. Spence, *The Search for Modern China* (New York: W. W. Norton, 1990), 415.

5. Steven I. Levine, "Introduction," in *China's Bitter Victory: The War with Japan, 1937–1945*, ed. James C. Hsiung and Steven I. Levine, xix (Armonk, NY: M. E. Sharpe, 1992).

6. William C. Kirby, "The Chinese War Economy," in Hsiung and Levine, *China's Bitter Victory*, 187–189.

7. Brian Crozier, *The Man Who Lost China: The First Full Biography of Chiang Kai-shek* (New York: Scribner's, 1976), 255–256.

8. Edmund O. Clubb, *20th Century China*, 3rd ed. (New York: Columbia University Press, 1978), 224.

9. R. J. Rummel, *Death By Government* (New Brunswick, NJ: Transaction Publishers, 1994), 134.

10. Edward L. Dreyer, *China at War 1901–1949* (London: Addison Wesley Longman, 1995), 314; Spence, *Modern China*, 507.

11. Charles F. Romanus and Riley Sutherland, *The United States Army in World War II: Time Runs Out in CBI* (Washington, DC: U.S. Government Printing Office, 1976), 245.

12. Hsi-sheng Ch'i, "The Military Dimension, 1942–1945," in Hsiung and Levine, *China's Bitter Victory*, 170.

13. Marvin Williamsen, "The Military Dimension 1937–1941," in Hsiung and Levine, *China's Bitter Victory*, 150.

14. Dreyer, *China at War*, 261, 266.

15. John W. Dower, *War without Mercy: Race and Power in the Pacific War* (New York: Pantheon, 1986), 164–169.

16. Immanuel C. Y. Hsü, *The Rise of Modern China* (Oxford: Oxford University Press, 2000), 601.

17. Barbara W. Tuchman, *Stilwell and the American Experience in China* (New York: Macmillan, 1971), 238.

18. Herbert Feis, *The China Tangle* (Princeton, NJ: Princeton University Press, 1972), 11.

19. Dreyer, *China at War*, 266–267.

20. Crozier, *The Man Who Lost China*, 236.

21. John W. Garver, "China's Wartime Diplomacy," in Hsiung and Levine, *China's Bitter Victory*, 20–22.

22. Laura Tyson Li, *Madame Chiang Kai-shek: China's Eternal First Lady* (New York: Grove Press, 2006), 202.

23. "Madame," *Time*, March 1, 1943, vol. XLI, no. 9, http://www.time.com/time/magazine/article/0,9171,932936,00.html?promoid=googlep, accessed October 17, 2007.

24. Tuchman, *Stilwell*, 250.

25. Crozier, *The Man Who Lost China*, 253.

26. Ibid., 307, 311.

27. T'ien-wei Wu, "The Chinese Communist Movement," in Hsiung and Levine, *China's Bitter Victory*, 79.

28. Kui-Kwong Shum, *The Chinese Communists' Road to Power: The Anti-Japanese National United Front, 1935–1945* (Oxford: Oxford University Press, 1988).

29. David M. Gordon, "The China-Japan War, 1931–1945," *Journal of Military History* 70, no. 1 (January 2006): 171.

30. Mao Zedong, *Selected Works of Mao Zedong*, Vol. II (Beijing: Foreign Languages Press, 1961), 140.

31. Odoric Y. K. Wou, *Mobilizing the Massses: Building Revolution in Henan* (Stanford, CA: Stanford University Press, 1994).

32. Hsü, *Rise of Modern China*, 599.

33. What follows is drawn from Denny Roy, *Taiwan: A Political History* (Ithaca, NY: Cornell University Press, 2003), 52–53.

34. Hsi-sheng Ch'i, "The Military Dimension, 1942–1945," in Hsiung and Levine, *China's Bitter Victory*, 180.

35. James C. Hsiung, "The War and After: World Politics in Historical Context," in Hsiung and Levine, *China's Bitter Victory*, 297.

CHAPTER 3: SINO-JAPAN WAR EXPANDS TO PACIFIC WAR

1. Stuart Creighton Miller, *"Benevolent Assimilation": The American Conquest of the Philippines, 1899–1903* (New Haven, CT: Yale University Press, 1982), 220.

2. Walter LaFeber, *The New Empire: An Interpretation of American Expansion, 1860–1898* (Ithaca, NY: Cornell University Press, 1998), 54.

3. William Appleman Williams, *The Tragedy of American Diplomacy* (New York: W. W. Norton, 1988), p. 51.

4. Walter LaFeber, *The Clash: U.S.-Japanese Relations Throughout History* (New York: W. W. Norton, 1997), 75.

5. Marius B. Jansen, *The Making of Modern Japan* (Cambridge, MA: Harvard University Press, 2002), p. 442.

6. Roosevelt to Hermann Speck von Sternberg, August 8, 1900, in Elting E. Morison, *The Letters of Theodore Roosevelt*, Vol. II, *The Years of Preparation, 1898–1900* (Cambridge, MA: Harvard University Press, 1951), 1394.

7. *New York Tribune*, March 18, 1898, p. 6.

8. *New York Times*, February 10, 1904, 8.

9. Elting E. Morison (ed.), *Letters of Theodore Roosevelt*, vol. 4 (Cambridge, MA: Harvard University Press, 1951), p. 1,202.

10. LaFeber, *The Clash*, 59, 78–84.

11. Ibid., 55–56.

12. Ibid.

13. Ibid., 106, 146.

14. Tomoko Akami, *Internationalizing the Pacific: The United States, Japan, and the Institute of Pacific Relations in War and Peace, 1919-45* (London: Routledge, 2002), p. 23.

15. Akira Iriye, *Power and Culture: The Japanese-American War 1941–1945* (Cambridge, MA: Harvard University Press, 1981), 2–3; LaFeber, *The Clash*, 154; Stephen R. Shalom, "VJ Day: Remembering the Pacific War," *Critical Asian Studies* 37, no. 2 (June 2005), http://www.zmag.org/zmag/articles/july95shalom.htm, accessed June 12, 2006.

16. George Friedman and Meredith LeBard, *The Coming War With Japan* (New York: St. Martin's Press, 1991), 63.

17. Ronald H. Spector, *Eagle Against the Sun: The American War with Japan* (New York: Vintage Books, 1985), 36.

18. LaFeber, *The Clash*, 168–169.

19. Lloyd C. Gardner, *Economic Aspects of New Deal Diplomacy* (Boston: Beacon Press, 1964), 70.

20. U.S. Department of State, *Foreign Relations of the United States, Japan: 1931–1941*, Vol. I (Washington, DC: U.S. Government Printing Office, 1943), 125.

21. Michael A. Barnhart, *Japan Prepares for Total War: The Search for Economic Security, 1919–1941* (Ithaca, NY: Cornell University Press, 1987), 90–101.

22. Friedman and LeBard, *The Coming War*, 57, 60.

23. Brooks Emeny, *The Strategy of Raw Materials: A Study of America in Peace and War* (New York: Macmillan, 1934), 23, 39, 174.

24. Barnhart, *Japan Prepares*, 131–132.

25. John K. Emmerson and Harrison M. Holland, *The Eagle and the Rising Sun: America and Japan in the Twentieth Century* (Reading, MA: Addison-Wesley, 1988), 56.

26. Barnhart, *Japan Prepares*, 146.

27. Spector, *Eagle*, 1.

28. Jonathan G. Utley, *Going to War with Japan 193–1941* (Knoxville: University of Tennessee Press, 1985), 34–35, 133; LaFeber, *The Clash*, 177.

29. Iriye, *Power and Culture*, 22.

30. The text of the Tripartite Pact is available online at http://avalon.law.yale.edu/wwii/triparti.asp, accessed December 12, 2008.

31. LaFeber, *The Clash*, 194–195; Utley, *Going to War*, 149.

32. Iriye, Power and Culture, 26–28.

33. John Costello, *The Pacific War* (New York: Rawson, Wade, 1981), 606.

34. Utley, *Going to War*, 162.

35. Robert A. Devine, *The Reluctant Belligerent: American Entry Into World War II* (New York: John A. Wiley & Sons, 1979), 126.

36. LeFeber, *The Clash*, 200.

37. Utley, *Going to War*, 151–153; Emmerson and Holland, *Eagle and Rising Sun*, 54.

38. Iriye, *Power and Culture*, 28.

39. *Oriental Economist*, no. 6 (September 1941): 450; Friedman and Lebard, *Coming War*, 75–76.

40. Okazaki Ayakoto, quoted in Ienaga Saburo, *The Pacific War 1931–1945* (New York: Pantheon, 1978), 133.

41. Barnhart, *Japan Prepares*, 264–266.

42. Gerhard L. Weinberg, *A World at Arms: A Global History of World War II* (New York: Cambridge University Press, 1994), 246.

43. Weinberg, *World at Arms*, 249, 253.

44. LaFeber, *The Clash*, 204.

45. Ienaga Saburo, *The Pacific War 1931–1945* (New York: Pantheon, 1978), 134.

46. Barnhart, *Japan Prepares*, 236.

47. Utley, *Going to War*, 170–173.

48. Emmerson and Holland, *Eagle and the Rising Sun*, 53.

49. LeFeber, *The Clash*, 208–213.

50. Spector, *Eagle*, 76.

51. Spector, *Eagle*, 44–45.

52. Memorandum of conversation, Secretary of State Cordell Hull with Japanese diplomatic delegation, Dec. 7, 1941, *Foreign Relations of the United States of America: Japan, 1931–1941*, Vol. II (Washington, DC: U.S. Government Printing Office, 1943), 787.

53. Sidney Fine and Gerald Saxon Brown, *The American Past: Conflicting Interpretations of the Great Issues* (New York: Macmillan, 1976), 464.

54. Associated Press, "Japanese Professor Rewrites Story of Pearl Harbor," December 9, 1999, posted at http://starbulletin.com/1999/12/09/news/story3.html, accessed August 18, 2006.

55. Spector, *Eagle*, 118.

56. Admiral Kemp Tolley, "The Strange Cruise of the Lanikai," *American Heritage Magazine* 24, no. 6 (October 1973), http://www.americanheritage.com/articles/magazine/ah/1973/6/1973_6_56.shtml; Mike Thompson, "Unlike George W. Bush, FDR Had Specific Warnings," Newsmax.com, April 13, 2004, http://www.newsmax.com/archives/articles/2004/4/13/94615.shtml, accessed February 2, 2006.

57. Barnhart, *Japan Prepares*, 123.

58. Edwin T. Layton, *And I Was There* (New York: William Morrow, 1985), 131–137, 259.

59. McCollum's memo is reprinted in Appendix A of Robert B. Stinnett, *Day of Deceit* (New York: Free Press, 2000); The Stimson quote is also found in Stinnett's book on p. 8.

60. See, for example, Stinnett, *Day of Deceit.*

61. Representative Alvin E. O'Konski had these figures read in to the *Congressional Record* of July 3, 1945, Vol. 91, A3692–3695.

62. Barnhart, *Japan Prepares*, 266–267.

63. United States Strategic Bombing Survey, *Summary Report (Pacific War)*, July 1, 1946, 20, online at http://www.anesi.com/ussbs01.htm, accessed June 30, 2005.

64. Richard Overy, *Why the Allies Won* (New York: W. W. Norton, 1997) 195, 197.

65. John Gorley Bunker, *Liberty Ships* (Salem, NH: Ayer Company, 1991), 3–17.

66. Williamson Murray and Allan Reed Millett, *A War to Be Won: Fighting the Second World War* (Cambridge, MA: Harvard University Press, 2000), 194.

67. Andrew Toppan, "World Aircraft Carriers List: Japanese Aircraft Carriers," March 2000, http://www.hazegray.org/navhist/carriers/ijn_cv.htm#kasa, accessed December 5, 2005; Toppan, "World Aircraft Carriers List: US Fleet Carriers, WWII Era," November 2001, http://www.hazegray.org/navhist/carriers/us_fleet.htm, accessed December 5, 2005.

68. Richard M. Leighton and Robert W. Coakley, *Global Logistics and Strategy, 1940–1943*, Vol. II, Appendix 82 (Washington, DC: Government Printing Office, 1955), 829.

69. United States Strategic Bombing Survey, *Summary Report (Pacific War)*, July 1, 1946, 13, 18.

70. Ibid.

71. Martin Van Creveld, *Supplying War* (New York: Cambridge University Press, 1977), 231.

72. Overy, *Why the Allies Won*, 205, 319.

73. Meirion Harries and Susie Harries, *Soldiers of the Sun: The Rise and Fall of the Imperial Japanese Army 1868–1945* (London: Heinemann, 1991), 296.

74. Michael C. C. Adams, *The Best War Ever: America and World War II* (Baltimore, MD: Johns Hopkins University Press, 1994), 67.

75. James F. Dunnigan and Albert A. Nofi, *Dirty Little Secrets of World War II* (New York: Perennial, 2003), 294–295.

CHAPTER 4: A RUTHLESS WAR

1. Dave Bartruff, "Tsuneko, Heroine of the Untold World War II Tsushima Maru Tragedy," *The World and I*, November 2004, online at http://www.worldandi.com/sub scribers/feature_detail.asp?num=24117, accessed September 1, 2006.

2. Dave Bartruff, "Tsuneko, Heroine of the Untold World War II Tsushima Maru Tragedy."

3. Denny Roy, Grant P. Skabelund, and Ray C. Hillam (eds.), *A Time to Kill: Reflections on War* (Salt Lake City, UT: Signature Books, 1992), 44–45.

4. "Night of broken glass," a government-incited rampage against Jews and Jewish-owned businesses in Germany and Austria in 1938.

5. Michael C. C. Adams, *The Best War Ever: America and World War II* (Baltimore, MD: Johns Hopkins University Press, 1994), 6.

6. Conrad C. Crane, *Bombs, Cities and Civilians: American Airpower Strategy in World War II* (Lawrence: University Press of Kansas, 1993), 58.

7. Paul Fussell, *Wartime: Understanding and Behavior in the Second World War.* (New York: Oxford University Press, 1989), 137, 138.

8. Mary Jarrell and Stuart Wright (eds.), *Randall Jarrell's Letters: An Autobiographical and Literary Selection* (Boston: Houghton Mifflin Company, 1985), 103.

9. Samuel A. Stouffer, Arthur A. Lumsdaine, Marion H. Lumsdaine, Robin M. Williams, Jr., M. Brewster Smith, Irving L. Janis, Shirley A. Star and Leonard S. Cotrell, *The American Soldier: Combat and Its Aftermath*, Vol. II (Princeton, NJ: Princeton University Press, 1949), 34.

10. Lemuel C. Shepard interview, Marine Corps Oral History Collection, 242, U.S. Marine Corps Historical Center; Ronald H. Spector, "The Pacific War and the Fourth Dimension of Strategy," in Gunter Bischof and Robert L. Dupont (eds.), *The Pacific War Revisited* (Baton Rouge: Louisiana State University Press, 1997), 46.

11. Norman V. Cooper, "The Military Career of General Holland M. Smith," PhD diss., University of Alabama, 1974, 240; Ronald H. Spector, "Fourth Dimension," 47.

12. John W. Dower, *War without Mercy: Race and Power in the Pacific War* (New York: Pantheon, 1986), 9, 55, 78–81.

13. Ibid.

14. Ronald H. Spector, *Eagle Against the Sun: The American War with Japan* (New York: Vintage Books, 1985), 410.

15. Dower, *War without Mercy*, 64–70.

16. Laurence Rees, *Horror in the East: Japan and the Atrocities of World War II* (Cambridge, MA: Da Capo Press, 2001), 133.

17. E. B. Sledge, *With the Old Breed at Peleliu and Okinawa* (Novato, CA: Presidio Press, 1981), 120.

18. Fussell, *Wartime*, 117.

19. Ulrich Straus, *The Anguish of Surrender: Japanese POWs of World War II.* (Seattle: University of Washington Press, 2003).

20. Frank Gibney, *Senso: The Japanese Remember the Pacific War* (Armonk, NY: M. E. Sharpe, 1995), 227.

21. The text of the agreement is posted at http://navyfield.g.hatena.ne.jp/BRNFC-Dartmouth/?word=*%5BHistory%5D, accessed December 12, 2008.

22. Nathan Miller, *War at Sea: A Naval History of World War II* (New York: Scribner, 1995), 480.

23. Gerhard L. Weinberg, *A World at Arms: A Global History of World War II* (New York: Cambridge University Press, 1994), 392–393.

24. Spector, *Eagle*, 484–485.

25. Williamson Murray and Allan Reed Millett, *A War to Be Won: Fighting the Second World War* (Cambridge, MA: Harvard University Press, 2000), 224–226; James F. Dunnigan and Albert A. Nofi, *Dirty Little Secrets of World War II* (New York: Perennial, 2003), 338–339; Walter J. Boyne, *Clash of the Titans: World War II at Sea* (New York: Simon and Schuster, 1995), 342; Kenneth J. Hagan, "American Submarine Warfare in the Pacific, 1941–1945: Guerre de Course Triumphant," in Bischof and Dupont, *The Pacific War Revisited*, 81–100; Weinberg, *A World at Arms*, 393; Spector, *Eagle*, 487.

26. John Costello, *The Pacific War* (New York: Rawson, Wade, 1981), 527–528.

27. Clay Blair, *Silent Victory: The U.S. Submarine War Against Japan* (New York: J. B. Lippincott, 1975), 851–852.

28. Roger Dingman, *Ghost of War: The Sinking of the Awa Maru and Japanese-American Relations, 1945–1995* (Annapolis, MD: Naval Institute Press, 1997), 103.

29. Ralph Modder, *The Singapore Chinese Massacre* (Singapore: Horizon Books, 2004), 21.

30. Yayori Matsui, "Women's International War Crimes Tribunal on Japan's Military Sexual Slavery: Memory, Identity and Society," in *Japanese War Crimes: The Search for Justice*, ed. Peter Li, 264 (New Brunswick, NJ: Transaction, 2003).

31. R. J. Rummel, *China's Bloody Century: Genocide and Mass Murder Since 1900* (Rutgers, NJ: Transaction Publishers, 1991), chap. 1.

32. R. J. Rummel, *Death by Government* (New Brunswick: Transaction, 1995), 144.

33. The most famous book on the Nanjing Massacre, although criticized for inflating casualty figures, is Iris Chang, *The Rape of Nanking: The Forgotten Holocaust of World War II* (New York: Basic Books, 1997); another is Honda Katsuichi, *The Nanjing Massacre: A Japanese Journalist Confronts Japan's National Shame* (New York: M. E. Sharpe, 1999).

34. "Pingdingshan Massacre Survivor Dies," *News Guangdong*, May 26, 2005, http://www.newsgd.com/specials/60thanniversaryofwaragainstjapaneseaggression/warmemoir/200508230113.htm, accessed October 20, 2006.

35. Diana Lary, "A Ravaged Place: The Devastation of the Xuzhou Region, 1938," in *Scars of War: The Impact of Warfare on Modern China*, ed. Diana Lary and Stephen MacKinnon (Vancouver: University of British Columbia Press, 2001), 98.

36. Chalmers A. Johnson, *Peasant Nationalism and Communist Power: The Emergence of Revolutionary China, 1937-1945* (Stanford: Stanford University Press, 1962), 194.

37. Linda Hoaglund, "Japanese Devils," *Persimmon: Asian Literature, Arts and Culture*, vol. III, no. 3 (Winter 2003), online version, http://www.persimmon-mag.com/winter2003/feature1.htm, accessed October 23, 2006.

38. Murray and Millett, *A War to Be Won*, 191.

39. Rees, *Horror in the East*, 36, 40.

40. Wang Zhenghua, "Air Bombing Survivors Demand Compensation," *China Daily*, July 19, 2004, http://www.chinadaily.com.cn/english/doc/2004–07/19/content_349635.htm, accessed October 20, 2006.

41. Associated Press, "China Finds Evidence of Japanese Germ Warfare During WWII," Aug. 13, 1996, http://www.kimsoft.com/korea/jp-germ4.htm, accessed October 13, 2006.

42. Xinhua, "Zhuanjia: qinhua rijun xijunzhan zhishao danhai yu 27 wan zhongguoren," August 9, 2005, online at http://politics.people.com.cn/GB/1026/36033391.html, accessed August 11, 2005.

43. Ienaga Saburo, *The Pacific War 1931–1945* (New York: Pantheon, 1978), 168–169.

44. Stephen MacKinnon, "Refugee Flight at the Outset of the Anti-Japanese War," in Lary and MacKinnon (eds.), *Scars of War*, 121–122; Rosario Renaud, *Le Diocese de Suchow (Chine): Champ apostolique des Jesuites canadiens de 1918 a 1954* (Montreal: Editions Bellarmin, 1982), 149; Lary, "A Ravaged Place," 105.

45. Peter Li, "Japan's Biochemical Warfare and Experimentation in China," in *Japanese War Crimes: The Search for Justice*, ed. Peter Li (New Brunswick, NJ: Transaction, 2003), 289–300.

46. Michael Zielenziger, "Ex-Japanese Soldier Deemed War Criminal," *Houston Chronicle*, July 3, 1998, A29.

47. Yuki Tanaka, *Hidden Horrors: Japanese War Crimes in World War II* (Boulder, CO: Westview Press, 1996), 162.

48. David Wise, "Wanted: Hitler's Scientists," *New York Times*, February 14, 1988, http://query.nytimes.com/gst/fullpage.html?res=940DE7D6123CF937A25751C0A 96E948260, accessed February 10, 2006; Tom Bower, *The Paperclip Conspiracy: The Hunt for the Nazi Scientists* (Boston: Little, Brown and Company, 1987).

49. "Japanese Unit 731 Biological Warfare Unit," World War II in the Pacific, http://www.ww2pacific.com/unit731.html, accessed February 10, 2006; Dunnigan and Nofi, *Dirty Little Secrets*, 242.

50. Charles A. Stenger, *American Prisoners of War in WWI, WWII, Korea, and Vietnam: Statistical Data Concerning Numbers Captured, Repatriated, and Still Alive* (Washington, DC: Veterans Health Administration, 1981), 3–4; Tanaka, *Hidden Horrors*, 2.

51. Tanaka, *Hidden Horrors*, 11.

52. Tanaka, *Hidden Horrors*, 39; Spector, *Eagle*, 398; Eugene C. Jacobs, *Blood Brothers: A Medic's Sketch Book* (New York: Carlton Press, 1985), http://www.infomo Wtions.com/etexts/gutenberg/dirs/etext05/blbro10.htm, accessed August 6, 2007.

53. Tanaka, *Hidden Horrors*, 95–101.

54. Yao Lan, "Surviving War Crimes," *Shanghai Star*, April 4, 2002, http://app1. chinadaily.com.cn/star/2002/0404/pr22–1.html, accessed October 19, 2006.

55. Ustinia Dolgopol and Snehal Paranjape, "Comfort Women: An Unfinished Ordeal," International Commission of Jurists, Geneva, Switzerland, [n.d.], http:// www.comfort-women.org/Unfinished.htm, accessed October 20, 2006.

56. Zeng Min, "Silent No More," *China Daily*, March 31, 2000, http://app1.china daily.com.cn/star/history/00–03–31/, accessed October 23, 2006.

57. Kankoku Teishin-tai Mondai Taisaku Kyogikai (ed.), *Shogen: Kyosci Renko Sareta Chosenjin Gun-ianfutachi* (Tokyo: Akashi Shoten, 1993), 125.

58. Richard P. Hallion, "Precision Weapons, Power Projection, and the Revolution in Military Affairs," Air Force Historical Studies Office, May 1999, https://www. airforcehistory.hq.af.mil/EARS/Hallionpapers/precisionweaponspower.htm, accessed September 7, 2007.

59. Ginowan Mayor Iha Yoichi's letter to President George W. Bush, October 15, 2003, posted at http://www.city.ginowan.okinawa.jp/DAT/LIB/WEB/1/00050_00004_ 001.pdf, accessed August 31, 2006; Russell F. Weigley, "Japan's Next-to-Last Stand," *New York Times*, August 30, 1992, http://query.nytimes.com/gst/fullpage.html?res=9E0 CE1DD163AF933A0575BC0A964958260, accessed October 23, 2006.

60. George Feifer, "The Rape of Okinawa," *World Policy Journal* XVII, no. 3 (Fall 2000), http://www.worldpolicy.org/journal/feifer.html, accessed October 26, 2006.

61. Ota Masahide, "Re-Examining the History of the Battle of Okinawa," in *Okinawa: Cold War Island*, ed. Chalmers Johnson (Cardiff, CA: Japan Policy Research Institute, 1999), 29.

62. James Brooke, "1945 Suicide Order Still a Trauma on Okinawa," *International Herald Tribune*, June 21, 2005, http://www.iht.com/articles/2005/06/20/news/oki.php, accessed Oct. 26, 2006.

63. Ota, "Re-Examining the History," 30.

64. Shinya Hattori, "Kerama Islands Haunted by Wartime Mass Suicides," *Japan Today*, April 2, 2005, http://www.japantoday.com/jp/feature/885, accessed October 23, 2006.

65. Brooke, "1945 Suicide Order."

66. Haroko Taya Cook and Theodore F. Cook, *Japan at War: An Oral History* (New York: The New Press, 1992), 364–365.

67. Nicholas D. Kristof, "Exploring the Darker Side of Okinawa," *New York Times*, January 21, 1996, http://query.nytimes.com/gst/fullpage.html?sec=travel&res=9A04E FDA1339F932A15752C0A960958260, accessed November 14, 2006.

68. Rees, *Horror*, 128–129; Cook and Cook, *Japan at War*, 364–365; Ienaga, *Pacific War*, 185; Shinya, "Kerama Islands Haunted by Wartime Mass Suicides."

69. Brooke, "1945 Suicide Order."

70. Chiyomi Sumida, "Horrors of Battle of Okinawa Lie Just below the Surface," *Stars and Stripes* (Pacific Edition), June 25, 2006, http://www.estripes.com/article.asp? section=104&article=37295&archive=true, accessed October 31, 2006.

71. Norma Field, *In the Realm of a Dying Emperor: Japan at Century's End* (New York: Vintage Books, 1993), 64.

72. Linda Sieg, "Battle of Okinawa Mass Suicides Recalled, Debated," Reuters News Service, June 22, 2005, http://www.tiscali.co.uk/news/newswire.php/news/ reuters/2005/06/22/world/battleofokinawamasssuicidesrecalleddebated.html, accessed October 31, 2006.

73. Field, *In the Realm*, 64–65.

74. *Youth Division of Soka Gakkai, Cries For Peace: Experiences of Japanese Victims of World War II* (Tokyo: The Japan Times Press, 1978), excerpts posted online at http://www.bookmice.net/darkchilde/japan/peace.html, accessed September 1, 2006.

75. Kyodo News Service, "Postwar60: Ex-Himeyuri Students Recall War, Hope for Peace," September 9, 2005, http://www.findarticles.com/p/articles/mi_m0WDQ/ is_2005_Sept_12/ai_n15403217, accessed October 27, 2006.

76. Kjeld Duits, "The Forgotten Grief of Okinawa," July 2, 2005, http://www. ikjeld.com/japannews/00000187.php, accessed October 27, 2006; "Himeyuri War Memorial and Himeyuri Peace Museum in Okinawa," http://www.japanesehistory. de/fotos/Okinawa_Himeyuri/, accessed October 27, 2006.

77. Jim Nelson, "The Causes of the Bataan Death March Revisited," http://www. us-japandialogueonpows.org/Nelson.htm, accessed September 14, 2007.

78. Ienaga, *The Pacific War*, 190.

79. A battle cruiser had the large guns of a battleship but less armor protection, sacrificing weight for increased speed.

80. Churchill's remarks to the House of Commons, December 11, 1941; Web site of the Churchill Centre, Washington, DC, http://www.winstonchurchill.org/i4a/ pages/index.cfm?pageid=371, accessed December 13, 2005.

81. Bert Wynn and Alan Matthews, "Shadows of the Ensign," Force Z Survivors Association Web site, http://www.forcez-survivors.org.uk/shadows4.html, accessed December 13, 2005; Alan Matthews, "The Sinking of the *Prince of Wales* and *Repulse:* A Series of Personal Accounts Compiled from Crew Members," http://www.microworks.net/pacific/personal/pow_repulse.htm, accessed December 13, 2005.

82. "Saburo Sakai," MyFairCW Legendary Aces of World War II, http://members. chello.be/kurt.weygantt/worldwariiaces.index.html_saburosakai.htm, accessed January 23, 2006; "An Interview with Saburo Sakai, 1916–2000," Microsoft.com, http://www. microsoft.com/games/combatfs2/articles_sakai.asp, accessed January 23, 2006.

83. Frank Gibney, *Senso: The Japanese Remember the Pacific War* (Armonk, NY: M. E. Sharpe, 1995), 72–73.

CHAPTER 5: STRATEGIC BOMBING IN THE PACIFIC WAR

1. Bernard Brodie, *Strategy in the Missile Age* (Princeton, NJ: Princeton University Press, 1959), 98.

2. John Ellis, *Brute Force: Allied Strategy and Tactics in the Second World War* (New York: Viking Penguin, 1990), 166.

3. Charles Webster and Noble Frankland, *The Strategic Air Offensive Against Germany 1939–1945*, vol. 4 (London: Her Majesty's Stationery Office, 1961), 71–83; A.J.P. Taylor, *English History, 1914–1945* (Oxford: Clarendon Press, 1965), 517–518.

4. The text of the resolution is available at http://www.dannen.com/decision/int law.html#D, accessed December 12, 2008.

5. *New York Times*, June 4, 1938; John W. Dower, *War without Mercy: Race and Power in the Pacific War* (New York: Pantheon, 1986), 38; U.S. Department of State, *Foreign Relations of the United States: Japan, 1931–1941*, Vol. I (Washington, DC: U.S. Government Printing Office, 1943), 506.

6. This speech is available online at http://www.millercenter.virginia.edu/scripps/diglibrary/prezspeeches/roosevelt/fdr_1937_1005.html, accessed April 13, 2006.

7. "Appeal of President Franklin D. Roosevelt on Aerial Bombardment of Civilian Populations," Sept. 1, 1939, posted at http://www.dannen.com/decision/int-law.html#E, accessed March 21, 2006.

8. This joint Anglo-French declaration is posted online at http://www.yale.edu/lawweb/avalon/wwii/yellow/ylbk369.htm, accessed March 28, 2006.

9. Robert Batchelder, *The Irreversible Decision, 1939–1950* (New York: Houghton Mifflin, 1961), 172–173.

10. "Address by Adolf Hitler, Chancellor of the Reich, before the Reichstag, September 1, 1939," available online at http://fcit.usf.edu/Holocaust/resource/document/HITLER1.htm, accessed April 13, 2006.

11. David Ian Hall, "Black, White and Grey: Wartime Arguments for and against the Strategic Bomber Offensive," posted on the Web site of the Laurier Centre for Military Strategic and Disarmament Studies, http://info.wlu.ca/~wwwmsds/CMH%20backissue%20pages/vol7n1hallbomber, accessed March 29, 2006.

12. David Jablonsky, *Churchill and Hitler: Essays on the Political-military Direction of Total War* (London: Taylor and Francis, 1994), 117.

13. Hall, "Black, White and Grey."

14. "Arthur Travers Harris," Wikipedia, March 3, 2006, http://en.wikipedia.org/w/index.php?title=Arthur_Travers_Harris&oldid=42107074, accessed March 9, 2006; Jonathan Glancey, "Our Last Occupation," *The Guardian*, April 19, 2003, http://www.guardian.co.uk/comment/story/0,3604,939608,00.html, accessed March 9, 2006; Alexander Cockburn, "Against the War? Be There!" *New York Press*, February 11, 2003, http://nypress.com/print.cfm?content_id=7704, accessed March 9, 2006; James S. Corum, "The Myth of Air Control: Reassessing the History," *Aerospace Power Journal*, Winter 2000, http://www.airpower.maxwell.af.mil/airchronicles/apj/apj00/win00/corum.htm, accessed March 9, 2006.

15. Edward Spannaus, "'Shock and Awe': Terror Bombing, From Wells and Russell to Cheney," *Executive Intelligence Review*, October 31, 2003, http://www.larouchepub.com/other/2003/3042shock_awe_wwii.html, accessed April 20, 2006.

16. Williamson Murray and Allan Reed Millett, *A War to Be Won: Fighting the Second World War* (Cambridge, MA: Harvard University Press, 2000), 320.

17. A. C. Grayling, "NS Essay—'If We Did Anything Questionable in the War, We Should Have the Maturity to Admit It and Learn from It,'" *New Statesman*, February 27, 2006, http://www.newstatesman.com/Ideas/200602270022, accessed March 29, 2006.

18. Conrad C. Crane, *Bombs, Cities and Civilians: American Airpower Strategy in World War II* (Lawrence: University Press of Kansas, 1993), 24.

19. The medium bombers of the Doolittle Raid dropped a few bombs on Tokyo and other cities in April 1942, but the first B-29 raids on the home islands began in June 1944.

20. E. Bartlett Kerr, *Flames Over Tokyo: The U.S. Army Air Forces' Incendiary Campaign Against Japan 1944–1945* (New York: Donald I. Fine, 1991), 7; Crane, *Bombs, Cities and Civilians*, 33.

21. Ronald Schaffer, *Wings of Judgment: American Bombing in World War II* (New York: Oxford University Press, 1985), 86–95, 55–58.

22. Crane, *Bombs, Cities and Civilians*, 88–89.

23. Schaffer, *Wings of Judgment*, 100; George Fowler, "Holocaust at Dresden," *The Barnes Review* (Washington, DC), February 1995, http://www.christusrex.org/www1/war/dresden6.html, accessed April 20, 2006; Kerr, *Flames Over Tokyo*, 145.

24. Kerr, *Flames Over Tokyo*, 133–137.

25. Herman S. Wolk, "General Arnold, the Atomic Bomb, and the Surrender of Japan," in *The Pacific War Revisited*, ed. Gunter Bischof and Robert L. Dupont, 165–166 (Baton Rouge: Louisiana State University Press, 1997).

26. Crane, *Bombs, Cities and Civilians*, 92.

27. Andrew J. Rotter, *Hiroshima: The World's Bomb* (Oxford, UK: Oxford University Press, 2008), 141.

28. Ibid., 126.

29. Carl Berger, *B-29: The Superfortress* (New York: Ballantine Books, 1970), 37.

30. Kerr, *Flames Over Tokyo*, 7.

31. Ibid., 30–44, 72, 83–84.

32. An example is Frank E. Vandiver, *1001 Things Everyone Should Know About World War II* (New York: Broadway Books, 2002), 228.

33. Robert S. Burrell, "Breaking the Cycle of Iwo Jima Mythology: A Strategic Study of Operation Detachment," *Journal of Military History*, no. 68 (October 2004): 1143–1186.

34. Spector, *Eagle*, 492.

35. Ibid., 539.

36. Charles F. Romanus and Riley Sutherland, *Stilwell's Mission to China* (Washington, DC: Department of the Army, 1953), 253; Martha Byrd, *Chennault: Giving Wings to the Tiger* (Tuscaloosa: University of Alabama Press, 1987), 155–158, 172–182.

37. Spector, *Eagle*, 341.

38. John Costello, *The Pacific War* (New York: Rawson, Wade, 1981), 525.

39. Spector, *Eagle*, 489.

40. Kerr, *Flames Over Tokyo*, 154.

41. General Curtis E. LeMay, "Race for the Superbomb," The American Experience Web site, Public Broadcasting System, http://www.pbs.org/wgbh/amex/bomb/peopleevents/pandeAMEX61.html, accessed May 4, 2006.

42. United States Strategic Bombing Survey (hereafter USSBS), Summary Report (Pacific War), July 1, 1946, 16, online at http://www.anesi.com/ussbs01.htm, accessed June 30, 2005.

43. General Curtis E. LeMay, "Race for the Superbomb," The American Experience Web site, Public Broadcasting System, http://www.pbs.org/wgbh/amex/bomb/peopleevents/pandeAMEX61.html, accessed May 4, 2006.

44. Costello, Pacific War, 548.

45. Ibid., 527.

46. Martin Caidin, *A Torch to the Enemy: The Fire Raid on Tokyo* (New York: Ballantine, 1960), 141.

47. Kerr, *Flames Over Tokyo*, 207, 211.

48. R. J. Rummel, "Was World War II American Urban Bombing Democide?" September 22, 2003, http://www.hawaii.edu/powerkills/COMM.10.5.03.HTM, accessed July 6, 2005. Other estimates are higher; in 1956 the Japanese League of War-Damaged Cities determined that 509,734 Japanese died in bombing raids. Kiroku Hanai, "No Sense of Proportionality," *Japan Times*, September 28, 2004, http://www.japantimes.co.jp/cgi-bin/makeprfy.pl5?eo20040928kh.htm, accessed Aug. 26, 2005.

49. USSBS, 16–17; Kerr, *Flames Over Tokyo*, p. 276; *Proceedings of the Eighth Military History Symposium*, United States Air Force Academy, Colorado Springs, CO, 1978, 187; Major T. J. Cronley, "Curtis E. LeMay: The Enduring 'Big Bomber Man,'" United States Marine Corps Command and Staff College, Quantico, VA, March 1986, posted at http://www.globalsecurity.org/wmd/library/report/1986/CTJ.htm, accessed August 7, 2007.

50. Keith Wheeler, *Bombers over Japan* (Alexandria, VA: Time Life Books, 1982), 180; Kerr, *Flames Over Tokyo*, 267.

51. USSBS, 15–19.

52. Ronald Takaki, *Hiroshima: Why America Dropped the Atomic Bomb* (New York: Little, Brown and Company, 1995), 29.

53. German bombing of London and other British cities, most heavily in 1940–41, which killed over 50,000 civilians during the war.

CHAPTER 6: THE ATOMIC BOMBS AND THE END OF THE WAR

1. Robert Dallek, *Franklin D. Roosevelt and America Foreign Policy, 1932–1945* (New York: Oxford University Press, 1979), 440; Forrest C. Pogue, *George C. Marshall: Organizer of Victory, 1943–1945* (New York: Viking Press, 1973), 350–351.

2. Charles F. Brower IV, "The Joint Chiefs of Staff and National Policy: American Strategy and the War with Japan, 1943–1945," PhD diss., University of Pennsylvania, 1987, 209–210.

3. Robert Butow, *Japan's Decision to Surrender* (Stanford, CA: Stanford University Press, 1954), 69.

4. Barton J. Bernstein, "The Perils and Politics of Surrender: Ending the War with Japan and Avoiding the Third Atomic Bomb," *Pacific Historical Review* XLVI (February 1977): 5.

5. Joseph C. Grew, *Turbulent Era: A Diplomatic Record of Forty Years 1904–1945*, Vol. II (Boston: Houghton Mifflin, 1952), 134–136.

6. Eiji Takemae, *Inside GHQ: The Allied Occupation of Japan and Its Legacy* (New York: Continuum International Publishing Group, 2002), 216.

7. Richard B. Frank, "Why Truman Dropped the Bomb: Sixty Years after Hiroshima, We Now Have the Secret Intercepts That Shaped His Decision," *Weekly Standard*, August 8, 2005, posted online at http://www.answers.com/topic/atomic bombings-of-hiroshima-and-nagasaki, accessed April 26, 2006.

8. Akira Iriye, *Power and Culture: The Japanese-American War 1941–1945* (Cambridge, MA: Harvard University Press, 1981), 252–254, 255–256.

9. Some historians have accused Truman of retroactively inflating the anticipated casualty figures to justify the A-bombings on the basis that the lives "saved" by averting an invasion through use of the bombs far exceeded the number killed at Hiroshima and Nagasaki. For evidence that U.S. planners indeed expected very high casualties from an invasion of the home islands, see D. M. Giangreco, "Casualty Projections for the U.S. Invasions of Japan: Planning and Policy Implications," *Journal of Military History* 62, no. 3 (Jul. 1998): 547–570.

10. United States Department of State, *Foreign Relations of the United States: Potsdam*, Vol. I (Washington, DC: U.S. Government Printing Office, 1960), 909.

11. Ronald H. Spector, *Eagle Against the Sun: The American War with Japan* (New York: Vintage Books, 1985), 543.

12. Stephen E. Ambrose and Brian Loring Villa, "Racism, the Atomic Bomb, and the Transformation of Japanese-American Relations," in *The Pacific War Revisited*, ed. Gunter Bischof and Robert L. Dupont, 185 (Baton Rouge: Louisiana State University Press, 1997).

13. D. M. Giangreco, "Harry Truman and the Price of Victory," *American Heritage Magazine* 54, no. 2 (April/May 2003), [n.p.], AmericanHeritage.com, http://www.americanheritage.com/articles/magazine/ah/2003/2/2003_2_13a.shtml, accessed July 10, 2007.

14. Richard B. Frank, *Downfall: The End of the Imperial Japanese Empire* (New York: Random House, 1999), 184–185.

15. Frank, *Downfall*, 188–189; Spector, *Eagle*, 543, 544.

16. Williamson Murray and Allan Reed Millett, *A War to Be Won: Fighting the Second World War* (Cambridge, MA: Harvard University Press, 2000), 520.

17. Bryan McNulty, "The Great Atomic Bomb Debate," Perspectives, Ohio University, January 1997, http://www.ohiou.edu/perspectives/9701t/bomb2.htm, accessed July 6, 2005.

18. Iriye, *Power and Culture*, 242–243.

19. Gerhard L. Weinberg, *A World at Arms: A Global History of World War II* (New York: Cambridge University Press, 1994), 882–883.

20. Frank, "Why Truman Dropped the Bomb."

21. Herman S. Wolk, "General Arnold, the Atomic Bomb, and the Surrender of Japan," in Bischof and Dupont, *Pacific War Revisited*, 173–174.

22. Ronald Schaffer, *Wings of Judgment: American Bombing in World War II* (New York: Oxford University Press, 1985), 144–146.

23. Hasegawa Tsuyoshi, *Racing the Enemy: Stalin, Truman and the Surrender of Japan* (Cambridge, MA: Belknap Press, 2005), 3.

24. Weinberg, *World At Arms*, 590.

25. Ibid., 655–656.

26. Hasegawa, *Racing*, 229.

27. The text is available at http://www.atomicarchive.com/Docs/Hiroshima/Potsdam.shtml, accessed December 13, 2008.

28. Hasegawa, *Racing*, 211. Hasegawa (pp. 166–168) also speculates that the Japanese press might have misquoted Suzuki.

29. Sadao Asada, "The Shock of the Atomic Bomb and Japan's Decision to Surrender: A Reconsideration," *Pacific Historical Review* vol. 67 no.4 (1998): 477–512.

30. U.S. Department of Defense, *Entry of the Soviet Union Into the War Against Japan: Military Plans 1941–1945* (Washington, DC: Government Printing Office, 1955), 70.

31. Michael Kort, *"Racing the Enemy:* A Critical Look," *Historically Speaking: The Bulletin of the Historical Society,* vol. 7, no. 3 (January/February 2006), http://www.bu.edu/historic/hs/kort.html, accessed August 13, 2007.

32. Gar Alperovitz, *Atomic Diplomacy: Hiroshima and Nagasaki* (New York: Simon & Schuster, 1965). For a thorough critique of Alperovitz, see Robert James Maddox, *Weapons for Victory: The Hiroshima Decision Fifty Years Later* (Columbia: University of Missouri Press, 1995).

33. Martin J. Sherwin, *A World Destroyed* (New York: Knopf, 1973), 194.

34. Paul F. Boller, *Not So! Popular Myths About America from Columbus to Clinton* (New York: Oxford University Press, 1995), 148–152.

35. William F. Halsey and Joseph J. Bryan III, *Admiral Halsey's Story* (New York: McGraw-Hill, 1947), 266.

36. Richard B. Frank, "HIROSHIMA: The Birth of Nuclear Warfare: An Ugly End, with or without the Atom Bomb," *San Francisco Chronicle,* July 31, 2005, http://www.sfgate.com/cgi-bin/article.cgi?f=/c/a/2005/07/31/ING4KDU0AN1.DTI., accessed April 26, 2006.

37. Edward Drea, *MacArthur's Ultra: Codebreaking and the War Against Japan, 1942–1945* (Lawrence: University Press of Kansas, 1992), 202–222.

38. Frank, "Why Truman Dropped the Bomb."

39. Hasegawa, *Racing,* 179.

40. C. L. Sulzberger and David G. McCullough, *World War II* (New York: American Heritage, 1966), 616.

41. Hasegawa, *Racing,* 180.

42. Schaffer, *Wings of Judgment,* 147–148.

43. "Surviving Nagasaki: Akiko Seitelbach," BBC News, August 5, 2005, http://news.bbc.co.uk/1/hi/world/asia-pacific/4748365.stm, accessed August 7, 2007.

44. Weinberg, *World at Arms,* 889.

45. Harry S. Truman primary sources Web site, "The American Experience: The Presidents," Public Broadcasting System, http://www.pbs.org/wgbh/amex/presidents/33_truman/psources/ps_japanwarn.html, accessed April 28, 2006.

46. Schaffer, *Wings of Judgment,* 171–174.

47. The section is informed by Hasegawa, *Racing,* 205–250.

48. Butow, *Japan's Decision to Surrender,* 75.

49. Hasegawa, *Racing,* 212.

50. Herbert P. Bix, "Japan's Delayed Surrender: A Reinterpretation," in *Hiroshima in History and Memory,* ed. Michael J. Hogan, 80–115 (New York: Cambridge University Press, 1996).

51. Robert Butow, Japan's Decision to Surrender (Stanford, CA: Stanford University Press, 1954), 245.

52. John Toland, The Rising Sun: The Decline and Fall of the Japanese Empire, 1936–1945 (New York: Random House, 1970), 936–937.

53. Paul Fussell, *Wartime: Understanding and Behavior in the Second World War* (New York: Oxford University Press, 1989), 120.

54. Hasegawa, *Racing,* 258–259, 285, 289.

55. Leo Maley III and Uday Mohan, "Second Guessing Hiroshima?" History News Service, July 29, 1998, http://www.h-net.org/~hns/articles/1998/072998a.html, accessed April 29, 2006; Mohan and Maley, "Military: Hiroshima . . . The Anniversary We Misremember," History News Service, Jul. 30, 2001, http://hnn.us/articles/167.html, accessed April 27, 2006.

56. William D. Leahy, *I Was There* (New York: Whittlesey House, 1950), 259.

57. Crane, *Bombs, Cities and Civilians*, 106, 38. Schaffer believes Spaatz was "ambivalent about attacking enemy civilians" and that his reservations were pragmatic rather than moral. Schaffer, *Wings of Judgment*, 105.

58. Ralph Bard, "Memorandum on the Use of S-1 Bomb," Harrison-Bundy Files, RG 77, microfilm publication M1108, folder 77, National Archives, Washington, DC.

59. Report of the Committee on Political and Social Problems, June 11, 1945, available at AtomicArchive.com, http://www.atomicarchive.com/Docs/Manhattan Project/FranckReport.shtml, accessed March 21, 2006.

60. The two versions of the Szilard petition are posted online at http://www.dannen.com/decision/45-07-17.html and http://www.dannen.com/decision/45-07-03.html, accessed March 21, 2006.

61. Ibid.

62. Sadao Asada, "The shocks of the Atomic Bomb and Japan's Decision to Surrender: A Reconsideration," *Pacific Historical Review* 67, no. 4 (1998): 510–511.

63. Barton Bernstein, "Compelling Japan's Surrender Without the A-Bomb, Soviet Entry, or Invasion: Reconsidering the U.S. Bombing Survey's Early-Surrender Conclusion," *Journal of Strategic Studies* 18, no. 2 (June 1995): 101–148.

64. An English translation of Hirohito's speech is available at http://www.mtholyoke.edu/acad/intrel/hirohito.htm, accessed December 13, 2008.

65. Hasegawa, *Racing*, 250.

66. Security studies scholar Robert Pape argues that Japan's surrender resulted from the U.S. Navy's sea blockade and the Soviet attack on Japanese forces in Manchuria, which convinced Japanese leaders that their plan for defending the home islands was untenable. Pape says these factors would have ended the war in mid-August even without the American strategic bombing campaign and without the atomic bomb. Robert A. Pape, Why Japan Surrendered," *International Security* 18, no. 2 (Fall 1993): 187–188, 199–200.

67. Nicholas D. Kristof, "Blood on Our Hands?" *New York Times*, August 5, 2003, http://www.nytimes.com/2003/08/05/opinion/05KRIS.html?ex=1375502400&en=bd 91752373a54fd2&ei=5007&partner=USERLAND, accessed August 8, 2007.

68. Butow, *Japan's Decision to Surrender*, 117–119, 175.

69. John W. Dower, *Empire and Aftermath: Yoshida Shigeru and the Japanese Experience, 1874–1954* (Cambridge, MA: Harvard University Press, 1979), 260–264.

70. The United States Strategic Bombing Survey (USSBS) concluded that "certainly prior to 31 December 1945, and in all probability prior to November 1, 1945, Japan would have surrendered even if the atomic bombs had not been dropped, even if Russia had not entered the war, and even if no invasion had been planned or contemplated." United States Strategic Bombing Survey, *Summary Report (Pacific War)*, July 1, 1946, online at http://www.anesi.com/ussbs01.htm, accessed June 30, 2005. Critics subsequently challenged this conclusion, alleging that USSBS leader Paul Nitze and his staff wrote their report with a bias in favor of demonstrating the efficacy of air power.

71. Paul Fussell claims that at the end of the war the Allies were still suffering 7,000 casualties per week fighting Japan. Fussell, *Thank God for the Atom Bomb and Other Essays* (New York: Summit Books, 1988), 18.

72. Richard B. Frank, "HIROSHIMA."

73. Yoshida Yutaka, *Showa tenno no Shusenshi* (Tokyo: Iwanami Shinsho, 1991), 33; Bix, "Hiroshima in History," 225.

74. The American Experience: Truman Web site, Public Broadcasting Corporation, http://www.pbs.org/wgbh/amex/truman/psources/ps_diary.html, accessed November 8, 2005.

CHAPTER 7: REGIME CHANGE IN KOREA, JAPAN, AND TAIWAN

1. Bruce Cumings, *Korea's Place in the Sun: A Modern History* (New York: W. W. Norton, 1997), 177–179; Kurt W. Tong, "Korea's Forgotten Atomic Bomb Victims," *Bulletin of Concerned Asian Scholars* 23, no. 1 (January–March 1991): 31; Lisa Yoneyama, "Memory Matters: Hiroshima's Korean Atom Bomb Memorial and the Politics of Ethnicity," in *Living With the Bomb: American and Japanese Cultural Conflicts in the Nuclear Age*, ed. Laura Hein and Mark Selden, 205 (Armonk, NY: M. E. Sharpe, 1997).

2. Cumings, *Korea's Place*, 179.

3. Geoff Simons, *Korea: The Search for Sovereignty* (New York: St. Martin's Press, 1995), 176.

4. Simons, *Search for Sovereignty*, 156.

5. United States Department of State, *Foreign Relations of the United States: Diplomatic Papers, 1945. The British Commonwealth, the Far East*, Vol. VI (Washington, DC: U.S. Government Printing Office, 1945), 1039.

6. Ki-baik Lee, *A New History of Korea* (Seoul: Ilchokak, 1984), 376.

7. United States Department of State, *Foreign Relations of the United States: Diplomatic Papers, 1945. The British Commonwealth, the Far East*, Vol. VI (Washington, DC: U.S. Government Printing Office, 1945), 1145.

8. Cumings, *Korea's Place*, 200–209, 223.

9. John R. Hodge to George C. Marshall, Jan. 3, 1948, U.S. Department of State Records, 895.00/1–348, National Archives; cited in James I. Matray, "Korea's Partition: Soviet-American Pursuit of Reunification, 1945–1948," *Parameters* XXVIII, no. 1 (1998): 150–162.

10. A. Wigfall Green, *Epic of Korea* (Washington, DC: Public Affairs Press, 1950), 95.

11. Cumings, *Korea's Place*, 217–223; Simons, *Search for Sovereignty*, 181–183.

12. Jon Halliday and Bruce Cumings, *Korea, The Unknown War* (London: Viking, 1988), 47.

13. United States Department of the Army, *Reports of General MacArthur*, vol. I, *MacArthur in Japan: The Occupation: Military Phase* (Washington, DC: U.S. Department of the Army, 1966), 158–159, 170–179, 191–193.

14. Hasegawa Tsuyoshi, *Racing the Enemy: Stalin, Truman and the Surrender of Japan* (Cambridge, MA: Belknap Press, 2005), 273.

15. "1945: Power No More: IN OUR PAGES:100, 75 AND 50 YEARS AGO," *International Herald Tribune*, Sept. 22, 1995, http://www.iht.com/articles/1995/09/22/edold.t_39.php, accessed October 26, 2007.

16. John W. Dower, *Embracing Defeat: Japan in the Wake of World War II* (New York: W. W. Norton, 1999), 27, 224, 419.

17. Greg Mitchell, "Special Report: Hiroshima Cover-up Exposed," *Editor and Publisher*, August 6, 2005, online at http://www.editorandpublisher.com/eandp/news/article_display.jsp?vnu_content_id=1001001583, accessed August 30, 2005.

18. Makabe Hiroshi, "Ikenie ni Sareta Nanamannin no Musumetachi," in *Tokyo Yakeato Yamiichi o Kiroku Suru Kai* (ed.), *Tokyo Yamiichi Kobo Shi* (Tokyo: Sofusha, 1978), 200–201.

19. Yuki Tanaka, *Hidden Horrors: Japanese War Crimes in World War II* (Boulder, CO: Westview Press, 1996), 105–105.

20. Dower, *Defeat*, 130.

21. Tsuchiyama Jitsuo, "Ironies of Japanese Defense and Disarmament Policy" in *Japanese Foreign Policy Today*, ed. Takashi Inoguchi and Purnendra Jain (New York: Palgrave Macmillan, 2000), 138.

22. Dower, *Defeat*, 447, 449.

23. NSC 13/2, "Report by the National Security Council on Recommendations with Respect to United States Policy Toward Japan," October 7, 1948, Harry S. Truman Library Documents, Record of the National Security Committee-Meetings, No. TRUMAN-4847, available at http://210.128.252.171/modern/e/img_r/M008/M008–002r.html, accessed October 29, 2007.

24. Dower, *Defeat*, 548.

25. Curtis Andressen, *A Short History of Japan: From Samurai to Sony* (Sydney: Allen & Unwin, 2003), 125.

26. Dower, *Defeat*, 561.

27. Chou Wan-yao, "Jihpen tsai T'aichunshih tungyuan yu T'aiwanjen ti haiwai ts'anchan chingyen, 1937–1945," *T'aiwan Shih Yenchiu* 2, no. 1 (June 1995): 93–96.

28. George H. Kerr, *Formosa Betrayed* (Boston: Houghton Mifflin, 1965), 72.

29. Lai Tse-han, Ramon H. Myers, and Wei Wou, *A Tragic Beginning: The Taiwan Uprising of February 28, 1947* (Stanford, CA: Stanford University Press, 1991), 149–164.

CHAPTER 8: PACIFIC WAR *RASHOMON*

1. Presidential Proclamation on "National Pearl Harbor Remembrance Day, 2003," the White House, Office of the Press Secretary, December 5, 2003, http://www.whitehouse.gov/news/releases/2003/12/20031205–10.html, accessed June 20, 2005.

2. "Pelosi Statement on the Anniversary of the Attack on Pearl Harbor," December 7, 2005, Congresswomen Nancy Pelosi's congressional Web site, http://www.house.gov/pelosi/press/releases/Dec05/pearl.html, accessed September 11, 2008; "Statement by Secretary R. James Nicholson on Pearl Harbor Day," December 6, 2005, U.S. Department of Veterans Affairs Web site, http://www1.va.gov/opa/press rel/pressrelease.cfm?id=1054, accessed July 24, 2006; "Remarks by Senator Bob Dole at Ground Zero," BobDole.org, April 10, 2003, http://www.bobdole.org/issues/arti cle.php?id=5, accessed August 15, 2006.

3. "Codey Signs Proclamation for Pearl Harbor Remembrance Day," December 7, 2005, http://politics.nexcess.net/pressrelease/2005/12/acting_governor_richard_codey_ 39.html, accessed July 24, 2006; "McCain Apologizes for Using Slur: GOP Candidate Renounces 'Bigoted' Language," *San Jose Mercury*, February 24, 2000, available at http://www.asianam.org/mccain.htm, accessed August 15, 2006; "Pearl Harbor Remembrance Day," Alaska state government press archives Web page, December 2, 2004, http://gov.state.ak.us/archive.php?id=1398&type=6, accessed August 15, 2006; "Governor Orders Flags Lowered to Half-Staff for Pearl Harbor Remembrance Day," Office of the [Ohio] Governor Web site, December 6, 2007, http://governor.ohio.gov/Default.aspx?tabid=511, accessed September 11, 2008; "Lowering of Flags in Honor of National Pearl Harbor Remembrance Day," Governor Haley Barbour web site, December 6, 2007, http://www.governorbarbour.com/proclamations/Executive%20Order%20H ome%20Page/PearlHarbor-EO993htm.htm, accessed September 11, 2008; "Executive Order #228," Office of [Wisconsin] Governor Jim Doyle Web site, December 6, 2007,

http://www.wisgov.state.wi.us/journal_media_detail_print.asp?prid=3050&locid=19, accessed September 11, 2008; Proclamation by Gov. Mark Sanford, December 7, 2003, available at http://72.14.209.104/search?q=cache:_viWiDMb8g8J:www.scgovernor. com/uploads/proclamations/Pearl%2520Harbor%2520Remembrance%2520Day%25 20_1203.pdf+%22Pearl+Harbor%22+%2B+%22without+provocation%22&hl=en&gl =us&ct=clnk&cd=41, accessed August 15, 2006.

4. Cal Thomas, "Act of War Shows Terrorists Must Go," *Baltimore Sun* online, September 12, 2001, http://www.baltimoresun.com/news/custom/attack/bal-op.thom as12sep12,0,2702221.story?coll=bal-attack-utility, accessed August 15, 2006; Michelle Malkin, "Look behind the Pokemon Curtain," *Jewish World Review*, December 9, 1999, http://www.jewishworldreview.com/michelle/malkin120999.asp, accessed October 20, 2006; "Gingrich, Col. North on Pearl Harbor, Memorial Day," Foxnews.com, May 25, 2007, http://www.realclearpolitics.com/articles/2007/05/gingrich_col_north_on_pearl_ ha.html, accessed September 11, 2008; Rush Limbaugh, "Unleash Israel, Win Peace," RushLimbaugh.com, December 7, 2001, http://www.rushlimbaugh.com/home/daily/ site_071706/content/unleash_israel.LogIn.html, accessed August 15, 2006; Barbara Simpson, "The Erosion of Anger," WorldNet Daily, September 13, 2004, http://www. worldnetdaily.com/news/article.asp?ARTICLE_ID=40419, accessed August 15, 2006.

5. Don Mitchell, "Japan Doesn't Deserve an Apology from U.S.," letter to the editor, *Honolulu Star-Bulletin*, March 10, 2001, http://starbulletin.com/2001/03/10/ editorial/letters.html, accessed August 15, 2006.

6. A *Newsweek* article, November 25, 1991, quoted in Margaret Quigley, "Inno-cent Americans, Predatory Asians," *Fairness and Accuracy in Reporting*, April/May 1992, http://www.fair.org/index.php?page=1203&printer_friendly=1, accessed July 24, 2006.

7. Ira Chernus, "The Pearl Harbor Myth," History News Network, December 8, 2001, online at http://hnn.us/articles/453.html, accessed June 29, 2005.

8. Internet editorial column by Ruth Talovich, "Pearl Harbor Revisited," December 10, 2005, Nguoi Viet Online, http://nguoi-viet.com/absolutenm/anmviewer. asp?a=36770&z=40, accessed July 24, 2006.

9. "Transcript of Bush speech on terrorism," CNN.com, March 8, 2005, http://www. cnn.com/2005/ALLPOLITICS/03/08/bush.transcript/, accessed December 8, 2005.

10. Michael Wright (ed.), *The World at Arms: The Reader's Digest Illustrated History of World War II* (New York: Reader's Digest Association, 1989), 138.

11. Joy Hakim, *A History of Us, Book 9: War, Peace and All That Jazz, 1918–1945* (New York: Oxford University Press, 1999), 109–110.

12. Ibid., 126–128.

13. Robert Leckie, *The Story of World War II* (New York: Random House, 1964), 67–69.

14. Kathleen Krull, *V Is for Victory: America Remembers World War II* (New York: Alfred A. Knopf, 1995), 6, 8, 10.

15. Alan Axelrod, *Complete Idiot's Guide to American History* (New York: Alpha Books, 1996), 248.

16. David C. King, *Children's Encyclopedia of American History* (New York: DK Pub-lishing House, 2003), 176, 180.

17. Agence France Presse, "Hiroshima Mayor Lashes Out at Bush on Atomic Bomb-ing Anniversary," August 6, 2003, http://www.commondreams.org/head lines03/0806–10.htm, accessed August 22, 2006; "The 1945 Tokyo Air Raids," *Asahi Shimbun*, March 10, 2005, asahi.com, http://www.asahi.com/english/opinion/TKY200503110174. html, accessed August 21, 2006.

18. Yaguchi Yujin, "War Memories Across the Pacific: Japanese Visitors at the USS *Arizona* Memorial," lecture at the USS *Bowfin* Museum, Honolulu, July 26, 2006; author interview with Dan Martinez, July 26, 2006.

19. Imperial Rescript on the Declaration of War, December 8, 1941, http://www.owensvalleyhistory.com/manzanar3/page14.html, accessed June 7, 2006.

20. There are several versions of the English translation of Hirohito's speech. The one I use here is from Japanese studies scholar William Wetherall, which he argues redresses the ambiguity and minor inaccuracies of commonly used versions such as that produced by the *Nippon Times* in 1945. William Wetherall, "Imperial Rescript Ending War: What Hirohito Really Said in His Surrender Speech," June 2007, http://members.jcom.home.ne.jp/yosha/nationalism/Imperial_rescript_1945-08-14.html, accessed November 8, 2007.

21. Yinan He, "Remembering and Forgetting the War: Elite Mythmaking, Mass Reaction, and Sino-Japanese Relations, 1950–2006," *History & Memory* 19, no. 2 (Fall/Winter 2007): 48.

22. "Abe Says World War II Leaders Tried by Allies Cannot Be Considered War Criminals," *Japan Today*, October 7, 2006, http://www.japantoday.com/jp/news/386506, accessed October 19, 2006.

23. *Shinpen—Atarashii Shakai: Rekishi* (Tokyo: Shoseki, 1998), 254.

24. Saito Sayuri, "Reconsidering History Education," *Daily Yomiuri*, September 18, 1997, 3.

25. *Asahi Shimbun*, October 17, 2005, 3; Alexander Bukh, "Japan's History Textbooks Debate: National Identity in Narratives of Victimhood and Victimization," *Asian Survey* XLVII, no. 5 (September/October 2007): 686.

26. Tawara Yoshifumi, "Junior High School History Textbooks: Whither 'Comfort Women' and the 'Nanking Massacre'?" *Sekai*, no. 68 (November 2000), http://www.iwanami.co.jp/jpworld/text/textbook01.html, accessed December 17, 2007.

27. Howard W. French, "Japan's Resurgent Far Right Tinkers With History," *The New York Times*, March 25, 2001, http://www.nytimes.com/2001/03/25/world/25JAPA.html?ex=1200459600&en=1be6725a173cd2f4&ei=5070, accessed January 14, 2008.

28. Alexander Bukh, "Japan's History Textbooks Debate: National Identity in Narratives of Victimhood and Victimization," *Asian Survey* XLVII, no. 5 (September/October 2007): 689.

29. Murakami Toshifumi, "A Study on Education about the Method to Be a Peace Builder: By the Investigation of Peace Consciousness of Junior High School Students," *Hiroshima Peace Science*, no. 28 (2006): 39, http://home.hiroshima-u.ac.jp/heiwa/JNL/28/Murakami.pdf, accessed December 19, 2007.

30. Philip A. Seaton, *Japan's Contested War Memories: The 'Memory Rifts' in Historical Consciousness of World War II* (London: Routledge, 2007).

31. Sayuri Saito, "Reconsidering History Education," *Daily Yomiuri*, September 18, 1997, 3; online documentary on "The Nanjing Massacre," section on "The Nanking Atrocities in the 1990s: III. The Controversy in Japan," online at http://www.geocities.com/nankingatrocities/1990s/nineties_03.htm, accessed August 12, 2005.

32. Hata Ikuhiko, *Nanking Jiken* (Tokyo: Chuo Koron, 1986), 184–215.

33. Chen Qian, "Japanese on lone inquest into atrocity," *China Daily* online, August 17, 2005, http://www2.chinadaily.com.cn/english/doc/2005-08/17/content_469808.htm, accessed August 17, 2005.

34. Michael J. Green, "Can Tojo Inspire Modern Japan?" *SAIS Review* 19, no. 2 (1999): 243–250.

35. *Lateline* program transcript for April 26, 2001, Australian Broadcasting Corporation, http://www.abc.net.au/lateline/stories/s283892.htm, accessed January 2, 2008.

36. Kyodo News Service, "Latest Japanese War Movie Offends Indonesians," March 22, 2001, posted at http://www.findarticles.com/p/articles/mi_m0WDQ/is_2001_March_26/ai_72697317, accessed August 17, 2006; Bo Xiong, "Indonesia Criticizes Japan for Distorting WWII History," *China News Digest*, May 18, 2001, http://www.cnd.org/CND-Global/CND-Global.01–05–17.html, accessed August 17, 2006.

37. Olivier Fabre, "Japan Nanjing Film Says War Criminals Were Martyrs," Reuters News Service, November 26, 2007, http://www.reuters.com/article/entertainmentNews/idUST30723520071126, accessed December 26, 2007.

38. "Ultranationalist manga gain popularity in Japan as regional tensions rise," *Mainichi* Daily News Online, December 1, 2005, http://mdn.mainichi-msn.co.jp/features/archive/news/2005/12/20051201p2g00m0fe022000c.html, accessed August 23, 2006; Norimitsu Onishi, "Ugly Images of Asian Rivals Become Best Sellers in Japan," *New York Times*, November 19, 2005, http://www.nytimes.com/2005/11/19/international/asia/19comics.html?ex=1290056400&en=b0d32e6a18339284&ei=5088&partner, accessed August 23, 2006.

39. Anthony Faiola, "Japan Honors War Dead and Opens Neighbors' Wounds," *Washington Post* (International Edition), April 23, 2005, A12.

40. Yui Daizaburo, "Between Pearl Harbor and Hiroshima/Nagasaki: Nationalism and Memory in Japan and the United States," in *Living with the Bomb: American and Japanese Cultural Conflicts in the Nuclear Age*, ed. Laura Hein and Mark Selden, 64 (New York: M. E. Sharpe, 1997).

41. Hun-Joo Cho, "Japanese Education Minister Distorts History Once Again," Dong-A Ilbo International, July 12, 2005, http://english.donga.com/srv/service.php3?bicode=060000&biid=2005071223648, accessed August 18, 2006.

42. Associated Press, "'No Massacre in Nanking,' Japanese Lawmakers Say," *International Herald Tribune*, June 19, 2007, http://www.iht.com/articles/2007/06/19/asia/nanking.1–78430.php, accessed December 20, 2007.

43. Mari Yamaguchi, "Ultra-rightist Tilt Posing Clear, Present Danger to Free Speech," *The Japan Times*, January 17, 2007, http://search.japantimes.co.jp/cgi-bin/nn20070117f1.html, accessed January 4, 2008.

44. Anthony Faiola, "Tokyo Teacher Is Punished for Pacifist Stance," *Washington Post*, August 30, 2005, A10; Justin McCurry, "A Touchy Subject," *Guardian* Unlimited, June 5, 2006, http://www.guardian.co.uk/elsewhere/journalist/story/0,,1790903,00.html, accessed December 28, 2007.

45. Yasukuni Jinja Web site, updated August 1, 2006, http://www.yasukuni.or.jp/english/, accessed August 17, 2006.

46. Sources for this section are Wakamiya Yoshibumi, "Zero Fighters in Chongqing and Pearl Harbor: Yasukuni's War Criminals as Martyrs?" *International Herald Tribune*, December 6, 2004,; available at Znet, http://www.zmag.org/content/showarticle.cfm?ItemID=6846, accessed August 18, 2006.

47. Sources for this section are my own notes from my visit to Yushukan in 2007; Paul Murphy, "Yasukuni Museum Tugs at Heartstrings to Keep Military Memories Alive," *Asahi Shimbun* News Service, August 15, 2002, posted at http://www.rense.com/general28/tudg.htm, accessed November 17, 2005; and Faiola, "Japan Honors War Dead and Opens Neighbors' Wounds," A12.

48. "Rightist Faces 12 Years in Torching of Kato Home," *The Japan Times*, April 19, 2007, http://search.japantimes.co.jp/cgi-bin/nn20070419a4.html, accessed January 2, 2008.

49. Jonathan Watts, "Japan's Revisionists Turn Emperor into a God Once More," *The Guardian*, August 21, 2002, http://www.guardian.co.uk/japan/story/0,7369,778007,00.html, accessed February 7, 2008.

50. Don Kirk, "Koreans Slice Their Fingers in Anti-Japan Rite," *The New York Times*, August 14, 2001, http://query.nytimes.com/gst/fullpage.html?res=9D04E0D7 1E3FF937A2575BC0A9679C8B63, accessed January 14, 2008.

51. Xinhua News Service, "Full Text: Chinese President's Speech on War Victory Commemoration," *People's Daily* Online, September 3, 2005, http://english.people.com.cn/200509/03/eng20050903_206351.html, accessed August 23, 2006; Xinhua News Service, "Japan Marks 60th Anniversary of Atomic Bombing on Hiroshima," August 6, 2005, http://news.xinhuanet.com/english/2005–08/06/content_3318096.htm, accessed August 26, 2006.

52. Xinhua News Service, "CPC Played a Pivotal Role in Resisting Japanese Aggression: People's Daily," August 15, 2005, http://english.peopledaily.com.cn/200508/15/print20050815_202410.html, accessed August 23, 2006.

53. Howard W. French, "China's Textbooks Twist and Omit History," *New York Times*, December 6, 2004, http://www.nytimes.com/2004/12/06/international/asia/06textbook.html?pagewanted=print&position, accessed November 16, 2007.

54. Xinhua News Agency, "Chinese Historians Say China Must Not Be Written Out of World War II," People's Daily Online, May 10, 2005, http://english.people.com.cn/200505/10/eng20050510_184293.html, accessed November 19, 2007.

55. Trevor N. Dupuy, *A Genius for War: The German Army and General Staff, 1807–1945* (Englewood Cliffs, NJ: Prentice Hall, 1977), 1–5, 234–235.

56. He, "Remembering and Forgetting," 66.

57. Ibid., 57.

58. Ibid., 57–59.

59. Hiroaki Sato, "High Price of Media-fabricated Heroism," *The Japan Times*, November 24, 2003, http://search.japantimes.co.jp/member/member.html?eo20031124hs.htm, accessed October 2, 2007; "Hyakunin-giri Kyoso," http://rene.malenfant.googlepages.com/hyakuningirikyousou, accessed October 2, 2007; Bob Tadashi Wakabayashi, "The Nanking 100-Man Killing Contest Debate: War Guilt amid Fabricated Illusions, 1971–75," *Journal of Japanese Studies* 26, no. 2 (Summer, 2000): 307–340.

60. French, "China's Textbooks Twist."

61. Pu Zhiqiang, "China's Selective Memory," *International Herald Tribune*, April 29, 2005, http://www.iht.com/articles/2005/04/28/opinion/edpu.php, accessed November 21, 2007.

62. Japan Criticizes China History Textbooks," NewsMax.com, April 25, 2005, http://archive.newsmax.com/archives/articles/2005/4/24/213543.shtml, accessed November 16, 2007.

63. "Taiwan Marks 70th Anniversary of Sino-Japanese War," *China Post* (Taiwan), July 8, 2007, chinapost.com.tw, http://www.chinapost.com.tw/print/114436.htm, accessed July 17, 2007.

64. Huang Qing, "There Were Two Main Anti-fascist War Battlefields," People's Daily Online, August 26, 2005, http://english.people.com.cn/200508/26/eng 20050826_204764.html, accessed November 10, 2006.

65. Xinhua, "Chinese Film on Trial of Japanese WWII War Criminals Debuts to Acclaim," People's Daily Online, September 3, 2006, http://english.people.com.cn/200609/03/eng20060903_299229.html, accessed November 10, 2006.

66. Xinhua, "China Joins Hands with U.S., U.K. to Shoot Movie on Nanjing Massacre," People's Daily Online, August 15, 2006, http://english.people.com.cn/200608/15/eng20060815_293061.html, accessed November 10, 2006.

67. Jun Hongo, "Filmmaker to Paint Nanjing Slaughter as Just Myth," *The Japan Times*, January 25, 2007, http://search.japantimes.co.jp/cgi-bin/nn20070125a3.html, accessed December 20, 2007.

CHAPTER 9: "COMFORT WOMEN" DISCOMFITURE

1. Bloomberg News, "S. Korea Protests Comment by Japan Official About Comfort Women," June 13, 2005, http://www.bloomberg.com/apps/news?pid=10000101&sid=alqoW0PqIavo, accessed January 29, 2008.

2. Quoted in Tessa Morris-Suzuki, "Japan's 'Comfort Women': It's Time for the Truth (in the Ordinary, Everyday Sense of the Word)," *Japan Focus*, March 8, 2007, http://www.japanfucus.org/products/topdf/2373, accessed January 9, 2008.

3. Gay J. McDougall, "Contemporary Forms of Slavery: Systematic Rape, Sexual Slavery and Slavery-like Practices during Armed Conflict," report for United Nations Commission on Human Rights, E/CN.4/Sub.2/1998/13, June 22, 1998, http://www.unhchr.ch/huridocda/huridoca.nsf/Documents?OpenFrameset, accessed January 9, 2008.

4. Larry Niksch, "Japanese Military's "Comfort Women" System," Congressional Research Service Memorandum, Washington, DC, April 3, 2007, 8, 11.

5. United Nations Committee Against Torture, "Consideration of Reports Submitted by States Parties Under Article 19 of the Convention: Conclusions and Recommendations of the Committee against Torture: Japan," August 3, 2007, CAT/C/JPN/CO/1, http://daccessdds.un.org/doc/UNDOC/GEN/G07/433/72/PDF/G0743372.pdf?OpenElement, accessed January 19, 2008.

6. Roy Lavon Brooks, *When Sorry Isn't Enough: The Controversy over Apologies and Reparations for Human Injustice* (New York: New York University Press, 1999), 118; Reiji Yoshida, "Evidence Documenting Sex-slave Coercion Revealed," *Japan Times Online*, April 18, 2007, http://search.japantimes.co.jp/cgi-bin/nn20070418a5.html, accessed January 15, 2008.

7. "Statement by the Chief Cabinet Secretary Yohei Kono on the Result of the Study on the Issue of 'Comfort Women,'" August 4, 1993, Japanese Ministry of Foreign Affairs Web site, http://www.mofa.go.jp/policy/women/fund/state9308.html, accessed January 9, 2008.

8. The Comfort Women Issue, Web site of the Japanese Embassy in the United States, [no date], http://www.us.emb-japan.go.jp/english/html/cw1.htm, accessed January 23, 2008.

9. Stephanie Strom, "Korea Won't Seek Japanese Reparations for WWII's 'Comfort' Women," *New York Times*, April 22, 1998, http://www.nautilus.org/archives/napsnet/dr/9804/APR22.html#item10, accessed January 10, 2008.

10. Norimitsu Onishi, "Tokyo's Attempts to Save Face Prolong Pain of 'Comfort Women,'" *Taipei Times*, April 27, 2007, http://www.taipeitimes.com/News/editorials/archives/2007/04/27/2003358455, accessed January 9, 2008.

11. Representative sources are *Yomiuri Shimbun*, "Background of 'Comfort Women' Issue: No Hard Evidence of Coercion in Recruitment of Comfort Women," Daily

Yomiuri Online, March 31, 2007, http://www.yomiuri.co.jp/dy/national/20070331dy02. htm, accessed January 9, 2008; "Truth of Comfort Women," http://resistance333.web. fc2.com/english/english_comfort_women1.htm, accessed January 9, 2008; "Summary of the Comfort Women Issue," November 22, 2007, http://orandazaka.wordpress. com/2007/11/22/summary-of-the-comort-women-issue/, accessed January 16, 2008; Nishioka Tsutomu, "THE TRUTH ABOUT THE COMFORT WOMEN? How Fiction Became Fact," September 18, 2007, http://trainingofenglish.blog.com/2091487/, accessed January 15, 2008; and "Background of 'Comfort Women' Issue: Comfort Station Originated in Government Regulated 'Civilian Prostitution,'" *Yomiuri Shimbun*, Daily Yomiuri Online, March 31, 2007, http://www.yomiuri.co.jp/dy/national/ 20070331dy01.htm, accessed January 8, 2008.

12. Nishioka, "THE TRUTH ABOUT THE COMFORT WOMEN."

13. Adam Gamble and Takesato Watanabe, *A Public Betrayed: An Inside Look at Japanese Media Atrocities and Their Warnings to the West* (Washington, DC: Regnery, 2004), 326.

14. David McNeill, "The Struggle for the Japanese Soul: Komori Yoshihisa, *Sankei Shimbun*, and the JIIA Controversy," *Japan Focus*, September 5, 2006, http://www. japanfocus.org/products/details/2212, accessed December 13, 2007.

15. "Truth of Comfort Women."

16. "Summary of the Comfort Women Issue."

17. "Background of 'Comfort Women' Issue: Comfort Station Originated in Government Regulated 'Civilian Prostitution.'"

18. The entire affair is reviewed in Norma Field, "The Courts, Japan's 'Military Comfort Women,' and the Conscience of Humanity: The Ruling in VAWW-Net Japan v. NHK," *Japan Focus*, February 10, 2007, http://www.japanfocus.org/products/ topdf/2352, accessed January 14, 2008.

19. Morris-Suzuki, "Japan's 'Comfort Women.'"

20. "Abe Remarks on Comfort Women Make Waves," *Chosun Ilbo*, March 5, 2007, http://english.chosun.com/w21data/html/news/200703/200703050022.html, accessed January 22, 2008; "Abe Digs In Heels Over Comfort Women," *Chosun Ilbo*, March 6, 2007, http://english.chosun.com/w21data/html/news/200703/200703060026. html, accessed January 22, 2008.

21. Norimitsu Onishi, "Japan Repeats Denial of Role in World War II Sex Slavery," *The New York Times*, March 17, 2007, http://www.nytimes.com/2007/03/17/ world/asia/17japan.html, accessed January 14, 2008.

22. Howard W. French, "Letter From China: In Asia, the Past Divides and Alienates," *International Herald Tribune*, March 8, 2007, http://www.iht.com/arti cles/2007/03/08/news/letter.php, accessed November 16, 2007.

23. Kyodo News Service, "U.S. Got Abe to Drop Denial over Sex Slaves," *The Japan Times*, November 9, 2007, http://search.japantimes.co.jp/rss/nn20071109a2. html, accessed January 22, 2008.

24. Stephanie Strom, "Seoul Won't Seek Japan Funds for War's Brothel Women," *New York Times*, April 22, 1998, A3.

25. "Japan Faces Joint Protest from Korean 'Comfort Women,'" BBC News, October 12, 1998, http://news.bbc.co.uk/1/hi/world/asia-pacific/191715.stm, accessed January 22, 2008.

26. Caroline Rose, *Sino-Japanese Relations: Facing the Past, Looking to the Future?* (London: Routledge, 2005), 73–76.

27. "60-Year Sadness of Chinese Comfort Women," *People's Daily* Online, September 18, 2000, http://english.peopledaily.com.cn/english/200009/18/eng20000918_50734.

html, accessed January 18, 2008; "Chinese 'Comfort Women' Exceeded 200,000: Expert," *People's Daily* Online, August 17, 2000, http://english.peopledaily.com.cn/eng lish/200008/17/eng20000817_48433.html, accessed January 18, 2008.

28. Reilly, James, "China's History Activism and Sino-Japanese Relations," *China: An International Journal* 4, no. 2 (September 2006), 197.

29. "60-Year Sadness of Chinese Comfort Women," *People's Daily* Online, September 18, 2000, http://english.peopledaily.com.cn/english/200009/18/eng20000918_50 734.html, accessed January 18, 2008.

30. Agence-France Presse, "Minister Touts Support for Sex-slave Remark," *Taipei Times*, July 12, 2005, http://www.taipeitimes.com/News/world/archives/2005/07/12/ 2003263199, accessed January 14, 2008.

31. "Foreign Ministry Spokesman Liu Jianchao's Press Conference on 12 July 2005," Web site of the Chinese Consulate in Los Angeles, July 13, 2005, http://los angeles.china-consulate.org/eng/news/confenrence/t203493.htm, accessed January 19, 2008.

32. Yuki Terazawa, "The Transnational Campaign for Redress for Wartime Rape by the Japanese Military: Cases for Survivors in Shanxi Province," *NWSA Journal* 18, no. 3 (Fall 2006).

33. Reilly, "China's History Activism," 204.

34. Xinhua, "China Blasts Japan Court's Rejection on WW2 Suits," China Daily, April 28, 2007, http://www.chinadaily.com.cn/china/2007–04/28/content_862488. htm, accessed January 23, 2008.

35. "Foreign Ministry Spokesman Qin Gang's Regular Press Conference on 28 June, 2007," web site of the People's Republic of China Embassy in the United Kingdom, June 30, 2007, http://www.chinese-embassy.org.uk/eng/zt/fyrth/t335373.htm, accessed January 19, 2008.

36. James Reilly, letter to the author, January 26, 2008.

37. Ken Silverstein, "Cold Comfort: the Japan Lobby Blocks Resolution on WWII Sex Slaves," *Harper's*, October 2006, http://www.harpers.org/archive/2006/10/sb cold-comfort-women-1160006345, accessed January 10, 2008.

38. Associated Press, "Bush Prods N. Korea on Nuclear Promise," April 27, 2007, MSNBC.com, http://www.msnbc.msn.com/id/18347775/, accessed August 2, 2007.

39. Associated Press, "House Seeks 'Comfort Women' Apology," June 26, 2007, http://www.msnbc.msn.com/id/19440435/, accessed January 14, 2008.

40. Richard Cowan, "House Seeks Japan's Apology on 'Comfort Women,'" Reuters News Service, July 30, 2007, http://www.reuters.com/article/politicsNews/ idUSN3041972020070730, accessed January 15, 2008.

41. Text of House Resolution 121 is available at http://www.govtrack.us/congress/ billtext.xpd?bill=hr110-121, accessed December 11, 2008.

42. "Get Facts Straight on Comfort Women," *Yomiuri Shimbun*, June 28, 2007, http://www.yomiuri.co.jp/dy/editorial/20070628TDY04005.htm, accessed January 16, 2008.

43. Xinhua, "China Focus: China Marks Japanese Surrender in Bitter Memory," *People's Daily* Online, August 16, 2005, http://english.peopledaily.com.cn/200508/16/ eng20050816_202603.html, accessed January 18, 2008; Edward Rothstein, "Onstage, the War Never Ends as Playwrights Pose Questions of Responsibility and Guilt," *New York Times*, November 8, 2004, http://www.nytimes.com/2004/11/08/theater/ reviews/08kazu.html, accessed January 18, 2008; Na Jeong-ju, "Japanese Lawmakers Propose Compensation for Sex Slavery Victims," *Korea Times*, February 12, 2003,

http://times.hankooki.com/lpage/nation/200302/kt2003021217052511970.htm, accessed January 18, 2008.

CHAPTER 10: CHINA AND THE "HISTORY CARD"

1. Xinhua, "U.S. 'Flying Tigers' to Have Memorial Park in SW China," November 2, 2007, http://news.xinhuanet.com/english/2007–11/02/content_7000288.htm, accessed December 20, 2007.

2. Yinan He, "History, Chinese Nationalism and the Emerging Sino-Japanese Conflict," *Journal of Contemporary China* 16, no. 50 (February 2007): 7.

3. *Asahi Shimbun*, June 5, 1987; Christopher Howe, *China and Japan: History, Trends, and Prospects* (Oxford: Oxford University Press, 1996), 63.

4. He, "History, Chinese Nationalism," 6.

5. Yinan He, "Remembering and Forgetting the War: Elite Mythmaking, Mass Reaction, and Sino-Japanese Relations, 1950–2006," *History & Memory* 19, no. 2 (Fall/Winter 2007): 53.

6. Chalmers Johnson, *Japan: Who Governs? The Rise of the Developmental State* (New York: W. W. Norton, 1995), 255.

7. Hidenori Ijiri, "Sino-Japanese Controversy Since the 1972 Normalization," in *China and Japan: History, Trends and Prospects*, ed. Christopher Howe, 65–67 (Oxford: Clarendon, 1996).

8. Japan Ministry of Foreign Affairs Web site, "Statement by Chief Cabinet Secretary Kiichi Miyazawa on History Textbooks," August 26, 1982, http://www.mofa.go.jp/policy/postwar/state8208.html, accessed December 13, 2007.

9. Howard W. French, "Letter From China: China Hails a Good Nazi and Makes Japan Take Notice," *New York Times*, March 15, 2006, http://www.nytimes.com/2006/03/15/international/asia/15letter.html?pagewanted=all, accessed November 16, 2007.

10. This is Yinan He's view. She writes that "Deng seized this opportunity to boost patriotism at home and appease the conservative faction" (He, "History, Chinese Nationalism," 6). She elaborates: "Japan's internal memory contestation, reported by the international media, created a profitable opportunity for the CCP that was baffled by all kinds of domestic problems at the time. Japan's internal fight about war memory had been going on for decades, but Beijing chose to ignore it until this point." (Yinan He, letter to the author, January 31, 2008).

11. He, "History, Chinese Nationalism," 6.

12. Peter Hays Gries, *China's New Nationalism: Pride, Politics, and Diplomacy* (Berkeley: University of California Press, 2004), 69–86; Peter Hays Gries, "Nationalism, Indignation and China's Japan Policy," *SAIS Review* XXV, no. 2 (Summer-Fall 2005): 109.

13. James Reilly, "China's History Activism and Sino-Japanese Relations," *China: An International Journal* 4, no. 2 (September 2006): 198–199.

14. Fang Lizhi, "Nihonjin no Seizai no Sensokan ni Tsuite," *Chuo Koron*, no. 8 (1987): 172–178.

15. Richard Corliss, "Beyond Cute," *Time*, March 22, 2004, http://www.time.com/time/magazine/article/0,9171,501040329–603270,00.html, accessed December 9, 2007.

16. "Toyota Apologizes to Chinese Consumers for Improper Ads," *People's Daily Online*, December 5, 2003, http://english.peopledaily.com.cn/200312/05/eng20031205_129766.shtml, accessed February 6, 2008.

17. He, "History, Chinese Nationalism," 11.

18. Denny Roy, "China-Japan Relations: Cooperation Amidst Antagonism," in *Asia's Bilateral Relations*, ed. Satu Limaye, 9.5 (Honolulu: Asia-Pacific Center for Security Studies, 2004).

19. Che-po Chan and Brian Bridges, "China, Japan and the Clash of Nationalisms," *Asian Perspective* 30, no. 1 (2006): 139–140.

20. Yui Daizaburo, "Between Pearl Harbor and Hiroshima/Nagasaki: Nationalism and Memory in Japan and the United States," in *Living with the Bomb: American and Japanese Cultural Conflicts in the Nuclear Age*, ed. Laura Hein and Mark Selden, 61–62 (New York: M. E. Sharpe, 1997).

21. Associated Press, "Chinese Hurt by Japanese WWII Poison Gas Demand Compensation," August 5, 2005, Sina.com, http://english.sina.com/china/1/2005/0805/41360.html, accessed February 6, 2008.

22. "Nakasone Denies Agreement Not to Worship at Shrine," BBC News, April 28, 2005, http://news.bbc.co.uk/chinese/trad/hi/newsid_4490000/newsid_4492500/4492503.stm, accessed December 9, 2007.

23. "China Accuses Japan of Worshipping War Criminals," Agence France-Presse, November 15, 2005, http://sg.news.yahoo.com/051115/1/3wi5w.html, accessed November 16, 2005.

24. Wakamiya Yoshibumi, "Zero Fighters in Chongqing and Pearl Harbor: Yasukuni's War Criminals as Martyrs?" *International Herald Tribune*, Dec. 6, 2004, posted at Znet, http://www.zmag.org/content/showarticle.cfm?ItemID=6846, accessed August 18, 2006.

25. Joseph Kahn, "Riot Police Called In to Calm Anti-Japanese Protests in China," *The New York Times*, April 10, 2005, http://www.nytimes.com/2005/04/10/international/10china.LONG.html?_r=1&oref=slogin, accessed February 7, 2008.

26. Joseph Kahn, "China Is Pushing and Scripting Anti-Japanese Protests," *New York Times*, April 15, 2005, http://www.nytimes.com/2005/04/15/international/asia/15china.html?pagewanted=print&position=, accessed January 22, 2008.

27. Joseph Kahn, "No Apology From China for Japan Protests," *The New York Times*, April 18, 2005, http://www.nytimes.com/2005/04/18/international/asia/18china.html, accessed February 8, 2008.

28. Chan and Bridges, "China, Japan and the Clash of Nationalisms," 128.

29. Gries, "Nationalism, Indignation," 111; Chan and Bridges, "China, Japan and the Clash of Nationalisms," 134; Phillip P. Pan, "Chinese Step Up Criticism of Japan," *Washington Post International Edition*, April 13, 2005, A14.

30. Shi Baohua, "Jing Hu Gaotie Cai Yong Lun Gui Ji Shu Qi Yong Cixuan Fu De Fa Ri Bao," *Jinghua Shibao*, January 15, 2004, http://bj.people.com.cn/GB/14545/2297992.html, accessed February 1, 2008.

CHAPTER 11: U.S.-JAPAN RELATIONS

1. Zbigniew Brzezinski, "America's New Geostrategy," *Foreign Affairs* 66, no. 4 (Spring 1988): 695–696.

2. U.S. Department of State, *Foreign Relations of the United States, 1949*, Vol. VII (Washington, DC: U.S. Government Printing Office, 1976), 927.

3. Walter LaFeber, *The Clash: U.S.-Japanese Relations Throughout History* (New York: W. W. Norton, 1997), 264, 281–282.

4. Memorandum dated July 31, 1951, John Foster Dulles Peace Treaty File, DOS, RG 59, Lot 54D423, Box 1, National Archives, Washington, DC; Timothy

D. Temerson, unpublished manuscript, "Double Containment and the Origins of the U.S.-Japan Security Alliance," Massachusetts Institute of Technology Japan Program, MITJP 91–14, 1992.

5. Text of the Treaty of Peace with Japan is available at http://www.international. ucla.edu/eas/documents/peace1951.htm, accessed December 15, 2008. Text of the U.S.-Japan Security Treaty is available at http://www.ioc.u-tokyo.ac.jp/~worldjpn/ documents/texts/docs/19510908.T2E.html, accessed December 15, 2008.

6. Fred Hiatt, "Marine General: U.S. Troops Must Stay in Japan," *The Washington Post*, March 27, 1990, A14, A20.

7. Gerald Curtis, "U.S. Policy Toward Japan, 1972–2000," in *New Perspectives on U.S.-Japan Relations*, ed. Gerald Curtis, 10 (Tokyo: Japan Center for International Exchange, 2000); Michael Schaller, *Altered States : The United States and Japan since the Occupation* (Oxford: Oxford University Press, 1997), 244.

8. Schaller, *Altered States*, 46.

9. "Soldier Kills Woman," *Los Angeles Times*, June 5, 1957, http://latimesblogs.lat imes.com/thedailymirror/2007/06/soldier_kills_w.html, accessed February 13, 2008.

10. Schaller, *Altered States*, 133–134, 141.

11. Dwight D. Eisenhower, *Public Papers of the Presidents of the United States: Dwight D. Eisenhower, 1954* (Washington, DC: U.S. Government Printing Office, 1958), 382–383.

12. Schaller, *Altered States*, 192–195.

13. Marc Gallicchio, "Occupation, Dominion, and Alliance: Japan in American Security Policy, 1945–69," in *Partnership: The United States and Japan 1951–2001*, ed. Akira Iriye and Robert A. Wampler, 130 (Tokyo: Kodansha International, 2001).

14. Michael Jonathan Green, "The Search for an Active Security Partnership: Lessons from the 1980s," in Iriye and Wampler, *Partnership*, 135.

15. Christopher Layne, "The Unipolar Illusion: Why New Great Powers Will Rise," *International Security* 17, no. 4 (Spring 1993): 39, 43; Kenneth N. Waltz, "The Emerging Structure of International Politics," *International Security* 18, no. 2 (Fall 1993): 65–66.

16. Jun Hongo, "Survivors of WWII Air Raids Begin Case for Compensation," *The Japan Times*, May 25, 2007, http://search.japantimes.co.jp/mail/nn20070525a4. html, accessed January 7, 2008.

17. LaFeber, *The Clash*, 339.

18. "Japan, Inc.: Winning the Most Important Battle," *Time*, May 10, 1971, http://www. time.com/time/magazine/article/0,9171,902974-2,00.html, accessed February 13, 2008.

19. Theodore H. White, "The Danger from Japan," *New York Times Magazine*, July 28, 1985, 19–58.

20. "Senator Jokes of Hiroshima Attack," *The New York Times*, March 4, 1992, 12.

21. Author interview with *Okinawa Times* editor Yara Tomohiro, April 2008.

22. Laura Hein and Mark Selden, "Culture, Power and Identity in Contemporary Okinawa," in *Islands of Discontent: Okinawan Responses to Japanese and American Power*, ed. Laura Hein and Mark Selden, 20 (Lanham, MD: Rowman & Littlefield, 2003).

23. Ishihara Masaie, "Memories of War and Okinawa," in *Perilous Memories: The Asia-Pacific War(s)*, ed. T. Fujitani, Geoffrey M. White, and Lisa Yoneyama, 88 (Durham, NC: Duke University Press, 2001).

24. Sono Ayako, "Okinawasen Shudanjiketsu o Meguru Rekishi Kyokasho no Kyomo," *Seiron*, no. 375 (2003): 112–117.

25. Koji Taira, "The Battle of Okinawa in Japanese History Books," in *Okinawa: Cold War Island*, ed. Chalmers Johnson (Cardiff, CA: Japan Policy Research Institute, 1999), 39.

26. Kyodo News Service, "Texts Stop Saying Army Forced Okinawa Suicides," *The Japan Times*, March 31, 2007, http://search.japantimes.co.jp/cgi-bin/nn20070331a5.html, accessed January 4, 2008.

27. Norimitsu Onishi, "Okinawans Protest Japan's Plan to Revise Bitter Chapter of World War II," *New York Times*, October 7, 2007, http://www.nytimes.com/2007/10/07/world/asia/07okinawa.html, accessed April 2, 2008.

28. "Okinawa City Rips Efforts to Alter Textbooks," *The Japan Times*, May 15, 2007, http://search.japantimes.co.jp/cgi-bin/nn20070515a2.html, accessed January 7, 2008; Kyodo News Service, "Okinawa 'Mass Suicide' Deletions Hit," *The Japan Times*, June 15, 2007, http://search.japantimes.co.jp/cgi-bin/nn20070615b1.html, accessed January 7, 2008.

29. Carolyn Brown Francis, "Women and Military Violence," in Johnson (ed.), *Cold War Island*, 201.

30. Mike Millard, "Okinawa, Then and Now," in Johnson (ed.), *Cold War Island*, 98; "The Number of Criminal Cases in Which SOFA Status People Have Been Arrested," Okinawa Prefectural Government Web site, Military Base Affairs Office, http://www3.pref.okinawa.jp/site/view/contview.jsp?cateid=14&id=666&page=1, accessed April 4, 2008.

31. "Cooperative Working Team Credits US Military with Reducing Crime Incidents," September 2005, web site of the U.S. consulate in Naha, http://naha.usconsulate.gov/wwwhhottopics1.html, accessed March 31, 2008; "Sex Crime Rate Involving U.S. Forces Is Extraordinarily High," *Japan Press Weekly*, March 25, 2008, http://www.japan-press.co.jp/2567/us_forces_5.html, accessed March 31, 2008.

32. Irvin Molotsky, "Admiral Has to Quit Over His Comments on Okinawa Rape," *New York Times*, November 18, 1995, http://query.nytimes.com/gst/fullpage.html?res=9502E6DA1239F93BA25752C1A963958260, accessed March 28, 2008.

33. Julia Yonetai, "Playing Base Politics in a Global Strategic Theater: Futenma Relocation, the G-8 Summit, and Okinawa," *Critical Asian Studies* 33, no. 1 (March 2001): 70–95.

34. Kato Yoichi, "INTERVIEW: Richard Lawless: Japan-U.S. Alliance Faces 'Priority Gap,'" *Asahi Shimbun*, May 22, 2008, http://www.asahi.com/english/Herald asahi/TKY200805220057.html, accessed September 3, 2008.

35. A.F.K. Organski and Jacek Kugler, "The Costs of Major Wars: The Phoenix Factor," *American Political Science Review* 71, no. 4 (December 1977): 1347–1366.

36. LaFeber, *The Clash*, 257.

37. Mike M. Mochizuki, "U.S.-Japan Relations in the Asia-Pacific Region," in Iriye and Wampler (eds.), *Partnership*, 14.

38. "Slave Wages," *The Economist*, March 30, 2006, http://www.economist.com/world/asia/displaystory.cfm?story_id=6748994, accessed January 14, 2008.

39. Tillman Durdin, James Reston, and Seymour Topping, *The New York Times: Report from Red China* (New York: Quadrangle Books, 1971), 92.

CHAPTER 12: ATOMIC RANCOR BETWEEN AMERICA AND JAPAN

1. The Editors, "Introduction," *CROSSROADS: A Journal of Nagasaki History and Culture*, no. 3 (Summer 1995), http://www.uwosh.edu/faculty_staff/earns/intro3.html, accessed March 6, 2008.

2. Victor Davis Hanson, "Remembering World War II: Revisionists Get It Wrong," National Review Online, May 13, 2005, http://www.nationalreview.com/hanson/hanson200505130808.asp, accessed September 7, 2005.

3. Tony Capaccio and Uday Mohan, "Missing the Target," *American Journalism Review*, July/August 1995, http://www.ajr.org/Article.asp?id=1285, accessed April 27, 2006; J. Samuel Walker, "The Decision to Use the Bomb: A Historiographical Update," *Diplomatic History* 14, no.1 (Winter 1990): 97–114.

4. Alan Axelrod, *The Complete Idiot's Guide to American History* (New York: Alpha Books, 1996), 258.

5. David C. King, *First Facts About U.S. History* (Woodbridge, CT: Blackbirch Press, 1996), 85.

6. Sherry Marker, *Illustrated History of the United States* (Greenwich, CT: Bison Books, 1988), 140.

7. Thomas J. Baerwald and Celeste Fraser, *World Geography: Building a Global Perspective* (Upper Saddle River, NJ: Prentice-Hall, 2003), 689.

8. Asada Sadao, "The Mushroom Cloud and National Psyches: Japanese and American Perceptions of the Atomic-Bomb Decision, 1945–1995," in *Living with the Bomb: American and Japanese Cultural Conflicts in the Nuclear Age*, ed. Laura Hein and Mark Selden, 184–186 (New York: M. E. Sharpe, 1997). Asada says this is not due to the influence of Gar Alperovitz's book *Atomic Diplomacy*, but rather stems from a popular but poorly documented 1951 book by British physicist P.M.S. Blackett called *Fear, War and the Bomb*.

9. Laura Hein and Mark Selden, "Commemoration and Silence: Fifty Years of Remembering the Bomb in America and Japan," in Hein and Selden (eds.), *Living with the Bomb*, 12.

10. Kiroku Hanai, "U.S. owes A-bomb apology," *The Japan Times*, July 23, 2007, http://search.japantimes.co.jp/cgi-bin/eo20070723kh.html, accessed March 6, 2008; "Opposition Prepares to Demand Defense Minister Resignation over A-bomb Remarks," *Japan News Review*, July 1, 2007, http://www.japannewsreview.com/politics/20070701page_id=251, accessed March 6, 2008.

11. The Editors, "Introduction," *CROSSROADS*.

12. Asada, "Mushroom Cloud," 175.

13. Kiroku Hanai, "U.S. Owes A-bomb Apology," *The Japan Times*, July 23, 2007, http://search.japantimes.co.jp/cgi-bin/eo20070723kh.html, accessed March 6, 2008.

14. Toru Hanai, "Japan Remembers Hiroshima," August 6, 2007, Reuters News Service, http://www.reuters.com/article/topNews/idUST23604520070806, accessed March 6, 2008.

15. Bay Fang, "Rethinking the Bomb," *U.S. News & World Report*, December 4, 2006, 34.

16. Hiroshi Matsubara, "Prejudice Haunts Atomic Bomb Survivors," *The Japan Times*, May 8, 2001, http://www.nci.org/0new/hibakusha-jt5701.htm, accessed March 6, 2008.

17. Beverly Deepe Keever, "Suffering, Secrecy, Exile: Bravo 50 Years Later," *Honolulu Weekly*, February 25, 2004, http://www.wagingpeace.org/articles/2004/05/24_keever_suffering-sccrecy-exile.htm, accessed August 22, 2007.

18. See the "Three Non-Nuclear Principles" page at the Japanese Foreign Ministry Web site, http://www.mofa.go.jp/policy/un/disarmament/nnp/announce.html, accessed December. 15, 2008.

19. Judith Miller, "U.S. Violated Nuclear Arms Pledge in Japan, Records Show," *New York Times*, December 12, 1999, http://query.nytimes.com/gst/fullpage.html?res=9D07EEDB1331F931A25751C1A96F958260, accessed December 15, 2008.

20. Edwin Reischauer, *My Life Between Japan and America* (New York: Harper and Row, 1986), 249–250.

21. "Ozawa Confirms Nuclear Weapons Potential of Japan's Plutonium Program as Further Nuclear Transports Loom," Greenpeace press release, April 7, 2002, http://archive.greenpeace.org/pressreleases/nucreprocess/2002apr7.html, accessed March 6, 2008.

22. Reuters News Service, "Japan Should Reexamine Its Nuclear Weapons Ban, Ruling Party Official Says," *Washington Post*, October 16, 2006, A15; "1 in 3 LDP Election Candidates Say Japan Should Reexamine Nuclear Weapons Stance," *Mainichi Shimbun*, July 26, 2007, http://mdn.mainichi-msn.co.jp/national/news/p20070716p2 a00m0na009000c.html, accessed July 16, 2007.

23. Douglas Holdstock and Frank Barnaby (eds.), *Hiroshima and Nagasaki: Retrospect and Prospect* (Oxford: Taylor and Francis, 1995), 48.

24. John T. Correll, "The Smithsonian and the Enola Gay: A Retrospective on the Controversy 10 Years Later," April 2004, Air Force Association Web site, http://www.afa.org/new_root/enolagay/, accessed March 6, 2008.

25. Ken Ringle, "2 Views of History Collide Over Smithsonian A-Bomb Exhibit," *Washington Post*, September 26, 1994, posted at www.h-net.org/~asia/threads/thrde nola.html, accessed June 29, 2007.

26. Yui Daizaburo, "Between Pearl Harbor and Hiroshima/Nagasaki: Nationalism and Memory in Japan and the United States," in Hein and Selden (eds.), *Living with the Bomb*, 55; Bill Gilbert, *Air Power: Heroes and Heroism in American Flight Missions, 1916 to Today* (New York: Citadel Press, 2003), 161–163.

27. The text of Senate Resolution 257 (1994) is available at http://digital.lib.lehigh. edu/trial/enola/files/round2/res257.pdf, accessed December 15, 2008.

28. Agence France Presse, "58 Years after Dropping Hiroshima Bomb, Enola Gay Ignites New Outrage," November 10, 2003, http://nucnews.net/nucnews/2003nn/ 0311nn/031110nn.htm#730, accessed March 6, 2008.

29. Elizabeth Olson, "Criticism Meets New Exhibit of Plane That Carried A-Bomb," *New York Times*, November 2, 2003, http://query.nytimes.com/gst/fullpage.html?res=9F 03E6DD1030F931A35752C1A9659C8B63, accessed March 6, 2008.

30. Asada Sadao, "Japanese Perceptions of the A-Bomb Decision, 1945–1980," in *The American Military and the Far East*, ed. Joe C. Dixon, 206–207 (Washington, DC: Government Printing Office, 1980).

31. T. R. Reid, "The Setting Sun of Akira Kurosawa; Japan's Famed Director Draws Yawns for Film Memoir," *Washington Post*, December 28, 1993, C1.

32. *Asahi Shinbun*, August 16, 1991, in Yui, "Between Pearl Harbor," 61.

33. Michael Wines, "President Rejects Apology to Japan," *New York Times*, December 2, 1991, A12; Steven R. Weisman, "Japanese Apology Over War Unlikely After Bush's Stand," *New York Times*, December 6, 1991, A1.

34. "World Notes Japan," *Time*, December 16, 1991, http://www.time.com/time/ magazine/article/0,9171,9774476,00.htmil, accessed February 12, 2008.

35. Asada, "Mushroom Cloud," p. 184.

36. Laura Hein and Mark Selden, "Commemoration and Silence: Fifty Years of Remembering the Bomb in America and Japan," in Hein and Selden (eds.), *Living with the Bomb*, 4, 7.

37. Hiroaki Sato, "Great Tokyo Air Raid Was a War Crime," *Japan Times* online, September 30, 2002, http://search.japantimes.co.jp/member/member.html?eo20020930hs. htm, accessed February 22, 2008.

38. Jeffery J. Roberts, "Peering through Different Bombsights: Military Historians, Diplomatic Historians, and the Decision to Drop the Atomic Bomb," *Airpower Journal* XII, no. 1 (Spring 1998): 68.

CHAPTER 13: CONCLUSION

1. Credit for this term goes to Kosaka Masataka; Yoichi Funabashi, "Japan and the New World Order," *Foreign Affairs* 70, no. 5 (Winter 1991/92): 65.

2. Text of the Treaty of Peace with Japan is available at http://www.international. ucla.edu/eas/documents/peace1951.htm, accessed December 15, 2008.

3. Tanaka Sakai, "The Northern Territories Impasse," Znet, October 28, 2006, http://www.zmag.org/znet/viewArticle/2876, accessed August 28, 2008.

4. Key Neorealist works are Kenneth N. Waltz, *Theory of International Politics* (Reading, MA: Addison-Wesley Press, 1979), and John Mearsheimer, *The Tragedy of Great Power Politics* (New York: W. W. Norton, 2001); for constructivism, see Alexander Wendt, "Anarchy Is What States Make of It: The Social Construction of Power Politics," *International Organization* 46, no. 3 (1992): 391–425.

5. See, for example, David Halberstam, "The History Boys," *Vanity Fair*, August 2007, 122–125, 168–169.

6. Paul Gattis, "Saban Invokes Images of War," *The Huntsville Times*, November 20, 2007, http://www.al.com/sports/huntsvilletimes/index.ssf?/base/sports/ 119555388219790.xml&coll=1, accessed December 9, 2007.

7. George H. W. Bush, Remarks to World War II Veterans and Families in Honolulu, Hawaii, December 7, 1991, Bush Presidential Library Web site, http:// bushlibrary.tamu.edu/research/papers/1989/89111306.html, accessed June 21, 2005.

8. "President Commemorates 60th Anniversary of V-J Day," White House press release, August 30, 2005, http://www.whitehouse.gov/news/releases/2005/08/200508 30–1.html, accessed September 6, 2005.

9. "President Bush Attends Veterans of Foreign Wars National Convention, Discusses War on Terror," August 22, 2007, Council on Foreign Relations "Essential Documents" Web page, http://www.cfr.org/publication/14075/president_bush_ attends_veterans_of_foreign_wars_national_convention_discusses_war_on_terror. html?breadcrumb=%2Fbios%2F11324%2Fgeorge_w_bush, accessed April 6, 2008.

Bibliography

Adams, Michael C. C. *The Best War Ever: America and World War II.* Baltimore, MD: Johns Hopkins University Press, 1994.

Akami Tomoko. *Internationalizing the Pacific: The United States, Japan, and the Institute of Pacific Relations in War and Peace, 1919–45.* London: Routledge, 2002.

Alperovitz, Gar. *Atomic Diplomacy: Hiroshima and Nagasaki.* New York: Simon & Schuster, 1965.

Ambrose, Stephen E. *Citizen Soldiers: The U.S. Army from the Normandy Beaches to the Bulge to the Surrender of Germany; June 7, 1944 to May 7, 1945.* New York: Simon and Schuster, 1997.

Ambrose, Stephen E., and Brian Loring Villa. "Racism, the Atomic Bomb, and the Transformation of Japanese-American Relations." In *The Pacific War Revisited*, edited by Gunter Bischof and Robert L. Dupont, 179–198. Baton Rouge: Louisiana State University Press, 1997.

Andressen, Curtis. *A Short History of Japan: From Samurai to Sony.* Sydney: Allen & Unwin, 2003.

Archibald, George. "Textbooks Flunk Test." *The Washington Times*, Mar. 28, 2004.

Asada Sadao. "Japanese Perceptions of the A-Bomb Decision, 1945–1980." In *The American Military and the Far East*, edited by Joe C. Dixon, 199–219. Washington, DC: U.S. Government Printing Office, 1980.

Asada Sadao. "The Mushroom Cloud and National Psyches: Japanese and American Perceptions of the Atomic-Bomb Decision, 1945–1995." In *Living with the Bomb: American and Japanese Cultural Conflicts in the Nuclear Age*, edited by Laura Hein and Mark Selden, 173–201. New York: M. E. Sharpe, 1997.

Asada Sadao. "The Shock of the Atomic Bomb and Japan's Decision to Surrender: A Reconsideration." *Pacific Historical Review* 67, no. 4 (1998): 477–512.

Axelrod, Alan. *The Complete Idiot's Guide to American History.* New York: Alpha Books, 1996.

Baerwald, Thomas J., and Celeste Fraser. *World Geography: Building a Global Perspective*. Upper Saddle River, NJ: Prentice-Hall, 2003.

Bard, Ralph. "Memorandum on the Use of S-1 Bomb." Harrison-Bundy Files, RG 77, microfilm publication M1108, folder 77, National Archives, Washington, DC.

Barnhart, Michael A. *Japan Prepares for Total War: The Search for Economic Security, 1919–1941*. Ithaca, NY: Cornell University Press, 1987.

Batchelder, Robert. *The Irreversible Decision, 1939–1950*. New York: Houghton Mifflin, 1961.

Bay Fang. "Rethinking the Bomb." *U.S. News & World Report*, Dec. 4, 2006.

Bellah, Robert N., Richard Madsen, William M. Sullivan, Ann Swidler, and Steven M. Tipton. *Habits of the Heart*. New York: Harper and Row, 1985.

Berger, Carl. *B-29: The Superfortress*. New York: Ballantine Books, 1970.

Bernstein, Barton J. "Compelling Japan's Surrender Without the A-Bomb, Soviet Entry, or Invasion: Reconsidering the U.S. Bombing Survey's Early-Surrender Conclusion." *Journal of Strategic Studies* 18, no. 2 (June 1995): 101–148.

Bernstein, Barton J. "The Perils and Politics of Surrender: Ending the War with Japan and Avoiding the Third Atomic Bomb." *Pacific Historical Review* XLVI, (February 1977): 1–27.

Bix, Herbert J. "Japan's Delayed Surrender: A Reinterpretation." In *Hiroshima in History and Memory*, edited by Michael J. Hogan, 80–115. New York: Cambridge University Press, 1996.

Blair, Clay. *Silent Victory: The U.S. Submarine War Against Japan*. New York: J. B. Lippincott, 1975.

Boller, Paul F. *Not So! Popular Myths About America from Columbus to Clinton*. New York: Oxford University Press, 1995.

Bower, Tom. *The Paperclip Conspiracy: The Hunt for the Nazi Scientists*. Boston: Little, Brown and Company, 1987.

Boyne, Walter J., *Clash of the Titans: World War II at Sea*. New York: Simon and Schuster, 1995.

Brodie, Bernard. *Strategy in the Missile Age*. Princeton, NJ: Princeton University Press, 1959.

Brokaw, Tom. *The Greatest Generation*. New York: Random House, 1998.

Brooks, Roy Lavon. *When Sorry Isn't Enough: The Controversy over Apologies and Reparations for Human Injustice*. New York: New York University Press, 1999.

Brower, Charles F., IV. "The Joint Chiefs of Staff and National Policy: American Strategy and the War with Japan, 1943–1945." PhD diss., University of Pennsylvania, 1987.

Brzezinski, Zbigniew. "America's New Geostrategy." *Foreign Affairs* 66, no. 4 (Spring 1988): 695–696.

Bukh, Alexander. "Japan's History Textbooks Debate: National Identity in Narratives of Victimhood and Victimization." *Asian Survey* XLVII, no. 5 (September/October 2007): 683–704.

Bunker, John Gorley. *Liberty Ships*. Salem, NH: Ayer Company, 1991.

Burrell, Robert S. "Breaking the Cycle of Iwo Jima Mythology: A Strategic Study of Operation Detachment." *Journal of Military History*, no. 68 (October 2004): 1143–1186.

Butow, Robert. *Japan's Decision to Surrender*. Stanford, CA: Stanford University Press, 1954.

Byrd, Martha. *Chennault: Giving Wings to the Tiger.* Tuscaloosa: University of Alabama Press, 1987.

Caidin, Martin. *A Torch to the Enemy: The Fire Raid on Tokyo.* New York: Ballantine, 1960.

Chan Che-po, and Brian Bridges. "China, Japan and the Clash of Nationalisms." *Asian Perspective* 30, no. 1 (2006): 127–156.

Chang, Iris. *The Rape of Nanking: The Forgotten Holocaust of World War II.* New York: Basic Books, 1997.

Ch'i Hsi-sheng. "The Military Dimension, 1942–1945." In *China's Bitter Victory: The War with Japan, 1937–1945,* edited by James C. Hsiung and Steven I. Levine, 157–184. Armonk, NY: M. E. Sharpe, 1992.

Chou Wan-yao. "Jihpen tsai T'aichunshih tungyuan yu T'aiwanjen ti haiwai ts'anchan chingyen, 1937–1945." *T'aiwan Shih Yenchiu* 2, no. 1 (June 1995): 93–96.

Clubb, Edmund O. *20th Century China.* New York: Columbia University Press, 1978.

Cook, Haroko Taya, and Theodore F. Cook. *Japan at War: An Oral History.* New York: The New Press, 1992.

Cooper, Norman V. "The Military Career of General Holland M. Smith." PhD diss., University of Alabama, 1974.

Costello, John. *The Pacific War.* New York: Rawson, Wade, 1981.

Crane, Conrad C. *Bombs, Cities and Civilians: American Airpower Strategy in World War II.* Lawrence: University Press of Kansas, 1993.

Crozier, Brian. *The Man Who Lost China.* New York: Charles Scribner's Sons, 1976.

Cumings, Bruce. *Korea's Place in the Sun: A Modern History.* New York: W. W. Norton, 1997.

Curtis, Gerald. "U.S. Policy Toward Japan from Nixon to Clinton." In *New Perspectives on US.-Japan Relations,* edited by Gerald Curtis, 1–38. Tokyo: Japan Center for International Exchange, 2000.

Dallek, Robert. *Franklin D. Roosevelt and America Foreign Policy, 1932–1945.* New York: Oxford University Press, 1979.

Devine, Robert A. *The Reluctant Belligerent: American Entry Into World War II.* New York: John A. Wiley & Sons, 1979.

Dingman, Roger. *Ghost of War: The Sinking of the Awa Maru and Japanese-American Relations, 1945–1995.* Annapolis, MD: Naval Institute Press, 1997.

Dower, John W. *Embracing Defeat: Japan in the Wake of World War II.* New York: W. W. Norton, 1999.

Dower, John W. *Empire and Aftermath: Yoshida Shigeru and the Japanese Experience, 1874–1954.* Cambridge, MA: Harvard University Press, 1979.

Dower, John W. *War without Mercy: Race and Power in the Pacific War.* New York: Pantheon, 1986.

Drea, Edward. *MacArthur's Ultra: Codebreaking and the War Against Japan, 1942–1945.* Lawrence: University Press of Kansas, 1992.

Dreyer, Edward L. *China at War 1901–1949.* London: Addison Wesley Longman, 1995.

Dunnigan, James F., and Albert A. Nofi. *Dirty Little Secrets of World War II.* New York: Perennial, 2003.

Dupuy, Trevor N. *A Genius for War: The German Army and General Staff, 1807–1945.* Englewood Cliffs, NJ: Prentice Hall, 1977.

Durdin, Tillman, James Reston, and Seymour Topping. *The New York Times: Report from Red China.* New York: Quadrangle Books, 1971.

Eisenhower, Dwight D. *Public Papers of the Presidents of the United States: Dwight D. Eisenhower, 1954.* Washington, DC: U.S. Government Printing Office, 1958.

Ellis, John. *Brute Force: Allied Strategy and Tactics in the Second World War.* New York: Viking Penguin, 1990.

Emeny, Brooks. *The Strategy of Raw Materials: A Study of America in Peace and War.* New York: Macmillan, 1934.

Emmerson, John K., and Harrison M. Holland. *The Eagle and the Rising Sun: America and Japan in the Twentieth Century.* Reading, MA: Addison-Wesley, 1988.

Faiola, Anthony. "Japan Honors War Dead and Opens Neighbors' Wounds." *Washington Post* (International Edition), Apr. 23, 2005, A12.

Faiola, Anthony, "Tokyo Teacher is Punished for Pacifist Stance." *Washington Post*, Aug. 30, 2005.

Fang Lizhi. "Nihonjin no Seizai no Sensokan ni Tsuite." *Chuo Koron*, no. 8 (1987): 172–178.

Feis, Herbert. *The China Tangle.* Princeton, NJ: Princeton University Press, 1972.

Field, Norma. *In the Realm of a Dying Emperor: Japan at Century's End.* New York: Vintage Books, 1993.

Francis, Carolyn Bowen. "Women and Military Violence." In *Okinawa: Cold War Island*, edited by Chalmers Johnson, 189–204. Cardiff, CA: Japan Policy Research Institute, 1999.

Frank, Richard B. *Downfall: The End of the Imperial Japanese Empire.* New York: Random House, 1999.

Friedman, George, and Meredith LeBard. *The Coming War With Japan.* New York: St. Martin's Press, 1991.

Funabashi Yoichi. "Japan and the New World Order." *Foreign Affairs* 70, no. 5 (Winter 1991/92): 58–74.

Fussell, Paul. *Thank God for the Atom Bomb and Other Essays.* New York: Summit Books, 1988.

Fussell, Paul. *Wartime: Understanding and Behavior in the Second World War.* New York: Oxford University Press, 1989.

Gallicchio, Marc. "Occupation, Dominion, and Alliance: Japan in American Security Policy, 1945–69." In *Partnership: The United States and Japan 1951–2001*, edited by Akira Iriye and Robert A. Wampler, 115–134. Tokyo: Kodansha International, 2001.

Gamble, Adam, and Takesato Watanabe. *A Public Betrayed: An Inside Look at Japanese Media Atrocities and Their Warnings to the West.* Washington, DC: Regnery, 2004.

Gardner, Lloyd C. *Economic Aspects of New Deal Diplomacy.* Boston: Beacon Press, 1964.

Garver, John W. "China's Wartime Diplomacy." In *China's Bitter Victory: The War with Japan, 1937–1945*, edited by James C. Hsiung and Steven I. Levine, 3–32. Armonk, NY: M. E. Sharpe, 1992.

Giangreco, D. M. "Casualty Projections for the U.S. Invasions of Japan: Planning and Policy Implications." *Journal of Military History* 62, no. 3 (Jul. 1998): 547–570.

Gibney, Frank (ed.). *Senso: The Japanese Remember the Pacific War.* Armonk, NY: M. E. Sharpe, 1995.

Gilbert, Bill. *Air Power: Heroes and Heroism in American Flight Missions, 1916 to Today.* New York: Citadel Press, 2003.

Gordon, David M. "The China-Japan War, 1931–1945." *Journal of Military History* 70, no. 1 (January 2006): 137–182.

Green, A. Wigfall. *Epic of Korea.* Washington, DC: Public Affairs Press, 1950.

Green, Michael J. "Can Tojo Inspire Modern Japan?" *SAIS Review* 19, no. 2 (1999): 243–250.

Green, Michael Jonathan. "The Search for an Active Security Partnership: Lessons from the 1980s." In *Partnership: The United States and Japan 1951–2001*, edited by Akira Iriye and Robert A. Wampler, 135–160. Tokyo: Kodansha International, 2001.

Grew, Joseph C. and Walter Johnson. *Turbulent Era: A Diplomatic Record of Forty Years 1904–1945.* Boston: Houghton Mifflin, 1952.

Gries, Peter Hays. *China's New Nationalism: Pride, Politics, and Diplomacy.* Berkeley: University of California Press, 2004.

Gries, Peter Hays. "Nationalism, Indignation and China's Japan Policy." *SAIS Review*, vol. XXV, no. 2 (Summer-Fall 2005): 105–114.

Hagan, Kenneth J. "American Submarine Warfare in the Pacific, 1941–1945: Guerre de Course Triumphant." In *The Pacific War Revisited*, edited by Gunter Bischof and Robert L. Dupont, 81–100. Baton Rouge: Louisiana State University Press, 1997.

Hakim, Joy. *A History of Us, Book 9: War, Peace and All That Jazz, 1918–1945.* New York: Oxford University Press, 1999.

Halberstam, David. "The History Boys." *Vanity Fair*, August 2007.

Halbwachs, Maurice. *On Collective Memory.* Chicago: University of Chicago Press, 1992.

Halliday, Jon, and Bruce Cumings. *Korea, The Unknown War.* London: Viking, 1988.

Halsey, William F., and Joseph J. Bryan III. *Admiral Halsey's Story.* New York: McGraw-Hill, 1947.

Harries, Meirion, and Susie Harries. *Soldiers of the Sun: The Rise and Fall of the Imperial Japanese Army 1868–1945.* London: Heinemann, 1991.

Hasegawa Tsuyoshi. *Racing the Enemy: Stalin, Truman and the Surrender of Japan.* Cambridge, MA: Belknap Press, 2005.

Hata Ikuhiko. *Nanking Jiken.* Tokyo: Chuo Koron, 1986.

He, Yinan. "History, Chinese Nationalism and the Emerging Sino-Japanese Conflict." *Journal of Contemporary China* 16, no. 50 (February 2007): 1–24.

He, Yinan. "Remembering and Forgetting the War: Elite Mythmaking, Mass Reaction, and Sino-Japanese Relations, 1950–2006." *History & Memory* 19, no. 2 (Fall/Winter 2007): 43–74.

Hein, Laura, and Mark Selden. "Culture, Power and Identity in Contemporary Okinawa." In *Islands of Discontent: Okinawan Responses to Japanese and American Power*, edited by Laura Hein and Mark Selden, 1–38. Lanham, MD: Rowman & Littlefield, 2003.

Hiatt, Fred. "Marine General: U.S. Troops Must Stay in Japan." *The Washington Post*, March 27, 1990.

Holdstock, Douglas, and Frank Barnaby (eds.). *Hiroshima and Nagasaki: Retrospect and Prospect.* Oxford, UK: Taylor and Francis, 1995.

Honda Katsuichi. *The Nanjing Massacre : A Japanese Journalist Confronts Japan's National Shame.* New York: M. E. Sharpe, 1999.

Howe, Christopher. *China and Japan: History, Trends, and Prospects.* Oxford, UK: Oxford University Press, 1996.

Hsiung, James C. "The War and After: World Politics in Historical Context." In *China's Bitter Victory: The War with Japan, 1937–1945*, edited by James C. Hsiung and Steven I. Levine, 295–306. Armonk, NY: M. E. Sharpe, 1992.

Hsü, Immanuel C. Y. *The Rise of Modern China*. Oxford, UK: Oxford University Press, 2000.

Ienaga Saburo. *The Pacific War 1931–1945*. New York: Pantheon, 1978.

Ijiri Hidenori. "Sino-Japanese Controversy Since the 1972 Normalization." In *China and Japan: History, Trends and Prospects*, edited by Christopher Howe, 60–82. Oxford, UK: Clarendon, 1996.

Iriye Akira. *Power and Culture: The Japanese-American War 1941–1945*. Cambridge, MA: Harvard University Press, 1981.

Ishihara Masaie. "Memories of War and Okinawa." In *Perilous Memories: The Asia-Pacific War(s)*, edited by T. Fujitani, Geoffrey M. White and Lisa Yoneyama, 87–106. Durham, NC: Duke University Press, 2001.

Jablonsky, David. *Churchill and Hitler: Essays on the Political-military Direction of Total War*. London: Taylor and Francis, 1994.

Jansen, Marius B. *The Making of Modern Japan*. Cambridge, MA: Harvard University Press, 2002.

Jarrell, Mary, and Stuart Wright (eds.). *Randall Jarrell's Letters: An Autobiographical and Literary Selection*. Boston: Houghton Mifflin Company, 1985.

Johnson, Chalmers. *Japan: Who Governs? The Rise of the Developmental State*. New York: W. W. Norton, 1995.

Johnson, Chalmers A. *Peasant Nationalism and Communist Power: The Emergence of Revolutionary China, 1937–1945*. Stanford: Stanford University Press, 1962.

Kankoku Teishin-tai Mondai Taisaku Kyogikai. *Shogen: Kyosei Renko Sareta Chosenjin Gun-ianfutachi*. Tokyo: Akashi Shoten, 1993.

Kerr, E. Bartlett. *Flames Over Tokyo: The U.S. Army Air Forces' Incendiary Campaign Against Japan 1944–1945*. New York: Donald I. Fine, 1991.

Kerr, George H. *Formosa Betrayed*. Boston: Houghton Mifflin, 1965.

King, David C. *Children's Encyclopedia of American History*. New York: DK Publishing House, 2003.

King, David C. *First Facts About U.S. History*. Woodbridge, CT: Blackbirch Press, 1996.

Kirby, William C. "The Chinese War Economy." In *China's Bitter Victory: The War with Japan, 1937–1945*, edited by James C. Hsiung and Steven I. Levine, 185–212. Armonk, NY: M. E. Sharpe, 1992.

Koji Taira. "The Battle of Okinawa in Japanese History Books." In *Okinawa: Cold War Island, edited by Chalmers Johnson, 39–49*. Cardiff, CA: Japan Policy Research Institute, 1999.

Krout, John A. *United States History From 1865*, 20th ed. New York: HarperCollins, 1991.

Krull, Kathleen. *V is for Victory: America Remembers World War II*. New York: Alfred A. Knopf, 1995.

Kyokuto Kokusai. *Gunji Saiban Sokkiroku*, Vol. 10. Tokyo: Yumatsudo, 1968.

LaFeber, Walter. *The Clash: U.S.-Japanese Relations Throughout History*. New York: W. W. Norton, 1997.

LaFeber, Walter. *The New Empire: An Interpretation of American Expansion, 1860–1898*. Ithaca, NY: Cornell University Press, 1998.

Lai Tse-han, Ramon H. Myers and Wei Wou. *A Tragic Beginning: The Taiwan Uprising of February 28, 1947*. Stanford, CA: Stanford University Press, 1991.

Lary, Diana. "A Ravaged Place: The Devastation of the Xuzhou Region, 1938." In *Scars of War: The Impact of Warfare on Modern China*, edited by Diana Lary and Stephen MacKinnon, 98–117. Vancouver: University of British Columbia Press, 2001.

Layne, Christopher. "The Unipolar Illusion: Why New Great Powers Will Rise." *International Security* 17, no. 4 (Spring 1993): 5–51.

Layton, Edwin T. *And I Was There*. New York: William Morrow, 1985.

Leahy, William D. *I Was There*. New York: Whittlesey House, 1950.

Leckie, Robert. *The Story of World War II*. New York: Random House, 1964.

Lee Ki-baik. *A New History of Korea*. Seoul: Ilchokak, 1984.

Leighton, Richard M., and Robert W. Coakley. *Global Logistics and Strategy, 1940–1943*, Vol. II. Washington DC: Government Printing Office, 1955.

Levine, Steven I. "Introduction." In *China's Bitter Victory: The War with Japan, 1937–1945*, edited by James C. Hsiung and Steven I. Levine, xvii–xxi. Armonk, NY: M. E. Sharpe, 1992.

Li, Laura Tyson. *Madame Chiang Kai-shek: China's Eternal First Lady*. New York: Grove Press, 2006.

Li, Peter. "Japan's Biochemical Warfare and Experimentation in China." In *Japanese War Crimes: The Search for Justice*, edited by Peter Li, 289–300. New Brunswick, NJ: Transaction, 2003.

MacKinnon, Stephen. "Refugee Flight at the Onset of the Anti-Japanese War." In *Scars of War: Impact of Warfare on Modern China*, edited by Diana Lary and Stephen Mackinnon, 118–135. Vancouver: University of British Columbia Press, 2001.

Maddox, Robert James. *Weapons for Victory: The Hiroshima Decision Fifty Years Later*. Columbia: University of Missouri Press, 1995.

Makabe Hiroshi. "Ikenie ni Sareta Nanamannin no Musumetachi." In *Tokyo Yamiichi Kobo Shi*, edited by Tokyo Yakeato Yamiichi o Kiroku Suru Kai, 192–217. Tokyo: Sofusha, 1978.

Mao Zedong. *Selected Works of Mao Zedong*, Vol. 2. Beijing: Foreign Languages Press, 1961.

Marker, Sherry. *Illustrated History of the United States*. Greenwich, CT: Bison Books, 1988.

Matray, James I. "Korea's Partition: Soviet-American Pursuit of Reunification, 1945–1948." *Parameters* 28, no. 1 (1998): 150–162.

Matsui Yayori. "Women's International War Crimes Tribunal on Japan's Military Sexual Slavery: Memory, Identity and Society." In *Japanese War Crimes: The Search for Justice*, edited by Peter Li, 259–280. Edison, NJ: Transaction, 2003.

Mearsheimer, John. *The Tragedy of Great Power Politics*. New York: W. W. Norton, 2001.

Millard, Mike. "Okinawa, Then and Now," In *Okinawa: Cold War Island*, edited by Chalmers Johnson, 93–98. Cardiff, CA: Japan Policy Research Institute, 1999.

Miller, Nathan. *War at Sea: A Naval History of World War II*. New York: Scribner, 1995.

Miller, Stuart Creighton. *"Benevolent Assimilation": The American Conquest of the Philippines, 1899–1903*. New Haven, CT: Yale University Press, 1982.

Mochizuki, Mike M. "U.S.-Japan Relations in the Asia-Pacific Region," In *Partnership: The United States and Japan 1951—2001*, edited by Akira Iriye and Robert A. Wampler, 13–32. Tokyo: Kodansha International, 2001.

Modder, Ralph. *The Singapore Chinese Massacre*. Singapore: Horizon Books, 2004.

Morison, Elting E., ed. *The Letters of Theodore Roosevelt, Vol. 2, The Years of Preparation, 1898–1900*. Cambridge, MA: Harvard University Press, 1951.

Murray, Williamson and Allan Reed Millett. *A War to be Won: Fighting the Second World War*. Cambridge, MA: Harvard University Press, 2000.

New York Times, "Senator Jokes of Hiroshima Attack," March 4, 1992.

Niksch, Larry. "Japanese Military's 'Comfort Women' System." Congressional Research Service, Apr. 3, 2007.

Organski, A.F.K., and Jacek Kugler. "The Costs of Major Wars: The Phoenix Factor." *American Political Science Review* 71, no. 4 (December 1977): 1347–1366.

Ota Masahide, "Re-Examining the History of the Battle of Okinawa," In *Okinawa: Cold War Island*, edited by Chalmers Johnson (Cardiff, CA: Japan Policy Research Institute, 1999), p. 29.

Overy, Richard. *Why the Allies Won*. New York: W. W. Norton, 1997.

Pan, Phillip P. "Chinese Step Up Criticism of Japan." Washington Post International Edition, April 13, 2005.

Pape, Robert A. "Why Japan Surrendered." *International Security* 18, no. 2 (Fall 1993): 154–201.

Pogue, Forrest C. and George C. Marshall. *Organizer of Victory, 1943—1945*. New York: Viking Press, 1973.

Proceedings of the Eighth Military History Symposium. United States Air Force Academy. Colorado Springs, CO, 1978.

Rees, Laurence. *Horror in the East: Japan and the Atrocities of World War II*. Cambridge, MA: Da Capo Press, 2001.

Reid, T. R. "The Setting Sun of Akira Kurosawa; Japan's Famed Director Draws Yawns for Film Memoir." *Washington Post*, December. 28, 1993.

Reilly, James. "China's History Activism and Sino-Japanese Relations." *China: An International Journal* 4, no. 2 (September 2006): 189–216.

Reischauer, Edwin. *My Life Between Japan and America*. New York: Harper and Row, 1986.

Renaud, Rosario. *Le Diocese de Suchow (Chine): Champ Apostolique des Jesuites Canadiens de 1918 a 1954*. Montreal: Editions Bellarmin, 1982.

Reuters News Service. "Japan Should Reexamine Its Nuclear Weapons Ban, Ruling Party Official Says." *Washington Post*, October 16, 2006.

Roberts, Jeffery J. "Peering through Different Bombsights: Military Historians, Diplomatic Historians, and the Decision to Drop the Atomic Bomb." *Airpower Journal* 12, no. 1 (Spring 1998): 66–78.

Rose, Caroline. *Sino-Japanese Relations: Facing the Past, Looking to the Future?* London: Routledge, 2005.

Romanus, Charles F. and Riley Sutherland. *Stilwell's Mission to China*. Washington, DC: Department of the Army, 1953.

Romanus, Charles F. and Riley Sutherland. *The United States Army in World War II: Time Runs Out in CBI*. Washington, D.C.: U.S. Government Printing Office, 1976.

Rotter, Andrew J. *Hiroshima: The World's Bomb*. Oxford, UK: Oxford University Press, 2008.

Roy, Denny. "China-Japan Relations: Cooperation Amidst Antagonism," In *Asia's Bilateral Relations*, edited by Satu Limaye, 9.1–9.8. Honolulu: Asia-Pacific Center for Security Studies, 2004.

Roy, Denny. *Taiwan: A Political History*. Ithaca, NY: Cornell University Press, 2003.

Roy, Denny, Grant P. Skabelund and Ray C. Hillam (eds.). *A Time To Kill: Reflections on War.* Salt Lake City, UT: Signature Books, 1992.

Rummel, R. J. *China's Bloody Century: Genocide and Mass Murder Since 1900.* Edison, NJ: Transaction Publishers, 1991.

Rummel, R. J. *Death By Government.* Edison, NJ: Transaction Publishers, 1994.

Saito Sayuri. "Reconsidering History Education." *Daily Yomiuri,* September 18, 1997, 3.

Schaffer, Ronald. *Wings of Judgment: American Bombing in World War II.* New York: Oxford University Press, 1985.

Schaller, Michael. *Altered States: The United States and Japan since the Occupation.* UK: Oxford University Press, 1997.

Schwartz, Barry. "Social Change and Collective Memory: The Democratization of George Washington." *American Sociological Review* 56 (1991): 221–36.

Schwartz, Barry. "The Social Context of Commemoration: A Study in Collective Memory." *Social Forces* 61 (1982): 374–402.

Seaton, Philip A. *Japan's Contested War Memories: The 'Memory Rifts' in Historical Consciousness of World War II.* London: Routledge, 2007.

Sherwin, Martin J. *A World Destroyed.* New York: Knopf, 1973.

Shinpen—Atarashii Shakai: Rekishi. Tokyo: Shoseki, 1998.

Shum Kui-Kwong. *The Chinese Communists' Road to Power: The Anti-Japanese National United Front, 1935–1945.* Oxford: Oxford University Press, 1988.

Simons, Geoff. *Korea: The Search for Sovereignty.* New York: St. Martin's Press, 1995.

Sledge, E. B. *With the Old Breed at Peleliu and Okinawa.* Novato, CA: Presidio Press, 1981.

Sono Ayako. "Okinawasen Shudanjiketsu o Meguru Rekishi Kyokasho no Kyomo." *Seiron* no. 375 (2003): 112–117.

Spector, Ronald H. *Eagle Against the Sun: The American War with Japan.* New York: Vintage Books, 1985.

Spector, Ronald H. "The Pacific War and the Fourth Dimension of Strategy." In *The Pacific War Revisited,* edited by Gunter Bischof and Robert L. Dupont, 41–56. Baton Rouge: Louisiana State University Press, 1997.

Spence, Jonathan D. *The Search for Modern China.* New York: W. W. Norton, 1990.

Stenger, Charles A. *American Prisoners of War in WWI, WWII, Korea, and Vietnam: Statistical Data Concerning Numbers Captured, Repatriated, and Still Alive.* Washington, DC: Veterans Health Administration, 1981.

Stinnett, Robert B. *Day of Deceit.* New York: Free Press, 2000.

Stouffer, Samuel A., Arthur A. Lumsdaine, Marion H. Lumsdaine, Robin M. Williams, Jr., M. Brewster Smith, Irving L. Janis, Shirley A. Star and Leonard S. Cotrell. *The American Soldier: Combat and Its Aftermath,* Vol. II. Princeton, NJ: Princeton University Press, 1949.

Straus, Ulrich. *The Anguish of Surrender: Japanese POWs of World War II.* Seattle: University of Washington Press, 2003.

Strom, Stephanie. "Seoul Won't Seek Japan Funds for War's Brothel Women." *New York Times,* Apr. 22, 1998.

Sulzberger, C. L., and David G. McCullough. *World War II.* New York: American Heritage, 1966.

Takaki, Ronald. *Hiroshima: Why America Dropped the Atomic Bomb.* New York: Little, Brown and Company, 1995.

Takashi Inoguchi, and Purnendra Jain (eds.). *Japanese Foreign Policy Today: A Reader.* New York: Palgrave Macmillan, 2000.

Takemae Eiji. *Inside GHQ: The Allied Occupation of Japan and Its Legacy*. New York: Continuum International Publishing Group, 2002.

Tanaka, Yuki. *Hidden Horrors: Japanese War Crimes in World War II*. Boulder, CO: Westview Press, 1996.

Taylor, A.J.P. *English History, 1914–1945*. Oxford: Clarendon Press, 1965.

Temerson, Timothy D. "Double Containment and the Origins of the U.S.-Japan Security Alliance." Unpublished manuscript, Massachusetts Institute of Technology Japan Program, MITJP 91–14, 1992.

Terazawa Yuki. "The Transnational Campaign for Redress for Wartime Rape by the Japanese Military: Cases for Survivors in Shanxi Province." *NWSA Journal* 18, no. 3 (Fall 2006): 133–145.

Thorne, Christopher. *The Issue of War*. New York: Oxford University Press, 1985.

Toland, John. *The Rising Sun: The Decline and Fall of the Japanese Empire, 1936–1945*. New York: Random House, 1970.

Tong, Kurt W. "Korea's Forgotten Atomic Bomb Victims." *Bulletin of Concerned Asian Scholars* 23, no. 1 (January—March 1991): 31–37.

Tsuchiyama Jitsuo. "Ironies of Japanese Defense and Disarmament Policy." In *Japanese Foreign Policy Today*, edited by Inoguchi Takashi and Purnendra Jain, 136–151. London: Macmillan, 2000.

Tuchman, Barbara W. *Stilwell and the American Experience in China*. New York: Macmillan, 1971.

United States Department of the Army. *Reports of General MacArthur*, Vol. I, *MacArthur in Japan: The Occupation: Military Phase*. Washington, DC: U.S. Department of the Army, 1966.

United States Department of Defense. *Entry of the Soviet Union Into the War Against Japan: Military Plans 1941–1945*. Washington, DC: U.S. Government Printing Office, 1955.

United States Department of State. *Foreign Relations of the United States, 1949*, Vol. VII. Washington, DC: U.S. Government Printing Office, 1976.

United States Department of State. *Foreign Relations of the United States: Diplomatic Papers, 1945. The British Commonwealth, the Far East*, Vol. VI. Washington, DC: U.S. Government Printing Office, 1945.

United States Department of State. *Foreign Relations of the United States: Japan, 1931–1941*, Vol. I. Washington, DC: U.S. Government Printing Office, 1943.

United States Department of State. *Foreign Relations of the United States: Potsdam*, Vol. I. Washington, DC: U.S. Government Printing Office, 1960.

United States Strategic Bombing Survey, *Summary Report (Pacific War)*. July 1, 1946. http://www.anesi.com/ussbs01.htm.

Utley, Jonathan G. *Going to War with Japan 193–1941*. Knoxville: University of Tennessee Press, 1985.

Van Creveld, Martin. *Supplying War*. New York: Cambridge University Press, 1977.

Vandiver, Frank E. *1001 Things Everyone Should Know About World War II*. New York: Broadway Books, 2002.

Wakabayashi, Bob Tadashi. "The Nanking 100-Man Killing Contest Debate: War Guilt amid Fabricated Illusions, 1971–75." *Journal of Japanese Studies* 26, no. 2 (Summer, 2000): 307–340.

Walker, J. Samuel. "The Decision to Use the Bomb: A Historiographical Update." *Diplomatic History* 14, no.1 (Winter 1990): 97–114.

Waltz, Kenneth N. "The Emerging Structure of International Politics." *International Security* 18, no. 2 (Fall 1993): 44–79.

Waltz, Kenneth N. *Theory of International Politics*. Reading, MA: Addison-Wesley Press, 1979.

Webster, Charles, and Noble Frankland. *The Strategic Air Offensive Against Germany 1939–1945*, Vol. 4. London: Her Majesty's Stationery Office, 1961.

Weinberg, Gerhard L. *A World at Arms: A Global History of World War II*. New York: Cambridge University Press, 1994.

Weisman, Steven R. "Japanese Apology Over War Unlikely After Bush's Stand." *New York Times*, Dec. 6, 1991.

Wendt, Alexander. "Anarchy Is What States Make of It: The Social Construction of Power Politics." *International Organization* 46, no. 3 (1992): 391–425.

Wheeler, Keith. *Bombers over Japan*. Alexandria, VA: Time Life Books, 1982.

Wou, Odoric Y. K. *Mobilizing the Masses: Building Revolution in Henan*. Stanford, CA: Stanford University Press, 1994.

White, Theodore H. "The Danger from Japan." *New York Times Magazine*, July 28, 1985.

Williams, William Appleman. *The Tragedy of American Diplomacy*. New York: W. W. Norton, 1988.

Williamsen, Marvin. "The Military Dimension 1937—1941." In *China's Bitter Victory: The War with Japan, 1937–1945*, edited by James C. Hsiung and Steven I. Levine, 135–156. Armonk, NY: M. E. Sharpe, 1992.

Wines, Michael. "President Rejects Apology to Japan." *New York Times*, Dec. 2, 1991.

Wolk, Herman S. "General Arnold, the Atomic Bomb, and the Surrender of Japan." In *The Pacific War Revisited*, edited by Gunter Bischof and Robert L. Dupont, 163–178. Baton Rouge: Louisiana State University Press, 1997.

Wright, Michael (ed.). *The World at Arms: The Reader's Digest Illustrated History of World War II*. New York: Reader's Digest Association, 1989.

Yaguchi Yujin. "War Memories Across the Pacific: Japanese Visitors at the USS Arizona Memorial." Lecture at the USS Bowfin Museum, Honolulu, July 26, 2006.

Yonetai, Julia. "Playing Base Politics in a Global Strategic Theater: Futenma Relocation, the G-8 Summit, and Okinawa." *Critical Asian Studies* 33, no. 1 (March 2001): 70–95.

Yoneyama, Lisa. "Memory Matters: Hiroshima's Korean Atom Bomb Memorial and the Politics of Ethnicity." In *Living With the Bomb: American and Japanese Cultural Conflicts in the Nuclear Age*, edited by Laura Hein and Mark Seldon, 202–231. Armonk, NY: M. E. Sharpe, 1997.

Yoshida Yutaka. *Showa tenno no Shusenshi*. Tokyo: Iwanami Shinsho, 1991.

Yui Daizaburo. "Between Pearl Harbor and Hiroshima/Nagasaki: Nationalism and Memory in Japan and the United States." In *Living with the Bomb: American and Japanese Cultural Conflicts in the Nuclear Age*, edited by Laura Hein and Mark Selden, 52–72. New York: M. E. Sharpe, 1997.

Zielenziger, Michael. "Ex-Japanese Soldier Deemed War Criminal." *Houston Chronicle*, July 3, 1998.

Index

About the Author

DENNY ROY is a Senior Fellow at the East-West Center, Honolulu. He has held faculty and research appointments in East Asian politics, history, and security issues at the Naval Postgraduate School, Asia-Pacific Center for Security Studies, Australian National University, National University of Singapore, and Brigham Young University. He is the author/editor of five books, including *Taiwan: A Political History* (2003), *The Politics of Human Rights in Asia* (2000), *China's Foreign Relations* (1998), and *The New Security Agenda in the Asia-Pacific Region* (1997). He has written for such scholarly journals as *International Security, Survival, Asian Survey, Security Dialogue, Contemporary Southeast Asia, Armed Forces & Society,* and *Issues & Studies.*